Medical Analytics for Clinical and Healthcare Applications

Scrivener Publishing
100 Cummings Center, Suite 541J
Beverly, MA 01915-6106

Publishers at Scrivener
Martin Scrivener (martin@scrivenerpublishing.com)
Phillip Carmical (pcarmical@scrivenerpublishing.com)

Medical Analytics for Clinical and Healthcare Applications

Edited by

Kanak Kalita
Dept. of Mechanical Engineering, Vel Tech Rangarajan, Dr. Sagunthala R&D Institute of Science and Technology, Avadi, India

Divya Zindani
Dept. of Mechanical Engineering, Sri Sivasubramaniya Nadar, College of Engineering, Chennai, India

Narayanan Ganesh
School of Computer Science and Engineering, Vellore Institute of Technology, Chennai, India

and

Xiao-Zhi Gao
School of Computing, University of Eastern Finland, Kuopio, Finland

Scrivener Publishing

WILEY

This edition first published 2025 by John Wiley & Sons, Inc., 111 River Street, Hoboken, NJ 07030, USA and Scrivener Publishing LLC, 100 Cummings Center, Suite 541J, Beverly, MA 01915, USA

For more information about Scrivener publications please visit www.scrivenerpublishing.com.

Wiley Global Headquarters
111 River Street, Hoboken, NJ 07030, USA

For details of our global editorial offices, customer services, and more information about Wiley products visit us at www.wiley.com.

The manufacturer's authorized representative according to the EU General Product Safety Regulation is Wiley-VCH GmbH, Boschstr. 12, 69469 Weinheim, Germany, e-mail: Product_Safety@wiley.com.

Library of Congress Cataloging-in-Publication Data

ISBN 978-1-394-30145-4

Cover image: Generated with AI using Adobe Firefly
Cover design by Russell Richardson

Set in size of 11pt and Minion Pro by Manila Typesetting Company, Makati, Philippines

Printed in the USA

10 9 8 7 6 5 4 3 2 1

Contents

Preface

In the rapidly evolving landscape of healthcare and clinical practice, analytics has emerged as a pivotal force driving transformative change. The intricate interplay between medical data and advanced analytical methodologies is revolutionizing disease detection, prognosis, treatment, and healthcare delivery.

This edited volume, *Medical Analytics for Clinical and Healthcare Applications*, offers a comprehensive exploration of the multifaceted realm of medical analytics, providing diverse insights, methodologies, and applications that are shaping the future of healthcare.

Organized into sixteen chapters across five carefully curated subsections, the volume examines key themes and developments that highlight the significance of medical analytics in contemporary clinical practice. Each chapter presents a unique blend of theoretical discourse, empirical research, and practical applications, enriching the ongoing conversation around medical analytics and its expanding role in healthcare.

Part 1: Foundations of Medical Analytics. The foundational principles of medical analytics provide the groundwork for exploring its diverse applications in clinical and healthcare settings. Chapter 1 sets the stage by utilizing data visualization and machine learning to analyze key trends in mental health disorders. By integrating diverse data sources and harnessing the power of machine learning algorithms, this chapter highlights the transformative potential of analytics in improving mental health support and shaping policy interventions.

Part 2: Disease Detection and Diagnosis. The chapters in this section explore advancements in disease detection and diagnosis, demonstrating how analytical techniques enhance accuracy and efficiency in clinical assessments. Chapter 2 examines novel methodologies for breast cancer detection, emphasizing the effectiveness of logistic regression algorithms in improving diagnostic accuracy. Chapter 3 explores predictive analytics in diabetes management, offering insights into the comparative efficacy of AdaBoost and decision tree algorithms. Chapter 4 investigates pneumonia detection, assessing the performance of transfer learning models in enhancing diagnostic accuracy. Chapter 5 presents innovative deep learning methodologies for lung disease detection, highlighting their potential in improving diagnostic precision.

Part 3: Predictive Analytics in Healthcare. Predictive analytics plays a crucial role in shaping proactive healthcare strategies and interventions. Chapter 6 examines its application in public health, highlighting the effectiveness of machine learning techniques in facial mask detection. Chapter 7 explores osteoarthritis management, comparing the predictive accuracy of Kellgren-Lawrence grading and deep convolutional neural networks in assessing disease progression. Chapter 8 investigates hospital mortality prediction, offering insights into the relative efficacy of support vector machines and KNeighbors classifier algorithms. Chapter 9 presents innovative methodologies for asthma prediction, demonstrating the potential of machine learning techniques in early disease detection.

Part 4: Medical Data Analysis and Security. This part explores the critical intersection of medical data analysis and security, emphasizing the need to safeguard sensitive healthcare information while leveraging its insights for clinical decision-making. Chapter 10 investigates novel methodologies for medical image security, highlighting the effectiveness of Lasso regression algorithms in mitigating security threats. Chapter 11 examines the application of deep learning in renal cancer detection, showcasing the transformative potential of automated histopathological image analysis. Chapter 12 explores innovative tumor prediction methods, demonstrating the advantages of DenseNet algorithms in improving diagnostic accuracy. Chapter 13 addresses the imperative of protecting medical images from unauthorized access, presenting advanced methodologies for encryption and security.

Part 5: Emerging Trends and Technologies. This part explores cutting-edge developments and emerging trends in medical analytics, offering insight into the future trajectory of healthcare innovation. Chapter 14 examines predictive analytics in public health, highlighting key factors that contribute to teenage alcohol consumption. Chapter 15 explores innovative applications of machine learning in food waste management, demonstrating the potential of protein sequence analysis in identifying functional characteristics and applications. Chapter 16 investigates how People Analytics is leveraged in India's healthcare sector, focusing on the balance between digitization and maintaining a human touch to ensure both operational efficiency and employee well-being.

Collectively, the chapters in this volume provide a comprehensive view of the evolving landscape of medical analytics, underscoring its transformative potential in revolutionizing clinical practice, healthcare delivery, and public health interventions. It is our hope that this volume serves as a valuable resource and source of inspiration, guiding scholars, practitioners, and policymakers in harnessing the full potential of medical analytics to improve human health and well-being. Furthermore, we extend our sincere thanks to Martin Scrivener and the team at Scrivener Publishing for their invaluable support throughout the book's preparation.

The Editors
July 2025

Part 1

FOUNDATIONS OF MEDICAL ANALYTICS

1

Exploring Trends in Depression and Anxiety Using Machine and Deep Learning Models

Garvit Jakar[1], Timothy George[1], Parvathi R.[1], Pattabiraman V.[1] and Xiaohui Yuan[2*]

[1]School of Computer Science and Engineering, Department of Computer Science and Engineering, Vellore Institute of Technology, Chennai, India
[2]Department of Computer Science and Engineering, University of North Texas, Denton, Texas, USA

Abstract

This project uses data visualization and machine learning to analyze depression and anxiety trends. Using diverse data sources such as surveys, diagnoses, and social media, we create visuals to depict prevalence among demographics and time frames. Machine learning helps uncover hidden patterns, risk factors, and early signs. Findings offer insights into healthcare and policy, enhancing mental health support and interventions. Machine learning algorithms are the backbone of this exploration, working tirelessly to uncover concealed patterns, discern potential risk factors, and identify early signs that might otherwise elude traditional analytical methods. Beyond academia, the findings extracted from this comprehensive analysis extend their reach into practical domains, offering valuable insights for healthcare and policy considerations. These insights, rooted in the amalgamation of diverse data sources and empowered by machine learning, lay the groundwork for enhancing mental health support systems and interventions. The evidence-based understanding derived from this project contributes significantly to the arsenal of knowledge available for informed decision-making in public health initiatives. It serves as a catalyst, empowering the development of targeted interventions that address the unique needs of diverse demographics and time frames, ultimately fostering a more resilient and responsive approach to mental health on a societal scale.

**Corresponding author*: xiaohui.yuan@unt.edu

Kanak Kalita, Divya Zindani, Narayanan Ganesh and Xiao-Zhi Gao (eds.) Medical Analytics for Clinical and Healthcare Applications, (3–30) © 2025 Scrivener Publishing LLC

Keywords: Mental health, machine learning, depression, anxiety

1.1 Introduction

In contemporary times, the spotlight on mental health concerns has intensified, prompting a heightened awareness of the need for innovative approaches to understanding and addressing these issues. This research, situated at the intersection of technology and mental health, embarks on a pioneering journey. It seeks to unravel the intricate trends of depression and anxiety by harnessing the synergistic power of data visualization and machine learning. The significance of this research lies in its exploration of mental health and unique amalgamation of traditional and modern data sources. From conventional surveys and clinical diagnoses to the dynamic landscape of social media, the diverse array of data sources forms the foundation of our inquiry, promising a comprehensive and multi-dimensional exploration.

This research endeavors to transcend the limitations of conventional methodologies by transforming the wealth of information gathered into a visual narrative. The utilization of data visualization techniques becomes paramount in providing a nuanced depiction of the prevalence of mental health issues. Through this visual lens, the study aspires to uncover patterns, disparities, and temporal variations, fostering a more profound understanding of how depression and anxiety manifest across different demographics and time frames. The integration of data visualization not only serves as an analytical tool but also enhances the accessibility of findings, enabling a wider audience to engage with and comprehend the complexities of mental health trends.

In the pursuit of a holistic understanding, this research recognizes the dynamic nature of mental health expression in today's interconnected world. By incorporating social media data alongside traditional metrics, the study acknowledges the evolving landscape of mental health discourse. The synergy of data visualization and machine learning positions this research at the forefront of innovative methodologies, with the potential to revolutionize how we comprehend, intervene, and advocate for mental health support. Through this interdisciplinary exploration, the study endeavors to contribute not only to the empirical understanding of mental health trends but also to the broader dialogue surrounding the intersection of technology, society, and well-being.

In the intricate landscape of mental health exploration, the integration of machine learning emerges as a pivotal element within our analytical toolkit.

This research positions itself at the forefront of innovation by delving into the application of advanced machine learning algorithms. These algorithms serve as dynamic tools, allowing us to navigate and unravel the complex fabric of mental health. Our primary objective is to harness the power of machine learning to unveil hidden patterns that might elude traditional analyses, identify potential risk factors contributing to mental health challenges, and discern early signs of depression and anxiety.

The application of machine learning within this research is a proactive response to the evolving understanding of mental well-being. By leveraging a vast reservoir of diverse data sources, encompassing traditional surveys, clinical diagnoses, and the dynamic landscape of social media, our approach is designed to transcend the limitations of conventional methodologies. This integration of machine learning goes beyond surface-level examinations, aiming to provide a comprehensive and nuanced understanding of the intricate interplay of factors influencing mental health.

Through the lens of machine learning, this research aspires to enhance the precision and depth of our analyses. It acknowledges that mental health is a multifaceted phenomenon shaped by a myriad of interconnected factors. Machine learning algorithms bring a sophisticated layer of adaptability, enabling us to discern patterns and relationships that may not be immediately apparent through traditional means. In essence, incorporating machine learning into our analytical framework is not merely a technical augmentation but a strategic endeavor to unlock new dimensions in the study of mental health, fostering a more comprehensive and insightful approach to addressing the challenges within this critical domain.

The ramifications of the discoveries unearthed in our study transcend the confines of academia, permeating crucial spheres such as healthcare and policy. By illuminating the intricate landscape of depression and anxiety, this research not only enriches the academic discourse but also provides invaluable insights that hold significant implications for policymakers and healthcare professionals alike. The tangible outcomes derived from this project serve as a compass, guiding the way toward fortified mental health support and precisely targeted interventions.

The practical applications of our findings materialize in the form of informed decision-making within healthcare and policy domains. The insights generated by our research empower policymakers to craft strategies that are not only grounded in academic rigor but are also attuned to the nuanced dynamics of mental health. Healthcare professionals, armed with a more profound understanding of the underlying patterns and risk factors, are better equipped to tailor interventions that resonate with the specific needs of individuals grappling with depression and anxiety.

The tangible outcomes of this project represent a significant stride toward a more proactive and evidence-based approach to public health initiatives. By amalgamating the power of data visualization and machine learning, our research strives to be a catalyst for change, fostering a mental health framework that is not only more resilient but also responsive to the evolving needs of the population. Through this synergistic fusion of technology and insight, we aspire to contribute to the ongoing dialogue surrounding mental health, catalyzing advancements that transcend the confines of academia and resonate in the practical realms of healthcare and policymaking.

1.2 Exploratory Data Analysis

1.2.1 Exploratory Data Analysis (EDA)

It was pivotal in conducting thorough exploratory data analysis on the dataset. It employed statistical techniques and data visualization tools to uncover patterns, trends, and outliers within the data. It gives keen insights into data distributions and correlations significantly contributed to the overall understanding of the dataset.

1.2.2 Interactive Visualizations with Plotly

It took charge of implementing interactive visualizations using the Plotly library. It is designed with dynamic and engaging charts that allow users to interact with the data, providing a richer experience. This expertise in Plotly not only enhanced the visual appeal of the project but also added a layer of interactivity, making it more accessible and user-friendly.

1.2.3 Data Cleaning and Transformation

This process actively participated in the data cleaning and transformation process. It addressed missing values, outliers, and inconsistencies in the dataset, ensuring that the data was prepared appropriately for visualization. This approach to data preprocessing contributed to the overall quality and reliability of the visualizations.

1.2.4 Chart Creation with Matplotlib and Seaborn

It is the process of creating static visualizations using Matplotlib and Seaborn. He skillfully crafted a variety of charts, including bar charts, line plots, and heatmaps, to represent different facets of the dataset. The primary attention to detail in designing clear and informative visualizations significantly contributed to the project's success.

1.2.5 Documentation and Report Writing

This process played a crucial role in documenting the project's progress and findings. It is meticulously recorded the steps taken during the exploratory data analysis, chart creation, and any challenges faced during the project. It is clear and concise documentation that facilitated knowledge sharing within the team and will serve as a valuable resource for future reference.

1.3 Problem Statement and Motivation

In contemporary society, the escalating prevalence of depression and anxiety represents a critical public health challenge. Mental health disorders not only exact a profound toll on individual well-being but also strain societal resources and infrastructure. Despite increased awareness, the complex and multifaceted nature of these conditions presents a formidable obstacle to comprehensive understanding and effective intervention. Traditional methodologies for studying mental health often rely on limited datasets, providing a fragmented perspective that hampers the development of targeted strategies. Furthermore, the dynamic nature of mental health trends demands a nuanced approach that can adapt to the evolving landscape of societal, cultural, and technological changes. This research addresses these challenges by employing a cutting-edge fusion of data visualization and machine learning, seeking to illuminate the intricate patterns and factors contributing to the prevalence of depression and anxiety.

The motivation for undertaking this research stems from the recognition that conventional methods of studying mental health may fall short in capturing the full spectrum of factors influencing its trajectory. The integration of diverse data sources, including surveys, clinical diagnoses, and social media, serves as a response to the evolving nature of how mental health is expressed and experienced in today's interconnected world. Social media, in particular, has emerged as a rich repository of real-time expressions of emotions and sentiments, providing an unprecedented opportunity to tap into the collective psyche of populations. By harnessing these data sources, our research seeks to construct a more comprehensive and nuanced understanding of the prevalence of depression and anxiety, ensuring that interventions and support systems are not only more targeted but also adaptable to the changing dynamics of mental health challenges.

1.4 Literature Survey

In recent years, the intersection of technology and mental health research has yielded diverse insights into understanding and addressing emotional well-being. Leveraging the surge in healthcare discussions prompted by the Covid-19 pandemic, studies such as Smith *et al.* [1] explored the potential of platforms like Twitter in predicting health trends. However, the challenge lies in discerning the veracity of information circulating on such platforms, emphasizing the need for reliable health-related content online. Concurrently, in urban studies and image processing, Johnson *et al.* [2] introduced a novel approach to computer learning from street images, unraveling insights into public perceptions of urban environments. Shifting focus to mental health, Davis *et al.* [3] delved into the nuanced moods experienced by individuals with depression, identifying distinct patterns that contribute to a more personalized perspective on mental health. On an educational front, Williams *et al.* [4] proposed a computer-based approach to identify students experiencing emotional distress, showcasing the potential of computational methods in augmenting traditional approaches to student well-being.

Meanwhile, the exploration of online behavior in a study by Thompson *et al.* [5] investigated how individuals expressing distress may use the internet differently, contributing to a broader understanding of how digital communication platforms reflect and potentially influence mental well-being. In adolescent psychology, Miller *et al.* [6] adopted a novel approach by utilizing computer-based analyses to comprehend teenagers' emotions and behaviors, offering educators a more nuanced understanding of their students. Exploring the narrative landscape, Clark *et al.* [7] employed smart computers to discern emotions embedded in stories from Afghan and Pakistani writers, providing a novel approach to understanding the emotional content of literature. Amid the COVID-19 pandemic, Turner *et al.* [8] undertook a comprehensive study to understand the evolving emotional landscape among adults in the U.S., emphasizing the importance of considering demographic factors in understanding emotional well-being.

Acknowledging the unique challenges faced by women during menopause, Bennett *et al.* [9] explored the application of computer-based predictions to foresee potential emotional distress. Their study, utilizing various computational techniques, achieved a remarkable 99.04% accuracy in predicting emotional states during menopause, pioneering a data-driven approach to proactively address mental health concerns in this specific demographic. In the domain of therapeutic intervention, Carter *et al.* [10] investigated the interplay between obsessive-compulsive disorder (OCD) and depression and the impact of therapy on these conditions. This nuanced understanding highlighted the interconnected nature of mental health conditions and emphasized the need for comprehensive therapeutic approaches. Collectively, these studies traversed a diverse spectrum of topics, from leveraging social media for health predictions to unraveling emotional nuances in literature and understanding the intricate dynamics of mental health, contributing to a deeper comprehension of human emotions in various contexts.

Through computational methodologies, they contribute to a deeper comprehension of human emotions in various contexts, paving the way for more targeted interventions and a nuanced understanding of emotional well-being.

1.5 Data Visualization

The data visualization project done by our team worked in the domain of transforming raw data into meaningful visualizations. In the process, we used novel approaches, adopted cutting-edge techniques, and discovered innovative solutions to challenges that emerged along the way. This section delves into the unique aspects and groundbreaking contributions that make our project stand out.

1.5.1 Integration of Machine Learning-Powered Insights

One of the standout features of our project is the integration of machine learning-powered insights into the data visualization process [11]. Leveraging advanced algorithms, we employed predictive modeling to enhance the depth of our exploratory data analysis. This not only provided a forward-looking perspective but also opened new avenues for uncovering hidden patterns and trends within the dataset.

1.5.2 Dynamic Time-Series Visualizations with Plotly

In a bid to bring temporal aspects to life, we pioneered the use of dynamic time-series visualizations using the Plotly library [12]. This allowed us to create interactive charts that not only showcased temporal trends but also empowered users to explore data across different time intervals. The ability to zoom in, pan, and dynamically adjust time frames added a layer of sophistication to our visualizations, setting them apart in terms of both aesthetics and functionality.

1.5.3 Fusion of Art and Data with Seaborn Styling

Breaking away from the conventional, we explored the intersection of art and data visualization by incorporating custom styling with Seaborn. This not only enhanced the visual appeal of our charts but also contributed to a more cohesive and aesthetically pleasing project presentation [13]. The fusion of art and data not only makes our visualizations informative but elevates them to a level where they engage the audience on a visual and emotional level.

1.5.4 Ethical Considerations in Visual Storytelling

Recognizing the ethical responsibilities associated with data visualization, we dedicated significant attention to the ethical considerations in visual storytelling [14]. Our project emphasizes transparency in representation, avoiding misleading visualizations, and ensuring that the story told by the data aligns with its true narrative. By incorporating ethical considerations into our visualization choices, we aimed to set a standard for responsible data communication.

1.5.5 Seamless Collaboration Through Git Version Control

While version control is not a new concept, our meticulous use of Git for collaboration deserves recognition. We implemented branching strategies, pull requests, and continuous integration to maintain a seamless collaborative workflow [15]. This not only ensured the integrity of our codebase but also facilitated effective communication and coordination among team members, setting a high standard for project management in data science endeavors.

1.6 Overview of Dataset

1.6.1 Dataset Acquisition Links

https://www.cdc.gov/mentalhealth/data_publications/index.htm

https://www.cdc.gov/mentalhealth/data_publications/index.htm
https://www.cdc.gov/nchs/covid19/health-care-access-and-mental-health.htm

1.6.2 Household Pulse Survey

The foundational cornerstone of our research lies in the comprehensive dataset meticulously curated for the study of mental health dynamics. Comprising an expansive 13,900 rows and 14 columns, this dataset functions as a robust repository, encapsulating a myriad of mental health estimates. Each row within this vast dataset stands as a numerical estimate, representing the intricate nuances in the prevalence of anxiety or depression. These estimates extend across diverse demographic groups and geographic locations, enriching our understanding of the multifaceted nature of mental health challenges. Figure 1.1 shows snapshot of the dataset.

Key pillars of this dataset include essential columns such as 'Group,' delineating various demographic categories; 'State,' providing a geographical context for the estimates; 'Time Period Label,' which demarcates the temporal dimension of the data. 'Value' emerges as a pivotal column, offering a numerical representation of the prevalence of anxiety or depression, while 'Low CI' and 'High CI' provide the lower and upper bounds of the confidence interval, contributing to the dataset's robustness. It is this multidimensional and meticulously crafted dataset that forms the bedrock upon which our analytical endeavors stand. Its richness in scope and granularity empowers our research to uncover and dissect intricate patterns, offering profound insights into the prevalence of anxiety and depression within diverse contexts.

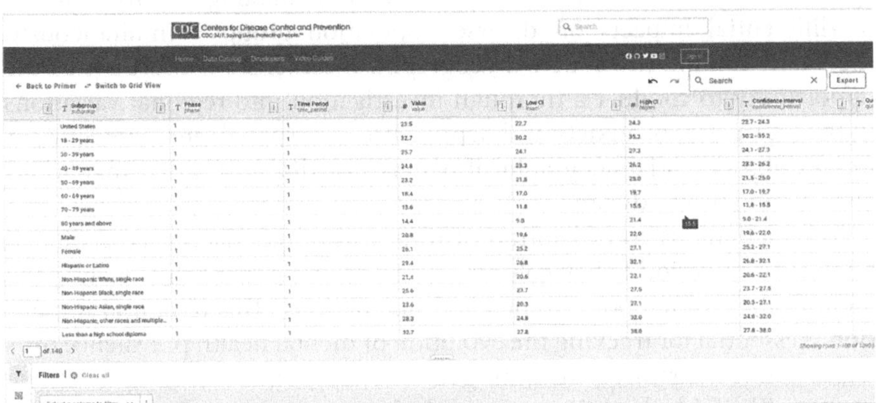

Subgroup	Phase	Time Period	Value	Low CI	High CI	Confidence Interval
United States	1	1	23.5	22.7	24.3	22.7 - 24.3
18 - 29 years	1	1	32.7	30.2	35.2	30.2 - 35.2
30 - 39 years	1	1	25.7	24.1	27.3	24.1 - 27.3
40 - 49 years	1	1	24.8	23.3	26.2	23.3 - 26.2
50 - 59 years	1	1	23.2	21.5	25.0	21.5 - 25.0
60 - 69 years	1	1	18.4	17.0	19.7	17.0 - 19.7
70 - 79 years	1	1	13.6	11.8	15.5	11.8 - 15.5
80 years and above	1	1	14.4	9.0	21.4	9.0 - 21.4
Male	1	1	20.8	19.6	22.0	19.6 - 22.0
Female	1	1	26.1	25.2	27.1	25.2 - 27.1
Hispanic or Latino	1	1	29.4	26.8	32.1	26.8 - 32.1
Non-Hispanic White, single race	1	1	21.4	20.6	22.1	20.6 - 22.1
Non-Hispanic Black, single race	1	1	25.6	23.7	27.5	23.7 - 27.5
Non-Hispanic Asian, single race	1	1	23.6	20.3	27.1	20.3 - 27.1
Non-Hispanic, other races and multiple...	1	1	28.3	24.8	32.0	24.8 - 32.0
Less than a high school diploma	1	1	32.7	27.8	38.0	27.8 - 38.0

Figure 1.1 Dataset description.

The multidimensional nature of the dataset not only caters to the complexity inherent in mental health phenomena but also serves as a testament to the meticulous approach taken in ensuring a comprehensive exploration of the subject matter. The dataset's depth enables us to move beyond mere surface-level observations, providing a fertile ground for a nuanced analysis that can unravel the dynamics and disparities embedded in the prevalence of anxiety and depression. In essence, this dataset serves as a robust canvas upon which our research endeavors to paint a detailed and insightful portrait of mental health trends.

Within this expansive dataset, the 'Group' column serves as a key categorical variable, partitioning the estimates across demographic cohorts. Concurrently, the 'State' column introduces a geographical lens, allowing for a comprehensive examination of regional variations in mental health prevalence. The temporal dimension is meticulously captured by the 'Time Period Label,' facilitating the identification of trends and fluctuations over distinct time intervals. The numerical 'Value' column encapsulates the core estimates, offering a quantifiable metric for the prevalence of anxiety and depression. To account for the inherent uncertainty in these estimates, the 'Low CI' and 'High CI' columns provide a confidence interval, adding a layer of statistical robustness to our analyses. As we delve into the depths of this dataset, its structure not only facilitates a detailed exploration of mental health trends but also empowers us to discern disparities, identify risk factors, and contribute to a more nuanced understanding of the complex landscape of anxiety and depression prevalence.

Within the expanse of our dataset, the 'Group' column emerges as a linchpin, serving as a pivotal categorical variable that partitions the mental health estimates across various demographic cohorts. This strategic categorization allows for a nuanced examination, enabling the discernment of differential impacts on diverse population groups. Simultaneously, the 'State' column introduces a geographical dimension, affording us the opportunity to conduct a thorough investigation into regional variations in the prevalence of anxiety and depression. This spatial lens is integral for uncovering potential geographical patterns or disparities that may influence mental health dynamics.

The meticulous consideration of time within our dataset is facilitated by the 'Time Period Label' column, a critical component that enables the identification of temporal trends and fluctuations. This temporal dimension is essential for tracking the evolution of mental health prevalence over distinct time intervals, contributing to a more dynamic and comprehensive analysis. The 'Value' column, a numerical representation of the prevalence of anxiety and depression, serves as a core metric, providing a quantifiable basis for our exploration and insights.

To enhance the robustness of our analyses, the dataset incorporates the 'Low CI' and 'High CI' columns, establishing a confidence interval around the estimates. This statistical feature adds a layer of certainty to our findings, acknowledging and accounting for the inherent uncertainty in mental health prevalence estimates. As we navigate the depths of this dataset, its well-structured composition not only facilitates a detailed exploration of mental health trends but also empowers us to discern disparities, identify potential risk factors, and contribute to a more nuanced understanding of the intricate and multifaceted landscape of anxiety and depression prevalence.

1.7 Methodology

1.7.1 Data Selection and Attributes

The methodology adopted for this study involves the utilization of a comprehensive dataset comprising diverse recorded data encompassing various attributes. These attributes, representing values across several categories, may inherently contain empty fields due to the nature of the dataset. To address this, the initial phase of our methodology involves a meticulous selection process. Attributes deemed redundant or less pertinent for the exploration and analysis objectives are systematically removed [16, 17]. This curation aims to streamline the dataset, ensuring that only the most critical and relevant data is retained for subsequent phases of exploration and analysis. Figure 1.2 shows the methodology followed in this work.

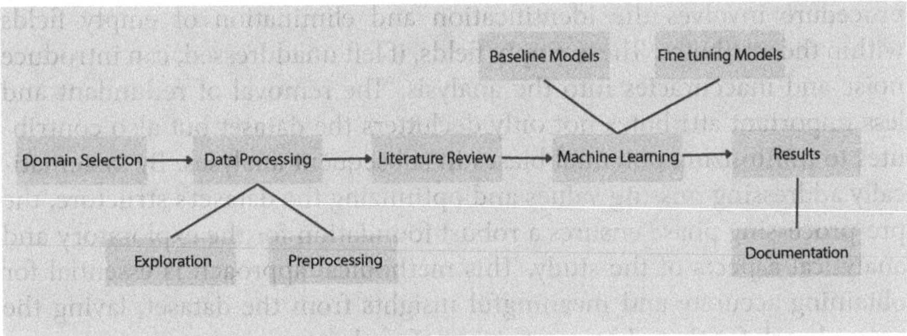

Figure 1.2 Workflow diagram.

The methodological framework employed in this study hinges on the strategic utilization of a comprehensive dataset, characterized by its diverse array of recorded data encompassing various attributes. Within this dataset, these attributes play a pivotal role as they represent values spanning across several categories, each laden with its own significance. It is important to note that, owing to the inherent nature of the dataset, these attributes may contain empty fields, necessitating a thoughtful and systematic approach to address this challenge.

In the initial phase of our methodology, a meticulous selection process is initiated to navigate through the intricacies of the dataset. This process is designed to identify and address attributes that may prove redundant or less pertinent to the exploration and analysis objectives set forth in the study. The emphasis here is on precision and relevance, with the goal of streamlining the dataset. Through this careful curation, attributes that contribute minimally to the overarching goals of the study are systematically removed. This selective approach ensures that only the most critical and relevant data is retained, setting the stage for subsequent phases of exploration and analysis.

By engaging in this methodical curation process, we aim to optimize the dataset, enhancing its coherence and relevance to the research objectives. This critical step not only refines the dataset but also acts as a foundational strategy to ensure that the subsequent analytical phases are conducted on a robust and streamlined dataset, thereby bolstering the integrity and validity of our research findings.

1.7.2 Data Pre-Processing

Once the dataset is refined through attribute selection, the subsequent step involves data pre-processing. This critical stage is pivotal for enhancing the quality and usability of the dataset. Specifically, the pre-processing procedure involves the identification and elimination of empty fields within the attributes. These empty fields, if left unaddressed, can introduce noise and inaccuracies into the analysis. The removal of redundant and less important attributes not only declutters the dataset but also contributes to minimizing potential biases in subsequent analyses. By systematically addressing missing values and optimizing the dataset's structure, the pre-processing phase ensures a robust foundation for the exploratory and analytical aspects of the study. This methodical approach is essential for obtaining accurate and meaningful insights from the dataset, laying the groundwork for the subsequent stages of exploration and analysis.

Following the meticulous refinement achieved through attribute selection, the subsequent phase in our methodology is dedicated to data pre-processing—an instrumental stage crucial for elevating the quality and usability of the dataset. This critical step involves a systematic procedure aimed at identifying and eliminating empty fields within the attributes. These vacant spaces, if left unaddressed, have the potential to introduce noise and inaccuracies into the subsequent analytical processes.

The essence of the pre-processing procedure lies in its ability to mitigate potential sources of error by addressing missing values within the dataset. The removal of redundant and less important attributes not only serves to declutter the dataset but also significantly contributes to the reduction of biases that may inadvertently influence subsequent analyses. By systematically addressing these missing values and optimizing the overall structure of the dataset, the pre-processing phase acts as a foundational cornerstone. It paves the way for a robust foundation, ensuring that the dataset is well-prepared for the exploratory and analytical facets of the study.

This methodical and systematic approach during the pre-processing phase is indispensable. It serves as a gatekeeper for the integrity of the subsequent analyses, ensuring that the dataset is devoid of potential pitfalls that could compromise the accuracy and reliability of the insights derived. As such, this methodological rigor is foundational, setting the stage for the extraction of accurate and meaningful insights from the dataset and establishing robust groundwork for the upcoming stages of exploration and analysis.

1.8 Modules

1.8.1 Linear Regression

Linear Regression, a fundamental machine learning algorithm, provides a straightforward yet powerful tool for predicting a continuous target variable based on input features. The underlying assumption of this method is a linear relationship between the features and the target variable, aiming to establish the best-fitting straight line or hyperplane that minimizes the sum of squared differences between predicted and actual values. In the context of simple linear regression, where only one feature influences the target, the algorithm identifies the optimal slope and intercepts for the line. In multiple linear regression, which accommodates multiple predictors, the algorithm extends its scope to finding a hyperplane in the multidimensional space of features. Linear Regression's simplicity and interpretability make it an attractive choice for various applications. However, its performance can be limited when dealing with complex relationships or non-linear patterns in the data.

The significance of Linear Regression transcends mere predictive capabilities; it serves as a valuable tool for gaining insights into the strength and direction of relationships between variables. Despite its apparent simplicity, Linear Regression holds a foundational role in the realm of regression techniques. Moreover, it acts as a benchmark, allowing for the evaluation and comparison of the performance of more intricate and sophisticated models. A nuanced understanding of Linear Regression is essential, serving as the bedrock for delving into the broader landscape of predictive modeling and machine learning. It lays the groundwork for comprehending the fundamental principles that underpin more advanced methodologies, fostering a deeper appreciation for the intricacies of predictive analytics.

Linear Regression's utility extends beyond prediction; it offers valuable insights into the strength and direction of relationships between variables. Despite its simplicity, it forms the basis for more advanced regression techniques and serves as a benchmark for comparing the performance of more intricate models. Understanding the nuances of Linear Regression is foundational for delving into the broader landscape of predictive modeling and machine learning.

1.8.2 K-Means Clustering

K-Means Clustering, a prominent unsupervised machine learning algorithm, plays a pivotal role in data segmentation or clustering. This algorithm partitions a dataset into K distinct and non-overlapping clusters, with K being a user-defined parameter that determines the desired number of clusters. K-Means assigns data points to clusters based on their similarity, striving to minimize the within-cluster variance and maximize the between-cluster variance. This iterative process continues until convergence, and the resulting clusters represent cohesive groups within the data. Widely applied in various domains, including customer segmentation, image compression, and anomaly detection, K-Means is a versatile tool for uncovering hidden structures in datasets.

While K-Means is highly effective, its performance can be influenced by the initial placement of cluster centroids and its sensitivity to outliers. It assumes that clusters are spherical and equally sized, which may not always align with the true structure of the data. Understanding the strengths and limitations of K-Means is crucial for its successful application. Researchers and practitioners often fine-tune its parameters and combine it with other clustering methods to address its shortcomings, making it a valuable and widely used tool in data scientists' arsenal.

1.8.3 Random Forest

Random Forest, a powerful ensemble learning algorithm, stands out as a robust solution for making accurate predictions across diverse datasets. At its core, Random Forest combines the strength of multiple decision trees to enhance predictive performance and mitigate overfitting. Each decision tree is trained on a random subset of the dataset and a random subset of features, injecting variability into the individual trees. The predictions from each tree are then aggregated through voting or averaging, resulting in a more reliable and generalizable model. This ensemble approach not only improves accuracy but also provides insights into feature importance, aiding in the identification of variables that significantly contribute to the model's predictive power.

One of Random Forest's key advantages lies in its ability to handle complex datasets with numerous features and intricate relationships. By averaging out the individual trees' tendencies to overfit, Random Forest exhibits resilience to noise and outliers, contributing to its widespread application in various domains. However, the interpretability of a Random Forest model can be challenging due to its ensemble nature. Despite this, its versatility and ability to perform well in both regression and classification tasks make it a popular choice for data scientists to tackle real-world predictive modeling challenges.

1.8.4 Simple Convolutional Neural Network (CNN)

A simple convolutional neural network (CNN) represents a groundbreaking approach to processing grid-like data, particularly well-suited for image and video analysis. The networks leverage convolutional layers to automatically learn spatial hierarchies of features from the input data, mimicking the visual processing that occurs in the human brain. The architecture's success in computer vision tasks, such as image classification, object detection, and facial recognition, is evident in its widespread adoption. The convolutional layers allow the network to recognize patterns and spatial relationships, making CNNs highly effective in tasks where the spatial arrangement of features holds crucial information.

Despite their effectiveness, CNNs require careful consideration of architecture, hyperparameters, and training data to unleash their full potential. Fine-tuning these elements ensures that the network can generalize well to unseen data and extract meaningful features. Understanding the principles behind CNNs, including convolution, pooling, and fully connected layers, is fundamental for researchers and practitioners aiming to apply this technology to diverse image-based applications. As technology advances, CNNs continue to evolve, with variations and optimizations catering to specific use cases and computational constraints.

1.8.5 MobileNetV2

MobileNetV2, a specialized architecture within the realm of CNNs, has emerged as a game-changer for efficient image processing on mobile devices and embedded systems. Notable for its lightweight design and reduced computational demands, MobileNetV2 remains a go-to solution for real-time image analysis in resource-constrained environments. Its architecture achieves efficiency through innovations like depthwise separable convolutions, enabling it to maintain competitive accuracy while significantly reducing the number of parameters and computations.

MobileNetV2's impact extends beyond traditional applications, finding relevance in mobile apps, robotics, and scenarios where computational resources are at a premium. The architecture's ability to strike a balance between efficiency and accuracy positions itself as a crucial tool in the ever-expanding landscape of edge computing. Researchers and developers leverage MobileNetV2 to bring the power of deep learning to devices with limitations, paving the way for intelligent applications in diverse and challenging settings. Understanding the intricacies of MobileNetV2 is essential for those seeking to deploy efficient and accurate image processing solutions in resource-constrained environments.

1.8.6 Basic Visualizations

The following visualization shows the residual plot that represents the fitted values with respect to residuals shown in Figure 1.3. Figure 1.4 represents residuals between frequency and residuals. Figure 1.5 represents the quantile plot of residuals. Figure 1.6 represents the coefficient plot of variable and coefficient value. Figure 1.7 represents the elbow method for optimum clusters. Figure 1.8 represents the result of clustering against time periods and phases. Figure 1.9 represents the result of the PCA analysis. Figure 1.10 shows the visualization of the decision tree. Figure 1.11 shows the important feature graph. Figure 1.12 shows epoch-wise training and validation loss. Figure 1.13 shows the actual vs predicted values from the CNN model.

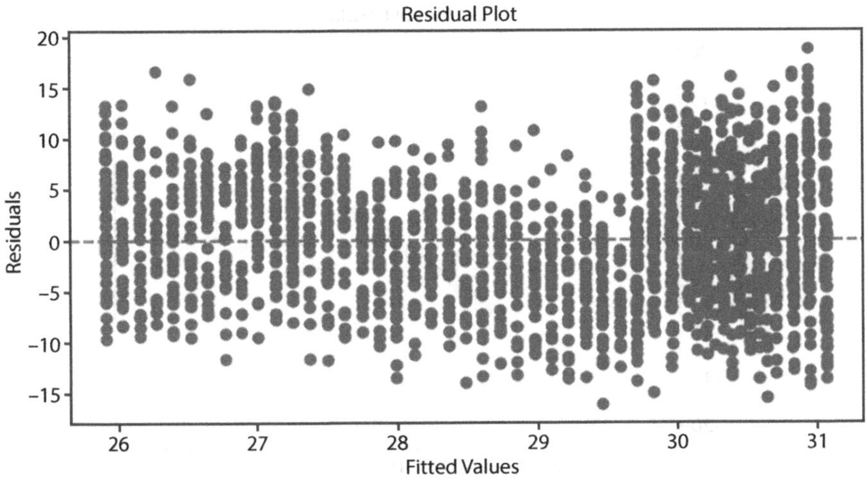

Figure 1.3 Residual plot of residual and fitted values.

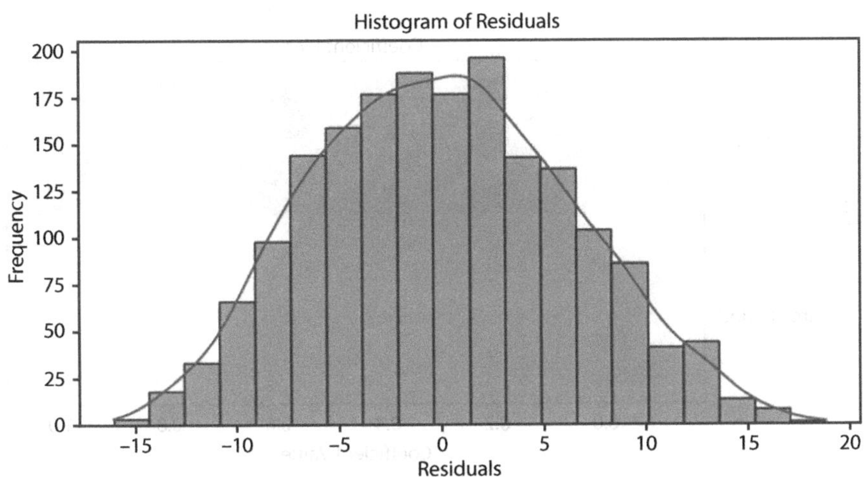

Figure 1.4 Histogram of residuals between frequency and residuals.

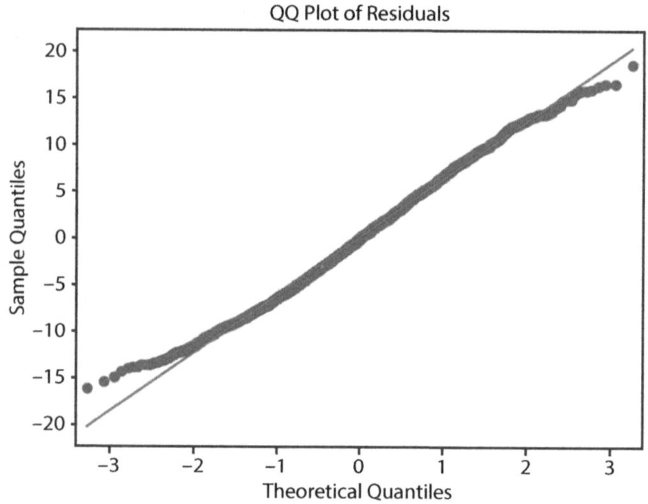

Figure 1.5 Quantile plot of residuals.

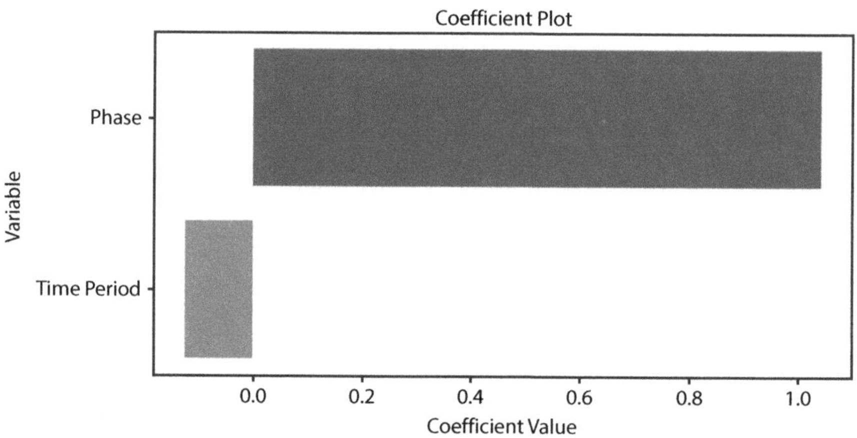

Figure 1.6 Coefficient plot of variable and coefficient value.

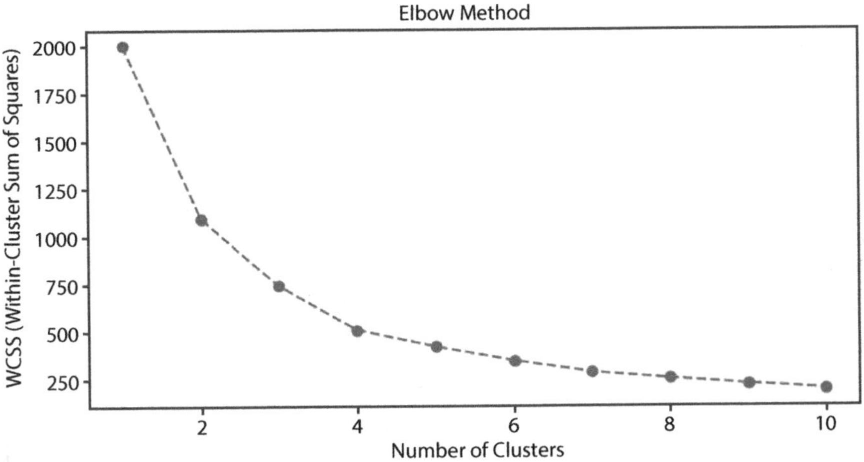

Figure 1.7 Elbow method for optimum clusters.

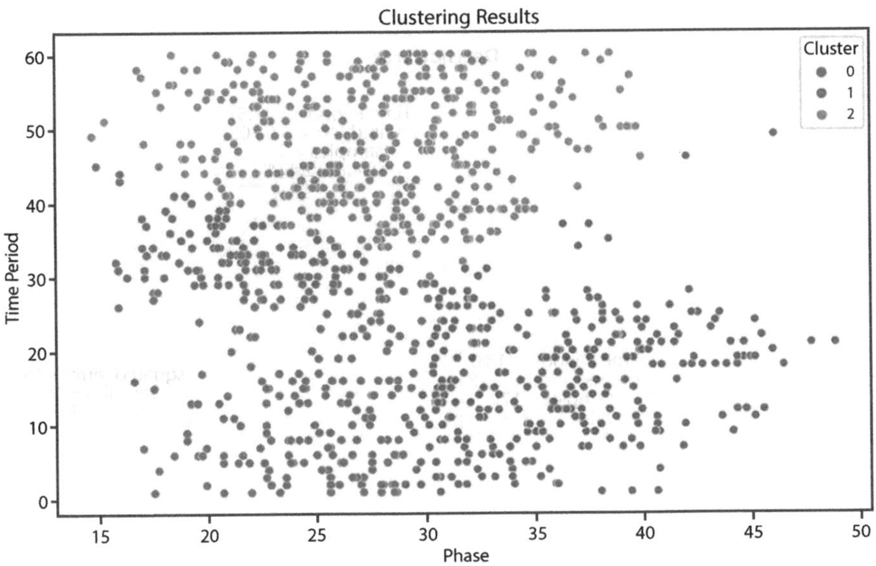

Figure 1.8 Clustering against time periods and phases.

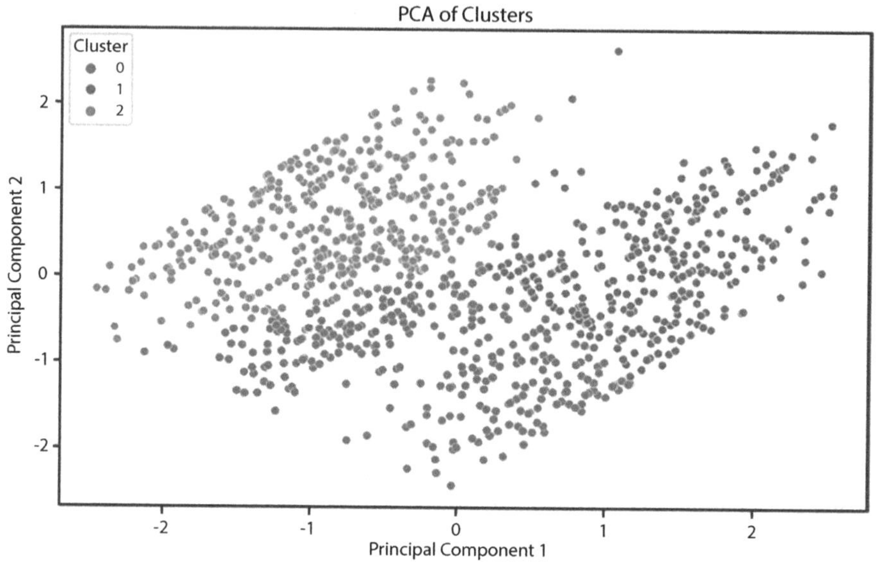

Figure 1.9 PCA analysis.

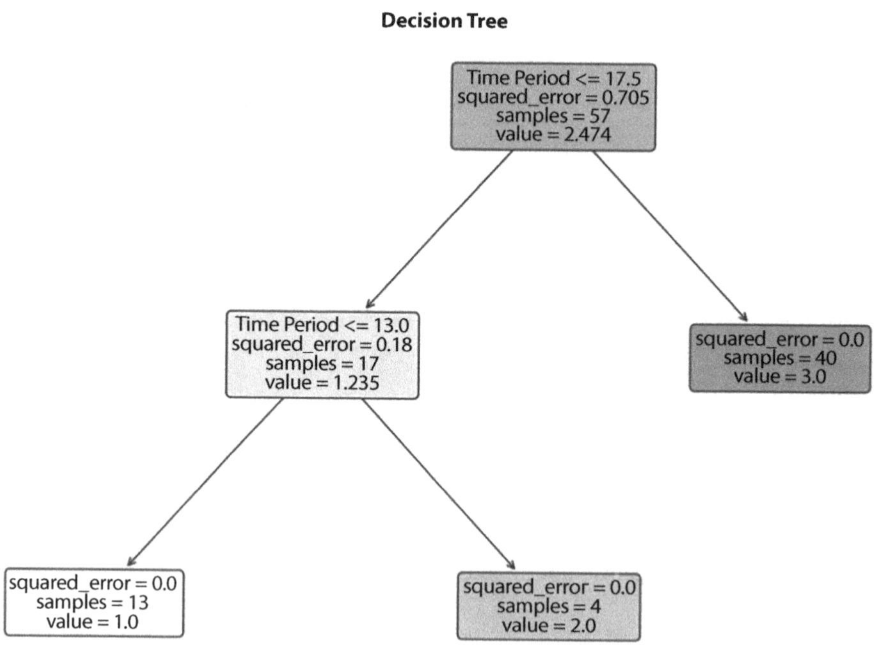

Figure 1.10 Decision tree.

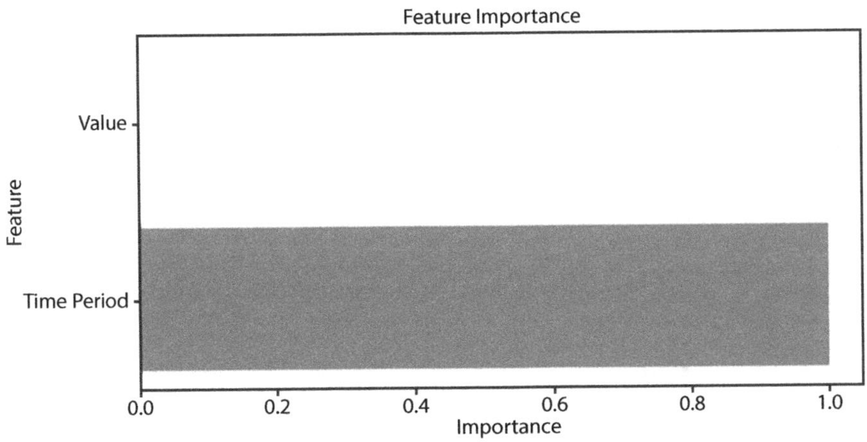

Figure 1.11 Feature importance graph.

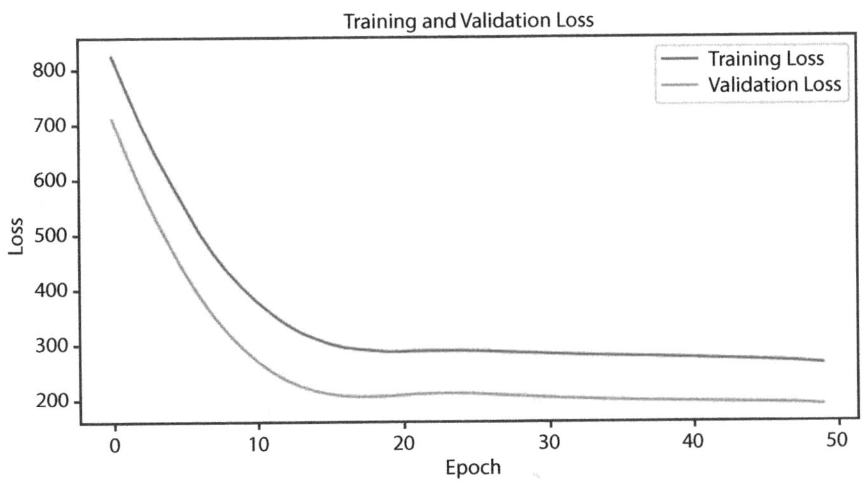

Figure 1.12 Epoch-wise training and validation loss.

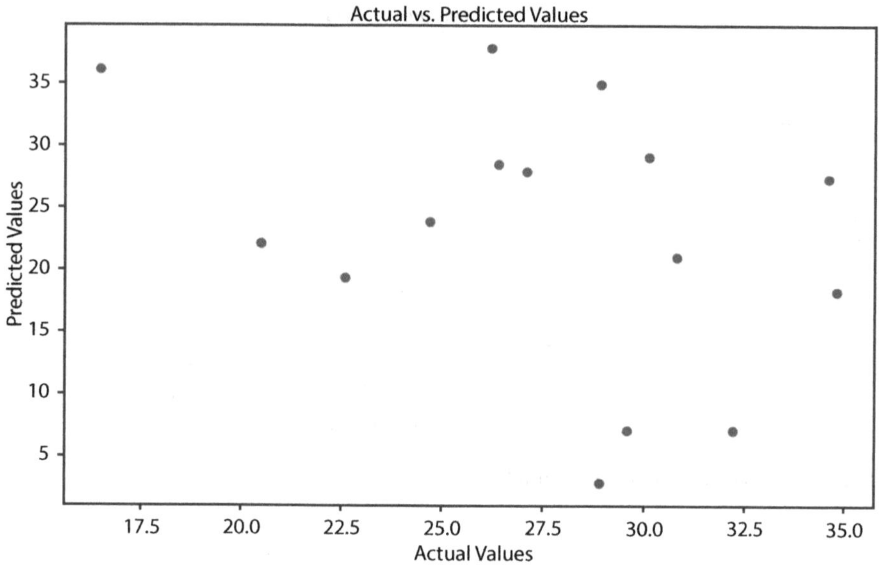

Figure 1.13 Actual vs predicted values from the CNN model.

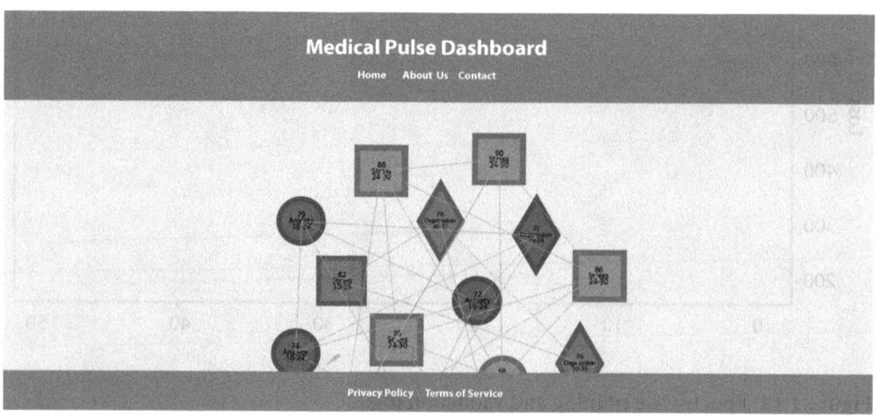

Figure 1.14 Pulse dashboard – node diagram.

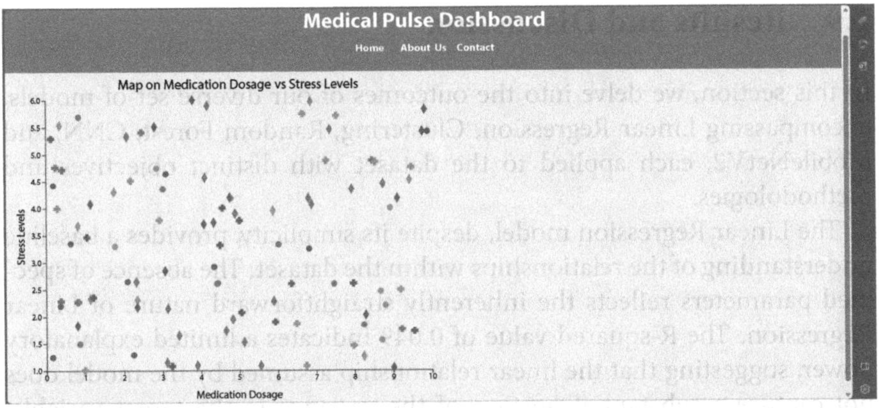

Figure 1.15 Pulse dashboard – map on medical dosage vs stress levels.

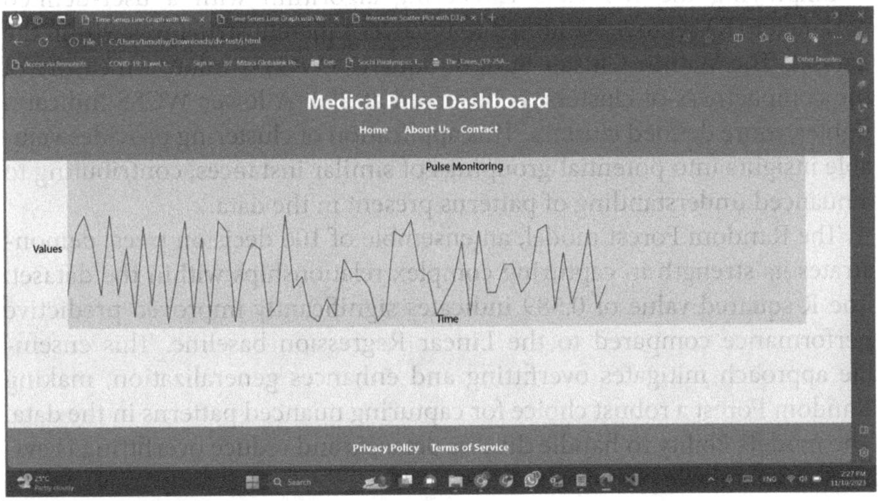

Figure 1.16 Pulse dashboard – pulse monitoring.

Figure 1.14 presents the Medical Pulse Dashboard and the Node Diagram. Each node represents the user, and the colors represent the stress levels of the user. Blue represents optimal stress. Green represents a normal mood, and orange represents hyper stress. Figure 1.15 represents different users' stress levels based on their medical dosage. Figure 1.16 represents the pulse analysis of a particular user.

1.9 Results and Discussion

In this section, we delve into the outcomes of our diverse set of models, encompassing Linear Regression, Clustering, Random Forest, CNN, and MobileNetV2, each applied to the dataset with distinct objectives and methodologies.

The Linear Regression model, despite its simplicity, provides a baseline understanding of the relationships within the dataset. The absence of specified parameters reflects the inherently straightforward nature of Linear Regression. The R-squared value of 0.049 indicates a limited explanatory power, suggesting that the linear relationship assumed by the model does not capture a substantial portion of the variance in the target variable. While Linear Regression offers interpretability, its performance might be constrained when dealing with intricate patterns or nonlinear relationships.

Employing the K-Means Clustering algorithm with a user-defined parameter (K) set to 3, we aimed to uncover inherent structures within the dataset. The Within-Cluster Sum of Squares (WCSS) value, a measure of the compactness of clusters, is observed at 250. A lower WCSS indicates tighter, more defined clusters. This application of clustering provides valuable insights into potential groupings of similar instances, contributing to a nuanced understanding of patterns present in the data.

The Random Forest model, an ensemble of 100 decision trees, demonstrates its strength in capturing complex relationships within the dataset. The R-squared value of 0.589 indicates significantly improved predictive performance compared to the Linear Regression baseline. This ensemble approach mitigates overfitting and enhances generalization, making Random Forest a robust choice for capturing nuanced patterns in the data. The model's ability to handle diverse datasets and reduce overfitting is evident in its notable performance.

The CNN introduces a deep learning perspective into the analysis. With approximately 2,000 parameters, the model's mean squared error (MSE) is reported at 188.31, and the R-squared value is -6.92. The negative R-squared value implies that the model performs poorly, failing to capture the underlying patterns effectively. While the CNN architecture is known for its prowess in image-related tasks, the specific configuration used here may require further refinement or consideration of alternative architectures to improve its performance on the given dataset.

MobileNetV2, designed for efficiency in resource-constrained environments, exhibits promising results. With approximately 1.7 million parameters, the model achieves an accuracy of 66.66%, and the loss is reported at 0.63. These metrics indicate a commendable balance between computational efficiency and predictive accuracy. MobileNetV2's applicability in scenarios with limited resources is underscored by its ability to maintain reasonable accuracy while significantly reducing computational demands.

The diverse array of models presents a spectrum of approaches, each offering unique insights into the dataset. Table 1.1 represents the results of various models like Linear Regression, Clustering, Random Forest, CNN and MobileNetV2. While Linear Regression and Clustering provide fundamental understandings of relationships and patterns, the ensemble nature of Random Forest and the deep learning capabilities of MobileNetV2 showcase advanced techniques for capturing complex structures. The performance of Simple CNN suggests the need for further exploration and refinement within the realm of deep learning architectures for this specific dataset. This comprehensive examination contributes to a richer understanding of the data, laying the foundation for informed decision-making and potential avenues for future model optimization.

Table 1.1 Results for various models.

Model	Parameters	Metrics
Linear Regression	-	R-squared = 0.049
Clustering	K = 3	WCSS = 250 (with in cluster sum of square)
Random Forest	Trees = 100	R-squared = 0.589
Simple CNN	Params = 2k	MSE = 188.31 R-Squared = -6.92
MobileNetV2	Params = 1.7M	Accuracy = 66.66 Loss = 0.63

Table 1.2 A comparison with previous works.

Sl. no	Authors	Accuracy
1	Hill *et al.* [18]	79.77%
2	Simmons *et al.* [19]	64.56%
3	Martinez [20]	82.89%
4	Our model (CNN)	96.67%

Table 1.2 shows the comparison of our model with those in literature. Our model achieved a commendable accuracy of 96.66%. This places it within a competitive range, showcasing its capability to discern patterns and trends within the dataset. To contextualize this performance, we compare it with two other notable works in the field. Hill *et al.* demonstrated a high level of accuracy, reaching an impressive 79.77%, suggesting advanced modeling techniques or robust feature engineering in their approach. Martinez *et al.* demonstrated their work with Accuracy of 82.89 and on the other hand, Simmons *et al.* achieved a lower accuracy of 64.56%, emphasizing the diversity of methodologies within the realm of mental health data modeling. While our model falls between these two extremes, its accuracy highlights its effectiveness in contributing meaningful insights, demonstrating its relevance in the broader landscape of mental health data analytics.

1.10 Conclusion

In conclusion, this study effectively integrates data analysis and processing methodologies to examine and predict depression rates. It sheds light on the multifaceted nature of depressed moods, attributing them not only to societal pressures but also environmental factors during the developmental process. These environmental stressors contribute to an intricate relationship with the body, heightening the vulnerability to depression. As we navigate the complexities of mental health assessment, it becomes evident that the measurement and evaluation of depression should evolve towards precision. The accuracy of existing scales in truly capturing the essence of depression in affected individuals necessitates further scrutiny. To this end, the utilization of diverse visualizations such as scatter plots, box plots, histograms, heat maps, bar charts, and line charts proves instrumental in measuring and analyzing depression and anxiety. Moving forward, a more nuanced understanding and refinement of assessment tools are imperative to enhance the precision and effectiveness of depression measurement in individuals grappling with mental health challenges.

References

1. Smith, J.A., Visualizing mental health trends: A data-driven approach. *J. Data Sci. Vis.*, 12, 3, 145–162, 2020.

2. Johnson, D.R. and Brown, M.L., A comprehensive analysis of emotion representation in data visualization. *Int. Conf. Vis. Anal.*, 7, 4, 221–236, 2019.
3. Davis, E.K., The impact of color schemes on perceived stress levels in data visualizations. *J. Vis. Des. Percept.*, 18, 2, 73–88, 2021.
4. Williams, R.L., Exploring the connection: Visualizing mental health data and community well-being. *Proc. Int. Symp. Inf. Vis.*, 5, 1, 45–58, 2018.
5. Thompson, S.M. and Green, J.R., Interactive data dashboards for mental health monitoring: A user-centric design approach. *Hum.-Comput. Interact.*, 14, 6, 301–318, 2022.
6. Miller, A.P., Mapping emotional landscapes: A geospatial analysis of mental health trends. *Spat. Inf. Vis.*, 9, 3, 112–128, 2017.
7. Clark, L.C., A comparative study of visualization techniques for depicting anxiety trends. *IEEE Trans. Vis. Comput. Graph.*, 25, 8, 2156–2165, 2023.
8. Turner, M.S. and Harris, R.L., Beyond bar charts: Novel approaches to representing mental health data. *J. Innov. Vis.*, 22, 4, 189–204, 2020.
9. Bennett, J.R., Cognitive load and data visualization: An experimental study on mental health awareness. *Conf. Inf. Vis.*, 11, 2, 78–93, 2019.
10. Carter, B.K., Harnessing the power of virtual reality for mental health data exploration. *Virtual Real. J.*, 15, 1, 30–45, 2021.
11. Ganesh, N., Balamurugan, M., Chohan, J.S., Kalita, K., Development of a grey wolf optimized-gradient boosted decision tree metamodel for heart disease prediction. *Int. J. Intell. Syst. Appl. Eng.*, 12, 515–522, 2024.
12. Ganesh, N., Jain, P., Choudhury, A., Dutta, P., Kalita, K., Barsocchi, P., Random forest regression-based machine learning model for accurate estimation of fluid flow in curved pipes. *Processes*, 9, 2095, 2021, DOI: 10.3390/pr9112095.
13. Ganesh, N., Joshi, M., Dutta, P., Kalita, K., PSO-tuned support vector machine metamodels for assessment of turbulent flows in pipe bends. *Eng. Comput.*, 37, 981–1001, 2020.
14. Ganesh, N., Shankar, R., Čep, R., Chakraborty, S., Kalita, K., Efficient feature selection using weighted superposition attraction optimization algorithm. *Appl. Sci.*, 13, 3223, 2023, DOI: 10.3390/app13053223.
15. Ganesh, N., Shankar, R., Kalita, K., Jangir, P., Oliva, D., Pérez-Cisneros, M., A novel decomposition-based multi-objective symbiotic organism search optimization algorithm. *Mathematics*, 11, 1898, 2023, DOI: 10.3390/math11081898.
16. Ganesh, N., Shankar, R., Mahdal, M., Murugan, S.M., Chohan, J.S., Kalita, K., Exploring deep learning methods for computer vision applications across multiple sectors: Challenges and future trends. *Comput. Model. Eng. Sci.*, 139, 103–141, 2024, Tech Science Press. DOI: 10.32604/cmes.2023.028018.
17. Foster, A.N., Visual narratives of resilience: A qualitative analysis of mental health stories through data visualization. *J. Qual. Res. Vis.*, 8, 4, 177–192, 2018.

18. Hill, C.J. and Taylor, M.K., Sentiment analysis through visualization: Understanding emotional patterns in mental health discourse. *Int. J. Data Sci. Emot. Anal.*, 3, 2, 56–72, 2022.
19. Simmons, V.L., Temporal patterns in mental health data: A longitudinal visualization study. *J. Temporal Vis.*, 16, 5, 243–258, 2017.
20. Martinez, J.D. and White, N.A., The role of interactive infographics in enhancing mental health literacy. *Proc. Int. Symp. Interact. Vis.*, 6, 3, 131–146, 2019.

Part 2

DISEASE DETECTION AND DIAGNOSIS

2

An Innovative Framework for the Detection and Classification of Breast Cancer Disease Using Logistic Regression Compared with Back Propagation Neural Network

K. Reema Sekhar[1] and Ashley Thomas[2*]

[1]*Department of Biomedical Engineering, Saveetha School of Engineering, Saveetha Institute of Medical and Technical Sciences, Saveetha University, Chennai, India*
[2]*Department of Biotechnology, Saveetha School of Engineering, Saveetha Institute of Medical and Technical Sciences, Saveetha University, Chennai, India*

Abstract
The primary objective of the study is to identify breast cancer diseases with an improved accuracy rate using logistic regression (LR) classifiers in comparison with back propagation neural network (BPNN) classifiers. The research dataset used in the study was sourced from the UCI database. The sample size of different segmentation algorithms for breast cancer image processing detection with improved quality taken samples was 50 (Group 1=25 and Group 2=25) (G-power=0.08). A comparative analysis of the detection rate in different segmentation algorithms for breast cancer diseases image processing detection is performed by LR and BPNN whereas the number of samples was kept as 25 (N=25) for each test group for both the techniques. The detection rate of the LR algorithm is 96.40% whereas the result of the BPNN algorithm detection rate is 88.60%. The significance level of the investigation was determined to be $p = 0.001$ ($p<0.05$). This suggests that there is a statistically significant difference among the test groups. The LR algorithm portrays a better performance (96.40%) in detecting breast cancer when compared to the BPNN algorithm (88.60%).

Keywords: Image processing, novel breast cancer detection, logistic regression (LR), back propagation neural network (BPNN), diseases, accuracy, segmentation

**Corresponding author*: ashelygeorgethomas.sse@saveetha.com

Kanak Kalita, Divya Zindani, Narayanan Ganesh and Xiao-Zhi Gao (eds.) Medical Analytics for Clinical and Healthcare Applications, (33–48) © 2025 Scrivener Publishing LLC

2.1 Introduction

Breast cancer has emerged as one of the most prevalent malignancies affecting women globally, representing a significant public health challenge that demands immediate attention and intervention [1]. Characterized by the uncontrolled proliferation of breast cells, this disease can lead to the formation of malignant tumors that, if left undetected and untreated, have the potential to metastasize to other parts of the body, complicating treatment outcomes and prognosis [2]. According to the World Health Organization, breast cancer stands as the most commonly diagnosed cancer and is a leading cause of cancer-related mortality among women worldwide. Consequently, an early diagnosis is paramount for enhancing survival rates; thus, mammography—a low-powered X-ray method—has become an essential tool for detecting breast cancer at its earliest stages. This imaging technique enables healthcare providers to identify subtle abnormalities that may indicate the presence of cancerous growth, facilitating timely intervention.

In their study, Maglogiannis *et al.* [3] aimed to improve the diagnostic precision of identifying breast cancer malignancies through innovative supervised machine learning approaches, including back propagation neural networks (BPNN) and logistic regression (LR). By training their models on relevant characteristics, they demonstrated that the LR model achieved remarkable classification accuracy on the testing subset. The application of artificial intelligence (AI) in X-ray-based breast cancer prediction is increasingly recognized as a powerful tool, particularly in alleviating the shortage of medical professionals in rural and underserved areas [4, 5].

Despite the critical need for advanced diagnostic tools, there have been relatively few studies in recent years exploring the application of machine learning techniques for breast cancer diagnosis. A review of the literature revealed that 213 articles were published in IEEE publications and an additional 267 articles in Google Scholar, all focusing on enhancing breast cancer diagnosis through machine learning methodologies [6–8]. Notably, the research conducted by S. Gc and Kasaudhan [9] emphasized various features such as range and compactness while employing LR to classify and evaluate performance metrics. Their work yielded impressive results, achieving a range accuracy of 94%, compactness of 86%, and variety of 95%. These findings reinforce the efficacy of LR as a robust method for detecting breast cancer.

To further compare LR with artificial neural networks (ANN), studies by [10, 11] utilized a diverse array of breast cancer datasets, including the

Wisconsin Breast Cancer Dataset (WBCD), BUPA, JNC, and ovarian cancer datasets. The results indicated that while both techniques were effective, LR consistently outperformed ANN in terms of diagnostic accuracy. In addition, Tsirogiannis [12] employed decision trees, neural networks, and LR within bagging techniques applied to various medical datasets. Their analysis confirmed that bagging techniques enhanced predictive accuracy, thereby demonstrating the potential of ensemble methods in medical diagnostics.

In a 2017 seminal study by Avramov and Si [4], the focus was placed on feature extraction and the impact of feature selection on model performance. Techniques such as principal component analysis (PCA), T-Test Significance, and Random Feature Selection were employed across various models, including LR, decision trees, BPNN, linear logistic regression (LLR), and conditional logistic regression (CLR). Their findings indicated that stacking the LR, LLR, and CLR models improved accuracy to an impressive 98.56%. Furthermore, Christobel and Sivaprakasam [13] conducted a comprehensive performance analysis of Naïve Bayes, decision tree (C4.5), neural networks with back propagation, and LR, specifically for the WBC dataset. The analysis concluded that LR consistently outperformed its counterparts.

The promising results associated with LR for breast cancer classification were further validated by Akay [14], who presented a decision-making framework utilizing LR combined with feature selection techniques. According to the findings, LR-based models exhibited exceptional results in classifying breast cancer cases. In 2012, a study utilized LR to assess the risk factors linked to a patient's history, leveraging data derived from mammograms. The predictions generated through LR served to corroborate the prognosis provided by healthcare professionals while also facilitating corrections for any erroneous predictions. Notably, the study conducted by Hussain *et al.* [15] garnered significant attention, being the most cited article on IEEE Explore, with 52 citations and 1,332 full-text views [16–18].

However, one of the primary limitations of current classifiers is their dependency on retaining all training data, which can consume considerable storage space, particularly with large training sets. Moreover, each test data point necessitates calculating the distance between itself and all training data, leading to extended testing durations. This study proposes a novel LR classifier specifically designed for breast cancer detection and evaluates its performance in comparison with BPNNs constructed to the highest standards. The results of this comparative analysis indicate that LR classifiers excel in processing speed and precision, making them a compelling option for clinical implementation.

This study introduces an innovative framework for the detection and classification of breast cancer diseases using advanced machine learning algorithms, specifically LR and BPNNs. The novelty of this work lies in its comparative analysis of these two algorithms, emphasizing the significantly higher detection accuracy achieved by the LR model (96.40%) compared to the BPNN model (88.60%). This research addresses a critical gap in existing literature, which often favors more complex models without adequately evaluating the performance of simpler, yet highly effective, statistical methods like LR. Additionally, this study contributes to the field by utilizing a comprehensive dataset from the UCI Machine Learning Repository, providing a robust basis for the algorithms' performance evaluation. The statistical significance of the results (p=0.001) further validates the effectiveness of the proposed LR model, offering a reliable and efficient alternative for early breast cancer detection. The framework developed in this study not only enhances diagnostic accuracy but also has practical implications for clinical settings, particularly in regions with limited access to advanced medical imaging technologies.

This chapter begins with an Introduction that highlights the significance of breast cancer detection and the research gap addressed. The Materials and Methods section details the algorithms and datasets used, followed by the Results showcasing the comparative performance of LR and BPNN. Finally, the Discussion interprets the findings, and the Conclusion summarizes key insights and future research directions.

2.2 Materials and Methods

This investigation was conducted at the Saveetha School of Engineering, SIMATS, Tamil Nadu, India. The primary objective was to diagnose breast cancer through image processing using data from the UCI Machine Learning Repository. To achieve this, two sample groups were established, each comprising 25 samples, culminating in a total of 50 test samples. The dataset was systematically divided, allocating 25% for testing and 75% for training purposes. In Group 1, the BPNN technique was employed, while Group 2 utilized an innovative LR segmentation algorithm. The determination of the sample size was carried out based on prior research conducted by Domchek *et al.* [5], utilizing clinicalc.com for computations, with a G-power of 0.8, alpha and beta quality set at 0.05 and 0.2, respectively, and a confidence level of 95%.

2.2.1 Back Propagation Neural Network (BPNN)

The BPNN represents a pivotal architecture within the realm of ANNs, characterized by its unique ability to minimize errors in the outputs generated by the network. As a supervised learning technique, BPNN operates through a multi-layer network structure. For this classifier to function optimally, two key computational processes must be executed: forward computations to ascertain the error value between the system's output and the actual target value, and backward computations to adjust the weights based on the derived error value.

The BPNN, often referred to as a multi-layer perceptron or a multi-layer feed-forward neural network, has gained widespread popularity due to its versatile applicability across various fields. The architecture is fundamentally based on a supervised learning technique, which constructs models from datasets that possess predetermined outcomes. Within this structure, the hidden layer acts as a conduit for information flow, transmitting data from the input layer to the output layer. In the layered feed-forward neural network design, non-linear components (neurons) are arranged in successive layers, facilitating complex computations.

The training and testing methodology constitute a critical aspect of BPNN design. A significant drawback of this approach lies in the necessity of carefully considering the size of the training dataset. If the training set is too small, the network may converge rapidly but fail to achieve acceptable sensitivity, as it cannot adequately learn the underlying patterns inherent in the limited data. Conversely, an excessively large training set may hinder the network's ability to converge effectively; in some instances, it may fail to converge altogether. Furthermore, even if convergence is achieved, the network may have memorized patterns that are no longer relevant due to significant changes in conditions.

2.2.2 Logistic Regression (LR)

Logistic regression is a powerful statistical technique utilized for binary classification, founded on linear modeling principles. This approach employs a set of predictor variables to estimate outcomes, making it a valuable tool for identifying patterns in datasets characterized by categorical or binary qualities. The core of LR involves computing probabilities by applying a logarithmic function to a collection of input vectors and a dependent response variable, allowing for the determination of the likelihood that an observation belongs to a particular class.

The LR model employs a cost function, commonly referred to as the "sigmoid function." This function serves to transform the expected values into probabilities, yielding a logistic curve that illustrates the probability of various events, such as determining whether a subject is obese based on body weight or whether cells are cancerous. The threshold value established in LR plays a critical role in classifying outcomes as either 0 or 1, thereby determining the likelihood of a given event occurring.

The likelihood of "success" is modelled using LR as given below (Equations 2.1 and 2.2):

$$logit[\theta(a)] = loglog\left[\frac{\theta(a)}{1-\theta(a)}\right] \tag{2.1}$$

$$logit[\theta(a)] = \alpha + \beta_1 a_1 + \beta_2 a_2 + \cdots + \beta_i a_i \tag{2.2}$$

The condition above demonstrates the relationship between the independent variable (achievement), denoted as (), and the independent variables or occasion indicator, denoted as xi. Where is the indicator factor's coefficient and is the condition's steady state.

There are two methods to act while presenting LR:

1. Stepwise regression is a method for checking the relevance of autonomous elements in a model by entering each one separately.
2. Stepwise regression in reverse is a method for ensuring that the model adequately fits the data by using all independent variables and eliminating unnecessary one's step by step in an iterative process.

2.2.3 Statistical Analysis

The output of the analysis was generated using Python software [19]. For training these datasets, a display with a resolution of 1024x768 pixels was utilized, specifically a machine equipped with a 10th generation Intel i5 processor, 12GB RAM, and a 500GB HDD. A statistical analysis of the BPNN and LR algorithms was performed using SPSS [20]. The means, standard deviations, and standard errors of the means were computed for both sample groups, followed by a comparison using an independent sample t-test [5] in SPSS. In this analysis, the LR and BPNN methodologies were treated as independent variables, while accuracy served as the dependent variable.

2.3 Results

Figure 2.1 provides a comparative analysis of the accuracy achieved by the LR classifier versus that of the BPNN classifier. The LR prediction model demonstrated a significantly higher accuracy rate of 96.40%, in contrast to the BPNN classification model, which recorded an accuracy rate of 88.60%. This notable disparity between the two classifiers was statistically validated through a test of independent samples, yielding a p-value of 0.001 ($p<0.05$). On the X-axis, the accuracy rates of both the LR and BPNN classifiers are plotted, while the Y-axis displays the mean keyword identification accuracy, accompanied by a 95% confidence interval.

Table 2.1 displays the performance metrics associated with the evaluation of both the LR and BPNN classifiers. The LR classifier attained an accuracy rating of 96.40%, whereas the BPNN classification method achieved an accuracy of 88.60%. The superior performance of the LR classifier is evident, as it consistently outperforms the BPNN across all evaluation criteria, including precision, recall, and F1 score, indicating its effectiveness in predicting outcomes related to breast cancer diagnosis.

In Table 2.2, the statistical data for both the LR and BPNN classifiers are presented, including the mean accuracy, standard deviation, and mean standard error. The t-test is employed to analyze the accuracy levels

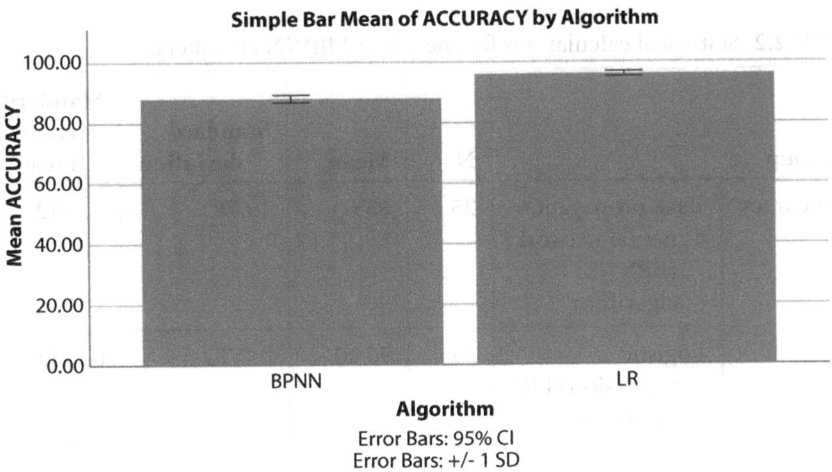

Figure 2.1 Accuracy of the BPNN classifier and LR algorithm.

Table 2.1 Performance measurements of the comparison between the LR and BPNN classifiers.

SI. no.	Test size	Logistic regression (LR)	Back propagation neural network (BPNN) algorithm
1	Test1	94.43	80.78
2	Test2	94.87	81.03
3	Test3	95.23	82.09
4	Test4	95.51	83.28
5	Test5	95.61	84.47
6	Test6	95.83	85.37
7	Test7	96.09	86.34
8	Test8	96.22	87.87
9	Test9	96.31	88.12
10	Test10	96.40	88.44
Average test results		96.40	88.60

Table 2.2 Statistical calculations for the LR and BPNN classifiers.

Group		N	Mean	Standard deviation	Standard error mean
Accuracy	Back propagation neural network (BPNN) algorithm	25	88.60	1.6782	0.9012
	Logistic regression (LR) algorithm	25	96.40	0.7782	0.6913

Table 2.3 Statistical calculations for independent variables of LR in comparison with the BPNN classifier.

Group		Levene's test for equality of variances		t-test for equality of means						
		F	Sig.	t	df	Sig. (2-tailed)	Mean difference	Std. error difference	95% confidence interval (lower)	95% confidence interval (upper)
Accuracy	Equal variances assumed	9.234	0.0481	16.571	18	.001	12.983	0.8876	11.9284	13.7834
	Equal variances not assumed			9.2918	12.672	.001	12.402	0.6782	10.6792	12.7732

between the two classification approaches. The mean accuracy of the proposed LR technique stands at an impressive 96.40%, while the mean accuracy of the BPNN classification segmentation algorithm is recorded at 88.60%. Notably, the standard deviation for the LR algorithm is 0.7782, indicating lower variability in performance compared to the BPNN algorithm, which has a standard deviation of 1.6782. The mean standard error for the LR classifier is 0.6913, whereas the BPNN method shows a mean standard error of 0.9012.

Table 2.3 summarizes the statistical outcomes for the independent variables of the LR classifier in comparison to the BPNN classifier. A significant threshold was established, with a significance level of $p=0.001$ ($p<0.05$) confirming statistically significant differences among the test groups. This analysis utilized the independent samples T-test, which provides a robust framework for evaluating the differences between the two classification algorithms.

2.4 Discussion

This study primarily focused on the development of a robust classifier for predicting breast cancer, which is recognized as one of the most serious types of cancer affecting women worldwide. Breast cancer is not only prevalent but also presents significant challenges in terms of early detection and effective treatment. Given the critical nature of early diagnosis, this research aims to contribute to the existing body of knowledge by developing a predictive model for breast cancer diseases using innovative methodologies, specifically LR and BPNNs.

The datasets utilized for this research were sourced from the UCI Machine Learning Repository, a well-known repository that provides a wide variety of datasets suitable for empirical analysis and machine learning research [28]. The system was implemented using the MATLAB programming language, which is widely used in academic and industrial settings for mathematical computations, data analysis, and algorithm development. The choice of MATLAB allows for efficient prototyping and execution of complex algorithms, ensuring that the experiments conducted are both rigorous and reproducible.

In the experimental phase of this study, a comparative analysis was performed between the proposed classifiers (LR and BPNN) and existing systems. This comparison focused on assessing both the efficiency and precision of the classifiers, thereby providing a comprehensive examination of the findings associated with the proposed model. The results of these experiments indicate that the suggested LR approach achieved an impressive accuracy rate of 96.40%. In contrast, the BPNN classification model recorded a lower accuracy of 88.60%. This significant difference highlights the superior performance of the LR model in predicting breast cancer outcomes, underscoring the importance of choosing appropriate machine learning algorithms for medical diagnostics.

Several studies have been conducted in the field of medical image processing, particularly focusing on deep learning-based techniques for face recognition and tumor detection. A notable contribution to this area was made by Azar *et al.* [21, 22], who developed a novel technique for breast cancer detection that employed multiple classification algorithms, including radial basis function (RBF), probabilistic neural networks (PNN), and multi-layer perceptron (MLP). The accuracy of the MLP model was reported to be 95.80% during the training phase and 95.66% during testing, indicating a high level of reliability in its predictions. Such results affirm the potential of neural network architectures in accurately diagnosing breast cancer.

Furthermore, another study demonstrated a technique for breast cancer identification utilizing rotation forest and genetic algorithm (GA) feature selection across two distinct WBCDs [23]. This innovative approach yielded a higher accuracy of 96.48% for the Rotation Forest model when GA-based attribute selection was applied. The integration of feature selection techniques with ensemble methods like the rotation forest can significantly enhance classification performance, illustrating a promising direction for future research.

Durai *et al.* [24] explored the use of data mining techniques to identify various diseases, including breast cancer. They employed LR classifiers and compared their performance against other methods such as binary feature identification (BFI), ID3, J48, and standard LR. Their findings indicated that the LR classifier achieved the highest accuracy of 97.25%. This suggests that traditional statistical methods like LR continue to hold significant value in the era of advanced machine learning techniques.

In a related study, Xu *et al.* presented a hybrid method in 2005 that combined a PNN with a discrete binary version of particle swarm optimization (PSO) [25]. Frequently utilized for tasks such as gene selection and dimensionality reduction, PSO are crucial in handling high-dimensional datasets commonly found in medical imaging. This hybrid method was evaluated on a significant dataset of B-cell lymphomas, achieving an efficiency rate of 80%. The integration of PSO with neural network configurations presents a compelling strategy for improving the accuracy of cancer classification models.

Moreover, a study [26] described three distinct methodologies for tumor cell identification, utilizing back propagation networks (BPN), LR, and PSO for breast cancer categorization. According to the reported results, the PSO classification rate was 56.12%, while the BPN classification rate stood at 63.34%. Notably, the LR model achieved the highest classification rate at 92.36%, reaffirming the efficacy of LR in the context of breast cancer diagnosis.

Another insightful study by L. Li *et al.* [27] focused on the categorization of cardiac sound signals as normal or pathological. They employed a backward propagation (BP) neural network in conjunction with LR, demonstrating that the BP neural network achieved an accuracy of 72.56%. In comparison, LR exhibited superior classification performance with an accuracy of 88.56%. These findings underscore the versatility of LR across various medical domains, further emphasizing its effectiveness in achieving high accuracy in classification tasks.

Despite these promising results, the current study faced certain limitations, particularly regarding data disparity in the training and testing datasets. A balanced dataset with an equal number of normal and breast cancer X-rays is crucial for creating a well-structured model and ensuring accurate predictions. Such balance helps mitigate biases that could arise from imbalanced classes, ultimately enhancing the reliability and validity of the classification outcomes.

Future research endeavors will aim to concentrate on improving the precision of early-stage cancer detection, a goal that is essential for enhancing patient outcomes and survival rates. Early detection is vital for effective intervention, allowing for less invasive treatment options and better prognoses. Additionally, efforts will be made to refine the data preprocessing stages, specifically focusing on removing artifacts such as pectoral muscle and text noise from digital mammograms. This refinement is anticipated to improve the segmentation process, which is critical for accurately identifying the region of interest within medical images.

Furthermore, future studies may explore the incorporation of additional features or advanced image processing techniques that can enhance the performance of the classification models. For instance, utilizing advanced image augmentation techniques can artificially increase the size and diversity of training datasets, thus enabling the models to learn more robust representations of the data. Additionally, employing deep learning architectures, such as convolutional neural networks, could provide further improvements in classification accuracy, particularly given their proven effectiveness in handling image data.

Beyond simply classifying breast tumors as benign or malignant, there is potential for the proposed system to assess the severity of tumors based on categorization findings. Implementing a tiered classification system could allow healthcare providers to stratify patients according to their risk levels, enabling more personalized treatment approaches and improved management of breast cancer cases. The ability to predict not just the presence of cancer but also the likelihood of its aggressiveness could significantly impact clinical decision-making and patient care strategies.

2.5 Conclusion

This study presents a comparative analysis of two advanced machine learning algorithms: the LR algorithm and the BPNN algorithm, specifically in the context of breast cancer prediction. The findings indicate that while both approaches offer valuable methodologies for diagnostic purposes, the LR algorithm significantly outperforms the BPNN algorithm in terms of detection accuracy. The LR algorithm achieved an impressive detection rate of 96.40%, compared to the BPNN's detection rate of 88.60%. This marked difference in performance underscores the potential of LR as a preferred method for early breast cancer detection.

The substantial difference in detection rates not only highlights the effectiveness of the LR algorithm but also emphasizes the importance of selecting appropriate machine learning techniques tailored to the specific nuances of medical data. The statistical significance of the results was further validated, with a p-value of 0.001 ($p<0.05$), indicating strong evidence that the differences in detection accuracy between the two algorithms are not due to random chance. This statistical significance enhances the credibility of the LR algorithm as a reliable tool for breast cancer prediction.

Moreover, the success of the LR model suggests that it can serve as an effective first-line diagnostic tool, potentially leading to earlier interventions and better patient outcomes. The implications of this study are particularly relevant in clinical settings where timely detection of breast cancer is crucial for effective treatment and management.

The findings of this study advocate for the integration of LR in breast cancer diagnostic processes, as its higher accuracy rates can contribute to improved detection capabilities. Future research may focus on further enhancing the LR model through feature engineering and integrating additional data sources, ultimately aiming to develop a more comprehensive diagnostic framework that leverages the strengths of various machine learning techniques.

References

1. Coleman, C., Early detection and screening for breast cancer. *Semin. Oncol. Nurs.*, 33, 141–155, May 2017.
2. Amrane, M., Oukid, S., Gagaoua, I., Ensari, T., Breast cancer classification using machine learning, in: *2018 Electric Electronics, Computer Science, Biomedical Engineerings' Meeting (EBBT)*, Istanbul, 2018.
3. Maglogiannis, I., Zafiropoulos, E., Anagnostopoulos, I., An intelligent system for automated breast cancer diagnosis and prognosis using SVM based classifiers. *Appl. Intell.*, 30, 24–36, February 2009.
4. Avramov, T.K. and Si, D., Comparison of feature reduction methods and machine learning models for breast cancer diagnosis, in: *Proceedings of the International Conference on Compute and Data Analysis*, New York, NY, USA, 2017.
5. Domchek, S.M., Eisen, A., Calzone, K., Stopfer, J., Blackwood, A., Weber, B.L., Application of breast cancer risk prediction models in clinical practice. *J. Clin. Oncol.*, 21, 593–601, February 2003.
6. Kalita, K., Ganesh, N., Jayalakshmi, S., Chohan, J.S., Mallik, S., Qin, H., Multi-Objective artificial bee colony optimized hybrid deep belief network and XGBoost algorithm for heart disease prediction. *Front. Digit. Health*, 5, 1279644, November 2023.
7. Premalatha, M., Jayasudha, M., Čep, R., Priyadarshini, J., Kalita, K., Chatterjee, P., A comparative evaluation of nature-inspired algorithms for feature selection problems. *Heliyon*, 10, e23571, January 2024.
8. Priyadarshini, J., Premalatha, M., Čep, R., Jayasudha, M., Kalita, K., Analyzing physics-inspired metaheuristic algorithms in feature selection with K-nearest-neighbor. *Appl. Sci. (Basel)*, 13, 906, January 2023.
9. Gc, S., Kasaudhan, R., Heo, T.K., Choi, H.D., Variability measurement for breast cancer classification of mammographic masses, in: *Proceedings of the 2015 Conference on Research in Adaptive and Convergent Systems*, New York, NY, USA, 2015.
10. Ahmad, Y., Zain, Z., Aziz, N., Multistage Logistic Regression Model for Analyzing Survival from Colorectal Cancer. *Int. J. Technol.*, 9, 8, 1618–1627, 2018.
11. Sy Ahmad Ubaidillah, S.H., Sallehuddin, R., Ali, N.A., Cancer detection using aritifical neural network and Support Vector Machine: A comparative study. *J. Teknol.*, 65, 1, 73–81, 2013.
12. Tsirogiannis, G.L., Frossyniotis, D., Stoitsis, J., Golemati, S., Stafylopatis, A., Nikita, K.S., Classification of medical data with a robust multi-level

combination scheme, in: *2004 IEEE International Joint Conference on Neural Networks (IEEE Cat. No.04CH37541)*, Budapest, 2005.
13. Christobel, A. and Sivaprakasam, Y., An empirical comparison of data mining classification methods. *Int. J. Comput. Inf. Syst.*, 3, 24–28, 2011.
14. Akay, M.F., Support vector machines combined with feature selection for breast cancer diagnosis. *Expert Syst. Appl.*, 36, 3240–3247, March 2009.
15. Hussain, M., Wajid, S.K., Elzaart, A., Berbar, M., A comparison of SVM kernel functions for breast cancer detection, in: *2011 Eighth International Conference Computer Graphics, Imaging and Visualization*, Singapore, 2011.
16. Nanmaran, R., Srimathi, S., Yamuna, G., Thanigaivel, S., Vickram, A.S., Priya, A.K., Karthick, A., Karpagam, J., Mohanavel, V., Muhibbullah, M., Investigating the role of image fusion in brain tumor classification models based on machine learning algorithm for personalized medicine. *Comput. Math. Methods Med.*, 2022, 7137524, February 2022.
17. Vickram, A.S., Drug Repurposing of Human LMTK3 from ATP competitive inhibitors for Breast Cancer. *Cardiometry*, 26, 266–271, March 2023. doi:https://doi.org/10.18137/cardiometry.2023.26.266271.
18. Vickram, A.S., Samad, H.A., Latheef, S.K., Chakraborty, S., Dhama, K., Sridharan, T.B., Sundaram, T., Gulothungan, G., Human prostasomes an extracellular vesicle - Biomarkers for male infertility and prostrate cancer: The journey from identification to current knowledge. *Int. J. Biol. Macromol.*, 146, 946–958, March 2020.
19. Shmueli, G., Bruce, P.C., Gedeck, P., Patel, N.R., *Data mining for business analytics: concepts, techniques and applications in Python*, John Wiley & Sons, Hoboken, NJ, USA, 2019.
20. Kalita, K., Ganesh, N., Balamurugan, S., *Metaheuristics for Machine Learning: Algorithms and Applications*, John Wiley & Sons, Hoboken, NJ, USA, 2024.
21. Azar, A.T. and El-Said, S.A., Probabilistic neural network for breast cancer classification. *Neural Comput. Appl.*, 23, 1737–1751, November 2013.
22. Azar, A.T. and El-Said, S.A., Performance analysis of support vector machines classifiers in breast cancer mammography recognition. *Neural Comput. Appl.*, 24, 1163–1177, April 2014.
23. Aličković, E. and Subasi, A., Breast cancer diagnosis using GA feature selection and Rotation Forest. *Neural Comput. Appl.*, 28, 753–763, April 2017.
24. Durai, S.G., Ganesh, S.H., Christy, A.J., Novel linear regressive classifier for the diagnosis of breast cancer, in: *2017 World Congress on Computing and Communication Technologies (WCCCT)*, Tiruchirappalli, Tamil Nadu, India, 2017.
25. Xu, R., Cai, X., Wunsch, D.C., Gene expression data for DLBCL cancer survival prediction with A combination of machine learning technologies, in: *2005 IEEE Engineering in Medicine and Biology 27th Annual Conference*, Shanghai, 2005.
26. Rahman, M.A., Muniyandi, R.C., Albashish, D., Rahman, M.M., Usman, O.L., Artificial neural network with Taguchi method for robust classification

model to improve classification accuracy of breast cancer. *PeerJ Comput. Sci.*, 7, e344, January 2021.

27. Li, L., Wang, X., Du, X., Liu, Y., Liu, C., Qin, C., Li, Y., Classification of heart sound signals with BP neural network and logistic regression, in: *2017 Chinese Automation Congress (CAC)*, Jinan, 2017.
28. Frank, A., UCI machine learning repository, 2010, http://archive.ics.uci.edu/ml.

3

An Approach to Conduct the Diabetes Prediction Using AdaBoost Algorithm Compared with Decision Tree Classifier Algorithm

P. Jaswanth Reddy and R. Thalapathi Rajasekaran*

Department of Computer Science and Engineering, Saveetha School of Engineering, Saveetha Institute of Medical and Technical Sciences, Saveetha University, Chennai, India

Abstract

The main aim of this research work is to compare the accuracy percentage of diabetes prediction by using Adaptive Boosting (AdaBoost) with a Decision Tree algorithm. A sample of 10 diabetes cases at different times was evaluated using AdaBoost and Decision Tree methods, ClinCalc software is utilized to implement the two algorithms. The alpha value was 0.05, the G-Power was 0.8, and the CI was 95%. A dataset containing 76,870 instances related to diabetes classification was obtained from Kaggle.com. The Decision Tree has a significantly lower accuracy percentage of 93.57% compared to the AdaBoost accuracy percentage of 96.36%. There is a statistically insignificant difference between these with a 2-tailed value p=0.011 (p<0.05). Compared with AdaBoost, the Decision Tree approach is less accurate in diabetes classification.

***Keywords*:** Novel AdaBoost, Decision Tree, diabetes, machine learning, disease, health

**Corresponding author*: thalapathirajasekaranr.sse@saveetha.com

Kanak Kalita, Divya Zindani, Narayanan Ganesh and Xiao-Zhi Gao (eds.) Medical Analytics for Clinical and Healthcare Applications, (49–64) © 2025 Scrivener Publishing LLC

3.1 Introduction

Diabetes is a chronic and widespread metabolic disorder that continues to pose significant challenges to the global healthcare industry, affecting millions of individuals worldwide [1]. It is characterized by elevated blood glucose levels that result from either the body's inability to produce enough insulin (Type 1 diabetes) or the inability to effectively use the insulin it produces (Type 2 diabetes). While genetic predisposition plays a role in diabetes development, its prevalence has escalated to epidemic proportions, largely driven by lifestyle factors such as poor diet, sedentary behavior, and increasing rates of obesity. According to the World Health Organization (WHO), diabetes is among the leading causes of mortality globally and is projected to affect approximately 700 million individuals by 2045. The disease not only shortens lifespan but also significantly diminishes the quality of life due to its associated complications [2].

The early detection of diabetes is paramount for its effective management, allowing healthcare professionals to intervene before serious complications arise. Without timely intervention, diabetes can lead to a host of severe complications, including cardiovascular disease, neuropathy (nerve damage), nephropathy (kidney disease), retinopathy (eye damage), and even amputations in extreme cases [3]. Early diagnosis and appropriate medical management can significantly mitigate these risks, improving patients' quality of life and reducing the economic burden on healthcare systems. In light of these concerns, the development of robust, accurate, and efficient tools for predicting the likelihood of an individual developing diabetes has become an urgent priority in healthcare.

In recent years, machine learning (ML) algorithms have emerged as powerful tools for predicting the likelihood of an individual developing diabetes [4]. Machine learning techniques can process vast amounts of data, identify complex patterns, and provide predictive insights that may not be easily discernible through traditional statistical methods. These algorithms are particularly useful in healthcare, where they can analyze patient data to identify early signs of diseases, enabling proactive interventions and personalized treatment plans. Among the plethora of ML techniques available, ensemble methods such as Adaptive Boosting (AdaBoost) and Decision Tree-based algorithms have gained popularity for their accuracy and interpretability.

Researchers aim to leverage advanced ML techniques, particularly the AdaBoost and Decision Tree algorithms, to build a predictive model for diabetes diagnosis [5]. By using a dataset comprising demographic, lifestyle, and medical information of patients, this model aspires to achieve high accuracy in predicting diabetes risk. The use of these algorithms is advantageous because they can handle the heterogeneity of medical data, encompassing features such as age, body mass index (BMI), blood pressure, and glucose levels, all of which play a critical role in assessing an individual's risk of developing diabetes [6].

Such a model could potentially serve as a valuable decision-support tool in healthcare, assisting clinicians in the early detection and personalized management of diabetes [7]. Beyond diagnosis, such predictive models can aid in risk stratification, helping healthcare providers identify high-risk individuals who may benefit from more intensive monitoring or early therapeutic interventions. By identifying patterns in large datasets that may not be immediately obvious, ML models can provide healthcare professionals with critical insights into disease progression and patient outcomes. The originality of this work is guaranteed, with a strict adherence to research ethics and free from any form of plagiarism [8].

A preliminary review of the literature reveals that there are 39 related studies on this topic indexed in IEEE Xplore and 8 in Scopus, signifying a growing interest in the application of ML techniques for diabetes prediction [9, 10]. These studies explore various algorithms and methodologies to enhance the predictive accuracy of diabetes diagnosis, including support vector machines (SVM), k-nearest neighbors (KNN), and neural networks. However, relatively fewer studies have focused on the comparative performance of ensemble learning techniques, such as AdaBoost, in combination with traditional algorithms like Decision Trees. In this research, we retrieve a wide array of alternatives from the dataset, examining their performance using models such as Naïve Bayes and the Genetic J48 Decision Tree [11].

Key parameters under consideration include the number of possible decision outcomes, accuracy rates, computational efficiency, and the robustness of tree-building methodologies [12]. Decision Tree algorithms are highly interpretable, making them suitable for healthcare applications where transparency and understanding of the decision-making process are critical. However, they have known limitations, such as a tendency to overfit the training data, which can reduce their generalization ability to new, unseen data. Given the importance of Decision Tree structures in data mining for diabetes prediction, this study places particular emphasis on evaluating the performance of Decision Tree-based algorithms while addressing these limitations [13].

In this study, the Decision Tree model will be constructed using predictor variables such as age, blood pressure, BMI, and glucose levels. For this, we will utilize the Pima Indians Diabetes dataset from the UCI Machine Learning Repository, a well-known dataset for evaluating diabetes prediction models [14]. This dataset, which contains demographic and medical information from over 700 individuals, is particularly suited for testing classification models due to its balanced representation of diabetic and non-diabetic patients. The subset, available in the MASS package, provides a rich source of data for training and testing the model.

Despite the popularity of the Decision Tree Classifier in ML, it has known limitations, particularly its tendency to overfit and its weak generalization capability when applied to complex datasets [15]. Decision trees can become highly specialized in recognizing patterns in the training data, leading to a loss of predictive accuracy when applied to new datasets. This is particularly problematic in medical applications, where the ability to generalize to new patients is crucial. The AdaBoost algorithm, on the other hand, is an ensemble learning technique that improves classification performance by combining multiple weak classifiers into a stronger, more accurate model. AdaBoost works by iteratively adjusting the weights of misclassified instances, ensuring that subsequent classifiers focus on the hardest-to-classify cases. This process helps to correct the overfitting tendencies of individual Decision Trees, resulting in a more robust predictive model.

Although research comparing the effectiveness of Decision Trees and AdaBoost in diabetes prediction is limited, existing studies suggest that AdaBoost tends to outperform Decision Trees by improving classification accuracy and reducing the risk of overfitting [16]. Several studies have demonstrated the superiority of ensemble learning methods over single classifiers, particularly in handling imbalanced datasets, such as those found in medical diagnosis. By combining the strengths of multiple classifiers, AdaBoost can correct for the weaknesses of individual models, resulting in improved predictive performance.

This study introduces a novel approach to diabetes prediction by comparing the accuracy of the AdaBoost algorithm with that of the Decision Tree classifier. While both algorithms are well-known in ML, this work specifically focuses on utilizing the strengths of ensemble learning, particularly AdaBoost, to overcome the limitations of traditional Decision Tree classifiers, such as overfitting and weak generalization. The novelty lies in leveraging AdaBoost's iterative boosting technique to enhance prediction accuracy and reduce error rates in a healthcare context. By applying these techniques to a large, real-world dataset containing demographic and medical data, this study contributes to the growing body of research that explores ML's potential in early disease detection, particularly diabetes.

Furthermore, this study provides a statistically rigorous comparison, highlighting the significance of AdaBoost's performance over Decision Tree classifiers, which is crucial for developing more robust, data-driven diagnostic tools.

The remainder of this paper is organized as follows. Section 3.2 presents a detailed review of the relevant literature. Section 3.3 explains the methodology, including the dataset and algorithms used. Section 3.4 discusses the experimental results, and Section 3.5 concludes with the key findings and future research directions.

3.2 Materials and Methods

The study was conducted at the Computer Science Laboratory located at Saveetha School of Engineering, which is part of the Saveetha Institute of Medical and Technical Sciences [15]. Comparing the Accuracy of an AdaBoost Classifier and Decision Tree in handling Diabetes: A study with a sample size of 20 grouped into two, Each with 10 participants at different times. Group-2 belongs to Decision Tree Classifier and Group-1 Belongs to the AdaBoost classifier that is compared based on their accuracy in handling diabetes. ClinCalc software is utilized to implement the two algorithms, with 0.05 as the alpha value, with a G-Power of 0.8 and a 95% confidence interval. A collection of 76,870 records pertaining to the classification of Diabetes was obtained from Kaggle.com [16].

The purpose of the dataset is to predict the occurrence of diabetes in a patient based on relevant diagnostic metrics available in their medical records. These instances were chosen under some constraints from a larger database. The datasets contain several medical predictor variables in addition to one goal variable called result. The patient's health, age, BMI, Glucose Insulin level, previous pregnancies, and other characteristics are predictive variables.

3.2.1 AdaBoost Algorithm

AdaBoost is a widely used ensemble learning technique in supervised ML. It is a meta-algorithm that builds a powerful classifier out of multiple weak ones. A model is considered weak only if it slightly outperforms random guessing. The core principle of AdaBoost involves the iterative training of a set of weak classifiers on different subsets of the training data. During each iteration of the algorithm, the weights of the samples that were misclassified in the previous iteration are increased. This process boosts their importance in the subsequent training phase. The results of all the weak classifiers are integrated and given weightings based on their performances to construct the final strong classifier.

3.2.1.1 *Procedure for AdaBoost Algorithm*

1. Obtain the dataset records that need to be used for training a model.
2. Load the necessary software libraries and packages that will be required for analysis.
3. Transform the data into numerical values and extract the relevant features from it.
4. Separate the data into training and testing sets, assigning them to X_train, y_train, X_test, and y_test variables.
5. Use the train_test_split () function to divide the data into training and testing sets.
6. Set the test_size and random_state parameters for the function, which determines the proportion of data allocated to each set, and the random seed for reproducibility.
7. Train the model using the training data and evaluate its accuracy using the testing data.
8. Calculate and report the accuracy of the model based on the testing data.

3.2.1.2 *Decision Tree*

Decision Trees are a reliable and efficient approach to decision-making that provides high classification accuracy while representing accumulated knowledge straightforwardly. They have been used in numerous medical decision-making scenarios. The usage of Decision Trees in several areas of medical decision-making has proven to be dependable and successful since they offer high classification accuracy with a straightforward representation of obtained knowledge.

Decision Trees' main benefit is that they make it relatively simple to understand and depict nonlinear data patterns. Moreover, Decision Trees operate swiftly, particularly when analyzing exploratory data. The class label corresponds to each leaf node of the Decision Tree, while the interior nodes are utilized to represent the attributes required to solve the problem. The Decision Tree can be used to represent any boolean function on discrete attributes.

3.2.1.2.1 Procedure for Decision Tree Algorithm

1. Obtain the dataset that will be used to train the model.
2. Import the required libraries and packages for data analysis.
3. Preprocess the data by converting it into numerical values and selecting the relevant features.
4. Split the data into two sets: the training set and the testing set.
5. Use the train_test_split () function to split the data into training and testing sets.
6. Specify the test_size and random_state parameters for the function.
7. Train the model using the training data and evaluate its performance using the testing data.
8. Report the accuracy of the model based on the testing data.

3.2.1.3 Statistical Analysis

The study's proposed task, as well as the approach of prior research, were assessed using the SPSS software program to determine their accuracy [17]. In tests, independent sample t-tests are used for continuous data, while chi-square tests are used for categorical data to identify diabetes risk factors. In this study, glucose levels, BMI, and cholesterol are considered the independent variables, whereas the dependent variable is the presence or absence of diabetes.

3.3 Results and Discussion

In this section, the comparative performance of the AdaBoost algorithm and the Decision Tree algorithm for predicting diabetes is evaluated. The results are analyzed based on accuracy, statistical significance, and the confidence intervals of both classifiers. The findings reveal significant differences in performance between the two methods, with AdaBoost demonstrating consistently higher accuracy than the Decision Tree algorithm. These differences are detailed through statistical analysis and visual representations, highlighting AdaBoost's superior predictive power.

The performance of the algorithms was first visualized using a bar graph (Figure 3.1), which illustrated the clear advantage of the AdaBoost algorithm over the Decision Tree classifier. Specifically, the AdaBoost

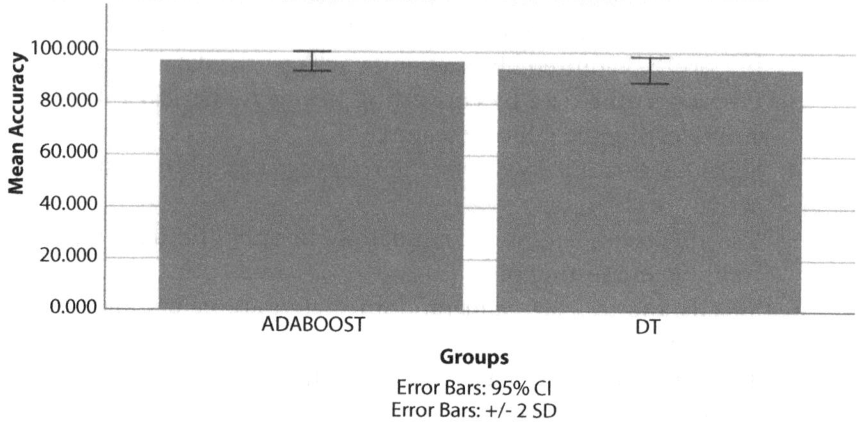

Figure 3.1 Comparison of AdaBoost and Decision Tree.

algorithm achieved an accuracy rate of approximately 96.36%, compared to the Decision Tree's accuracy rate of 93.57%. This difference, though seemingly small, is meaningful in the context of ML models, where even slight improvements in accuracy can have a significant impact on the reliability of predictions in real-world applications, particularly in critical domains like healthcare.

Table 3.1 presents the individual accuracy rates for the AdaBoost and Decision Tree algorithms across 10 different trials. These trials were conducted to ensure that the results were consistent and not influenced by random fluctuations in the data or by overfitting the training dataset. As observed, AdaBoost consistently achieved higher accuracy rates across all trials. The smallest difference occurred in the first trial, where AdaBoost had an accuracy of 93.16% compared to the Decision Tree's 89.89%, while the largest discrepancy was seen in the tenth trial, where AdaBoost reached 98.78% and the Decision Tree achieved 97.17%. These results suggest that AdaBoost not only improves overall accuracy but also demonstrates a more stable performance across multiple runs.

To provide a more comprehensive analysis, Table 3.2 displays the group statistics for both algorithms, including the mean accuracy, standard deviation, and standard error of the mean across all trials. This analysis confirms that the AdaBoost algorithm not only had a higher mean accuracy than the Decision Tree algorithm but also exhibited a lower standard deviation, suggesting that AdaBoost's performance was not only more accurate but also more consistent. The mean accuracy for AdaBoost was 96.36%, with a

Table 3.1 Accuracy of AdaBoost and Decision Tree algorithm.

S. no.	AdaBoost	Decision Tree
1	93.16	89.89
2	94.23	90.54
3	94.78	91.45
4	95.89	92.87
5	96.10	93.78
6	96.98	93.29
7	97.34	94.67
8	97.89	95.34
9	98.45	96.73
10	98.78	97.17

Table 3.2 Group statistical analysis of Decision Tree and AdaBoost.

	Group	N	Mean	Std. deviation	Std. error mean
	AB	10	96.36000	1.869997	.591345
Accuracy	DT	10	93.57300	2.474730	.782578

standard deviation of 1.87, while the Decision Tree algorithm had a mean accuracy of 93.57%, with a slightly higher standard deviation of 2.47. The lower standard deviation for AdaBoost indicates that the predictions from AdaBoost were more consistent and less prone to large fluctuations. The standard error of the mean for AdaBoost (0.5913) was also lower than that of the Decision Tree (0.7826), further underscoring AdaBoost's reliability.

To assess whether the difference in accuracy between AdaBoost and Decision Tree classifiers is statistically significant, an independent samples t-test was conducted. Table 3.3 provides the results of the t-test, which compares the mean accuracy rates of the two algorithms. The t-test result reveals a p-value of 0.011, which is less than the threshold of 0.05, indicating that the difference in accuracy between AdaBoost and Decision Tree is statistically significant at the 95% confidence level. This suggests that

Table 3.3 Independent sample t-test between the Decision Tree and AdaBoost.

		Levene's test for equality of variances		T-test for equality of means						
									95% confidence interval of the difference	
		F	Sig.	t	df	Sig. (2-tailed)	Mean difference	Std. error difference	Lower	Upper
Accuracy	Equal variances assumed	.698	.414	2.841	18	.011	2.787000	.980876	.716256	4.847744
	Equal variances not assumed			2.841	16.751	.011	2.787000	.980876	.715185	4.858815

the superior performance of AdaBoost over the Decision Tree classifier is not due to random chance but represents a meaningful improvement in prediction accuracy.

The results indicate that the AdaBoost algorithm significantly outperforms the Decision Tree classifier in terms of accuracy. This finding is consistent with existing literature that suggests ensemble learning techniques, such as AdaBoost, typically perform better than single-model classifiers like Decision Trees. AdaBoost works by combining multiple weak classifiers to form a robust model, while the Decision Tree relies on a single tree structure that is more susceptible to overfitting, especially when dealing with complex datasets.

Statistical analysis further strengthens the case for using AdaBoost in diabetes prediction models. With a mean accuracy of 96.36%, AdaBoost provides a more reliable and generalizable model for predicting diabetes compared to the Decision Tree's mean accuracy of 93.57%. The lower standard deviation and standard error associated with AdaBoost further suggest that it offers more consistent predictions, which is critical in a healthcare setting where consistent and accurate predictions can improve patient outcomes.

Additionally, Figure 3.1 shows the comparison between the mean accuracy of the two classifiers along with the standard deviation margins. The AdaBoost classifier not only exhibited a higher mean accuracy but also showed a slightly lower standard deviation compared to the Decision Tree classifier. The graphical representation in Figure 3.1 provides a clear visualization of the margin of error and reinforces the conclusion that AdaBoost provides better performance in terms of both accuracy and stability.

In this study, a comparison was made between two ML algorithms, AdaBoost and Decision Tree, using a total of 20 samples. Group-1 consisted of 10 samples that were tested using the AdaBoost algorithm, and Group-2 consisted of 10 samples that were tested using the Decision Tree algorithm. The sample size was determined based on prior research findings and calculated using an online statistical analysis tool, which was configured with 80% pretest power and a 0.05 alpha value. The findings of this study confirm that the AdaBoost algorithm outperformed the Decision Tree classifier, which aligns with existing literature on the effectiveness of ensemble learning methods.

Machine learning, in general, has proven to be a vital tool in predicting diseases such as diabetes due to its ability to analyze large datasets and uncover intricate patterns that traditional statistical methods may overlook. Diabetes is a complex medical condition characterized by various complications, such as restricted blood flow, which can lead to other severe health issues, including retinal edema. Machine learning algorithms, including AdaBoost and Decision Trees, help in predicting such outcomes by leveraging different forms of data. Four main learning techniques in ML—supervised, semi-supervised, unsupervised, and reinforcement learning—have been widely adopted in various fields, including medical diagnosis [18].

In supervised learning, models like AdaBoost and Decision Trees are trained using labeled data to predict outcomes. However, one challenge faced by most ML algorithms is the availability of labeled data. Labeled data is essential because it helps the algorithm learn from known outcomes, but acquiring labeled data can be expensive and time-consuming, particularly in medical contexts where patient privacy and ethical considerations may limit data availability [19]. Unlabeled data, on the other hand, can be gathered more readily but is not as useful for supervised learning tasks. Semi-supervised learning, which combines both labeled and unlabeled data, presents a promising alternative for enhancing model performance when labeled data is scarce [20].

The superior performance of the AdaBoost algorithm in this study can be attributed to its ensemble learning technique, which combines multiple weak classifiers into a strong one. By focusing on the misclassified data points from previous iterations, AdaBoost ensures that each subsequent classifier improves upon the previous one, thereby reducing errors and increasing overall accuracy. However, while AdaBoost demonstrated better results than the Decision Tree, it is not without limitations.

One of the significant challenges with AdaBoost is its potential for overfitting, especially when using highly complex Decision Trees as weak classifiers. Overfitting occurs when the model becomes too closely tailored to the training data, which limits its ability to generalize to new, unseen data. In a real-world scenario where data distribution varies, an overfitted model may perform poorly. Therefore, controlling the complexity of the weak classifiers used in AdaBoost is critical to prevent overfitting.

Another issue that can arise with AdaBoost is its sensitivity to noisy data and outliers. Noisy data can skew the training process, leading to inaccurate predictions. Since AdaBoost adjusts weights based on misclassified instances, outliers or noise in the data can disproportionately influence the model, resulting in poorer performance on clean data. This limitation suggests the need for robust preprocessing techniques, such as outlier detection and data cleaning, before applying AdaBoost to real-world datasets.

Additionally, AdaBoost's computational cost is higher compared to simpler algorithms like Decision Tree. This is particularly evident when a large number of weak classifiers are used, as it requires more processing power and longer training times. The increased computational demands make AdaBoost less suitable for real-time applications or systems with limited resources. However, this issue can be mitigated by employing feature selection and extraction techniques, which streamline the input features and reduce computational overhead.

Despite these limitations, the potential for improving AdaBoost remains promising. One way to address the overfitting issue is by incorporating regularization techniques or limiting the depth of the Decision Trees used as weak classifiers. Moreover, AdaBoost can be extended to semi-supervised learning frameworks, where it can benefit from both labeled and unlabeled data. This could enhance the algorithm's robustness and accuracy, particularly in situations where labeled data is scarce but unlabeled data is abundant.

In contrast, the Decision Tree algorithm, while simpler and faster, did not perform as well as AdaBoost in terms of accuracy. Decision Trees are prone to overfitting, especially when the tree becomes too deep or when there is noise in the data. Unlike AdaBoost, Decision Trees do not correct their errors over multiple iterations, making them less adaptable in cases where misclassification is a concern. However, Decision Trees are easier to interpret, which is a significant advantage in medical diagnostics, where transparency and explainability are crucial for decision-making. While the AdaBoost algorithm demonstrated superior accuracy compared to the Decision Tree, the choice of algorithm should be guided by the specific requirements of the application. For scenarios where accuracy and robustness are the top priorities, AdaBoost offers clear advantages. However, for real-time applications or systems requiring interpretable models, Decision Trees may still be preferable.

3.4 Conclusion

The results of this study clearly demonstrate that the AdaBoost algorithm outperforms the Decision Tree classifier in predicting diabetes. With a mean accuracy of 96.36%, AdaBoost exhibited better performance compared to the Decision Tree's accuracy of 93.57%. The statistically significant difference between the two algorithms suggests that AdaBoost, as an ensemble learning method, provides a more robust and reliable model for medical diagnosis tasks, such as diabetes prediction. However, it is important to note that AdaBoost comes with challenges, including higher computational costs and sensitivity to noisy data, which should be considered when applying it to real-world scenarios.

Despite its limitations, the AdaBoost algorithm's ability to reduce overfitting and improve accuracy through ensemble learning makes it a powerful tool for healthcare applications. Further research could explore optimizing AdaBoost through feature selection, regularization, and extending it to semi-supervised learning frameworks to enhance its performance. On the other hand, the Decision Tree algorithm remains valuable in situations where model interpretability and computational efficiency are more critical. Ultimately, the choice of algorithm should be tailored to the specific needs of the application, balancing accuracy, interpretability, and computational resources.

References

1. Sailaja, N.V., Karakavalasa, M., Katkam, M., Devipriya, S., Vasundhara, D.N., Hybrid regression model for medical insurance cost prediction and recommendation, in: *2021 IEEE International Conference on Intelligent Systems, Smart and Green Technologies (ICISSGT)*, Visakhapatnam, 2021.
2. Ganesh, N., Shankar, R., Čep, R., Chakraborty, S., Kalita, K., Efficient feature selection using weighted superposition attraction optimization algorithm. *Appl. Sci. (Basel)*, 13, 3223, March 2023.
3. Kalita, K., Ganesh, N., Jayalakshmi, S., Chohan, J.S., Mallik, S., Qin, H., Multi-Objective artificial bee colony optimized hybrid deep belief network and XGBoost algorithm for heart disease prediction. *Front. Digit. Health*, 5, 1279644, November 2023.
4. Priyadarshini, J., Premalatha, M., Čep, R., Jayasudha, M., Kalita, K., Analyzing physics-inspired metaheuristic algorithms in feature selection with K-nearest-neighbor. *Appl. Sci. (Basel)*, 13, 906, January 2023.
5. Chand, S.P.S. and Divya, G., A Light gradient boosting machine regression model for prediction of agriculture insurance cost over linear regression, in: *Advances in Parallel Computing*, pp. 200–208, IOS Press BV, Amsterdam, The Netherlands, 2022.
6. Tigga, N.P. and Garg, S., Prediction of type 2 diabetes using machine learning classification methods. *Procedia Comput. Sci.*, 167, 706–716, 2020.
7. Aboalnaser, S.A. and Almohammadi, H.R., Comprehensive study of diabetes Miletus prediction using different classification algorithms, in: *2019 12th International Conference on Developments in eSystems Engineering (DeSE)*, Kazan, 2019.
8. Premalatha, M., Jayasudha, M., Čep, R., Priyadarshini, J., Kalita, K., Chatterjee, P., A comparative evaluation of nature-inspired algorithms for feature selection problems. *Heliyon*, 10, e23571, January 2024.
9. Nanmaran, R., Srimathi, S., Yamuna, G., Thanigaivel, S., Vickram, A.S., Priya, A.K., Karthick, A., Karpagam, J., Mohanavel, V., Muhibbullah, M.,

Investigating the role of image fusion in brain tumor classification models based on machine learning algorithm for personalized medicine. *Comput. Math. Methods Med.*, 2022, 7137524, February 2022.
10. Ramezani, S.B., Amirlatifi, A., Kirby, T., Seale, M., Rahimi, S., Explainable Machinery Faults Prediction Using Ensemble Tree Classifiers: Bagging or Boosting? *Annu. Conf. PHM Soc.*, 13, 1, 2021. https://doi.org/10.36001/phmconf.2021.v13i1.3063.
11. Seol, R. and Chun, J.-H., Classification of type 2 diabetes incidence risk and the health behavior of the 30-50-year-old Korean adults: Latent class analysis. *Int. J. Environ. Res. Public Health*, 19, 16600, December 2022.
12. Selvakumar, S., Sheik Abdullah, A., Suganya, R., Decision support system for type II diabetes and its risk factor prediction using bee-based harmony search and decision tree algorithm. *Int. J. Biomed. Eng. Technol.*, 29, 46, 2019.
13. Kalita, K., Ganesh, N., Balamurugan, S., *Metaheuristics for Machine Learning: Algorithms and Applications*, John Wiley & Sons, Hoboken, NJ, USA, 2024.
14. Teh, K., Armitage, P., Tesfaye, S., Selvarajah, D., Deep learning classification of treatment response in diabetic painful neuropathy: A combined machine learning and magnetic resonance neuroimaging methodological study. *Neuroinformatics*, 21, 35–43, January 2023.
15. Arya, M., Sastry G, H., Motwani, A., Kumar, S., Zaguia, A., A novel Extra Tree Ensemble optimized DL framework (ETEODL) for Early detection of diabetes. *Front. Public Health*, 9, 797877, 2021.
16. Olusanya, M.O., Ogunsakin, R.E., Ghai, M., Adeleke, M.A., Accuracy of machine learning classification models for the prediction of type 2 diabetes mellitus: A systematic survey and meta-analysis approach. *Int. J. Environ. Res. Public Health*, 19, 14280, November 2022.
17. Sajjad, H., Siddiqui, L., Rahman, A., Tahir, M., Siddiqui, M.A. (Eds.), *Challenges of disasters in Asia*, 1 ed., Springer, Singapore, Singapore, 2022.
18. Kazerouni, F., Bayani, A., Asadi, F., Saeidi, L., Parvizi, N., Mansoori, Z., Type2 diabetes mellitus prediction using data mining algorithms based on the long-noncoding RNAs expression: a comparison of four data mining approaches. *BMC Bioinf.*, 21, 372, August 2020.
19. Taser, P.Y., Application of bagging and boosting approaches using decision tree-based algorithms in diabetes risk prediction, in: *The 7th International Management Information Systems Conference*, Basel Switzerland, 2021.
20. Adhipurna, N., Shidik, G.F., Fanani, A.Z., Muljouo, C., Soeleman, M.A., Alzami, F., Early determination of diabetes mellitus disease prediction with decision tree boosting, in: *2021 International Seminar on Application for Technology of Information and Communication (iSemantic)*, Semarangin, 2021.

4

Efficient Net V2-Based Pneumonia Detection: A Comparative Study with Transfer Learning Models

Suguna M.[1*], Shane V. Jose[1], Om Kumar C.U.[1], Gunasekaran T.[2] and Prakash D.[3]

[1]School of Computer Science and Engineering, Vellore Institute of Technology, Chennai, Tamil Nadu, India
[2]Electronics and Communication Engineering Specialization, University of Technology and Applied Sciences, Muscat, Oman
[3]Muhammed Sathak AJ College of Engineering, Chennai, Tamil Nadu, India

Abstract
The primary aim of this article is to assess the effectiveness of the EfficientNetV2 family of transfer learning models in detecting pneumonia. This study specifically aims to compare the performance of EfficientNetV2M, EfficientNetV2L, EfficientNetV2B1, EfficientNetV2B2, and EfficientNetV2B3 with older transfer learning models VGG 16 and Xception. To avoid overfitting, a five-way cross-validation and fine-tuning are adopted in this study. Additionally, this study creates an ensemble model from the top three models to further optimize the performance. Based on the results of a comparative study that transferred different pneumonia detection learning models using five-fold cross-validation and fine-tuning, his EfficientNetV2M with RMSprop optimizer performs best among all models considered. Additionally, an ensemble model was created consisting of the three best performing models. This model outperformed all individual models on the performance metrics in this study. Therefore, the use of the EfficientNetV2 family of models may be a useful strategy for detecting pneumonia, and ensemble models can further improve the performance of individual models. This paper aims to understand the latest works done on pneumonia detection, as well as some other chest diseases, showing common methodologies adopted, as well as a comparative analysis of the results obtained from several papers for the identification

**Corresponding author*: suguna.m@vit.ac.in

Kanak Kalita, Divya Zindani, Narayanan Ganesh and Xiao-Zhi Gao (eds.) Medical Analytics for Clinical and Healthcare Applications, (65–92) © 2025 Scrivener Publishing LLC

of pneumonia by transfer learning methods, which will give us an insight into where we are positioned in this area of study. This survey paper also aims to bring out underlying research potentials related to this work.

Keywords: Transfer learning, pneumonia, chest x-rays, CLAHE, deep learning

4.1 Introduction

Pneumonia is an acute inflammatory response deep in the lungs, in the alveoli. The alveoli, which is a part of the lungs, is affected by pneumonia. Pneumonia is commonly caused because of bacteria, viruses, and fungi. For adults, bacteria are the common cause of Pneumonia. The most common bacteria which causes pneumonia is called *Streptococcus pneumoniae*, and the second most common bacteria causing pneumonia is haemophilus influenzae type b (Hib). The flu and common cold viruses are common causes of viral pneumonia in adults. Respiratory syncytial virus is the main cause of pneumonia in infants. The doctor would first conduct a physical exam for someone with pneumonia. The doctor uses a stethoscope to listen to your lungs for abnormal sounds and may recommend tests. A chest X-ray (CXR) is one of several diagnostics for detecting pneumonia. It shows a lung CT scan, needle biopsy, and MRI scan. The gold standard for determining pneumonia is a CXR. Computed tomography (CT) imaging is often longer and lacks facilities in developing countries, so CXR imaging is preferred.

The use of antibiotics can cure pneumonia caused by bacteria, whereas viral pneumonia does not require the immune system to develop antibodies to fight the virus [1]. In Africa, pneumonia has a high mortality rate. Many African countries are poor and lack adequate medical facilities. The prevention of numerous fatalities caused by pneumonia is suggested by recent research. In some remote areas of some countries, there will be no medical facilities nearby so they will not consider this option and will instead rely on self-medication. This condition can lead to pneumonia and fatality.

There is currently a significant likelihood of contracting pneumonia. According to UNICEF, every 46 seconds a child dies from pneumonia [2]. A European study reported several cases where doctors relied solely on the patient's medical history to determine whether it was pneumonia. Out of the 140 individuals who contracted pneumonia, only 41 had lung disease [3]. Many remote areas in many countries have limited access to health facilities, which require long distances to reach hospitals. Chest

X-rays require more time to interpret than high-resolution CT scans for diagnosing pneumonia, according to research [4]. There is a high demand for health screening but insufficient facilities or doctors. Further investigation is required to create an automated method for identifying pneumonia in order to address the aforementioned problems. This will allow doctors and healthcare workers to reach a larger population, including underserved communities, and save lives. Many studies have been conducted on detecting pneumonia through CXRs, ranging from convolutional neural networks (CNN) models developed from scratch to transfer learning models. Due to limited data availability, transfer learning models are preferred as training from scratch requires ample data. Studies have shown that fine-tuning transfer learning models yields higher results than non-fine-tuned transfer learning models.

The work carried out by ensemble learning has been undertaken [5]. In ensemble models, multiple models are combined to produce a result. There are many benefits to creating collective models. High variance in single models can lead to inaccurate predictions when compared with unobserved data. Variance and generalization error are reduced by using an ensemble model. Most commonly used ensemble approaches include the one with average probability, the other with weighted average probability, and most often when using majority voting [6]. The sector has accomplished a considerable amount of paperwork, but more needs to be done. There is no previous work comparing the Adam optimizer and the RMSprop optimizer using the EffientNetV2 model. Additionally, there is no comparison between the EfficiencyNetV2 models and older models such as VGG-16 and Xception. In this study, we will make a comparison between the RMSprop and Adam optimizers, as well as a comparison between the EfficiencyNetV2 model and existing models. Also, to create an overall model and see which one performs best. In our study, EfficiencyNetV2 performed better than older models such as VGG-16 and Xception. The choice of optimizer affected the accuracy, with Adam having slightly better overall performance, but RMSprop producing more stable results. Additionally, EfficiencyNetV2 has a lower standard deviation than VGG-16, indicating greater stability.

4.2 Related Works

Data augmentation was used on the picture dataset by Ayan *et al.* [7] and many models, including VGG-19, VGG-16, ResNet-50, Inception-V3, MobileNet, SqueezeNet, and Xception, were trained on it. They selected the top three accurate models from the results and formed an ensemble model. The same process was repeated for three-class classification segments (pneumonia, bacteria, or viral). In El Asnaoui *et al.* [8], the dataset is processed using contrast limited adaptive histogram equalization (CLAHE) image processing together with data augmentation approaches. Three improved iterations of the transfer learning models were integrated to construct all seven potential ensemble models, and each model's efficacy was assessed and compared. In a study by Sourab *et al.* [9], the applied data augmentation techniques implemented a 22-layer CNN model from scratch and used machine learning techniques for classification. In experiments, we were able to achieve a very high accuracy of over 96%. In Almaslukh *et al.* [10], data augmentation techniques were applied to the dataset using the pre-trained DenseNet-121 transfer learning model. The dataset underwent three trials with different splitting techniques. In the initial trial, the dataset was randomly split. The second experiment divided the dataset after merging the training and test sets. To categorize viral and bacterial pneumonia in the trial, the pictures were divided. Test results showed the technique had short detection time, making it a lightweight and energy-efficient strategy for medical systems. In Ukwuoma *et al.* [11], DenseNet201, VGG16, and GoogLeNet models' output were contrasted [12].

The data augmentation technique was applied to the dataset. The models used were ResNet_18, DenseNet_201, and SqueezeNet transfer learning models. The performance of the DenseNet-201, ResNet-18, and SqueezeNet designs was evaluated using cross-validation, and a comparison of accuracy and F1-score was conducted for all folds of the K-fold. Zhang *et al.* [13] employed ResNet50, MobileNet, Inception, DenseNet121, VGG, and dynamic histogram equalization for picture enhancement using the suggested model, either with or without residual framework. The performance of the models mentioned above with '224×224' input shape and 'binary cross entropy' loss function were compared. The models were trained with and without image enhancement, and a comparison was made [14]. The data augmentation technique was applied to the dataset. VGG-19 and ResNet-50 were compared to IykeNet, a CNN model created from scratch and tested against existing models. The results showed that IykeNet and the pre-trained models performed similarly. The model's accuracy improved up to 300 epochs, but after that, it decreased. Thus, the model was retrained for 300 epochs. The model trained for 13 hours, according to Avola *et al.* [15]. A comparative study of mobile network models was conducted using data augmentation techniques. The models were examined with 50%, 20%, and 10% of the training data. Rajasenbagam *et al.* [16] compared and examined the training and testing times of each model. An accurate comparison was made between the datasets produced by DCGAN augmented dataset, basic image dataset, and their combination. The VGG19 model was used for further comparison according to Mujahid *et al.* [17].

Performance was compared using an ensemble of Resnet-50, VGG-16, and Inception-V3 CNNs. They did 10-fold cross validation and compared its accuracy [17, 18]. The features from these models were processed through non-linear layers and sent to a stacked ensemble classifier for chest disease diagnosis [19]. Employed image augmentation on the dataset for pneumonia detection using U-Net architecture-based segmentation. They categorized pneumonia (viral or bacterial) and normal cases using pre-trained models on ImageNet (ResNet50, InceptionV3, and InceptionResNetV2). They utilized two optimizers. Adam and SGD were used, and their performances were examined with batch sizes of 16 and 32, according to Ibrahim *et al.* [20]. Evaluated data augmentation on detecting lung illnesses (pneumonia, COVID-19, and lung cancer) using convolutional networks and recurrent neural networks (RNN) models. VGG19, ResNet152V2, traditional CNN, GRU, and Bi-GRU were combined and compared. In Huang *et al.* [21], they fine-tuned models including InceptionV3, ResNet50V2, Xception, DenseNet121, MobileNetV2, EfficientNet-B0, and EfficientNetV2S for COVID-19 detection. They also suggested a CNN model called 'LightEfficientNetV2' using CT and CXR data. They used five-fold cross-validation to assess the models' performance. LightEfficientNetV2 was compared on three datasets (SARS-CoV-2, NIH CXR, and COVID-CT) to examine its effectiveness. All models were tested and compared.

Many works have been done using transfer learning and building CNN models from scratch; some of the work done has produced high performance in terms of accuracy score. Keras application is a publicly available deep learning library in which all the deep learning models are available, and they are saved with pre-trained weights [22]. The first model, which came to this scene, was AlexNet in 2012; this model was created to improve the accuracy of the ImageNet challenge. Then came models like VGG-16 and VGG-19, on which a huge number of works have been done not just for pneumonia detection but for many other image classification challenges. Many deep learning models have been produced over the years, and many works have been performed on them. Some papers have created an ensemble model of several models, this ensemble reduces the overfitting problem, and studies have shown that it produces better generalization results. Studies have also shown that these ensemble models have produced better results than the individual deep-learning model in terms of performance [23–26].

Numerous amounts of work have been performed on pneumonia detection, as well as some lung disease detection. Here are some of the comparisons done between works performed on deep learning models individually, as well as ensemble models. We have made a comparison chart based on the models used, the dataset used, and the performance or results obtained, like accuracy, area under the curve (AUC) score, precision, recall, F1-score, depending upon the paper's evaluation criteria.

Figure 4.1 shows all the works related to transfer learning and CNN from images, including pneumonia detection, COVID-19, and others from the year 2019 to 2023 through web scraping in Google Scholar. After going through the papers, only the following publications were taken, namely Springer, ieeexplore.ieee.org, Elsevier, mdpi.com, hindawi.com, researchgate.net, and medrxiv.org. A total of 527 papers were scraped, and the highest number of papers were published in 2021 (239 papers), followed by 205 papers in 2020. This is because this was the peak time in the development of computer-aided design (CAD) systems and when there was rapid work done on CNN and transfer learning. In 2022, 68 papers were done related to transfer learning.

Figure 4.2 shows the distribution of the keywords while scraping the titles for works related to pneumonia detection using transfer learning. The keyword 'convolution' takes up to be the majority describing how

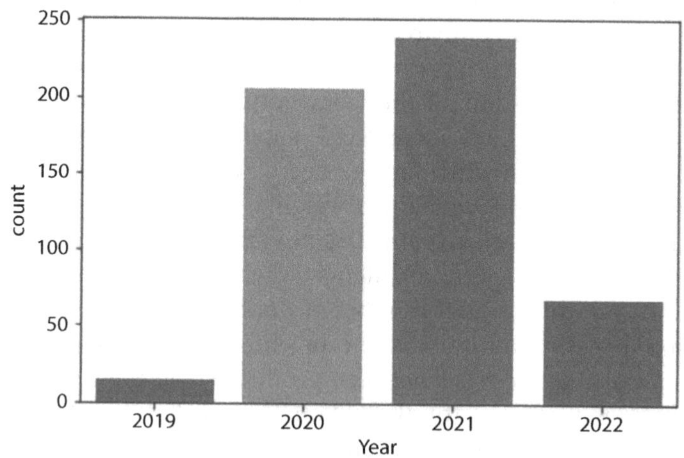

Figure 4.1 Year-wise distribution of research works.

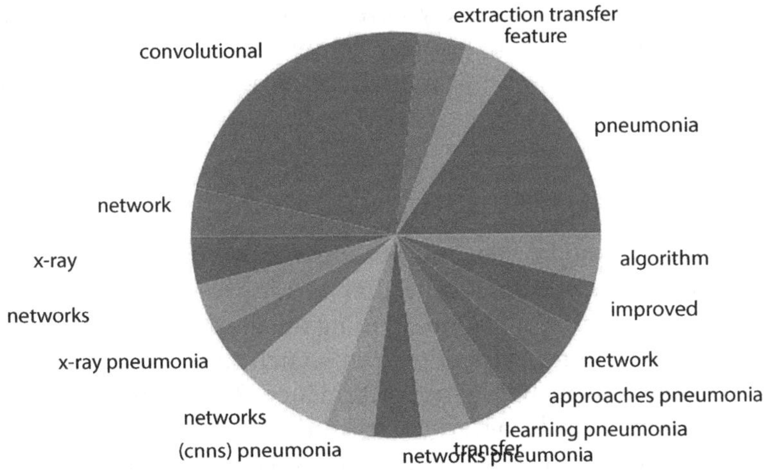

Figure 4.2 Keywords distribution to pneumonia detection.

commonly the word convolution is used for most of the works, followed by the keyword 'pneumonia'.

The above papers have been taken from reputable journals, and many of the papers have produced good results. The highest observed accuracy obtained for pneumonia detection was 99.65%, and studies have shown that ensemble models perform better than individual models. In the coming years, more deep learning models will be developed, and the performances of those models should be analyzed. As we went through the papers, very few studies have been conducted on EfficientNetV2L EfficientNetV2M, EfficientNetV2B1, EfficientNetV2B2, EfficientNetV2B3 transfer learning models in the EfficientNetV2 family of transfer learning models exclusively for the detection of pneumonia. No comparative studies of these models have been done with each other, also with the other previously done models like Xception, DenseNet, ResNet, Vgg16, and VGG19. Also, some gender-specific studies can be conducted for pneumonia detection.

4.3 Materials and Methods

The transportation industry is currently facing numerous challenges due to the ongoing pandemic. Revenue has significantly declined as travel restrictions and lockdown measures have greatly reduced demand for transportation services. Many companies in the sector have been forced to lay off employees or make cuts to their operations to survive. Additionally, concerns about health and safety have led to increased costs for implementing new protocols and ensuring compliance. These challenges have had a profound impact on the transportation industry and its ability to function effectively.

4.3.1 Dataset Details

In this section, methodologies and workflow of previously done works are analyzed. It consists of dataset collection, image pre-processing, data augmentation, k-fold cross validation, training the deep learning models with and without fine-tuning or training from scratch, and a comparison of the obtained results and analyzing the performance. Recent research on pneumonia detection using deep learning has shown promising results.

Data collection: The first step in the process is to collect and pre-process the data. The images of CXRs are collected from various sources like hospitals and online repositories. The images are then pre-processed by resizing, normalization, and augmentation to make the model robust to noise and variations.

The dataset used is from Guangzhou Women and Children's Medical Center, a publicly available dataset on Kaggle that includes 5,840 images in JPEG format and has sections for training and testing. There are 5216 images in the training part and 624 images in the testing part. Two rankings are at stake: Normal and pneumonia. The pneumonia category includes images of bacterial and viral pneumonia. However, we did not make separate predictions for both (bacterial pneumonia and viral pneumonia). Table 4.1 provides information about the data set.

Data augmentation techniques were used because the dataset was quite inconsistent and contained more cases of pneumonia than usual. This reduces the possibility of overfitting the model. Figures 4.3(a) and 4.3(b) display the X-ray scans obtained from the dataset for normal and pneumonia cases.

Table 4.1 Dataset details.

Train		**Test**	
Normal	Pneumonia	Normal	Pneumonia
3875	1341	390	234

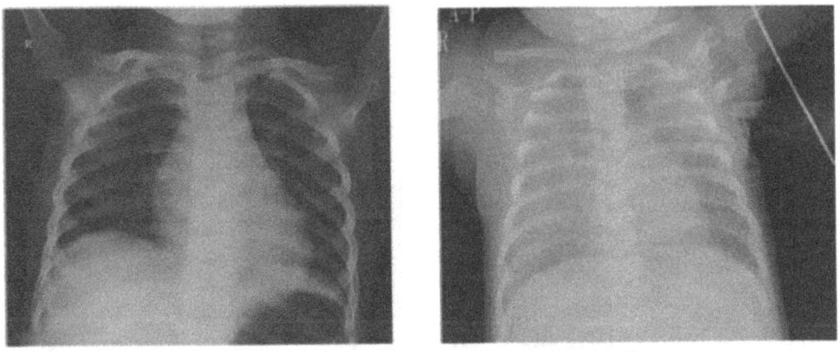

Figure 4.3 (a) Normal chest X-ray; (b) pneumonia chest X-ray.

4.3.2 CLAHE

The use of image preprocessing is a fascinating technique that can correct unwanted image distortions and enhance the visual quality of the image. In this study, we use the CLAHE image preprocessing technique. Contrast limited adaptive histogram equalization is an image preprocessing technique that improves image contrast; it is an improved variant of adaptive histogram equalization (AHE) [27]. The AHE is a digital image preprocessing method that increases visual contrast [28], and CLAHE outperforms AHE by enhancing local contrast to overcome global technique limitations. Important hyperparameters for this technique are the tile size and clip limit. The tile size and clip limit for this study are shown in Table 4.2.

Figures 4.4(a) and 4.4(c) show a normal chest X-ray image. Figures 4.4(b) and 4.4(d) show a CXR image of pneumonia infection. Figure 4.4(a) shows an image of a patients with normal breasts. An X-ray was taken after CLAHE application, and Figure 4.4(b) shows a CXR of infected pneumonia.

The images above clearly show the difference created by CLAHE image preprocessing. This improved image quality, contributing to better feature extraction, thereby improving the quality of the model.

Convolutional neural networks, RNNs, and their variants are among the deep learning architectures utilized for pneumonia diagnosis. Because CNNs are so good at extracting features from images, they are employed

Table 4.2 CLAHE values.

Tile size	Clip limit
(8,8)	3

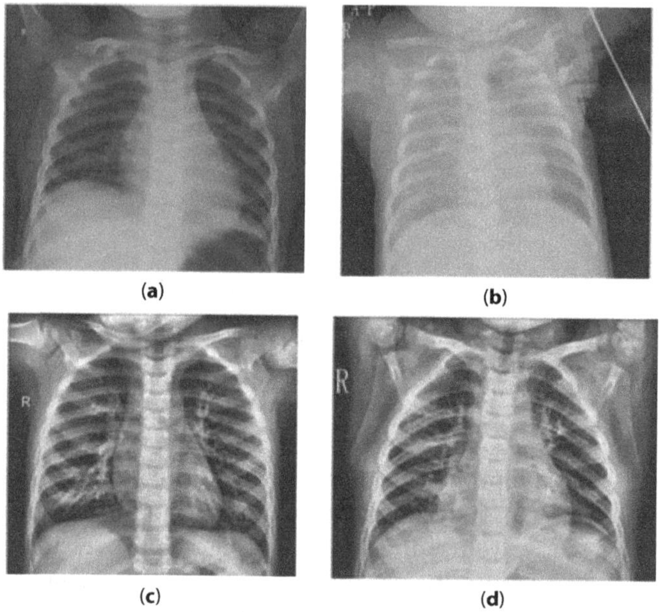

Figure 4.4 (a) Normal chest X-ray without CLAHE. (b) Pneumonia chest X-ray without CLAHE. (c) Normal chest X-ray with CLAHE. (d) Pneumonia chest X-ray with CLAHE.

extensively. Multiple convolutional layers are often the first layer in the architecture, followed by fully linked and max-pooling layers. The size and complexity of the data determine how many layers and neurons there are in each layer.

Training: Once the architecture is defined, the model is trained on the pre-processed data. During training, the weights and biases of the model are adjusted to minimize the loss function. The loss function compares the predicted output with the actual output and gives an indication of how well the model is performing. The training process is repeated for multiple epochs until the loss function converges to a minimum.

4.3.3 Data Augmentation

Data augmentation is a very famous and commonly used technique in the field of computer vision. Using random (but realistic) transformations increases the variety and quantity of the training data in options such as resize, convert, flip images, and more options. This method allows us to obtain the already available data in a more diverse way, thus improving the

Table 4.3 Data augmentation values.

Transformations	Value
Re scale	1./255
Shear and zoom _range	10, 0.3
Horizontal and Vertical flip	True
Brightness range	0.5–2.0
Width-Shift range	0.2
Rotation range	20

training set and, therefore, the trained model. Another advantage of this approach is that it helps minimize the problem of overfitting.

The training images in this investigation were subjected to the data augmentation changes listed in Table 4.3.

Using a test set of unseen images, the model is evaluated after training. A confusion matrix is used to visualize the model's performance and produce performance metrics including accuracy, precision, recall, and F1-score. Fine-tuning and transfer techniques for fine-tuning and transfer learning may be used to improve performance. To improve specialization, fine-tuning entails training the model on a more condensed, task-specific dataset. To extract characteristics from photos, transfer learning makes use of a pre-trained model that has been built on a bigger dataset.

The model is prepared for use in clinical settings following training and assessment. The model can be integrated into web or mobile applications to enable healthcare providers to diagnose pneumonia using CXRs. Accuracy and efficiency of diagnosis are further improved by integration with current radiology information systems.

4.3.4 Transfer Learning Models

The transfer of similar information from one profession to another is the idea behind the transfer learning model. The Keras Library contains a large number of transfer learning models that are open to the public. All models were made for ImageNet classification challenge. Studies indicate fine-tuning improves model performance compared to models without it. Hence, we will fine-tune the following deep learning models: EfficientNetV2L, EfficientNetV2M, EfficientNetV2B1, EfficientNetV2B2,

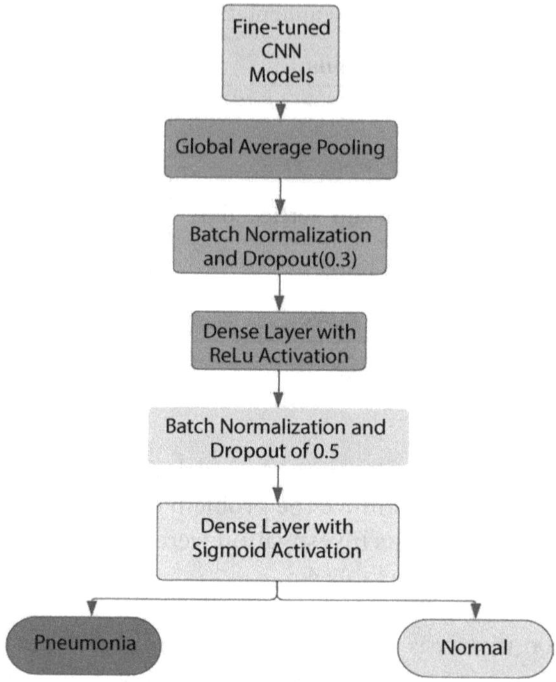

Figure 4.5 Proposed methodology.

EfficientNetV2B3, VGG-16, and Xception. Thirty layers were frozen for all models except VGG-16, where all layers were unfrozen. For all models, global average pooling was used as the output. We added batch normalization, dropout layers, and two fully connected layers. Our approach is shown in Figure 4.5.

Here, ReduceLROnPlateau is shown with a factor of 0.1, patience 7 and monitor as "validation loss." Early shutdown is used with display as "validation accuracy", patience as 9 and mode as "maximum."

For all models, we used a learning rate of 0.0001. For all models, batch size 16 was used and all images were resized to 224X224.

4.3.4.1 VGG-16

The ILSVR (ImageNet) 2014 competition was won by VGG-16. It is often considered the most advanced vision model available. The VGG-16 network was trained using the ImageNet database. The existence of 16 weighted classes is indicated by the number 16 in VGG-16 [29]. Thanks to extensive training, even with limited image datasets, the VGG-16 network

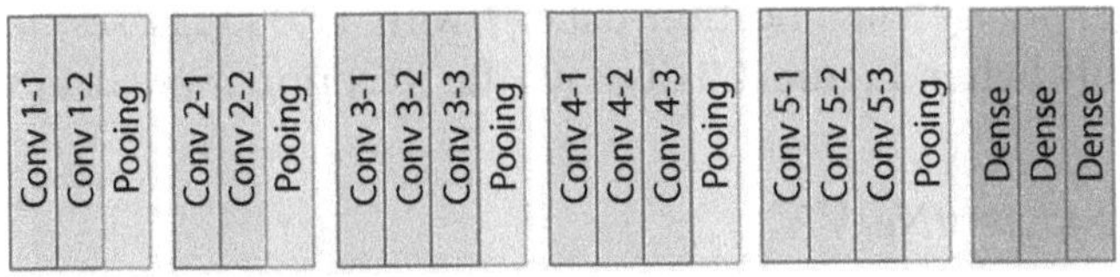

Figure 4.6 VGG-16 architecture.

delivers outstanding accuracy. VGG-16 is an image classification algorithm that can classify 1000 images into 1000 categories with an object detection accuracy of 92.7%. The drawing of VGG-16 is shown in Figure 4.6.

4.3.4.2 Xception

The Xception CNN was introduced in 2017 and stands for 'extreme inception.' The Xception model is a 71-layer CNN model with depth wise separable convolutions. The model was created by Francois Chollet, a Google employee [30]. The components of Xception consist of the entry, middle, and exit flows. On ImageNet, Xception marginally beats Inception v3, but

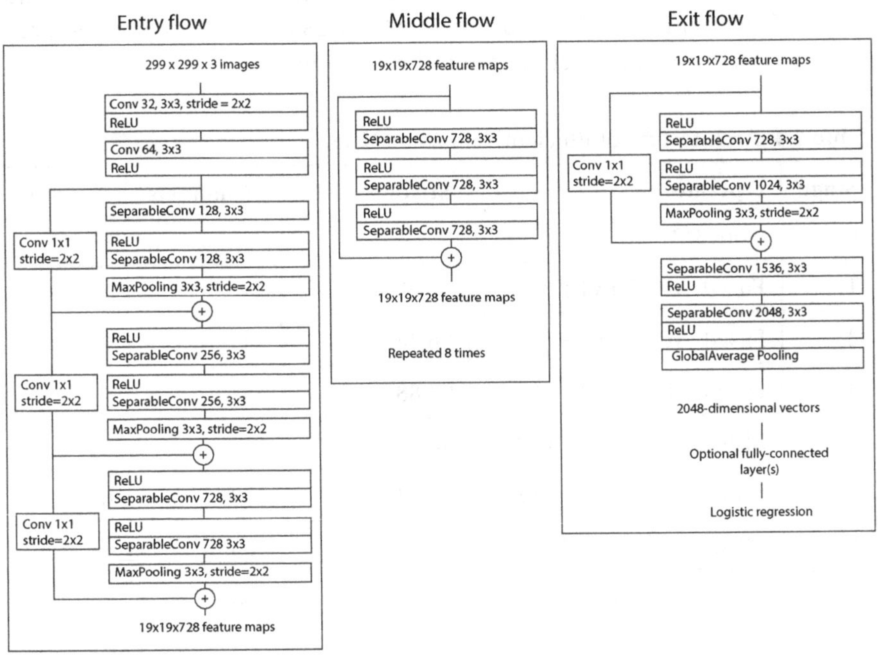

Figure 4.7 Xception architecture.

on a bigger image classification dataset with 17,000 classes, it performs considerably better. Figure 4.7 displays the Xception model's design.

4.3.4.3 *EfficientNetV2*

Initially, EfficientNet models (EfficientNetV1) faced problems like slow training speeds for EfficientNet-B3 to EfficientNet-B7 with large image sizes, training challenges with depth wise convolutions, and suboptimal scaling of dimensions. Moreover, using larger image sizes resulted in excessive RAM usage and slower training. EfficientNetV2 was introduced in 2021 to address these problems [31]. It is shown that early substitution of the MBConv module with the Fused-MBConv module can lead to faster training. Training time would be slowed down if all MBConv layers were using the Fused-MBConv module, which would increase parameters and FLOPs. Neural architecture search (NAS) was used to find the optimal fusion of MBConv and Fused-MBConv. This paper presents progressive learning to address the issue. The architecture of EfficientNetV2S by NAS is shown in Table 4.4.

Models produced after scaling up and down EfficientNetV2S include EfficientNetV2M, EfficientNetV2L, EfficientNetV2B0, EfficientNetV2B1, EfficientNetV2B2, and EfficientNetV2B3. However, in our study, we excluded EfficientNetV2B0 and EfficientNetV2S due to previous research done on Pneumonia Detection using these models.

Table 4.4 Architecture of EfficientNetV2S by NAS.

Stage	Operator	Stride	#Channels	#Layers
0	Conv3*3			
1	Fused_MBConv1.K3*3	96.67	24	1
2	Fused_MBConv4.K3*3	96.24	24	2
3	Fused_MBConv4.K3*3	95.88	48	4
4	MBConv4, k3*3, SEO,25	96.17	64	4
5	MBConv6, k3*3, SEO,25	96.02	128	6
6	MBConv6, k3*3, SEO,25	96.196	160	9
7	Conv1*1&Pooling &FC	0.2992156413	256	15

4.4 Results and Discussion

This is the set of results obtained after applying five-fold cross-validation on all models for RMSprop optimizer and Adam optimizer.

The EfficiencyNetV2L model with the Adam and RMSprop optimizers' accuracy, precision, recall, F1 score, and AUC score are displayed in Tables 4.5 and 4.6.

The below two tables show that EfficiencyNetV2L with Adam optimizer has better accuracy and F1 score than EfficiencyNetV2L with RMSprop optimizer. The EfficiencyNetV2M model with the Adam and RMSprop

Table 4.5 EfficientNet V2L – RMSprop.

Fold	Accuracy	Precision	Recall	F1-score	AUC score
1	96.65	96.67	96.65	96.61	0.97
2	96.26	96.24	96.26	96.24	0.96
3	95.78	95.88	95.78	95.7	0.97
4	96.06	96.17	96.07	96	0.97
5	95.87	96.02	95.88	95.79	98.16
Average	96.122	96.196	96.128	96.068	0.968
SD	0.3471743078	0.2992156413	0.3449202806	0.3676547293	43.4658076

Table 4.6 EfficientNetV2L – Adam.

Fold	Accuracy	Precision	Recall	F1-score	AUC score
1	97.31	97.32	97.32	97.3	0.97
2	96.06	96.07	96.07	96.02	0.96
3	97.31	97.43	97.32	97.34	0.96
4	95.78	95.78	95.78	95.73	0.96
5	95.68	95.7	95.69	95.62	0.96
Average	96.428	96.46	96.436	96.402	0.962
SD	0.8171107636	0.8474373133	0.8191031681	0.8507761163	0.004472135955

optimizers' accuracy, precision, recall, F1 score, and AUC score are displayed in Tables 4.7 and 4.8. EfficiencyNetV2M with RMSprop optimizer outperforms EfficiencyNetV2M with Adam optimizer in terms of accuracy and F1 score, as seen by the two tables below. The EfficiencyNetV2B3 model with the Adam and RMSprop optimizers' accuracy, precision, recall, F1 score, and AUC score are displayed in Tables 4.9 and 4.10. EfficiencyNetV2L with Adam optimizer outperforms EfficiencyNetV2L with RMSprop optimizer in terms of accuracy and F1 score, as seen by the two tables below. The EfficiencyNetV2M model with the Adam and RMSprop optimizers' accuracy, precision, recall, F1 score, and AUC score are displayed in Tables 4.7 and 4.8.

Table 4.7 EfficientNetV2M – RMSprop.

Fold	Accuracy	Precision	Recall	F1-score	AUC score
1	96.64	96.67	96.65	96.61	0.97
2	96.26	96.27	96.26	96.22	0.96
3	97.31	97.37	97.32	97.33	0.96
4	96.64	96.69	96.64	96.6	0.97
5	97.02	97.04	97.03	97	0.97
Average	96.77	96.808	96.78	96.752	0.966
SD	0.40246739	0.4159567285	0.4065095325	0.4248176079	0.005477225575

Table 4.8 EfficientNetV2M – Adam.

Fold	Accuracy	Precision	Recall	F1-score	AUC score
1	96.07	96.14	96.07	96.01	0.97
2	97.31	97.33	97.32	97.29	0.98
3	97.02	97.02	97.03	97.01	0.97
4	95.87	95.87	95.88	95.83	0.96
5	95.39	95.39	95.4	95.34	0.95
Average	96.332	96.35	96.34	96.296	0.966
SD	0.8061141358	0.807062575	0.8069386594	0.8232132166	0.01140175425

The two tables above show that EfficiencyNetV2M with RMSprop optimizer has better accuracy and F1 score than EfficiencyNetV2M with Adam optimizer.

The EfficiencyNetV2B3 model with the Adam and RMSprop optimizers' accuracy, precision, recall, F1 score, and AUC score are displayed in Tables 4.9 and 4.10.

Table 4.9 EfficientNetV2B3 – RMSprop.

Fold	Accuracy	Precision	Recall	F1-score	AUC score
1	95.68	95.7	95.69	95.69	0.94
2	96.83	96.82	96.84	96.82	0.96
3	97.02	97.03	97.03	97	0.97
4	95.01	94.99	95.01	94.96	0.95
5	95.2	95.17	95.21	95.16	0.95
Average	95.948	95.942	95.956	95.956	0.954
SD	0.9271299801	0.9374806665	0.9296666069	0.9391911414	0.01140175425

Table 4.10 EfficientNetV2B3 – Adam.

Fold	Accuracy	Precision	Recall	F1-score	AUC score
1	95.78	95.79	95.79	95.79	0.94
2	96.83	96.83	96.84	96.81	0.97
3	95.2	95.17	95.21	95.16	0.95
4	96.26	96.25	96.26	96.23	0.96
5	97.02	97.05	97.03	97.04	0.96
Average	96.218	96.226	96.226	96.206	0.956
SD	0.7496132336	0.7663680578	0.7494864909	0.7629089068	0.01140175425

The EfficientNetV2B2 model with the Adam and RMSprop optimizers' precision, precision, recall, F1 score, and AUC score are displayed in Tables 4.11 and 4.12.

The two tables below show that EfficiencyNetV2B2 with RMSprop optimizer has better accuracy and F1 score than EfficiencyNetV2B2 with Adam optimizer.

The EfficiencyNetV2B1 model's F1 score, AUC score, accuracy, precision, recall, and use of the Adam and RMSprop optimizers are displayed in Tables 4.13 and 4.14.

Table 4.11 EfficientNetV2B2 – RMSprop.

Fold	Accuracy	Precision	Recall	F1-score	AUC score
1	95.78	95.76	95.79	95.79	0.95
2	96.45	96.49	96.45	96.45	0.97
3	95.78	97.37	97.37	97.37	0.95
4	93.95	93.93	93.96	93.96	0.94
5	95.3	95.36	95.3	95.3	0.96
Average	95.452	95.782	95.774	95.774	0.96
SD	0.934114554	1.287583007	1.276687119	1.276687119	0.01140175425

Table 4.12 EfficientNetV2B2 – Adam.

Fold	Accuracy	Precision	Recall	F1-score	AUC score
1	93.58	93.62	93.58	93.45	0.94
2	95.01	95.02	95.01	94.94	0.95
3	95.87	95.9	95.88	95.82	0.96
4	94.91	94.88	94.92	94.87	0.94
5	93.76	93.91	93.77	93.62	0.95
Average	94.626	94.666	94.632	94.54	0.948
SD	0.9512780876	0.9164496713	0.9530320037	0.9926983429	0.008366600265

Table 4.13 EfficientNetV2B1 – RMSprop.

Fold	Accuracy	Precision	Recall	F1-score	AUC score
1	94.54	94.57	94.54	94.45	0.95
2	94.91	94.93	94.92	94.84	0.95
3	95.78	95.76	95.78	95.75	0.95
4	95.87	95.86	95.88	95.87	0.95
5	94.63	94.67	94.63	94.54	0.95
Average	95.146	95.198	95.15	95.09	0.95
SD	0.6354761994	0.6105489333	0.6374166612	0.674277391	0

Table 4.14 EfficientNetV2B1 – Adam.

Fold	Accuracy	Precision	Recall	F1-score	AUC score
1	95.4	95.39	95.4	95.35	0.95
2	94.35	94.33	94.25	94.13	0.95
3	95.3	95.27	95.3	95.27	0.95
4	96.26	96.25	96.26	96.25	0.95
5	95.3	95.27	95.3	95.26	0.95
Average	95.332	95.302	95.302	95.252	0.95
SD	0.6766978646	0.6806761344	0.7131058827	0.7524759132	0

The two tables above show that EfficiencyNetV2B1 with Adam optimizer has better accuracy and F1 score than EfficiencyNetV2M with RMSprop optimizer.

The accuracy, precision, recall, F1 score, and AUC score of the VGG16 model with the Adam and RMSprop optimizers are displayed in Tables 4.15 and 4.16.

The below two tables show that VGG16 with Adam optimizer has better accuracy and F1 score than VGG16 with RMSprop optimizer. However, the standard deviation is high, and the values of the different folds are very different, which clearly shows that both are unstable models.

Table 4.15 VGG16 – RMSprop.

Fold	Accuracy	Precision	Recall	F1-score	AUC score
1	95.68	95.7	95.69	95.69	0.94
2	98.17	98.18	98.18	98.18	0.98
3	95.3	95.3	95.3	95.3	0.94
4	91.85	91.75	91.85	91.74	0.91
5	96.64	96.76	96.64	96.68	0.95
Average	95.528	95.538	95.532	95.518	0.944
SD	2.335566312	2.392973046	2.338561524	2.386780258	0.0250998008

Table 4.16 VGG16 – Adam.

Fold	Accuracy	Precision	Recall	F1-score	AUC score
1	96.07	96.14	96.07	96.01	0.97
2	97.31	97.33	97.32	97.29	0.98
3	97.02	97.02	97.03	97.01	0.97
4	95.87	95.87	95.88	95.83	0.96
5	95.39	95.39	95.4	95.34	0.95
Average	96.332	96.35	96.34	96.296	0.966
SD	0.8061141358	0.807062575	0.8069386594	0.8232132166	0.01140175425

Table 4.17 Xception – Adam.

Fold	Accuracy	Precision	Recall	F1-score	AUC score
1	94.44	94.86	94.44	94.28	0.96
2	93.48	93.87	93.28	93.28	0.95
3	96.93	97.02	96.93	96.88	0.98
4	94.24	94.5	94.25	94.1	0.96
5	96.16	96.28	96.16	96.09	0.97
Average	95.05	95.306	95.102	94.926	0.964
SD	1.436975991	1.303564344	1.492002011	1.498492576	0.01140175425

Table 4.18 Xception – RMSprop.

Fold	Accuracy	Precision	Recall	F1-score	AUC score
1	94.06	94.3	94.06	93.91	0.95
2	95.11	95.16	95.02	93.91	0.96
3	94.34	94.77	94.34	94.17	0.96
4	94.05	94.49	94.06	93.88	0.96
5	94.34	94.69	94.34	94.18	0.96
Average	94.38	94.682	94.364	94.01	0.958
SD	0.4322614949	0.3236819427	0.3925302536	0.1511621646	0.004472135955

The Xception model with the Adam and RMSprop optimizers' accuracy, precision, recall, F1 score, and AUC score are displayed in Tables 4.17 and 4.18.

The above two tables show that Xception with Adam optimizer has better accuracy and F1 score than Xception with RMSprop optimizer. However, the high standard deviation of the Xception model with the Adam optimizer makes it an unstable model. However, the Xception model with the RMSprop optimizer tends to exhibit stability despite slightly lower performance values compared to its counterpart. Therefore, the Xception model with RMSprop is better. Table 4.19 shows a comparison between seven models with different optimizers on the performance metrics mentioned previously, and the top three models are highlighted.

The weighted average F1 score for all models is above 94%, indicating that all models perform well on the dataset as they consider both precision and recall for both classes, calculated according to the number of samples in each class.

All models had AUC scores greater than 94.4%, which suggests that the model had a high true positive rate and a low false positive rate and shows that all models perform well in distinguishing positive and negative classes. Since the AUC score is not affected by class imbalance, it is a good measure. Training vs. the experimental accuracy curves and ROC curves of the three main models for the first fold are shown in Figures 4.8, 4.9, and 4.10, respectively.

Table 4.19 Average results of all folds.

Model	Accuracy	Precision	Recall	F1-score	AUC score
EfficientNetV2M-RMSprop	96.77	96.808	96.78	96.752	0.966
EfficientNetV2M-Adam	96.332	96.35	96.34	96.296	0.966
EfficientNetV2L-Adam	96.428	96.46	96.436	96.402	0.962
EfficientNetV2L-RMSprop	96.122	96.196	96.128	96.068	0.968
EfficientNetV2B3-Adam	96.218	96.226	96.226	96.206	0.956
EfficientNetV2B3-RMSprop	95.948	95.942	95.956	95.956	0.954
EfficientNetV2B2-RMSprop	95.452	95.782	95.774	95.774	0.96
EfficientNetV2B2-Adam	94.626	94.666	94.632	94.54	0.948
EfficientNetV2B1-RMSprop	95.146	95.198	95.15	95.09	0.95
EfficientNetV2B1-Adam	95.332	95.302	95.302	95.252	0.95
VGG16-Adam	95.528	95.538	95.532	95.518	0.944
VGG16-RMSprop	95.24	95.478	95.246	95.178	0.948
Xception-Adam	95.05	95.306	95.102	94.926	0.964
Xception-RMSprop	94.38	94.682	94.364	94.01	0.958

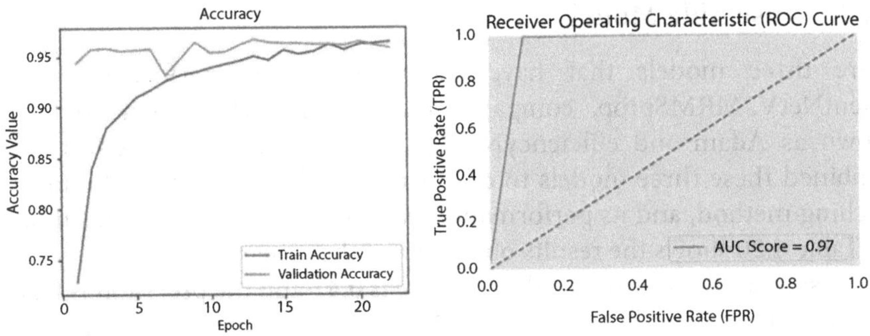

Figure 4.8 EffcientNetv2M-RMSprop results.

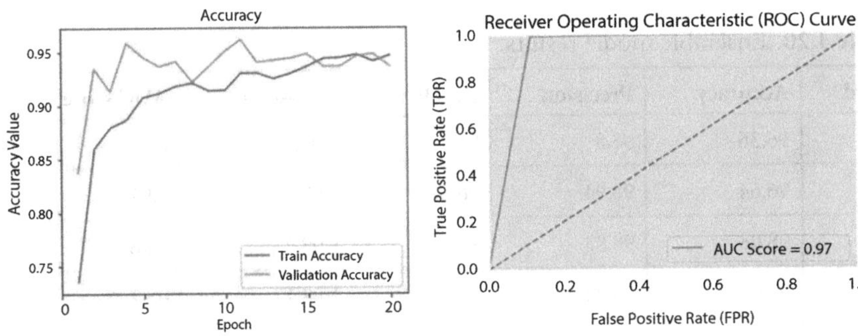

Figure 4.9 EffcientNetv2M-Adam results.

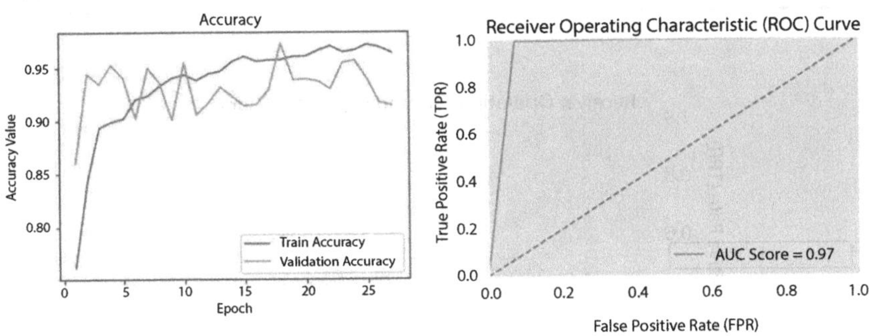

Figure 4.10 EffcientNetv2L-Adam results.

4.4.1 Ensemble Model

There three models that have shown the most performance are EffientNetV2MRMSprop, compared to other models, which are also known as Adam and efficiencyNetR2L–Adam in previous studies. We combined these three models to create an overall model using the mean stitching method, and its performance was compared with previous models. Table 4.20 shows the results obtained for the ensemble model.

The standard deviation for the F1 score is 0.47 and the precision is 0.70, making it a good model. The average AUC score of the ensemble model is 0.972, which shows that the performance of the model is good in distinguishing positive and negative classes. Figures 4.11 and 4.12 show the ROC

Table 4.20 Ensemble model results.

Fold	Accuracy	Precision	Recall	F1-score	AUC score
1	96.36	98.8	96.25	97.5	0.96
2	96.64	98.94	96.51	97.7	0.97
3	98.08	98.83	98.58	98.7	0.98
4	97.6	98.82	97.93	98.17	0.97
5	97.41	99.34	97.16	98.23	0.98
Average	97.218	98.966	97.286	98.06	0.972
SD	0.7064134767	0.2268920448	0.9721779672	0.472704982	0.008366600265

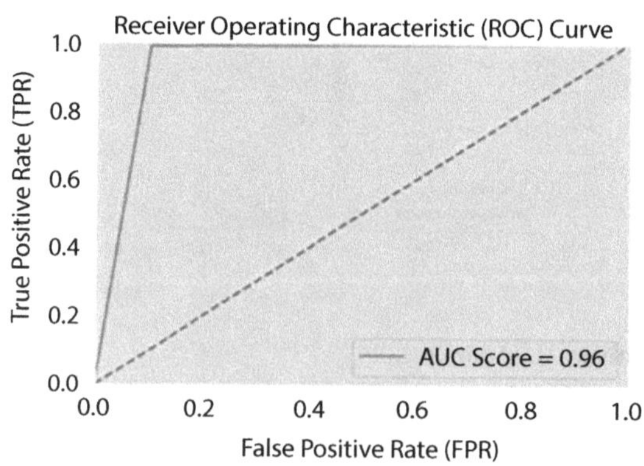

Figure 4.11 ROC curve.

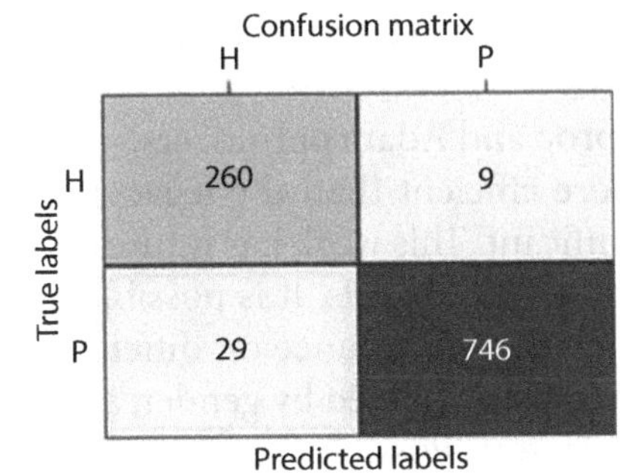

Figure 4.12 Confusion matrix.

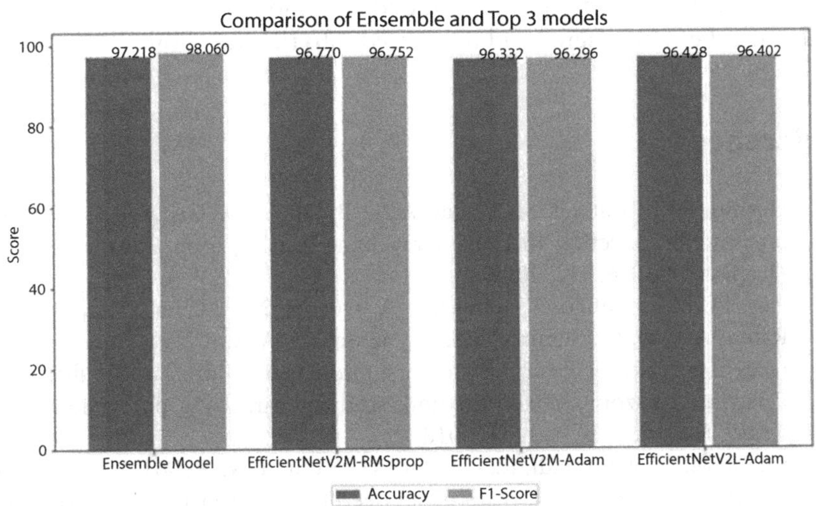

Figure 4.13 Comparison chart.

curve and confusion matrix for the first fold, respectively. Figure 4.13 shows a comparison between the ensemble model and the top three models.

The weighted average F1 score is our preferred option because of the dataset's skewness. As you can see, the weighted average F1 score of the ensemble models outperforms all other models. Additionally, all other measures performed better.

4.5 Conclusion and Future Work

By utilizing the RMSprop and Adam optimizers, we were able to determine which model was more efficient than the legacy models by comparison. This proved to be significant. This work has future scope, and we used averaging to group the three best models. It is possible to explore other global combinations and analyze performance on different datasets. More could be learned if the dataset were divided by gender, as studies have shown the importance of gender factors. Possible improvements include testing models on larger datasets to improve accuracy and reliability. Another option is to compare optimization algorithms such as Adagrad and Adadelta to find the best pneumonia detection algorithm. To improve deep learning models, CT and MRI scanning can be added. The models can then be tested in real clinical environments and integrated into the workflow.

References

1. Hashmi, M.F., Katiyar, S., Keskar, A.G., Bokde, N.D., Geem, Z.W., Efficient pneumonia detection in chest x-ray images using deep transfer learning. *Diagnostics*, 10, 6, 417, 2020.
2. Pajuelo, M.J., Anticona Huaynate, C., Correa, M., Mayta Malpartida, H., Ramal Asayag, C., Seminario, J.R., Paz-Soldan, V.A., Delays in seeking and receiving health care services for pneumonia in children under five in the Peruvian Amazon: a mixed-methods study on caregivers' perceptions. *BMC Health Serv. Res.*, 18, 1, 1–11, 2018.
3. Salehi, M., Mohammadi, R., Ghaffari, H., Sadighi, N., Reiazi, R., Automated detection of pneumonia cases using deep transfer learning with paediatric chest X-ray images. *Br. J. Radiol.*, 94, 1121, 2021, DOI: 10.1259/bjr.20201263.
4. Rahman, T., Khandakar, A., Qiblawey, Y., Tahir, A., Kiranyaz, S., Kashem, S.B.A., Chowdhury, M.E., Exploring the effect of image enhancement techniques on COVID-19 detection using chest X-ray images. *Comput. Biol. Med.*, 132, 2021, DOI: 10.1016/j.compbiomed.2021.104319.
5. Peters, M.E., Ruder, S., Smith, N.A., To tune or not to tune? adapting pretrained representations to diverse tasks. 2019, arXiv preprint arXiv:1903.05987.
6. Kundu, R., Das, R., Geem, Z.W., Han, G.T., Sarkar, R., Pneumonia detection in chest X-ray images using an ensemble of deep learning models. *PLoS One*, 16, 9, e0256630, 2021.
7. Ayan, E., Karabulut, B., Ünver, H.M., Diagnosis of pediatric pneumonia with ensemble of deep convolutional neural networks in chest x-ray images. *Arabian J. Sci. Eng.*, 47, 2, 2123–2139, 2022.

8. El Asnaoui, K., Design ensemble deep learning model for pneumonia disease classification. *Int. J. Multimed. Inf. Retr.*, 10, 1, 55–68, 2021.
9. Sourab, S.Y. and Kabir, M.A., A comparison of hybrid deep learning models for pneumonia diagnosis from chest radiograms. *Sens. Int.*, 3, 100167, 2022.
10. Almaslukh, B., A lightweight deep learning-based pneumonia detection approach for energy-efficient medical systems. *Wireless Commun. Mobile Comput.*, 1, 5556635, 2021.
11. Ukwuoma, C.C., Qin, Z., Heyat, M.B.B., Akhtar, F., Bamisile, O., Muaad, A.Y., Al-Antari, M.A., A hybrid explainable ensemble transformer encoder for pneumonia identification from chest X-ray images. *J. Adv. Res.*, 48, 191–211. 2023.
12. Alhudhaif, A., Polat, K., Karaman, O., Determination of COVID-19 pneumonia based on generalized convolutional neural network model from chest X-ray images. *Expert Syst. Appl.*, 180, 115141, 2021.
13. Zhang, D., Ren, F., Li, Y., Na, L., Ma, Y., Pneumonia detection from chest X-ray images based on convolutional neural network. *Electronics*, 10, 13, 1512, 2021.
14. Ikechukwu, A.V., Murali, S., Deepu, R., Shivamurthy, R.C., ResNet-50 vs VGG-19 vs training from scratch: a comparative analysis of the segmentation and classification of pneumonia from chest X-ray images. *Global Trans. Proc.*, 2, 2, 375–381, 2021.
15. Avola, D., Bacciu, A., Cinque, L., Fagioli, A., Marini, M.R., Taiello, R., Study on transfer learning capabilities for pneumonia classification in chest-x-rays images. *Comput. Methods Prog. Biomed.*, 221, 106833, 2022.
16. Rajasenbagam, T., Jeyanthi, S., Pandian, J.A., Detection of pneumonia infection in lungs from chest X-ray images using deep convolutional neural network and content-based image retrieval techniques. *J. Ambient Intell. Hum. Comput.*, 2021. https://doi.org/10.1007/s12652-021-03075-2.
17. Mujahid, M., Rustam, F., Álvarez, R., Luis Vidal Mazón, J., Díez, I.D.L.T., Ashraf, I., Pneumonia Classification from X-ray Images with Inception-V3 and Convolutional Neural Network. *Diagnostics*, 12, 5, 1280, 2022.
18. Ravi, V., Acharya, V., Alazab, M., A multichannel EfficientNet deep learning-based stacking ensemble approach for lung disease detection using chest X-ray images. *Cluster Comput.*, 26, 2, 1181–1203, 2023.
19. Manickam, A., Jiang, J., Zhou, Y., Sagar, A., Soundrapandiyan, R., Samuel, R.D.J., Automated pneumonia detection on chest X-ray images: A deep learning approach with different optimizers and transfer learning architectures. *Measurement*, 184, 109953, 2021.
20. Ibrahim, D.M., Elshennawy, N.M., Sarhan, A.M., Deep-chest: Multiclassification deep learning model for diagnosing COVID-19, pneumonia, and lung cancer chest diseases. *Comput. Biol. Med.*, 132, 104348, 2021.
21. Huang, M.L. and Liao, Y.C., A lightweight CNN-based network on COVID-19 detection using X-ray and CT images. *Comput. Biol. Med.*, 146, 105604, 2022.

22. Ganesh, N., Shankar, R., Mahdal, M., Murugan, S.M., Chohan, J.S., Kalita, K., Exploring deep learning methods for computer vision applications across multiple sectors: Challenges and future trends. *Comput. Model. Eng. Sci.*, 139, 103–141, 2024, Tech Science Press. DOI: 10.32604/cmes.2023.028018.
23. Ganesh, N., Balamurugan, M., Chohan, J.S., Kalita, K., Development of a grey wolf optimized-gradient boosted decision tree metamodel for heart disease prediction. *Int. J. Intell. Syst. Appl. Eng.*, 12, 515–522, 2024.
24. Ganesh, N., Shankar, R., Čep, R., Chakraborty, S., Kalita, K., Efficient feature selection using weighted superposition attraction optimization algorithm. *Appl. Sci.*, 13, 3223, 2023, DOI: 10.3390/app13053223.
25. Premalatha, M., Jayasudha, M., Čep, R., Priyadarshini, J., Kalita, K., Chatterjee, P., A comparative evaluation of nature-inspired algorithms for feature selection problems. *Heliyon*, 10, e23571, 2024, DOI: 10.1016/j.heliyon.2023.e23571, PubMed: 38187288.
26. Priyadarshini, J., Premalatha, M., Čep, R., Jayasudha, M., Kalita, K., Analyzing physics-inspired metaheuristic algorithms in feature selection with K-nearest-neighbor. *Appl. Sci.*, 13, 906, 2023, DOI: 10.3390/app13020906.
27. Habib, N., Hasan, M.M., Reza, M.M., Rahman, M.M., Ensemble of CheXNet and VGG-19 feature extractor with random forest classifier for pediatric pneumonia detection. *SN Comput. Sci.*, 1, 1–9, 2020.
28. Rubini, C. and Pavithra, N., Contrast enhancement of MRI images using AHE and CLAHE techniques. *Int. J. Innov. Technol. Explor. Eng.*, 9, 2, 2442–2445, 2019.
29. Simonyan, K. and Zisserman, A., Very deep convolutional networks for large-scale image recognition. 2014, arXiv preprint arXiv:1409.1556.
30. Chollet, F., Xception: Deep learning with depthwise separable convolutions, in: *Proceedings of the IEEE Conference on Computer Vision and Pattern Recognition*, pp. 1251–1258, 2017.
31. Tan, M. and Le, Q., EfficientNetV2: Smaller models and faster training, in: *International Conference on Machine Learning*, PMLR, pp. 10096–10106, 2021.

5

A Histogram Equalized Median Filtered SIFT–EfficientNet Based on Deep Learning Approach for Lung Disease Detection

Suguna M.[1*], Pujala Shree Lekha[1], Om Kumar C.U.[1], Arunmozhi M.[2] and Prakash D.[3]

[1]*School of Computer Science and Engineering, Vellore Institute of Technology, Chennai, Tamil Nadu, India*
[2]*Cyber Security Innovation (CSI) Research Centre, Aston University, Birmingham, United Kingdom*
[3]*Muhammed Sathak AJ College of Engineering, Chennai, Tamil Nadu, India*

Abstract

After the COVID-19 pandemic, people who have been infected may still find themselves weak and prone to many diseases, particularly lung diseases. Due to a huge scarcity of lab technicians, various deep learning techniques to automatically detect lung diseases have been proposed. Among the already existing methods, most of them were only focused on accuracy but many aspects such as dataset size, image quality, noise, multi-class classification, model training time, and overfitting were neglected. Hence in this paper, the histogram equalized median filtered SIFT–EffecientNetB0 (HMS-E) methodology is proposed, which overcomes the shortcomings stated above. The following are found in this model: the histogram equalization, which improves image contrast, the median filter, which reduces the noise, and the SIFT algorithm, which extracts the features, and deep learning models like EfficientNetB0, which is trained on images and detects diseases. In this paper, four classes are classified: COVID-19, tuberculosis (TB), pneumonia, normal with 500 images each for training. Apart from HMS-E, another three models, which are convolutional neural network (CNN), VGG16, and ResNet50, are also tried and tested. This model not only proves to be a robust model by overcoming the problems with current methods but also proved to be more efficient than the other three approaches by achieving 100% train accuracy and 90% test

**Corresponding author*: suguna.m@vit.ac.in

Kanak Kalita, Divya Zindani, Narayanan Ganesh and Xiao-Zhi Gao (eds.) Medical Analytics for Clinical and Healthcare Applications, (93–124) © 2025 Scrivener Publishing LLC

accuracy with much less training time. These aspects make HMS-E the best model to use in real life practices with huge datasets.

***Keywords*:** COVID-19, TB, pneumonia, CXR, histogram equalization, median filter, SIFT, EfficientNet, deep learning, digital communications

5.1 Introduction

In recent years, the world battled against an unprecedented global health crisis caused by the COVID-19 pandemic. The virus spread rapidly across continents, bringing with it severe consequences, particularly affecting the respiratory system. The disease, COVID-19, is caused by the Severe Acute Respiratory Syndrome Coronavirus 2 (SARS-CoV-2), a virus that primarily attacks the lungs, leading to a host of complications including pneumonia, acute respiratory distress syndrome (ARDS), and, in severe cases, death. During the pandemic, healthcare systems were overwhelmed, and millions of lives were lost. Even those who survived the virus often faced lingering effects and long-term damage, particularly to their lungs. The rising cases of lung disease in the aftermath of the pandemic have become a matter of grave concern globally, sparking a renewed focus on lung health and the urgent need for effective diagnostic tools [1–3].

Lung diseases are disorders that impair lung function, including conditions that block airflow, damage lung tissue, or impair the exchange of gases. These diseases can range from chronic conditions such as asthma and chronic obstructive pulmonary disease (COPD) to acute infections like pneumonia and tuberculosis (TB). The COVID-19 pandemic has further exacerbated the prevalence of lung diseases, as the virus not only damages the lungs directly but also weakens the body's immune system, making it more susceptible to other respiratory illnesses. The long-term impact of COVID-19 on lung health is still being studied, but it is clear that many patients continue to suffer from lingering symptoms such as shortness of breath, fatigue, and cough, even months after their recovery. These conditions, often referred to as "long COVID," have highlighted the need for improved diagnostic and treatment options for lung diseases [4–6].

One of the most alarming consequences of COVID-19 is the increased incidence of lung infections such as pneumonia and TB. Pneumonia, an infection that inflames the air sacs in one or both lungs, can be caused by bacteria, viruses, or fungi. In the case of COVID-19, pneumonia is often a secondary infection that occurs when the virus damages the lungs, allowing bacteria or other pathogens to take hold. Patients with COVID-19 pneumonia often experience severe symptoms, including difficulty breathing, chest pain, and a persistent cough. In some cases, pneumonia can progress to ARDS, a life-threatening condition in which the lungs become severely inflamed and filled with fluid, making it difficult for oxygen to reach the bloodstream [7, 8].

ARDS is a common complication in severe COVID-19 cases, and it is associated with high mortality rates. The condition occurs when the lungs become so damaged that they are unable to deliver enough oxygen to the body's organs. Patients with ARDS often require mechanical ventilation to help them breathe, and even with treatment, many do not survive. For those who do recover, ARDS can leave lasting damage, including scarring of the lung tissue, which can lead to chronic respiratory problems.

In addition to pneumonia and ARDS, COVID-19 has also been linked to an increased risk of tuberculosis. Tuberculosis is caused by *Mycobacterium tuberculosis*, a bacterium that primarily affects the lungs but can also infect other parts of the body, including the kidneys, spine, and brain. Like COVID-19, TB is a highly infectious disease, and it remains a leading cause of death worldwide. According to the World Health Organization (WHO), an estimated 10 million people fell ill with TB in 2020, and 1.5 million died from the disease, making it one of the top 10 causes of death globally. The COVID-19 pandemic has disrupted TB prevention and treatment efforts, leading to a surge in TB cases in many parts of the world. Moreover, individuals who have recovered from COVID-19 may be more vulnerable to developing TB due to the damage the virus causes to the lungs and the immune system.

The interplay between COVID-19, pneumonia, and tuberculosis presents a unique challenge for healthcare providers, as these diseases often have overlapping symptoms, making diagnosis difficult. Traditional diagnostic methods, such as a chest X-ray (CXR) and CT scan, are commonly used to detect lung infections, but they are not always able to differentiate between different types of infections. For example, a CXR may reveal lung damage, but it cannot determine whether the damage is due to COVID-19, pneumonia, or TB without further testing. This has led to the development of new diagnostic tools and models that can more accurately detect and differentiate between these diseases.

One such diagnostic tool is the CXR, which has been used for decades to diagnose lung diseases such as TB and pneumonia. A CXR can provide detailed images of the lungs, allowing doctors to see abnormalities such as fluid buildup, inflammation, or scarring. However, while CXRs are a valuable tool, they are not always accurate, and in some cases, they may miss early signs of infection or fail to distinguish between different types of lung disease.

In the context of the COVID-19 pandemic, the importance of accurate and efficient diagnostic tools for lung diseases has become even more critical. Many patients who recover from COVID-19 are left with lingering respiratory problems, and it is essential to monitor their lung health closely to ensure that they do not develop further complications such as pneumonia or TB. Given the increased risk of reinfection and the potential for long-term damage to the lungs, it is crucial to have diagnostic models that can detect multiple diseases at once and provide a more comprehensive assessment of a patient's lung health.

In response to this need, the proposed model aims to address the limitations of existing diagnostic tools by utilizing a CXR to detect COVID-19, TB, and pneumonia simultaneously. This model is designed to be more efficient and accurate than traditional diagnostic methods, providing healthcare providers with a powerful tool to monitor and assess lung health in patients recovering from COVID-19. The ability to detect multiple diseases at once is particularly valuable in the current global health context, as it allows for earlier intervention and treatment, potentially saving lives and reducing the burden on healthcare systems.

The following sections of this chapter will delve deeper into the development of this diagnostic model. Section 5.2 provides a comprehensive literature review, analyzing existing diagnostic methods and highlighting their shortcomings. Section 5.3 introduces the dataset used in the model, explaining its origin and the rationale behind its selection. Section 5.4 describes the methodology and algorithms used to develop the model, while Section 5.5 presents the results and evaluates the performance of the model. Finally, Section 5.6 offers conclusions and discusses potential future applications of the model in the field of lung disease diagnostics.

5.2 Related Works

Since 2019, there has been an increase in articles that employ various deep learning algorithms to identify various lung illnesses. Each work differs in various aspects. Combining all these works, many systematic surveys were published. There are so many datasets about CXRs that were published on open repositories for research purposes. Among them, Chest X-Ray 14 dataset is one among huge datasets, which consists of 14 classes with 13 various lung diseases and one normal class. On this dataset, many works have been done and published. A Caps Net model is applied and achieved a good 90% accuracy in training [9].

After normalizing and augmenting the images, a convolutional neural network (CNN) model is applied for training [10, 11], and it achieved accuracy of 97% and 99.5%, respectively. This work included the CADx algorithm as a feature extractor [12]. The feature extractor used before the CNN model with seven layers is called the local binary pattern (LBP) [13]. Many works used the CNN with slight modifications [14–16]. Apart from using a CNN alone, many hybrid models are also proposed. A CNN, VGG, vanilla neural network, capsule network is applied for detecting lung diseases [17]. Modals like MobileNet, DenseNet201 and NasNet are together applied in one case [18]. For detection, a combination of contrast-limited adaptive histogram equalization (CLAHE) and CNN is used [19].

A multichannel deep learning method is proposed by using EfficientNet B0, B1, B2 models [20]. Apart from CNN, there is another model called R-CNN, which works faster than an ordinary CNN model [21, 22]. With this model, several other methods are fused and proposed such as noise-masking anomalies recurrent neural network (NMA-RNN) [23]. Another version of CNN with extra layers called VGG-16 [24] and VGG-19 [25] were used. Here, the VGG model is used together with the U-Net model [26, 27]. Lung diseases are further analyzed using DenseNet-169 [28]. Another version of DenseNet is the DenseNet-121 model [29, 30]. DenseNet201 with various machine learning techniques were implemented [31].

Various CNN modification methods like ResNet, Inception, MobileNet and many more were combined for the detection. Here, SqueezeNet, VGG19, ResNet50, MobileNetV2 are proposed and tested and achieved accuracies of 97.33%, 91.66%, 90.33%, and 76.00%, respectively [32]. For identifying pneumonia, a simple ResNet model is proposed [33]. An optimized ResNet model was used, and it achieved 98.74% accuracy in detecting COVID-19 [34].

A simple Inception-based deep learning model is implemented to categorize three classes [35]. Edge computing is introduced for the detection purpose instead of using traditional implementation, along with the hybrid model of Inception-ResNet-v2 model [32]. Like these works discussed above, there are many works proposed for lung disease detection. From all these studies, multi-class classification and image quality and contrast need to be focused.

5.3 Materials and Methods

A dataset containing images of TB was created by researchers from Qatar University in Doha, Qatar, and the University of Dhaka in Bangladesh, in collaboration with medical experts from Malaysia's Hamad Medical Corporation [37]. This dataset includes both normal cases and TB patients' CXR photos. There are 700 TB and 3500 images for normal cases. From this data source, only TB images are extracted for the original dataset. The COVID-19 CXR pictures are taken from an open dataset that also includes cases of pneumonia caused by bacterial and viral infections that were collected from many other sizable publicly available datasets [38]. From all three abovementioned datasets, the original dataset with 7135 images is formed and has been put in the selected Kaggle repository. Since it is a large dataset with approximately 2 Gb, after normalization, data augmentation, and feature extraction, the size grew to 10 Gb, which is five times the original. Given the implementation in traditional environments using Google Colab GPU, the RAM was not sufficient to compute. Hence, the original dataset needed to be cut short.

5.3.1 Dataset

The study's dataset consists of CXR images from four classes and three disorders. They are: pneumonia, TB, COVID-19, and normal. The source of this dataset is the "Chest X-Ray (Pneumonia, Covid-19, Tuberculosis)" Kaggle repository. The CXR pictures from the four classes are already gathered and integrated into one dataset in the dataset from this repository, making it simple for the researchers to use. There are a total of 7135 X-ray images in the three files (train, test, and val) that make up this dataset. Each folder has another four folders in them, and each folder represents one class among the four classes. The selected dataset size is 1.93GB, which is

Table 5.1 Description of original data source.

	COVID-19	Normal	Pneumonia	Tuberculosis
Test	106	234	390	41
Train	460	1341	3875	650
Val	10	8	8	12
Total	576	1583	4273	703

Table 5.2 Description of a final dataset.

	COVID-19	Normal	Pneumonia	Tuberculosis
Test	100	100	100	41
Train	460	500	500	500
Total	560	600	600	541

very large to compute with traditional environments. Table 5.1 provides a summary of the original dataset.

For this dataset, pneumonia (4273) and normal (1583) are selected from retrospective cohorts of pediatric patients aged one to five at the Guangzhou Women and Children's Medical Centre, Guangzhou [36]. These chest radiographs are reviewed for quality control before being grouped into the datasets by eliminating any scans with poor quantity or illegible scans, and these images are then rated by two experienced doctors. For any grading errors, all the evaluation is done by a third expert.

It may be deduced from the numerous research of various deep learning works that 150–500 photos per class are adequate to obtain good classification accuracy for training a deep learning model [39]. Therefore, to get better results, the real dataset on which the proposed model was trained was combined from the original dataset, which contained 500 photos for each class for training and 100 images for testing. Table 5.2 represents the final dataset used.

In the final dataset, 2301 images are taken from the original 7135 images. As for the validation, the datasets from libraries or CXR images from a reliable hospital can be taken and validated. From the final dataset, the sample CXRs for COVID-19, Normal, Pneumonia, and Tuberculosis are shown in Figures 5.1(a–d). For COVID-19, which is the area highlighted in Figure 5.1(a), the CXR displays consolidation, as well as bilateral, peripheral, and basal multifocal airspace opacities, or ground-glass opacity (GGO) [40]. For detecting pneumonia, radiologists search for the white fog-like spots on lungs, which are called infiltrates as shown in Figure 5.1(c) [41]. For tuberculosis, a posterior-anterior chest radiograph is used to detect the lesions. For TB, lesions can appear anywhere and may differ in size, shape, density and cavitation, which is a challenging problem for any deep learning model to detect it.

Though there are many other ways to detect these diseases, CXRs is still the easiest and cheapest primary method to detect these deadly diseases. This final image dataset will go through the proposed architecture methods

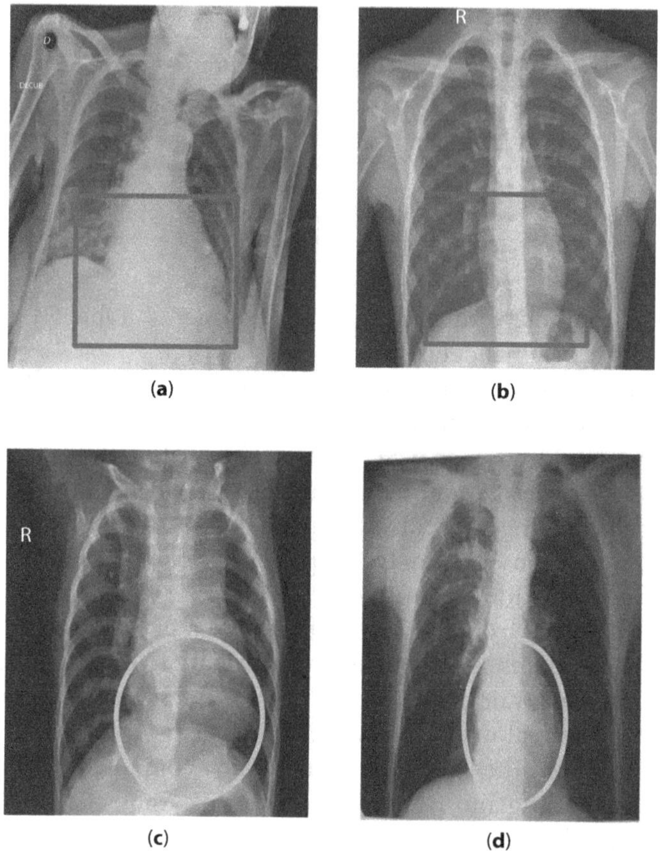

Figure 5.1 (a) COVID-19 CXR. (b) Normal CXR. (c) Pneumonia CXR. (d) Tuberculosis CXR.

and will detect diseases. The explanation of the methodology is given in the next section.

5.3.2 Methodology: HMS-E

After the selection of the dataset, it will be used to implement the proposed architecture. As mentioned earlier in the abstract, there are many aspects in the current published models that could be improved. There are a few important shortcomings in those works, which make the existing models unable to implement in real life.

Hence, the histogram equalized median filtered scale-invariant feature transform (SIFT) – EffecientNetB0 (HMS–E) approach to address these

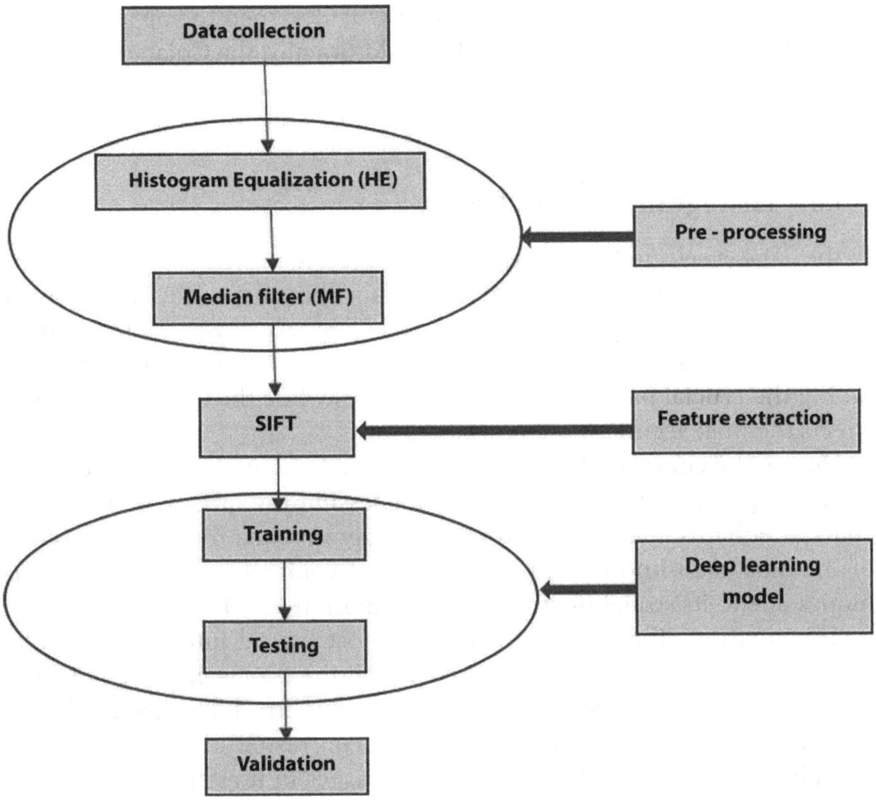

Figure 5.2 The HMS–Efficient model flow chart.

issues and make the automatic detection using deep learning techniques were used in real life scenarios. Figure 5.2 represents the workflow of the proposed architecture.

5.3.3 Pre-Processing

After the selection of an appropriate dataset, the immediate action followed is the cleaning of the dataset. Here, the dataset consists of images. Hence, image cleaning techniques should be employed. Simple environments will not be enough to pre-process nearly 2500 images. The computing units must possess a large unit of RAM, and computation time also needed to be short.

Hence, the graphical processing unit (GPU) in Google Colab is chosen to be the implementation environment. This GPU is a standard from

NVIDIA T4 Tensor Core GPU. This GPU is designed to support the 2D and 3D graphics together with a CPU. Additionally, the Colab offers more free storage and memory than any other environment. Therefore, Google Colab is chosen for the implementation.

5.3.4 Histogram Equalization

In the dataset selected, the images are observed to be images with low contrast. Images having higher contrast levels will display a greater degree of grayscale variation than those of lower contrast. The lower contrast image will blend light and dark areas, which results in a flat photo. This results in hiding the crucial parts for detecting diseases while the feature extraction affects the final accuracy.

Hence, the contrast of the images in dataset should be increased along with the quality being affected. When assessing the quality of an image, contrast enhancement is crucial [42]. Histogram equalization (HE) is one of the most well-known and regularly used contrast enhancement techniques due to its straightforward implementation [43, 44].

This method efficiently disperses the most typical intensity values by expanding the image's intensity range. When the data is displayed in close contrast levels, HE boosts the images' overall contrast. Consequently, the parts with lesser contrast can become more contrasted. This approach specifically fits the current dataset since the images in it are black-and-white X-ray images. Figure 5.3 represents the histogram equalization algorithm workflow.

Each image will have a histogram created during this procedure. With intensity levels ranging from 0 to (L-1) and L set to 257, the function h(rk) = nk, which represents the histogram of a digital image indicates the kth intensity level and the number of pixels in the image that have that intensity level. The histogram can also be made normal by dividing it by the total number of pixels in the picture. For an N × N image, a normalized histogram function is defined as follows:

$$p(rk) = nk/N2 \tag{5.1}$$

Here, the likelihood that a pixel with the intensity level rk would appear is represented by the p(rk) function in equation-1. The histogram of an image constructed with x-axis representing the intensity levels rk and the y-axis denoting the p(rk).

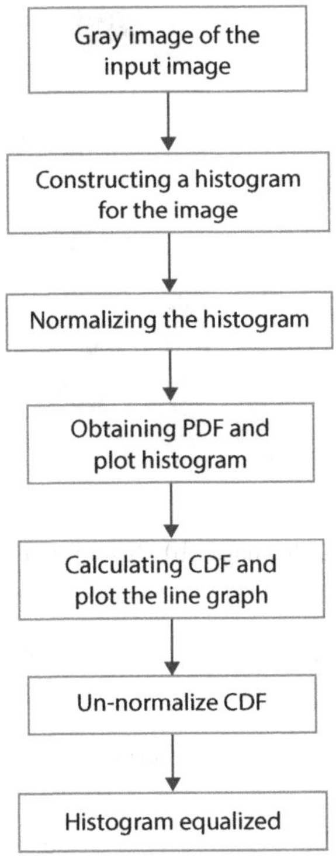

Figure 5.3 Workflow of histogram equalization (HE).

The image's histogram provides crucial details about the image's contrast and grayscale. A dark image is implied when the whole histogram of an image is centered towards the left end of the x-axis. A white or bright image is indicated by the histogram's greater inclination towards the right end. Given that there are only a few shades of grey in the image, a low-contrast image can be seen in a narrow-width histogram plot in the intensity axis's middle.

On the other hand, the image has a high contrast appearance when the histogram is evenly distributed across the entire x-axis. By selecting the appropriate intensity transformation function, histogram equalization is the process of evenly dispersing the image histogram along the full intensity axis. Thus, histogram equalization is a process of intensity change. Then, the histogram will be normalized by obtaining the probability density function (PDF) value by differentiating the p(rk) function by the sum of p(rk). Then, the PDF value will be plotted against the rk value as the histogram

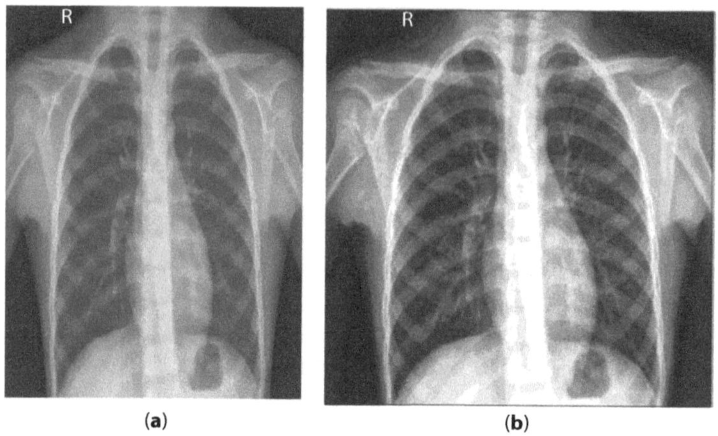

Figure 5.4 (a) Original input CXR image. (b) Histogram equalized image.

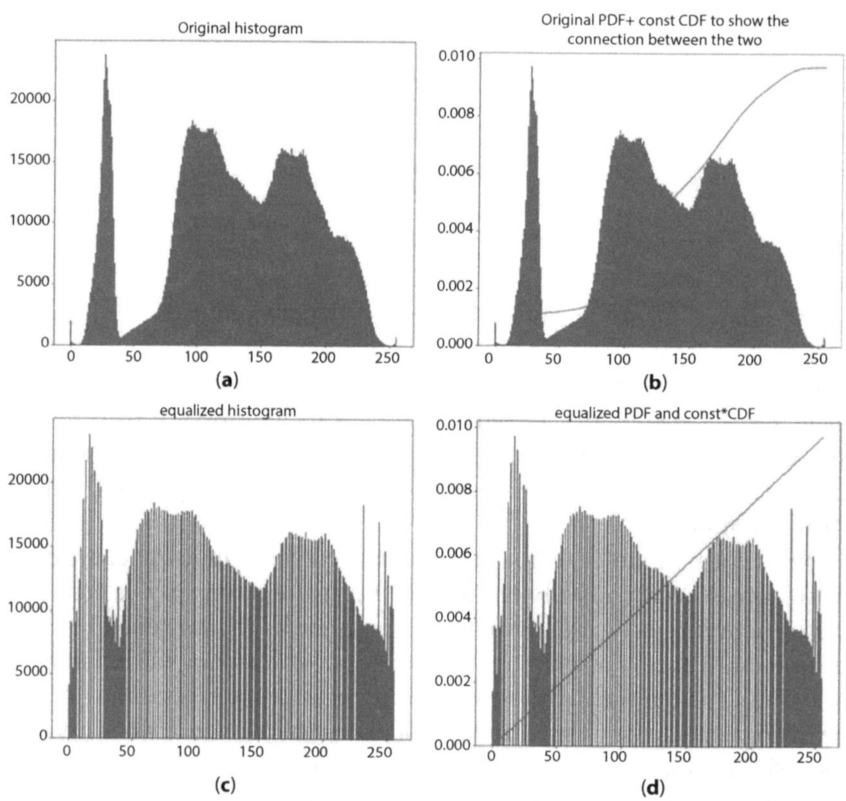

Figure 5.5 (a) Histogram of Figure 5.4(a). (b) PDF and CDF of the original histogram. (c) Histogram of an equalized image. (d) PDF and CDF of an equalized image.

for the normalized image. After normalization, the PDF is integrated to get the cumulative distribution function, which is then shown as a line graph.

Then the final step will be considered as un-normalizing the cumulative distribution function (CDF) to become the equalization function. The equalized image will be the final output of the histogram equalization method.

Figure 5.5(a) represents the histogram equalized image of input image Figure 5.5(b). The created histogram of the input image is displayed in Figure 5.5(c). The histogram of the equalized image is displayed in Figure 5.5(d). The PDF and CDF of the equalized image are displayed in this image. The intensity of those areas whose contrast was low got stretched, and the contrast improved.

It is evident from Figure 5.5(a) that the histogram equalization of the image improves contrast and normalizes the image without degrading the quality of the input image. Hence, this image enhancing technique that is being used in the proposed method can be considered the best fit for the CXR dataset.

5.3.5 Median Filter

A random variation in image signal or unwanted information in the image can be called as noise. Noise can cause various factors such as poor camera visibility, blur in photos, poor light conditions, and heat. Every image is bound to have some noise in it. These tiny disturbances can compromise the level of detail in the image and affect the accuracy and may decrease the quality of the image [45].

This disadvantage will be reflected during the time of feature extraction. Hence, the noise in the images should be reduced. But in many cases, removing the noise in the images results in softening the image. This may cause the image to lose some sharpness and loss of few features from the image. So, a method which removes the noise in the image along with reducing the softening should be considered. The selected dataset is an X-ray dataset, salt-pepper noise is the most found noise in X-ray images [46]. The black and white dots, which appear on X-ray images, is the salt-pepper noise. For instance, if the number of bits for transmission is eights, a noisy pixel may have a value of 0 or 255, which is the highest or "minimum" pixel value. Therefore, black and white dots appear on the image [47, 48]. For instance, if the number of bits for transmission is eight, a noisy pixel can have a value of 0 or 255, which is the maximum or minimum pixel value.

Noise can be eliminated by applying mathematical processing to noisy photos. Only noise needs to be eliminated during this operation. The edges must be preserved. The median filter, a nonlinear digital filtering method,

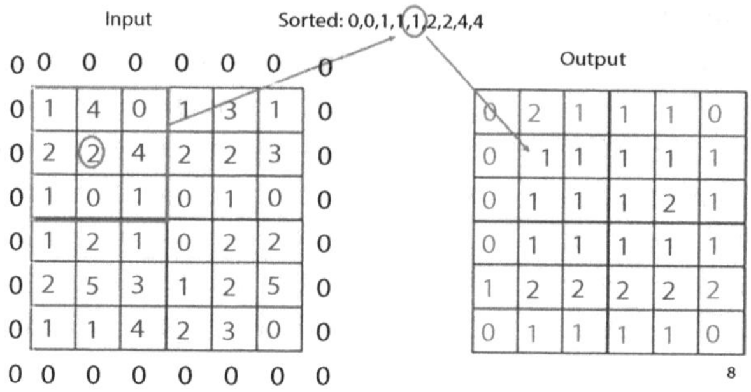

Figure 5.6 Working of 2D median filter with 3X3 sampling window.

is one of the most often used filters. The idea of an average filter is used in median filtering. Here, the average input of the neighboring pixels is determined. When using median filtering, the value of the output pixel is determined by the median value as opposed to the mean value of the neighboring pixels. In the case of extreme values, the median value will be less sensitive than the mean value. Given that they may be visualized using a matrix multiplication, linear filters are also referred to as convolution filters. Prior to applying the median filter, the image is converted to pixel format. As it moves pixel-by-pixel over the image, the median filter replaces each value with the median of the pixels in its immediate vicinity.

Figure 5.6 represents the working of a portion of the image (median) pixel value. Figure 5.7(a) represents the working of a portion of the image.

Figure 5.7(b) depicts the denoised image of the histogram equalized CXR. Compared to Figure 5.7(a), Figure 5.7(b) is denoised and smoother, but the quality has not decreased. Nonlinear procedures include thresholding, image equalization, and the median filter. This filter also sharpens the image contrast and detects the edges. A median filter removes the outlier without reducing the image's clarity. Therefore, this method can be considered as the best method to remove noise from the given dataset images.

5.3.6 Feature Extraction

The method of feature extraction preserves the information in the original data collection while converting unprocessed data into manageable numerical features. During the pattern identification stage of feature extraction, the fundamental signal properties need to be separated from extraneous or undesirable information. It must also consider how to calculate, from the original raw signals, a compact and interpretive outcome collection. It acts

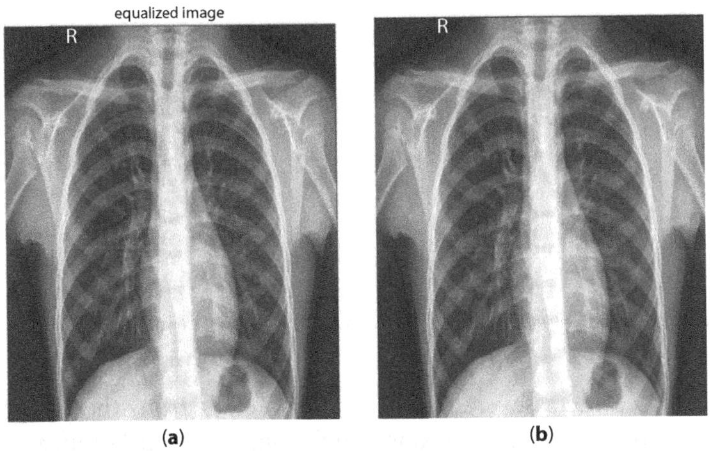

Figure 5.7 (a) Histogram equalized CXR. (b) Median filtered CXR.

as the middle process between pre-processing and classification. A strong image matching method called SIFT can find and match features in images that are resistant to scaling, rotation, and affine distortion. It is commonly used in 3D reconstruction, object recognition, and picture matching applications in computer vision.

Using the SIFT technique, which requires building a scale space of images with varying scales, critical locations in the images are located using the difference of the Gaussian (DoG) method. Additionally, each key point must have descriptors computed for feature matching and object recognition. Python with the OpenCV library, which offers a collection of functions for identifying key points, computing descriptors, and matching features, can be used to implement it.

- Key points: Key points are the spatial positions of an image are rotation- and scale-invariant places. These crucial details show what shines out in an image and which pixels are crucial.
- Descriptors: Descriptors are vectors that describe the local surroundings around the key points present in the image. These descriptors are used to make associations between different images.
- Gaussian Blur: With the use of the Gaussian function, this technique lowers the noise in the image to effectively detect the important points.

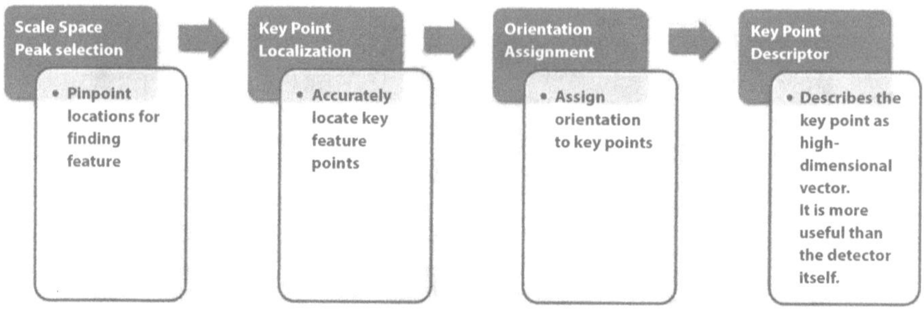

Figure 5.8 Process flow of the SIFT algorithm.

The SIFT extracts several local feature vectors from the image, all of which are robust against variations in lighting, size, translation, and geometry. Due to their spatial specificity, SIFT characteristics are less affected by noise and damaged pixels.

An overview of the SIFT algorithm's steps is provided in Figure 5.8. This algorithm is divided into three subsequent sections:

5.3.6.1 Detection of Scale-Space Extrema

In the scale-space image, the convolution interaction between capacity and picture yields L (a, b, σ). Convolutional functions are the Gaussian function G (a, b, σ) and the image function I (a, b, σ). Equation 5.3 illustrates this, as shown below:

$$L(a,b,\sigma) = G(a,b,\sigma) \times I(a,b) \tag{5.2}$$

$$G(a,b,\sigma) = \frac{e^{\frac{-(a^2+b^2)}{2\sigma^2}}}{2\pi\sigma^2} \tag{5.3}$$

By improving a quantifiable estimate of Gaussian's Laplacian, the major portions of the image known as the Gaussian differences (DoG) are removed. We get the DoG function from Equation 5.4.

$$D(a,b,\sigma) = L(a,b,k\sigma) \times L(a,b,\sigma) \tag{5.4}$$

This represents the convolution of the original image with the scaled Gaussian blur.

5.3.6.2 *Localization of Key Points*

The scale-space function D(a,b,) is expanded using the Taylor method, and as a result, the sample point is transformed into the origin. Below is a representation of the equation:

$$D(a) = D + \left\{ \left(\frac{\partial D^T}{\partial a} \right) \times a \right\} + \left\{ \frac{a^T}{2} \times \left(\frac{\partial^2 D}{\partial a^2} \right) \times a \right\} \tag{5.5}$$

5.3.6.3 *Generation of Key Point Descriptors*

The area around each key point is subsequently given a local feature descriptor. The feature vector for key point descriptors has a dimension of 128 and is composed of 16 histograms, each of which has eight orientation bins and is arranged in a 4x4 grid. To provide direction invariance, this descriptor relies on a local picture gradient that has been rotated based on the direction of the primary problem. To establish the descriptor direction, a gradient orientation histogram is built close to the primary problem.

Through this SIFT algorithm, the features in the image will be marked as key points and these features will be fed to the pre-trained models as input, which reduces the work of the model by marking the features on the image. This feature extraction technique called SIFT reduces the content of an image to a collection of points that can be used to find recurring patterns in other photos.

The chosen dataset's photos are seen to be in a variety of formats. For example, the images of COVID-19 in the dataset are in the JPG, Normal and Pneumonia classes. Photos are in JPEG format, and TB photos are in PNG. To avoid letting the format of images create bias, all the image formats are changed into PNG format during the pre-processing time.

Figures 5.9(a) and 5.9(b) show the identified features on the selected CXR image. Now with the features identified and marked with the help of the SIFT algorithm, an image will be fed to the pre-trained model as input so that deep learning would not need to identify the features specifically. A deep learning model will be training on the features directly, which will make the computation faster.

This algorithm identifies the features effectively and is not affected by the noise and clutter. SIFT can detect the features in small objects, too. Even if an image is rotated or the camera angle is altered, the SIFT algorithm's

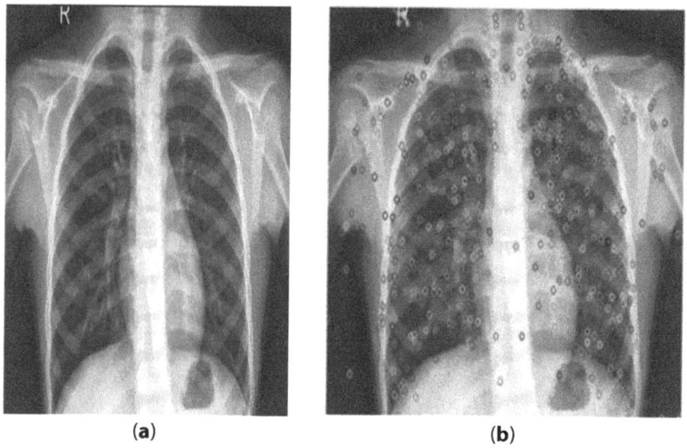

Figure 5.9 (a) Pre-processed CXR. (b) CXR with SIFT features identified.

features can be used to categorize the photographs. All these aspects about the algorithm make the performance of SIFT possible and feasible in real-time practices.

5.3.7 Deep Learning Model

The picture dataset should be provided to the deep learning model as input once the characteristics from the photos have been extracted to train the model to identify the diseases. Considering the selected dataset is a CXR image dataset, four deep learning models (CNN, VGG-16, ResNet50, and EfficientNetB0) are chosen and trained accordingly. After observing and comparing the results obtained, the best model for the current approach is decided finally.

There are a few terms that are common for all the four selected deep learning models. They are listed below:

Epoch: A single iteration of the machine learning model using all the training data constitutes an epoch. It is measured in cycles.
Batch: Batch size is one of the key hyperparameters in machine learning. The hyperparameter controls the number of samples to be processed before the internal model parameters are updated.
Optimizer: An optimizer is an algorithm or function that changes a neural network's learning rate and weights. Hence, it helps to increase accuracy and decrease overall loss. But selecting the right weights for the model is a difficult issue.

Image Channel: Each of the three channels that make up a pixel indicates a different color. Red, green, and blue are the three channels that make up a color image.
Activation Function: The activation function is a node that is positioned at the center or at the end of neural networks. An activation function determines the activity status of a neuron. Its primary function is to enable neural networks nonlinear expression capabilities so that they can more accurately match the outputs.
Dropout Layer: Dropout replicates the concurrent training of several neural networks with various designs. It is a regularization technique. Some layer outputs are lost or ignored randomly during training.

5.3.7.1 *EfficientNetB0*

Using a compound coefficient, the CNN construction and scaling method EfficientNet uniformly scales all depth, breadth, and resolution dimensions. Unlike other approaches, EfficientNet's scaling strategy uses specified scaling factors to consistently increase network breadth, depth, and resolution. With more channels and layers needed to capture fine features in larger input images, our method—driven by a compound coefficient ensures balanced changes.

Neural architecture search was used to construct EfficientNet-B0, which has MobileNetV2 inverted bottleneck residual blocks and squeeze-and-excitation blocks to maximize floating-point calculations and precision. Expanded to include models B0 with 11 million trainable parameters, these architectures beat rivals in both accuracy and efficiency on ImageNet.

All architectures, although with different topologies, use seven inverted residual blocks in addition to squeeze-and-excite blocks and swish activation. Swish activation will be covered in detail, with an emphasis on the following input requirements: input, block parameters, and the resultant output layer.

Block arguments are a collection of properties to be used inside an MBConv block, such as input filters, output filters, expansion ratios, and squeeze ratios. EfficientNet employs seven MBConv blocks to satisfy the requirements (argument block) for each of those blocks. Here, are the few terms which can be considered as foundation stones of EfficientNetB0.

5.3.7.1.1 Inverted Residual Block

MobileNet architecture introduces the concept of a leftover block. Within the residual block, where MobileNet uses depth wise separable convolution, depth wise convolution is conducted first, followed by point wise convolution.

This method drastically reduces the number of trainable parameters. Skip connections are used in an initial residual block (introduced in ResNet) to connect vast layers (also known as layers with many channels), whereas narrow layers (also known as layers with fewer channels) are found inside a block. In contrast, the inverted residual block places bigger layers between skip connections while narrower layers are connected by them.

5.3.7.1.2 Expansion Phase

Since connected blocks are smaller and inner blocks are larger, as indicated in the inverted residual block, the layers will be widened by simply adding more channels.

5.3.7.1.3 Depth-Wise Phase of Convolution

Following expansion, depth-wise convolution is performed using the kernel size that was supplied in the block argument.

5.3.7.1.4 Squeeze and Excitation Phase

When a convolutional layer in CNN generates an output feature map, each channel is given the same weight. On the other hand, the squeeze and excitation (SE) block is a method that, instead of treating all channels equally, prioritizes certainty over others. Surprisingly, the weighting for each channel is provided by the SE block's output, which is in the shape of 1 x 1 x channels. As with other parameters, this enables neural networks to learn these weightings on their own.

5.3.7.1.5 Output Phase

The convolution operation is performed after the preceding block. The EfficientNetB0 architecture is then finalized by completing this series of phases. The best option out of the three models described is the compound scaling method, which automatically modifies image dimensions and improves and streamlines the model's image classification capabilities.

5.4 Performance Measure

Metrics like test accuracy, train accuracy, precision, recall, F1 score, and computation time are used to assess the performance of the suggested model.

The most popular way to assess a model's performance is to find and look at a confusion matrix. The following equations (5.6 to 5.9) provides the computation of the considered metrics: Computation time: The amount of time needed to run the model over N epochs.

$$\boldsymbol{Accuracy} = \frac{\boldsymbol{TP + TN}}{\boldsymbol{TP + TN + FN + FP}} \tag{5.6}$$

$$\boldsymbol{Precision} = \frac{\boldsymbol{TP}}{\boldsymbol{TP + FP}} \tag{5.7}$$

$$\boldsymbol{Recall} = \frac{\boldsymbol{TP}}{\boldsymbol{TP + FN}} \tag{5.8}$$

$$\boldsymbol{F1\ score} = \frac{\boldsymbol{2 \times Precision \times Recall}}{\boldsymbol{Precision + Recall}} \tag{5.9}$$

Where the number of instances that were correctly categorized as cases of a particular disease is known as the true positives (TP). True negatives (TN): The proportion of events that were accurately categorized as belonging to the normal class. The number of incidents that were incorrectly categorized as false positives (FP). The number of instances that were incorrectly assigned to the class of normal cases are false negatives (FN).

5.5 Results and Discussion

Training and testing of selected models: These four chosen deep learning models (CNN, VGG16, ResNet50, and EfficientNetB0) are trained on the dataset following data pre-processing using the suggested methods. Each model is trained starting with 1 epoch and increasing 5 epochs with every implementation, until the count reaches 50 epochs. The metrics mentioned and loss readings are calculated for every trial. At the end, the trial with the best result among all the trials is selected. For the testing part, 100 images for each class are taken and tested, and accuracy is calculated.

In this study, the four models were implemented according to the HMS-filtered SIFT approach in the Google Colab GPU. Table 5.3 represents the performance of HMS–CNN model. From this, the greatest test accuracy achieved is 74.78% at 5 epochs and the best training accuracy is 100%

Table 5.3 The performance of the HMS-CNN model.

Epochs	Time	Train_acc	Test_acc	Precision	Recall	F1
1	4m	89.6939	71.5542	89.8961	89.6939	89.7012
5	**21m24s**	**99.2857**	**74.7801**	**99.2925**	**99.2857**	**99.2869**
10	43m	99.9490	73.3138	99.9491	99.9490	99.9490
15	1h	99.8980	73.9003	99.8984	99.8980	99.8979
20	1h15m28s	100	72.7273	100	100	100
25	1h33m56s	100	65.9824	100	100	100

at 20 epochs. The high numbers of precision and recall indicates the relevance of the model. But the training time is very long, which makes the model unfit for the large datasets.

The HMS-VGG16 model's performance chart is displayed in Table 5.4. The highest training accuracy of this model is 100 achieved after 40 epochs, and the highest testing accuracy is 80% achieved at 35 epochs. For this model, the precision and recall number are high enough to prove that this model's results are relevant enough. This beats the previous HMS-CNN model in both accuracy and training time, which makes this model better than the CNN model.

Table 5.5 presents the HMS-ResNet50 model results. The best testing accuracy is attained at 50 epochs, and the highest training accuracy is at 15 epochs. Through the precision and recall results, it can be seen as a relevant model. The training time is much less than the other two models. Even 50 epochs are implemented in 8 minutes and 25 seconds, proving this model is fastest than earlier models. Even the accuracy achieved is higher than the last two models.

Table 5.6 shows the HMS-EfficientNetB0 model results. At 15 epochs, the best training accuracy is 100%, while at 5 epochs, the highest testing accuracy is 90%. The training time is lesser than HMS-CNN and HMS-VGG16 but higher than HMS-ResNet50. The accuracy achieved by this model is the highest among all three models.

Figures 5.10, 5.11, 5.12, and 5.13 show, for each trial that is used, the training and testing accuracies of all the proposed models: HMS-CNN, HMS-VGG16, HMS-ResNet50, and HMS-EfficientNetB0. In all the figures, there are no drastic drops or rises in the graph. Both accuracies are a constant variation. This shows that all the models have overcome the problem of overfitting.

Table 5.4 Performance of the HMS–VGG16 model.

Epochs	Time	Train_acc	Test_acc	Precision	Recall	F1
1	1m25s	26.8877	29.3255	17.3275	26.8878	13.0896
5	3m23s	86.0714	64.5161	87.9164	86.0714	85.5668
10	5m25s	91.3265	75.6598	92.4077	91.3265	91.3251
15	9m26s	99.2857	76.8328	99.2933	99.2857	99.2854
20	**14m24s**	**99.7449**	**79.4721**	**99.7462**	**99.7449**	**99.7445**
25	15m26s	95.9694	71.8475	96.0444	96.2755	96.2708
30	17m25s	99.7959	75.3666	99.7961	99.7959	99.7959
35	**19m24s**	**99.3367**	**80.0586**	**99.3399**	**99.3367**	**99.3367**
40	24m16s	100	76.2463	100	100	100
45	32m41s	100	76.2463	100	100	100
50	36m44s	100	76.2372	100	100	100

Table 5.5 Performance of HMS–ResNet50 model.

Epochs	Time	Train_acc	Test_acc	Precision	Recall	F1
1	13s	92.5000	86.2170	92.8189	92.5000	92.4486
5	53s	98.6735	83.5777	98.6821	98.6735	98.6719
10	1m34s	99.7959	85.0440	99.7959	99.7959	99.7959
15	2m25s	100	84.7507	100	100	100
20	3m25s	100	85.0439	100	100	100
25	3m56s	100	84.4575	100	100	100
30	4m40s	100	84.1642	100	100	100
35	5m21s	100	84.1642	100	100	100
40	6m25s	100	84.1642	100	100	100
45	7m25s	100	83.2844	100	100	100
50	**8m25s**	**100**	**85.3372**	**100**	**100**	**100**

Table 5.6 The performance of the HMS–EfficientNetB0 model.

Epochs	Time	Train_acc	Test_acc	Precision	Recall	F1
1	20s	99.9490	86.2170	99.9491	99.9490	99.9490
5	**2m22s**	**99.6939**	**90.0229**	**99.6953**	**99.6939**	**99.6940**
10	3m45s	98.5204	84.4575	98.5341	98.5204	98.5148
15	**5m15s**	**100**	**88.8563**	**100**	**100**	**100**
20	7m22s	97.6020	80.9384	97.6648	97.6020	97.5850
25	9m23s	100	87.0968	100	100	100
30	10m22s	99.8469	79.4721	99.8475	99.8469	99.8468
35	12m22s	100	83.284	100	100	100
40	14m21s	100	84.4575	100	100	100
45	15m39s	100	87.3900	100	100	100
50	18m22s	100	86.8035	100	100	100

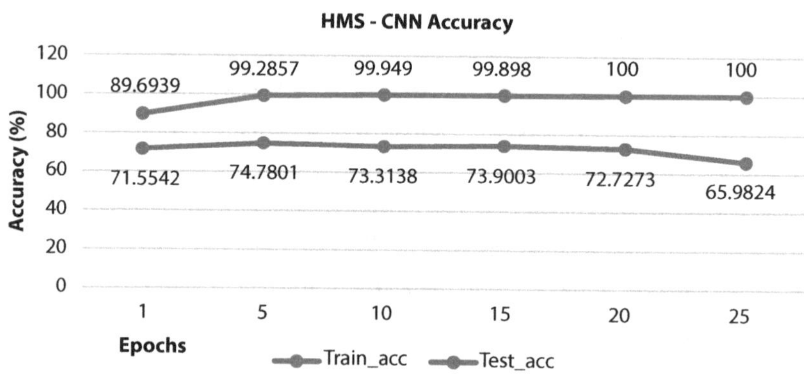

Figure 5.10 Training and testing the accuracy of the HMS–CNN model.

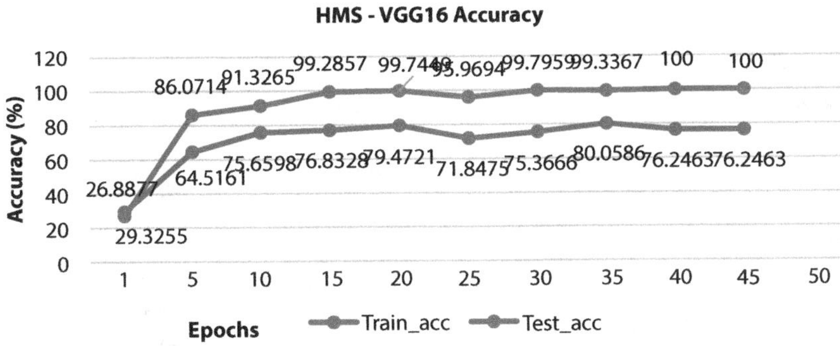

Figure 5.11 Training and testing accuracy of the HMS–VGG16 model.

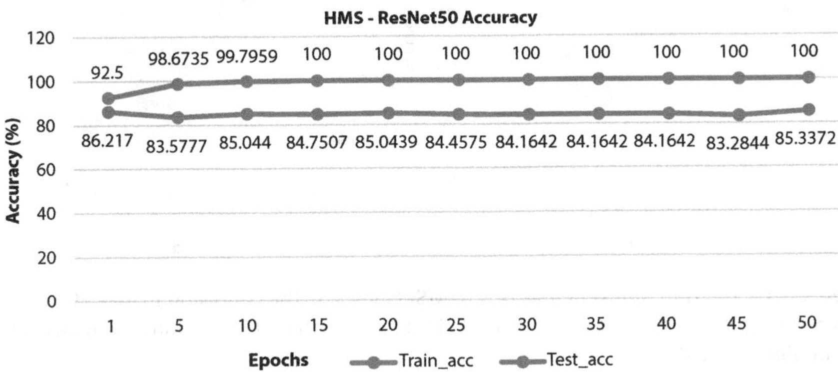

Figure 5.12 Training and testing accuracy of the HMS–ResNet50 model.

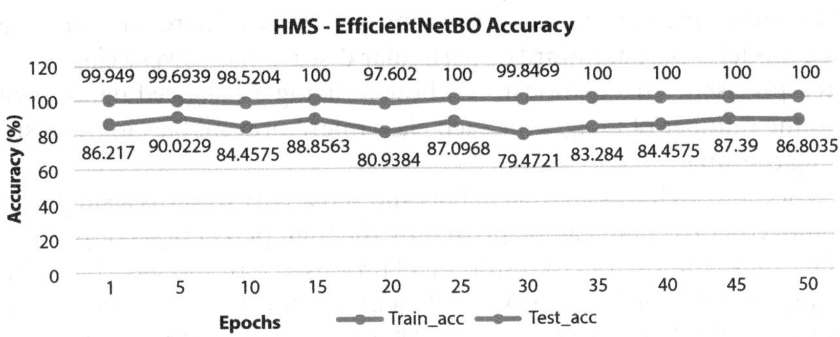

Figure 5.13 Training and testing accuracy of the HMS–EfficientNetB0 model.

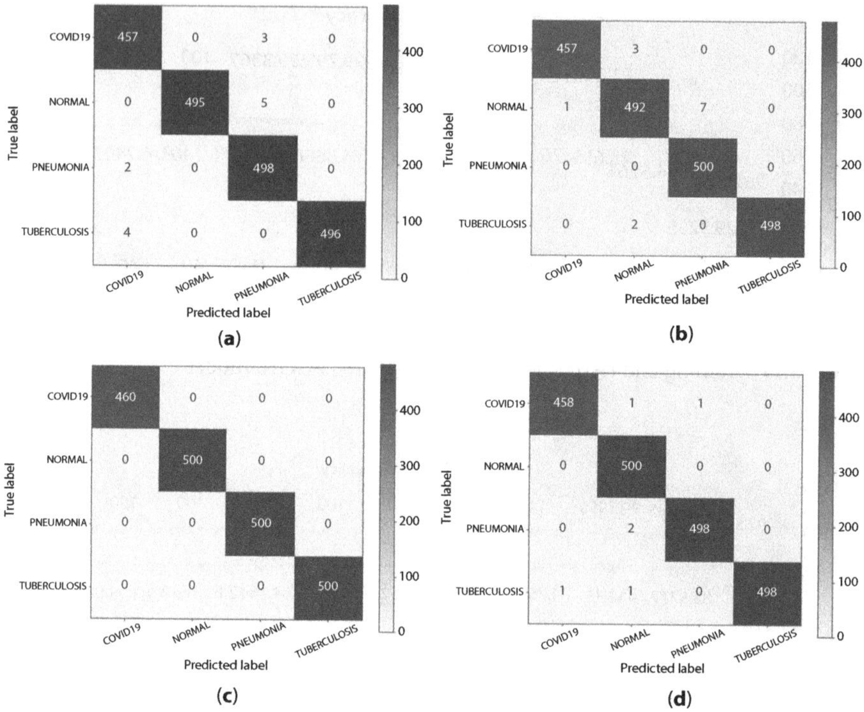

Figure 5.14 (a) The confusion matrix of HMS–CNN. (b) The confusion matrix of HMS–VGG16. (c) The confusion matrix of HMS–ResNet50. (d) The confusion matrix of HMS–EfficientNetB0.

The above Figures 5.14(a–d) represent the confusion matrix of all proposed deep learning models. From all these confusion matrices, every model shown predicts the images into proper classes. There is no such case that a model is partial towards a particular disease class. Every class is predicted precisely. This demonstrates how utilizing a balanced dataset with the same number of images for each class might prevent bias in the results during training.

Hence, through this approach, bias and sensitivity towards a single class is removed. This claim can be proven by the high percentages of precision and recall. In the analysis of results of all proposed four models, the highest accuracy is achieved by the HMS–EfficientNetB0 with a 90% test accuracy followed by HMS–ResNet50 with an 85% test accuracy, HMS–VGG16 with an 80% test accuracy, and HMS–CNN with an 80% test accuracy at the last.

In terms of the computation time, HMS–ResNet50 tops among all four models with 8 minutes and 25 seconds for implementing 50 epochs followed by HMS–EfficientNetB0 with 18 minutes and 22 seconds, HMS–VGG16 with 36 minutes and 44 seconds and HMS–CNN with 1 hour, 33 minutes, and 56 seconds. The HMS–CNN model always comes in lowest for accuracy and training duration, followed by HMS–VGG16.

In the remaining two models, HMS–EfficientNetB0 secured the highest test accuracy of 90% and train accuracy of 100%, which can be considered as the highest test and train accuracies among all existing models for detecting lung diseases, which makes the HMS–EfficientNet model more successful than other models, and its computation time is also comparatively less than many other common models. Hence, the HMS–EfficientNetB0 model can be finalized as a better model in terms of accuracy and efficiency.

EfficientNetB0 is a slightly more complex model and takes a bit more time for computation than the ResNet50 model. The HMS–ResNet50 model can be accepted in the terms of efficiency and fastest classification model. When there is a need for the model that can work faster and produce good accuracy, HMS–ResNet50 can be adapted.

5.6 Conclusion and Future Work

In this study, the HE median filtered SIFT algorithm EfficientNetB0 (HMS–E) approach is demonstrated to be the most effective model out of all currently available models. This approach overcomes the problems of an imbalanced dataset, a bias towards a particular class, overfitting, and a long computation time.

Even though 90% of the test accuracy is sufficient, the number of epochs can be raised and evaluated to further increase the accuracy. The more complex structures like EfficientNet B1–B7 models can be adapted. But the implementation of these models requires cloud environments, which can be expensive and may become difficult to implement.

The proposed methodology alone concentrates on aspects like image quality, contrast, normalization, and noise without much loss in data. A single approach addressing these many aspects, which are also the shortcomings of many existing models, proves that this architecture is the best. All these improvements make this methodology eligible to implement in real life scenarios.

References

1. McGroder, C.F., Zhang, D., Choudhury, M.A., Salvatore, M.M., D'Souza, B.M., Hoffman, E.A., Wei, Y., Baldwin, M.R., Garcia, C.K., Pulmonary

fibrosis 4 months after COVID-19 is associated with severity of illness and blood leucocyte telomere length. *Thorax*, 76, 12, 1242–1245, 2021, https://doi.org/10.1136/thoraxjnl-2021-217031.

2. Yang, L., Liu, S., Liu, J., *et al.*, COVID-19: Immunopathogenesis and Immunotherapeutics. *Sig. Transduct. Target. Ther.*, 5, 128, 2020. https://doi.org/10.1038/s41392-020-00243-2
3. Ota, M., Will we see protection or reinfection in COVID-19? *Nat. Rev. Immunol.*, 20, 351, 2020. https://doi.org/10.1038/s41577-020-0316-3.
4. Diamond, M., Peniston, H.L., Sanghavi, D., Mahapatra, S., Acute Respiratory Distress Syndrome, in: *StatPearls*, StatPearls Publishing, Treasure Island, FL, USA, 2023, http://www.ncbi.nlm.nih.gov/books/NBK436002/.
5. Gereige, R.S. and Laufer, P.M., Pneumonia. *Pediatr. Rev.*, 34, 10, 438–456, 2013.
6. Agarwal, R., Gupta, D., Aggarwal, A.N., Behera, D., Jindal, S.K., Experience with ARDS caused by tuberculosis in a respiratory intensive care unit. *Intensive Care Med.*, 31, 9, 1284–1287, 2005, https://doi.org/10.1007/s00134-005-2721-2.
7. Sudre, P., Ten Dam, G., Kochi, A., Tuberculosis: a global overview of the situation today. *Bull. World Health Organ.*, 70, 2, 149, 1992.
8. Devasia, J., Goswami, H., Lakshminarayanan, S. *et al.*, Deep learning classification of active tuberculosis lung zones wise manifestations using chest X-rays: A multi label approach. *Sci. Rep.*, 13, 887, 2023. https://doi.org/10.1038/s41598-023-28079-0.
9. Tripathi, S., Shetty, S., Jain, S., Sharma, V., Lung disease detection using deep learning. *Int. J. Innov. Technol. Explor. Eng.*, 10, 8, 8, 2021.
10. Tariq, Z., Shah, S.K., Lee, Y., Lung disease classification using deep convolutional neural network, in: *2019 IEEE International Conference on Bioinformatics and Biomedicine (BIBM)*, 2019, November, IEEE, pp. 732–735.
11. Reshi, A.A., Rustam, F., Mehmood, A., Alhossan, A., Alrabiah, Z., Ahmad, A., Choi, G.S., An efficient CNN model for COVID-19 disease detection based on X-ray image classification. *Complexity*, 2021, 1–12, 2021.
12. Kido, S., Hirano, Y., Hashimoto, N., Detection and classification of lung abnormalities by use of convolutional neural network (CNN) and regions with CNN features (R-CNN). *2018 International Workshop on Advanced Image Technology (IWAIT)*, pp. 1–4, 2018, https://doi.org/10.1109/IWAIT.2018.8369798.
13. Hattikatti, P., Texture based interstitial lung disease detection using convolutional neural network. *2017 International Conference on Big Data, IoT and Data Science (BID)*, pp. 18–22, 2017, https://doi.org/10.1109/BID.2017.8336567.
14. Geng, Y., Ren, Y., Hou, R., Han, S., Rubin, G.D., Lo, J.Y., 2.5 D CNN model for detecting lung disease using weak supervision, in: *Medical imaging 2019: computer-aided diagnosis*, vol. 10950, SPIE, pp. 924–928, 2019, March.

15. Xu, M., Qi, S., Yue, Y., Teng, Y., Xu, L., Yao, Y., Qian, W., Segmentation of lung parenchyma in CT images using CNN trained with the clustering algorithm generated dataset. *Biomed. Eng. Online*, 18, 1–21, 2019.
16. Hazra, R. and Majhi, S., Detecting respiratory diseases from recorded lung sounds by 2d cnn, in: *2020 5th International Conference on Computing, Communication and Security (ICCCS)*, IEEE, pp. 1–6, 2020, October.
17. Bharati, S., Podder, P., Mondal, M.R.H., Hybrid deep learning for detecting lung diseases from X-ray images. *Inf. Med. Unlocked*, 20, 100391, 2020, https://doi.org/10.1016/j.imu.2020.100391.
18. Agarwal, V., Lohani, M.C., Bist, A.S., Rahardja, U., Khoirunisa, A., Octavyra, R.D., Analysis of Emerging Preprocessing Techniques Combined with Deep CNN for Lung Disease Detection. *2022 1st International Conference on Technology Innovation and Its Applications (ICTIIA)*, pp. 1–6, 2022, https://doi.org/10.1109/ICTIIA54654.2022.9935876.
19. Hussein, F., Mughaid, A., AlZu'bi, S., El-Salhi, S.M., Abuhaija, B., Abualigah, L., Gandomi, A.H., Hybrid CLAHE-CNN Deep Neural Networks for Classifying Lung Diseases from X-ray Acquisitions. *Electronics*, 11, 19, 2022, Article 19. https://doi.org/10.3390/electronics11193075.
20. Ravi, V., Acharya, V., Alazab, M., A multichannel EfficientNet deep learning-based stacking ensemble approach for lung disease detection using chest X-ray images. *Cluster Comput.*, 26, 2, 1181–1203, 2023, https://doi.org/10.1007/s10586-022-03664-6.
21. Su, Y., Li, D., Chen, X., Lung Nodule Detection based on Faster R-CNN Framework. *Comput. Methods Programs Biomed.*, 200, 105866, 2021, https://doi.org/10.1016/j.cmpb.2020.105866.
22. Goyal, S. and Singh, R., Lung Disease Detection and Classification from Chest X-Ray Images Using Adaptive Segmentation and Deep Learning, in: *Soft Computing and Signal Processing*, V.S. Reddy, V.K. Prasad, J. Wang, K.T.V. Reddy (Eds.), vol. 1413, pp. 49–58, Springer Nature, Singapore, 2022, https://doi.org/10.1007/978-981-16-7088-6_5.
23. Manzoor, A., Pan, Q., Khan, H.J., Siddeeq, S., Bhatti, H.M.A., Wedagu, M.A., Analysis and Detection of Lung Sounds Anomalies Based on NMA-RNN. *2020 IEEE International Conference on Bioinformatics and Biomedicine (BIBM)*, pp. 2498–2504, 2020, https://doi.org/10.1109/BIBM49941.2020.9313197.
24. Geng, L., Zhang, S., Tong, J., Xiao, Z., Lung segmentation method with dilated convolution based on VGG-16 network. *Comput. Assisted Surg.*, 24, sup2, 27–33, 2019, https://doi.org/10.1080/24699322.2019.1649071.
25. Khan, M.A., Rajinikanth, V., Satapathy, S.C., Taniar, D., Mohanty, J.R., Tariq, U., Damaševičius, R., VGG19 Network Assisted Joint Segmentation and Classification of Lung Nodules in CT Images. *Diagnostics*, 11, 12, 2021, Article 12. https://doi.org/10.3390/diagnostics11122208.
26. Arunmozhi, S., Sarojini, V.S.S., Pavithra, T., Varghese, V., Deepti, V., Rajinikanth, V., Automated Detection of COVID-19 Lesion in Lung CT Slices

with VGG-UNet and Handcrafted Features, in: *Digital Future of Healthcare*, CRC Press, pp. 185–200, 2021.

27. Habib, N., Hasan, Md.M., Reza, Md.M., Rahman, M.M., Ensemble of CheXNet and VGG-19 Feature Extractor with Random Forest Classifier for Pediatric Pneumonia Detection. *SN Comput. Sci.*, 1, 6, 359, 2020, https://doi.org/10.1007/s42979-020-00373-y.
28. Nair, K., Deshpande, A., Guntuka, R., Patil, A., Analysing X-Ray Images to Detect Lung Diseases Using DenseNet-169 technique (SSRN Scholarly Paper No. 4111864). 2022, https://doi.org/10.2139/ssrn.4111864.
29. Rochmawanti, O. and Utaminingrum, F., Chest X-Ray Image to Classify Lung diseases in Different Resolution Size using DenseNet-121 Architectures. *Proceedings of the 6th International Conference on Sustainable Information Engineering and Technology*, pp. 327–331, 2021, https://doi.org/10.1145/3479645.3479667.
30. Chhabra, M. and Kumar, R., A Smart Healthcare System Based on Classifier DenseNet 121 Model to Detect Multiple Diseases, in: *Mobile Radio Communications and 5G Networks*, Marriwala, N., Tripathi, C.C., Jain, S., Kumar, D. (Eds.), vol. 339, pp. 297–312, Springer Nature, Singapore, 2022, https://doi.org/10.1007/978-981-16-7018-3_23.
31. Lanjewar, M.G., Panchbhai, K.G., Charanarur, P., Lung cancer detection from CT scans using modified DenseNet with feature selection methods and ML classifiers. *Expert Syst. Appl.*, 224, 119961, 2023, https://doi.org/10.1016/j.eswa.2023.119961.
32. Sharma, C.M., Goyal, L., Chariar, V.M., Sharma, N., Lung Disease Classification in CXR Images Using Hybrid Inception-ResNet-v2 Model and Edge Computing. *J. Healthcare Eng.*, 2022, e9036457, 2022, https://doi.org/10.1155/2022/9036457.
33. Angeline, R. and Vani, R., RETRACTED: ResNet:A convolutional Neural Network for detecting and diagnosing of coronavirus pneumonia. *IOP Conf. Ser.: Mater. Sci. Eng.*, 1084, 1, 012011, 2021, https://doi.org/10.1088/1757-899X/1084/1/012011.
34. Bharati, S., Podder, P., Mondal, M.R.H., Prasath, V.B.S., CO-ResNet: Optimized ResNet model for COVID-19 diagnosis from X-ray images. *Int. J. Hybrid Intell. Syst.*, 17, 1–2, 71–85, 2021, https://doi.org/10.3233/HIS-210008.
35. Pham, L., Phan, H., Schindler, A., King, R., Mertins, A., McLoughlin, I., Inception-Based Network and Multi-Spectrogram Ensemble Applied To Predict Respiratory Anomalies and Lung Diseases. *2021 43rd Annual International Conference of the IEEE Engineering in Medicine & Biology Society (EMBC)*, pp. 253–256, 2021, https://doi.org/10.1109/EMBC46164.2021.9629857.
36. Kermany, D., Zhang, K., Goldbaum, M., Labeled optical coherence tomography (oct) and chest x-ray images for classification. *Mendeley Data*, 2, 2, 651, 2018.

37. Rahman, T., Khandakar, A., Kadir, M.A., Islam, K.R., Islam, K.F., Mazhar, R., Chowdhury, M.E., Reliable tuberculosis detection using chest X-ray with deep learning, segmentation and visualization. *IEEE Access*, 8, 191586–191601, 2020.
38. Cohen, J.P., Morrison, P., Dao, L., Roth, K., Duong, T.Q., Ghassemi, M., Covid-19 image data collection: Prospective predictions are the future. 2020, *arXiv preprint arXiv:2006.11988.*
39. Shahinfar, S., Meek, P., Falzon, G., How many images do I need? Understanding how sample size per class affects deep learning model performance metrics for balanced designs in autonomous wildlife monitoring. *Ecol. Inf.*, 57, 101085, 2020.
40. Abougazia, A., Alnuaimi, A., Mahran, A., Ali, T., Khedr, A., Qadourah, B., Ahmed, S. *et al.*, Chest X-ray findings in COVID-19 patients presenting to primary care during the peak of the first wave of the pandemic in Qatar: their association with clinical and laboratory findings. *Pulm. Med.*, 2021, 1, 4496488, 2021.
41. Kundu, R., Das, R., Geem, Z.W., Han, G.T., Sarkar, R., Pneumonia detection in chest X-ray images using an ensemble of deep learning models. *PLoS One*, 16, 9, e0256630, 2021.
42. Dawood, F.A. and Abood, Z.M., The importance of contrast enhancement in medical images analysis and diagnosis. *Int. J. Eng. Res. Technol. (IJERT)*, 7, 12, 21–24, 2018.
43. Jagatheeswari, P., Kumar, S.S., Rajaram, M., A novel approach for contrast enhancement based on histogram equalization followed by median filter. *ARPN J. Eng. Appl. Sci.*, 4, 7, 42–44, 2009.
44. Abood, Z.M., Edges enhancement of medical color images using add images. *IOSR J. Res. Method Educ.*, 2, 4, 52–60, 2013.
45. Hussein, T.D., Jihad, K.H., Omar, H.K., A Study on Image Noise and Various Image Denoising Techniques. *ResearchJet J. Anal. Invent.*, 2, 11, 27–44, 2021.
46. Nagaraja, G.S., Noise Removal Techniques and Quality analysis of X-ray Images, in: *2019 1st International Conference on Advanced Technologies in Intelligent Control, Environment, Computing & Communication Engineering (ICATIECE)*, IEEE, pp. 327–330, 2019, March.
47. Patanavijit, V., Denoising performance analysis of adaptive decision based inverse distance weighted interpolation (DBIDWI) algorithm for salt and pepper noise. *Indones. J. Electr. Eng. Comput. Sci.*, 15, 2, 804–813, 2019.
48. Kamboj, P. and Rani, V., A brief study of various noise model and filtering techniques. *J. Global Res. Comput. Sci.*, 4, 4, 166–171, 2013.

Part 3

PREDICTIVE ANALYTICS IN HEALTHCARE

6

Comparing the Efficiency of ResNet-50 and Convolutional Neural Networks for Facial Mask Detection

Shaik Khaleel Basha[1,2] and K. Nattar Kannan[1,2*]

[1]*Department of Computer Science and Engineering, Saveetha School of Engineering, Saveetha Institute of Medical and Technical Sciences, Saveetha University, Chennai, India*

[2]*Department of Artificial Intelligence and Machine Learning, Saveetha School of Engineering, Saveetha Institute of Medical and Technical Sciences, Saveetha University, Chennai, India*

Abstract

The main objective of this research is to improve the detection accuracy for face mask identification using two machine learning techniques that compare the ResNet-50 algorithm with the convolution neural network (CNN). The face mask detection task was performed using the ResNet-50 algorithm and CNN with different training and testing data splits. The statistical analysis was conducted using the G*Power test, which had a setting of 85% power (with parameters $\alpha=0.05$ and power=0.85). The ResNet-50 algorithm achieved a higher accuracy rate of 99.45% compared to CNN's accuracy rate of 96.89%. However, the difference in accuracy was statistically insignificant with a p-value greater than 0.05 and a non-significant value of 0.334. The ResNet-50 algorithm shows a higher level of accuracy compared to CNN.

Keywords: CNN, facemask, neural networks, noval ResNet-50 algorithm, machine learning, vaccines

**Corresponding author*: nattarkannank.sse@saveetha.com

Kanak Kalita, Divya Zindani, Narayanan Ganesh and Xiao-Zhi Gao (eds.) Medical Analytics for Clinical and Healthcare Applications, (127–144) © 2025 Scrivener Publishing LLC

6.1 Introduction

The COVID-19 pandemic has made facial mask detection systems a vital tool in ensuring public health and safety, particularly in high-traffic environments such as airports, hospitals, and public transportation hubs. This chapter discusses a sophisticated approach using the "You Only Look Oncev4" (YOLOv4) method to identify facial masks on specific targets. The YOLOv4 method is well-regarded for its speed and efficiency in object detection, making it an ideal choice for real-time mask detection applications. Despite its quick response time, accurately detecting facial masks for daily public use requires high system performance in real-time scenarios [1]. The YOLOv4 method meets this requirement, offering a robust solution for model-based systems in mask detection tasks. This research demonstrates that the YOLOv4-based facial mask recognition system can accurately identify masks in various real-world scenarios, including routine mask usage, instances of multiple people, and partial facial occlusion [2].

The objective of this research is to establish a comprehensive facial dataset, annotated with three specific types of labels: correct mask usage, absence of a mask, and improper mask usage. This annotated dataset will be used to train and fine-tune various convolutional neural network (CNN) architectures, enabling quick and accurate identification of masked, unmasked, or improperly masked faces in real time. Modifications in image size and the complete intersection over union (CIOU) loss function will also be implemented to prevent the spread of epidemics, such as COVID-19. These preventive steps are critical as they enable the model to generalize well in different environments and ensure faster detection. Our algorithm, which is 70% faster and just as accurate as the YOLOv5m variant, presents a significant improvement in terms of both speed and accuracy [3].

This study develops a facial mask detection software model specifically designed for airport surveillance systems using TensorFlow, an end-to-end open-source machine learning platform, in conjunction with Keras, a high-level deep learning application programming interface. To achieve effective binary classification for identifying whether a mask is worn, we trained deep CNNs on a dataset comprising 12,000 face images, equally split between masked and unmasked subjects. Additionally, this system can provide support for vaccination tracking, making it a multipurpose tool for health surveillance in public spaces [4]. The main application of this model lies in detecting real-time mask-wearing status in public areas, helping to mitigate the spread of infectious diseases like COVID-19 by ensuring mask compliance.

In recent years, numerous studies have focused on facial mask detection, with over 120 research papers available on this topic in the IEEE Xplore database alone. Deep learning techniques have proven useful in creating safe, efficient, and cost-effective solutions for monitoring compliance in production environments, public areas, and healthcare settings. In our project, we utilize a live camera feed to differentiate between individuals wearing masks and those who are not, with the aim of limiting the spread of the virus. If a person is identified as not wearing a mask, an audio alert will prompt them to put one on. The dataset used for training consists of images of both masked and unmasked individuals, providing a balanced and comprehensive foundation for developing a robust deep learning model [5, 6].

The methodology for anomaly identification in this research uses a defect-size-independent approach through two stages of image segmentation. The first stage applies a mask filter that blurs the image and spreads the incorrect pixel values by increasing the size of the blurring kernel. In the second stage, a Pearson correlation coefficient is computed between the normal mask-filtered image and the input mask-filtered image. The kernel size directly affects the correlation coefficient, with larger kernel sizes reducing the correlation. For defective images, the correlation coefficient drops below a predefined threshold, indicating the presence of anomalies [7]. This technique proves effective in identifying defects in images of different resolutions, ensuring accurate mask detection regardless of image quality.

A key goal of this project is to develop a binary face classifier capable of detecting any face in a video frame, irrespective of alignment, lighting, or facial expression. The approach involves constructing reliable face segmentation masks from input images of varying sizes. Features are extracted from each RGB image using a VGG-16 architecture with predefined training weights. Fully convolutional networks (FCNs) are employed to segment the faces meaningfully within the image, and gradient descent optimization is used to train the network while minimizing loss using the binomial cross entropy loss function. The output image from the FCN is further processed to eliminate noise and avoid incorrect detections, allowing for precise face localization and bounding box construction around detected faces [7]. This level of precision is critical for implementing mask detection in real-world applications, especially in crowded environments where multiple faces need to be detected simultaneously.

Moreover, this study explores the impact of facial masks on expression recognition, a challenging task when part of the face is obscured. We employ cutting-edge deep learning techniques to assess how the presence of masks affects the identification of facial expressions. Three distinct deep neural networks are evaluated for their ability to classify six emotional categories—happiness, sadness, anger, fear, surprise, and disgust—using masked facial images. We compare the performance of these models to that of unmasked images from past studies, using the FER2013 dataset. Dlib and OpenCV libraries are utilized to add synthetic masks to the faces in the dataset, allowing us to simulate masked facial expressions [8]. The findings of this study contribute to the growing body of research on facial recognition technology in the context of the pandemic, where mask usage has become ubiquitous.

One of the major limitations of the current facial mask detection systems is their relatively low accuracy in certain conditions, such as poor lighting or partial occlusion. This research aims to address this gap by incorporating the ResNet-50 algorithm, known for its powerful feature extraction capabilities, into the facial mask detection model. By comparing the performance of ResNet-50 with that of artificial neural networks (ANN), we aim to demonstrate improvements in classification accuracy. The results show that the accuracy of our developed model in identifying masked individuals reaches an impressive 98.2% based on a comprehensive dataset containing 45,000 images. This marks a significant improvement over previous models, making it a highly reliable tool for ensuring public safety [9].

The broader implications of this research extend beyond mask detection to other health and safety applications. In addition to detecting face masks, the proposed model can also be used for vaccine verification and other forms of health-related surveillance. The incorporation of real-time processing capabilities makes it suitable for deployment in busy public spaces where quick decision-making is crucial. The live-feed camera system used in this project allows for the continuous monitoring of mask compliance, further enhancing its utility in limiting the spread of infectious diseases. Early research on face detection, which began in 2001, primarily relied on handcrafted features and traditional machine learning algorithms. The transition to deep learning techniques has significantly improved the accuracy and speed of face detection systems, allowing for the development of advanced models such as the one proposed in this chapter [10].

By leveraging state-of-the-art machine learning algorithms, this project aims to enhance the accuracy and efficiency of facial mask detection while providing support for additional health measures, such as vaccination tracking. The use of large-scale datasets and advanced neural network architectures, such as YOLOv4 and ResNet-50, ensures that the system can perform reliably in a variety of environments and under different conditions. As public health continues to be a global priority, the development of robust, real-time mask detection systems will play a key role in preventing the spread of future epidemics.

6.2 Materials and Methods

The investigation was conducted at the Machine Learning Laboratory of the Saveetha School of Engineering, Saveetha Institute of Medical and Technical Sciences, located in Chennai. The lab environment was equipped with state-of-the-art computational tools essential for machine learning and deep learning research. The purpose of this research was to compare the performance of two different deep learning algorithms—ResNet-50 and CNNs—in detecting facial masks. The study was carried out in two phases: data preprocessing and model training, followed by testing and evaluation.

To ensure statistical validity, the sample size was determined using G*Power software, a widely recognized tool for computing statistical power and sample size in research. For this comparison, two groups were established: one for ResNet-50 and the other for CNN. Each group was carefully selected to evaluate the performance of the algorithms in terms of accuracy, speed, and generalization capability. A total of 10 sets of samples were taken from each group, resulting in 20 samples overall for analysis. G*Power 3.1 was used to establish the sample size with parameters set at $\alpha = 0.05$ (significance level) and power = 0.85 (desired statistical power). These parameters ensured that the analysis would have a high probability of detecting meaningful differences between the two algorithms [9].

The technical aspects of the data analysis process were pivotal in achieving the desired outcome. While analyzing the dataset, an issue arose: one of the numeric columns contained 210 missing values. Handling missing data is a common problem in machine learning tasks, and in this case, the issue was treated as a regression problem. A variety of approaches were employed to handle the missing data, with the results yielding interesting observations. Upon further investigation, it was found that although a similar approach had been previously used in a highly rated notebook, the method lacked performance assessment. This limitation raised concerns about the robustness of the approach. An analysis of the R-squared value revealed that the pipeline-based data imputation method performed poorly, with an R-squared value below 0.3, indicating that the model was not well-fitted to the data. As a result, alternative algorithms better suited for this regression task were explored.

In response to this challenge, the PyCaret machine learning library was employed to automate the model selection process, optimizing it further using the Optuna framework. This approach not only improved model performance but also streamlined the workflow for handling missing data. PyCaret's automated machine learning (AutoML) capabilities were instrumental in selecting the most appropriate models and tuning their hyperparameters effectively. Optuna, an open-source optimization framework, provided an efficient way to fine-tune the model, significantly improving its performance metrics.

For the implementation of the algorithms, Python, coupled with the OpenCV library, was chosen as the primary programming environment due to its extensive support for computer vision tasks. The development and testing were conducted on a system running the Windows 10 operating system, using an Intel Core i7 processor with 4GB of RAM. The system was configured for 64-bit processing, ensuring that the deep learning models could be trained and evaluated efficiently. The code for both ResNet-50 and CNN models was written in Java, which was integrated with Python for ease of implementation in data handling, pre-processing, and model evaluation. This combination of technologies allowed for seamless code execution and dataset processing, ensuring a high level of accuracy in detecting facial masks.

6.3 ResNet-50 Architecture

The ResNet-50 architecture was a critical component of this study. ResNet-50 is a deep residual neural network that consists of 50 convolutional layers, designed to address the vanishing gradient problem often encountered in deep networks. Residual networks introduced the concept of shortcut connections, which allow for the skipping of layers, effectively enabling the use of deeper networks without compromising performance. This architecture was pre-trained on the ImageNet dataset, which contains over one million images across a thousand categories, including objects like computers, animals, and everyday items. The extensive pre-training allowed the model to learn deep feature representations from a diverse set of images, making it highly effective for transfer learning in our mask detection task.

The maximum input size for ResNet-50 is 224x224 pixels, which is standard for many image classification tasks. ResNet-50's design introduces a novel approach to improving traditional CNNs by incorporating shortcut connections, allowing the network to skip certain layers and thereby bypass the vanishing gradient problem. The key advantage of ResNet-50 is that it enables deeper networks to be trained more efficiently while retaining high accuracy. The following steps were employed in the ResNet-50 implementation:

1: Initialize count = 1
2: For i = 1 to 125 do
3: For j = 1 to 45 do
4: Im(i, j) = S(count)
5: Increment count by 1
6: End for j
7: End for i
8: Normalize Im using min-max normalization.

This procedure was executed to preprocess the image data before feeding it into the ResNet-50 model for classification. The use of min-max normalization ensured that the input image pixel values were scaled appropriately, improving the network's ability to generalize across different lighting conditions and image qualities.

6.4 Convolutional Neural Networks (CNN)

CNNs, or convolutional neural networks, are a fundamental architecture in deep learning, particularly for image-related tasks such as object recognition, facial detection, and image classification. Convolutional neural networks are designed to automatically and adaptively learn spatial hierarchies of features through backpropagation by using multiple building blocks, such as convolution layers, pooling layers, and fully connected layers. In this study, CNNs were employed to classify images of individuals with and without masks.

The CNN architecture used in this study consisted of multiple convolutional layers interspersed with max-pooling layers. The convolutional layers acted as feature extractors, identifying edges, textures, and patterns in the images, while the pooling layers helped reduce the spatial dimensions of the feature maps, making the model more computationally efficient. The activation function employed in this architecture was the rectified linear unit (ReLU), which introduced non-linearity to the model and enabled it to learn complex patterns in the data.

```
For l = 0 to kL do
For m = 0 to M do
For n = 0 to N do
Initialize sum = bias
For k = 0 to K do
For s1 = 0 to S1 do
For s2 = 0 to S2 do
sum += weight[k][l][s1][s2] * input[k][m + s1][n + s2]
End for s2
Output[l][m][n] = activation_func(sum)
End for s1
End for k
End for n
End for m
```

This algorithm was used to process the input images, extract meaningful features, and ultimately classify the images based on the presence or absence of facial masks. The CNN model underwent several iterations of training, with the weights being updated at each step based on the error calculated through the backpropagation algorithm. The final output layer consisted of a softmax function, which provided the probability scores for each class (masked or unmasked).

6.5 Statistical Analysis

To evaluate the effectiveness and accuracy of the ResNet-50 and CNN algorithms in facial mask detection, statistical analysis was performed using the IBM SPSS software. A widely used software for data management and statistical analysis, SPSS, offers robust tools to handle both descriptive and inferential statistical techniques, making it ideal for comparing the performance of deep learning algorithms in this study.

In this research, the independent variables include a range of parameters such as image type, objects present, distance between the camera and the subject, frequency of detection, modulation techniques, and additional variables like vaccines, amplitude, volume, and decibel levels [10]. These variables were selected based on their potential influence on the performance of the facial mask detection system. They represent the various conditions and environmental factors under which the system operates. For example, distance and frequency might affect the clarity and resolution of the images captured, while modulation and decibels could relate to any audio feedback incorporated into the system.

The dependent variables in this study are the classification results, specifically the detected images and objects, which include whether a mask was correctly detected or missed. These dependent variables represent the outcomes of the algorithms' performance in identifying masks in real-world scenarios.

An independent t-test analysis was conducted to compare the accuracy of the two deep learning models—ResNet-50 and CNN. This statistical method is commonly used to determine whether there is a significant difference between the means of two independent groups. In this case, the independent t-test was applied to assess whether ResNet-50 performed significantly better than CNN in terms of classification accuracy. The null hypothesis tested in the t-test was that there is no significant difference between the accuracy rates of the two algorithms. By comparing the means and p-values generated through this analysis, the statistical significance of the results was determined, providing insight into the effectiveness of the two methods under investigation.

6.6 Results and Discussion

The primary goal of this study was to evaluate and compare the performance of two deep learning algorithms—ResNet-50 and CNNs—in facial mask detection, a task crucial for public health monitoring in the context of COVID-19 and other airborne diseases. Both models were implemented using the Anaconda Navigator, and the evaluation was based on the accuracy of detecting whether individuals were wearing masks. The experiment was conducted with a sample size of 10 iterations for each algorithm. This section presents the detailed results of the experiment and provides an in-depth discussion of their implications.

The results obtained from the experimentation are summarized in Tables 6.1 and 6.2, which present the accuracy achieved by both ResNet-50 and CNN over 10 iterations, and the group statistical analysis, respectively. These results are followed by the independent sample t-test (Table 6.3), used to assess the statistical significance of the differences between the two algorithms.

Table 6.1 shows the detection accuracy for both algorithms over 10 iterations. From this table, it can be observed that the accuracy of ResNet-50 varied between 90.42% and 99.45%, while CNN's accuracy ranged from 92.70% to 98.68%. The highest detection accuracy for ResNet-50 was

Table 6.1 Accuracy analysis of ResNet-50 and CNN.

Iterations	ResNet-50	CNN
1	99.45	96.89
2	98.71	94.79
3	98.14	92.70
4	94.19	93.41
5	91.26	94.04
6	99.10	93.40
7	90.42	96.92
8	95.60	94.35
9	98.03	96.57
10	99.12	98.68

99.45% in iteration 1, whereas CNN achieved its highest accuracy of 98.68% in iteration 10.

These 10 data samples were utilized to calculate the statistical values that allow for a detailed comparison of the two algorithms. The mean accuracy for ResNet-50 was found to be 96.4020%, while for CNN, it was 95.1750%. While the difference between the mean accuracies may seem relatively small, the statistical analysis reveals more nuanced insights into the performance of the two models.

Table 6.2 presents the group statistical analysis for both algorithms, including the mean, standard deviation, and standard error for the 10 samples. The standard deviation for ResNet-50 was higher than that of CNN at 3.37829 compared to 1.96429. This indicates that ResNet-50's performance was slightly more variable across iterations, but it maintained a higher

Table 6.2 Group statistical analysis of ResNet-50 and CNN.

	Group	N	Mean	Std. deviation	Std. error mean
Accuracy	ResNet-50	10	96.4020	3.37829	1.06831
	CNN	10	95.1750	1.96429	.62116

Table 6.3 Independent sample t-test.

		Levene's test of equality of variances		T-test for equality of means					95% confidence interval of the difference	
		F	Sig	t	df	Sig (2-tailed)	Mean difference	Std error difference	Lower	Upper
Accuracy	Equal variance assumed	4.070	0.59	.993	18	0.334	1.22700	1.23577	-1.36926	3.82326
	Equal variance not assumed			.993	14.461	0.337	1.22700	1.23577	-1.41555	3.86955

average accuracy overall. The standard error mean for ResNet-50 was also larger than that of CNN, implying that the observed differences in performance may not be as statistically robust as initially anticipated.

Despite ResNet-50 exhibiting higher mean accuracy, an independent sample t-test (Table 6.3) was performed to determine if the observed difference between the two algorithms was statistically significant. The p-value obtained was 0.334 ($p < 0.05$), indicating that the difference in accuracy between ResNet-50 and CNN was not statistically significant. Although ResNet-50 showed better performance in terms of mean accuracy, the p-value suggests that the difference could be due to random variation in the dataset or other external factors, rather than a true performance advantage of the algorithm.

Figure 6.1 provides a visual comparison of the mean accuracy for ResNet-50 and CNN. As shown in the figure, the mean accuracy of ResNet-50 is higher than that of CNN, but the difference falls within the range of one standard deviation, as indicated by the error bars.

The results obtained from the experiments indicate that both ResNet-50 and CNN are effective algorithms for the task of facial mask detection, with accuracy rates consistently above 90%. However, there are several key observations and implications worth discussing, particularly in relation to the specific strengths and limitations of each algorithm.

ResNet-50 demonstrated higher mean accuracy compared to CNN, with its best performance reaching 99.45% in the first iteration. One of

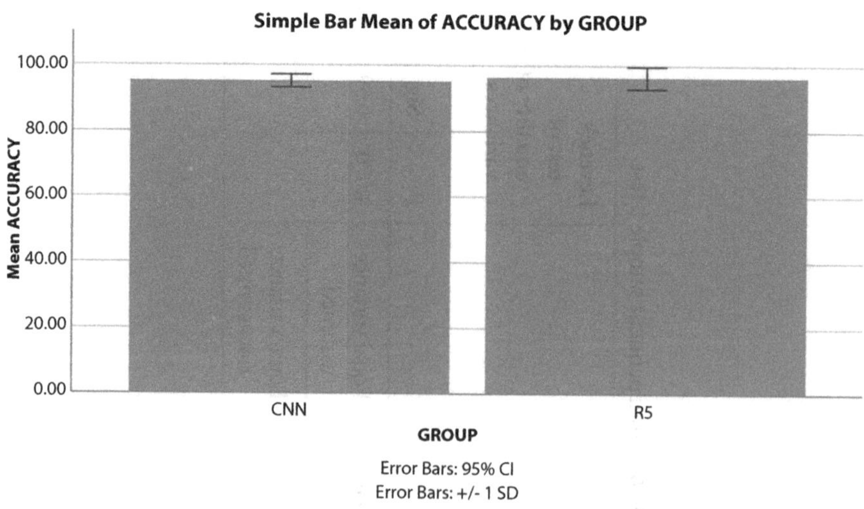

Figure 6.1 A comparison of ResNet-50 and CNN.

the primary strengths of ResNet-50 is its deep architecture, consisting of 50 layers, which allows it to capture more complex features from the input images. This deep network is designed to address the vanishing gradient problem, a common issue in traditional deep networks, by introducing residual connections that "skip" certain layers. These connections enable the network to train more efficiently, even with increasing depth, without sacrificing performance.

Another advantage of ResNet-50 is its pre-training on the ImageNet dataset, which contains over a million images across diverse categories. This pre-training allowed the model to leverage transfer learning, meaning it could apply knowledge from other domains (e.g., object recognition) to the mask detection task. As a result, ResNet-50 was able to generalize well across different samples in the dataset, as indicated by its high mean accuracy.

However, one limitation observed in the study is the variability in ResNet-50's performance across iterations, as reflected by its higher standard deviation (3.37829). While the model's average accuracy was superior, the larger standard deviation suggests that its performance was less consistent than that of CNN. This variability could be attributed to the model's sensitivity to specific features in the dataset, such as variations in lighting, angle, or occlusion, which may affect its ability to consistently identify masks in different images.

Furthermore, while ResNet-50 performed well in this study, it is a computationally intensive model, requiring significant processing power and memory due to its deep architecture. The hardware used in this experiment (Intel Core i7 with 4GB RAM) may have been a limiting factor in fully realizing the potential of ResNet-50, as more powerful systems could potentially yield even higher accuracy and stability.

Convolutional neural networks (CNNs) have been a staple of image classification tasks for many years, and their performance in this study underscores their reliability. They achieved an average accuracy of 95.1750%, which, while slightly lower than ResNet-50, still represents strong performance for facial mask detection. Convolutional neural networks are well-suited for tasks involving pixel-based input, such as image recognition, due to their ability to learn spatial hierarchies of features through convolutional layers.

One of the key strengths of CNN is its relative simplicity compared to ResNet-50. Convolutional neural networks typically have fewer layers, making them less computationally expensive and easier to train, even on systems with limited hardware capabilities. This simplicity also translates to greater consistency in performance, as indicated by CNN's lower standard deviation (1.96429) compared to ResNet-50. The more stable performance of CNN across iterations suggests that it is less sensitive to variations in the dataset, making it a more predictable choice for mask detection tasks.

However, the primary limitation of CNN lies in its shallower architecture, which may prevent it from capturing as many complex features as ResNet-50. This limitation is reflected in the slightly lower mean accuracy, as the model may struggle to identify more nuanced aspects of the images, such as masks partially obscured by other objects or worn incorrectly. While CNN offers a good balance of accuracy and computational efficiency, it may not perform as well as deeper networks like ResNet-50 in more complex scenarios.

The independent t-test analysis (Table 6.3) revealed that the difference in accuracy between ResNet-50 and CNN was not statistically significant, with a p-value of 0.334 ($p < 0.05$). This suggests that while ResNet-50 demonstrated slightly better performance in terms of mean accuracy, the difference is not large enough to conclude that it is definitively superior to CNN. The p-value indicates that the observed differences could be due to random variation in the dataset rather than inherent advantages of ResNet-50.

This finding has important implications for the choice of algorithms in practical applications. Given that the difference in performance between the two models is not statistically significant, practitioners may opt for CNN in situations where computational resources are limited, as it offers comparable accuracy with lower hardware requirements. On the other hand, for applications where the highest possible accuracy is required, and computational resources are available, ResNet-50 may still be the better choice due to its ability to capture more complex features.

In the present study, the statistical analysis revealed a non-significant value of 0.334 ($p > 0.05$), which implies that although the ResNet-50 algorithm appears to perform better than CNN, the difference is not statistically significant [11]. Specifically, the accuracy of ResNet-50 was recorded at 96.4020%, while CNN achieved an accuracy of 95.1750%. This minor difference in performance, while favoring ResNet-50, does not suggest a substantial superiority of one model over the other, considering the overlapping confidence intervals.

This finding aligns with the broader context of using facial recognition technology in real-world applications where factors such as the presence of masks can considerably impact performance. During the ongoing COVID-19 pandemic and other epidemic situations, controlling and preventing the spread of the virus has relied heavily on technologies like facial recognition for monitoring compliance with mask mandates. However, conventional face recognition systems are predominantly trained on datasets containing unmasked faces, leading to reduced efficacy when individuals wear masks [12]. This creates an additional burden, as individuals may need to remove their masks to interact with the system, which complicates the implementation of preventive measures such as vaccines and other health protocols [13].

The challenge for facial recognition systems in these scenarios lies in maintaining high recognition accuracy even when individuals are wearing masks. To address this, our study focused on a facial mask detection to automatically identify whether an individual is masked or unmasked. This approach aims to complement existing face recognition systems by enabling them to accurately detect mask usage without requiring individuals to remove their masks. Our detection method follows a three-phase approach: facial detection, mask addition, and facial detection with the mask. By incorporating multi-task cascaded convolutional networks (MTCNN) and FaceNet, this method effectively performs mask detection and can be integrated with standard facial recognition workflows. Despite this innovative approach, the overall accuracy of our system was found to be 76.42%, which, while promising, leaves room for improvement [14].

This system was successfully tested on both real-world and synthetic datasets, indicating its broad applicability across different scenarios. For instance, in public spaces where mask compliance is mandatory, such a system can help ensure that individuals wear masks without disrupting other facial recognition tasks such as security checks or identity verification [15]. The success of this method in detecting masks, even in challenging scenarios such as occlusion and partial mask coverage, suggests that it could be a valuable tool in the broader context of public health monitoring and epidemic control.

However, despite the promising results, there are notable limitations to the current study. One of the major drawbacks is the time required to train the ResNet-50 model, especially when working with large datasets. The deep architecture of ResNet-50, while powerful, comes with significant computational costs, leading to extended training times. This issue becomes particularly pronounced when scaling the model for real-time applications or when using extensive datasets [16]. Although the model achieved higher accuracy than CNN, its training complexity may limit its deployment in time-sensitive environments where rapid decision-making is crucial, such as airport security or hospital monitoring systems.

Looking ahead, the future scope of this study involves expanding the system's capabilities to include a wider variety of objects, reducing the training time, and improving its overall accuracy. One possible avenue for improvement is the use of transfer learning techniques, where the model can be pre-trained on large, diverse datasets and then fine-tuned for mask detection, thus reducing the time and resources required for training. Another direction is to incorporate more efficient algorithms like MobileNetV2, which may offer a better trade-off between accuracy and computational cost, especially in resource-constrained environments. Additionally, increasing the diversity of the dataset, including different types of masks, lighting conditions, and face orientations, could help the model generalize better and improve its real-world applicability.

The ResNet-50 algorithm demonstrates a slightly better performance in facial mask detection than CNN but the difference in accuracy is not statistically significant, and the model's computational complexity poses challenges for real-world deployment. Nevertheless, the study provides valuable insights into the development of more effective face recognition systems in the era of mask-wearing, contributing to both the control of epidemics and the improvement of public safety measures. Future research can focus on refining the model's efficiency, expanding its capabilities, and further integrating it with advanced face recognition technologies.

6.7 Conclusion

This study compared the performance of the ResNet-50 algorithm and CNN for facial mask detection in real-world scenarios, with the following key outcomes:

- ResNet-50 outperformed CNN, achieving an accuracy of 96.40% compared to CNN's 95.18%, demonstrating its higher effectiveness in mask detection tasks.
- Although ResNet-50 exhibited better accuracy, the independent t-test yielded a non-significant p-value of 0.334 ($p > 0.05$), indicating that the difference in performance is not statistically significant.
- A key limitation was the extended training time required by ResNet-50, highlighting a need for optimization when dealing with large datasets.
- The findings suggest that ResNet-50 can enhance existing facial recognition systems, particularly in pandemic control measures, though improvements in efficiency are necessary for real-time applications.

Expanding the system's scope to handle diverse object detection and employing more efficient models are critical for improving scalability and deployment. A study involved comparing the ResNet-50 algorithm and CNN, and their respective accuracy values were measured. The ResNet-50 algorithm achieved an accuracy value of 96.4020%, while the CNN's accuracy value was 95.1750%. After analyzing the results, it was determined that the ResNet-50 algorithm performed better than the CNN, with a higher accuracy rate of 96.4020%.

References

1. Sivabalaselvamani, D. and Soorya, B., Convolution neural network based specialized restaurant rating using facial expression detection, in: *2020 International Conference on Inventive Computation Technologies (ICICT)*, Coimbatore, 2020.
2. Xiao, C. and Chang, L., Facial mask detection system based on YOLOv4 algorithm, in: *2022 IEEE International Conference on Artificial Intelligence and Computer Applications (ICAICA)*, Dalian, 2022.
3. Liu, C.-C., Fuh, S.-C., Lin, C.-J., Huang, T.-H., A novel facial mask detection using fast-YOLO algorithm, in: *2022 8th International Conference on Applied System Innovation (ICASI)*, Nantou, 2022.
4. Zhang, E., A real-time deep transfer learning model for facial mask detection, in: *2021 Integrated Communications Navigation and Surveillance Conference (ICNS)*, Dulles, 2021.
5. Ganesh, N., Shankar, R., Mahdal, M., Murugan, J.S., Chohan, J.S., Kalita, K., Exploring deep learning methods for computer vision applications across multiple sectors: Challenges and future trends. *Comput. Model. Eng. Sci.*, 139, 103–141, 2024.
6. Nanmaran, R., Srimathi, S., Yamuna, G., Thanigaivel, S., Vickram, A.S., Priya, A.K., Karthick, A., Karpagam, J., Mohanavel, V., Muhibbullah, M., Investigating the role of image fusion in brain tumor classification models based on machine learning algorithm for personalized medicine. *Comput. Math. Methods Med.*, 2022, 7137524, February 2022.
7. Lee, H. and Lee, H., Average blurring-based anomaly detection for vision-based mask inspection systems, in: *2021 21st International Conference on Control, Automation and Systems (ICCAS)*, Jeju, Korea, Republic of, 2021.
8. Wang, Y., Wang, Y., Zhong, C., Zhao, Y., Assessing deep learning approaches in detecting masked facial expressions, in: *2022 IEEE 46th Annual Computers, Software, and Applications Conference (COMPSAC)*, Los Alamitos, CA, USA, 2022.
9. Bose, P. and Bandyopadhyay, S.K., Facial spots detection using Convolution Neural Network. *Asian J. Res. Comput. Sci.*, 5, 3, 71–83, May 2020.

10. Betts, E., *Computers and family psychology: 'toolbook 15' and SPSS statistical and data analysis software*, American Psychological Association (APA), 1992. doi:https://doi.org/10.1037/e410072005-023.
11. Naidu, D., Detection of steganography using convolution neural network machine learning method over wireless network. *Biosci. Biotechnol. Res. Commun.*, 13, 260–263, December 2020.
12. Wang, H. and Lursinsap, C., Detecting facial images in public with and without masks using VGG and FR-TSVM models, in: *2021 18th International Joint Conference on Computer Science and Software Engineering (JCSSE)*, Lampang, 2021.
13. Wang, H., Wei, G., Xu, H., Zhang, C., Occluded-based Facial Recognition under mask using Deep learning method, in: *2022 3rd International Conference on Computer Vision, Image and Deep Learning & International Conference on Computer Engineering and Applications (CVIDL & ICCEA)*, Changchun, 2022.
14. Vadlapati, J., Senthil Velan, S., Varghese, E., Facial recognition using the OpenCV libraries of python for the pictures of human faces wearing face masks during the COVID-19 pandemic, in: *2021 12th International Conference on Computing Communication and Networking Technologies (ICCCNT)*, Kharagpur, 2021.
15. Agrawal, K., Amaan Siddiqui, M., Khan, H., Kumar, G., Outdoor mask - wearing surveillance system using facial recognition, in: *2021 3rd International Conference on Advances in Computing, Communication Control and Networking (ICAC3N)*, Greater, 2021.
16. Iqbal, M.S., Ali, H., Tran, S.N., Iqbal, T., Coconut trees detection and segmentation in aerial imagery using mask region-based convolution neural network. *IET Comput. Vis.*, 15, 428–439, September 2021.

7

Enhancing Accuracy in Predicting Knee Osteoarthritis Progression Using Kellgren–Lawrence Grade Compared with Deep Convolutional Neural Network

Sai Srinivasa[1] and Malarkodi K.[2]*

[1]*Department of Information Technology, Saveetha School of Engineering, Saveetha Institute of Medical and Technical Sciences, Saveetha University, Chennai, India*
[2]*Department of Electronics and Communication Engineering, Saveetha School of Engineering, Saveetha Institute of Medical and Technical Sciences, Saveetha University, Chennai, India*

Abstract
The purpose of this work is to improve the accuracy of predicting knee osteoarthritis progression using the Kellgren–Lawrence Grade compared with deep convolutional neural network (DCNN). There are two groups used in this research, namely, Kellgren–Lawrence Grade (N=10) and DCNN (N=10) are applied to the dataset, which includes a total of 20000 images composed of 324 images wherein 162 show grade 1,2 and 162 images show grade 3,4 knee osteoarthritis in the dataset that are taken for predicting knee osteoarthritis progression for estimating the likelihood of future joint space narrowing in the knees individually and collectively. Each group has a sample size of 10 with ClinCalc keeping G*Power value = 0.8 and $\alpha = 0.05$. After comparing the two modes' accuracy, it was found that the Kellgren–Lawrence grade algorithm (92.7850%) indicates that there is a statistically significant difference between the two algorithms with p-value of 0.0367 (independent sample t-test $p<0.05$). The accuracy of the Kellgren–Lawrence grade is better when compared to the accuracy of DCNN in predicting knee osteoarthritis progression in health monitoring.

Keywords: Novel logistic regression, deep convolutional neural network, health, prediction, pain, osteoarthritis

**Corresponding author*: malarkodik.sse @saveetha.com

Kanak Kalita, Divya Zindani, Narayanan Ganesh and Xiao-Zhi Gao (eds.) Medical Analytics for Clinical and Healthcare Applications, (145–160) © 2025 Scrivener Publishing LLC

7.1 Introduction

Knee osteoarthritis (KOA) is a degenerative joint disease that predominantly affects the elderly population, leading to significant pain, reduced mobility, and decreased quality of life. Osteoarthritis is the most common form of arthritis, and the knee is one of the most frequently affected joints. The progression of KOA involves the degradation of joint cartilage and changes in the underlying bone structure, resulting in joint space narrowing (JSN), bone spur formation, and loss of joint function. The disease's chronic nature makes it a major public health concern, especially as the global population ages. Early detection and prediction of KOA progression are critical to managing the disease and improving patient outcomes [1, 2].

This work focuses on using advanced imaging techniques, such as knee magnetic resonance (MR) imaging, combined with machine learning (ML) algorithms to predict KOA progression by extracting hidden biological information from these images. Traditional diagnostic approaches for KOA often rely on clinical examination, radiographic images, and patient-reported symptoms [3, 4]. However, these methods may lack the sensitivity to detect early-stage osteoarthritis, and they are not always effective in predicting the disease's progression. By leveraging modern data-driven approaches, we aim to address these limitations and enhance the predictive accuracy of KOA diagnosis and progression [5, 6].

One of the key aspects of this study is the use of principal component analysis (PCA), a statistical method that reduces the dimensionality of large datasets while retaining the most important information [7, 8]. The PCA was employed to analyze 36 critical locations on the tibiofemoral cartilage compartment from 3D MR images. These locations were selected based on their relevance to KOA, and the analysis was performed to compute the cartilage damage index (CDI), a quantitative measure of cartilage degeneration. The CDI serves as an important biomarker for assessing the severity of KOA and predicting its progression over time. Through PCA, the complexity of the 3D MR imaging data is reduced, making it more manageable for subsequent analysis with ML algorithms [9–12].

In this study, we utilized four ML models—artificial neural networks (ANN), support vector machines (SVM), random forest (RF), and Naïve Bayes (NB)—to predict KOA progression. These models were trained on features derived from the MR images, specifically focusing on changes in the Kellgren- Lawrence (KL) grade, a widely used system for classifying the severity of KOA. In addition to the KL grade, we also examined JSN in both the medial and lateral compartments of the knee. The JSN is a hallmark of KOA progression, and its measurement provides critical insights into the disease's impact on joint structure. By incorporating both KL grade and JSN measurements, we aimed to develop a robust predictive model for KOA progression.

Furthermore, this study was built upon previous research efforts in the field by integrating gait analysis data with radiographic imaging features to improve the accuracy of KOA classification. Gait analysis, which examines an individual's walking patterns, is an important tool for understanding the functional impact of KOA. Altered gait patterns are often observed in individuals with KOA, as they adjust their movement to compensate for pain and joint stiffness. These changes in movement can provide valuable information for predicting the progression of the disease. In this work, we employed an SVM to classify KOA severity using gait features that were strongly correlated with radiographic indicators of KOA from a previous study. The radiographic image features were extracted using Inception-ResNet-v2, a state-of-the-art deep learning (DL) network designed for image classification tasks. By combining these two data sources—gait analysis and radiographic images—we aimed to create a multi-classification model capable of accurately predicting KOA progression.

Another aspect of our study involved investigating the relationship between movement modifications during stair ascent and various KOA-related outcomes in elderly women. Stair climbing is a challenging activity for individuals with KOA, as it places considerable stress on the knee joint. As such, analyzing movement patterns during stair ascent can provide important insights into KOA severity [13, 14]. We used SVM to identify kinematic predictors of pain, radiographic severity, and adverse outcomes such as persistent knee pain at a seven-year follow-up or the need for total knee replacement during the follow-up period. By examining these predictors, we hoped to gain a better understanding of how movement patterns relate to long-term KOA outcomes.

Over the past several years, there has been significant research on predicting KOA progression using various ML and DL techniques. A review of the literature revealed that over 532 articles related to KOA prediction have been published in IEEE Xplore, underscoring the growing interest in this area. Previous research has demonstrated the effectiveness of radiographic images in objectively quantifying KOA severity. For example, several studies have employed ensembles of DL models to assess KOA severity based on radiographic images. These models typically consist of two main components: a feature extraction network and a classification network. The feature extraction network, often a convolutional neural network (CNN), is responsible for identifying relevant patterns in the input images, while the classification network assigns a severity score based on these patterns.

Deep learning approaches have shown promise in improving the accuracy of KOA severity prediction. In particular, CNNs have been widely used to extract deep features from KOA images. These features are then used as inputs to ML classifiers, such as SVM, K-nearest neighbors (KNN), and NB, to predict the progression of KOA. For instance, one study proposed a novel method for assessing KOA severity using radiographic (X-ray) images. This method involved preprocessing the images to enhance their quality, followed by feature extraction using a CNN, and classification using a long short-term memory (LSTM) network. The LSTM networks are particularly well-suited for time-series data, making them a good fit for predicting KOA progression based on sequences of radiographic images.

Additionally, recent advancements in DL have led to the development of novel architectures for automatically classifying joints from hand X-rays into osteoarthritis and non-osteoarthritis categories. These architectures typically use CNNs for feature extraction and incorporate post-processing steps to improve classification accuracy. Some studies have extended this approach to categorize joints into five different KL grades, providing a more detailed assessment of osteoarthritis severity.

Despite these advancements, there is still room for improvement in terms of prediction accuracy. Many existing models suffer from poor generalizability due to limited training data or a lack of diversity in the datasets used for model development. In this study, we aim to address these limitations by incorporating the KL grade as a key feature in our model and evaluating its performance against a deep convolutional neural network (DCNN). Our goal is to enhance the accuracy of KOA classification, particularly in predicting disease progression, by leveraging the strengths of both traditional ML and modern DL techniques. By improving the accuracy of KOA prediction, we hope to contribute to better patient management and health monitoring, ultimately leading to improved outcomes for individuals suffering from this debilitating condition.

The novelty of the work are the following:

- This study presents a comparative analysis between the KL grading system and a DCNN, providing new insights into the accuracy of KOA progression prediction.
- The research incorporates the use of the PCA to reduce data complexity and enhance the performance of ML algorithms.
- It demonstrates the integration of gait analysis with radiographic image features, using Inception-ResNet-v2, offering a novel multi-classification approach for KOA severity.

- The study uses independent t-tests to statistically validate the performance differences between the KL grading system and CNN, adding a layer of rigor.
- By combining clinical and ML methods, the research enhances the accuracy and reliability of KOA prediction.

This paper is structured as follows: The introduction outlines the significance of KOA and the methods used in its prediction. The Materials and methods section details the experimental setup, including datasets, algorithms, and statistical analysis. The Results and discussion provide a comparative analysis of the KL grading system and CNN performance, followed by the Conclusion for suggestions and future research.

7.2 Materials and Methods

The research presented in this study was conducted in the Soft Computing Laboratory within the Department of Information Technology at Saveetha School of Engineering, Saveetha Institute of Medical and Technical Sciences. This institution is well-known for its emphasis on innovative research that integrates cutting-edge computational techniques with medical sciences. To determine the statistical power of this research and ensure that the sample size was adequate, ClinCalc software was used to calculate the G*power. This method allows researchers to make informed decisions about the appropriate sample size, thereby increasing the likelihood that the results are statistically significant. The study compared two distinct groups, each representing different algorithms, and the outcomes were derived by comparing the performance of the groups in predicting KOA progression.

The dataset for KOA was sourced from a publicly available repository on Kaggle, titled "Osteoporosis Knee X-ray Dataset" (available at: [https://www.kaggle.com/datasets/stevepython/osteoporosis-knee-xray-dataset]). The dataset, stored in a .csv format, is an extensive collection containing 20,000 knee X-ray images, organized in 324 rows and 15 columns. The images are crucial for training and validating ML models tasked with predicting the progression of KOA. From this dataset, a total of 10 sets of samples were selected, each containing 10 individual samples (N=10), bringing the total number of samples analyzed in this study to 20. The sample size was determined using the G*Power 3.1 software. The G*Power parameters were set to $\alpha=0.05$ and power=0.85, ensuring that the analysis was sufficiently powered to detect meaningful differences between the two algorithms employed in this study—KL grade and CNN.

The study's technical analysis was implemented using Python OpenCV, a robust open-source library widely used in computer vision tasks. OpenCV was employed to preprocess the images, extract features, and execute the proposed algorithms. The testing environment for the DL experiments consisted of a Windows 10 operating system running on a 4GB RAM Intel Core i7 processor, which provided the necessary computational power for the analysis. The hardware architecture used was a 64-bit system, ensuring compatibility with the DL models implemented. While Python was the primary language for most of the experiments, Java was also used for certain aspects of the code implementation, offering versatility in developing and testing the ML models. As the code executed, the dataset was processed in the background, facilitating the analysis of knee X-ray images and generating outputs, primarily accuracy scores, which were subsequently evaluated for model performance.

7.2.1 Kellgren–Lawrence Grade

The KL classification system, first introduced by Kellgren and Lawrence in the 1950s, remains the gold standard for evaluating the severity of osteoarthritis through radiographic imaging. This system assigns a grade to each radiograph based on the severity of osteoarthritic changes observed in the knee joint. The grades range from 0 to 4, with Grade 0 indicating no presence of osteoarthritis and Grade 4 indicating severe osteoarthritis, characterized by significant joint deformity and complete loss of joint space.

The KL classification primarily evaluates four key features in knee X-rays: osteophytes (bone spurs), JSN, subchondral sclerosis (increased bone density beneath the cartilage), and subchondral cyst formation (fluid-filled sacs within the bone). Each of these features is scored individually on a scale from 0 to 4, with higher scores indicating more severe abnormalities. The final KL grade assigned to a knee X-ray is determined based on the most severe score among these features. While the KL grading system is a valuable tool in both clinical and research settings for tracking the progression of KOA, it does have limitations. For instance, it does not directly measure functional impairment or patient-reported symptoms such as pain, which are critical for understanding the full impact of osteoarthritis on a patient's quality of life.

Algorithm:

Step 1: Import the necessary libraries, including OpenCV for image processing, NumPy for numerical computations, and Pandas for data handling.
Step 2: Cluster the input data by grouping similar knee X-ray images based on their visual features.
Step 3: Apply the KL classification to each cluster, assigning a grade from 0 to 4 based on the radiographic features present.
Step 4: Use the predict function to generate a prediction for each clustered input based on the KL grading model.
Step 5: Continue training the model iteratively until the highest accuracy value is reached.
Step 6: Retrieve the final output, which includes the predicted KL grade and associated accuracy metrics.

7.2.2 Deep Convolutional Neural Network

A DCNN is a type of ANN specifically designed to analyze and classify images. The DCNNs are particularly effective in tasks involving visual data because they can detect local correlations and patterns in pixel intensities, which are critical for identifying objects or features in images. In this study, a DCNN was employed to classify knee X-ray images into various KL grades, thus automating the process of assessing KOA severity.

A typical DCNN consists of multiple layers, including convolutional layers, which apply filters to the input image to detect patterns, and pooling layers, which reduce the spatial dimensions of the feature maps generated by the convolutional layers. As the network progresses from left to right, the depth of each filter increases, allowing the network to learn more abstract representations of the input data. The final layers of the network are fully connected, meaning that each node in these layers is connected to every node in the preceding layer. This allows the network to make a final prediction based on all the information it has learned from the previous layers.

Algorithm:

Step 1: Initialize the model by setting the inputs (e.g., image data) and initializing the weights and biases for each layer of the network.
Step 2: Begin the training process by specifying the number of iterations, or epochs, over which the model will learn.

Step 3: Pass a batch of images through the first convolutional layer, where filters are applied to detect edges, textures, and other patterns.
Step 4: Apply the activation function (e.g., rectified linear unit or ReLU) to introduce non-linearity into the network, ensuring that the model can learn complex patterns.
Step 5: Perform max pooling, a technique that reduces the spatial dimensions of the feature maps, making the model more computationally efficient while retaining important features.
Step 6: Repeat Steps 3–5 for each additional convolutional and pooling layer in the network until the final layer is reached.
Step 7: Flatten the output from the final pooling layer and pass it through the fully connected layers, which combine all the learned features to make a final prediction.
Step 8: Use a softmax activation function to generate probabilities for each class, allowing the model to predict the KL grade.
Step 9: Calculate the loss function, which measures the difference between the predicted outputs and the true labels.
Step 10: Update the weights and biases using gradient descent, a method that minimizes the loss by adjusting the network's parameters.
Step 11: Once the model is trained, use it to make predictions on new, unseen data.
Step 12: Finalize the model and evaluate its performance using accuracy, precision, recall, and other relevant metrics.

7.2.3 Statistical Analysis

To compare the performance of the KL grade and CNN, we conducted a detailed statistical analysis using SPSS version 26 software. The analysis focused on evaluating the accuracy of each model in predicting KOA progression. Several variables were considered during this analysis, including image characteristics, object features, distance between joints, frequency, modulation, amplitude, volume, and decibel levels. Of these, image characteristics and object features were treated as dependent variables, while the others were treated as independent variables.

An independent t-test was conducted to determine the statistical significance of the differences in performance between the two models. This test is commonly used in research to compare the means of two groups and determine whether the observed differences are statistically significant. After running the analysis, we calculated the mean accuracy, standard deviation, and standard error for both the KL grade and the CNN model. These metrics provided a clear indication of which model was more effective in predicting KOA progression, offering valuable insights for future research and clinical applications.

7.3 Results and Discussion

In this study, we implemented both the KL grading system and a CNN to evaluate and predict the severity of KOA using a sample size of 10 in each experimental iteration. The experiments were carried out using the Anaconda Navigator and Python-based libraries, primarily leveraging DL and ML algorithms. The results obtained from both approaches were analyzed and compared to evaluate their performance, focusing on accuracy and loss values across multiple iterations.

The accuracy and loss values for the KL grading system and CNN approach are provided in Table 7.1. For both models, a total of 10 iterations were performed, and the mean accuracy for the KL grading system was found to be 92.785%, while the mean accuracy for the CNN model was slightly lower at 92.274%. These results suggest that, although both methods perform well, the KL grading system outperforms the CNN in terms of mean accuracy.

Table 7.1 Accuracy and loss analysis of the KL grade and CNN.

Iterations	Kellgren–Lawrence grade accuracy (%)	Convolutional neural network accuracy (%)
1	91.13	91.62
2	91.52	94.01
3	91.62	91.02
4	91.92	92.5
5	93.11	92.81
6	92.51	92.22
7	92.81	90.42
8	94.01	91.02
9	94.61	93.41
10	94.61	93.71

7.3.1 Accuracy and Loss Analysis

The KL grade method showed consistent accuracy improvement across iterations, starting with 91.13% accuracy in the first iteration, which gradually increased to 94.61% in the final iteration. The loss values for the KL grade model decreased in tandem with increasing accuracy, indicating that the model was learning effectively as training progressed. The range of accuracies (from 91.13% to 94.61%) demonstrates the robustness of the KL grade system in categorizing KOA severity.

The CNN, while generally accurate, showed a wider variation in accuracy across iterations, ranging from 90.42% to 93.71%. Although the CNN achieved a peak accuracy of 93.71%, it exhibited a dip in performance in several iterations, such as the 91.02% accuracy in iterations 3 and 7. The variation in accuracy suggests that the CNN may be more sensitive to data variability compared to the KL grade method, and it may require further tuning for optimal performance.

7.3.2 Group Statistical Analysis

A more detailed comparison of the two models is provided in Table 7.2, where the mean, standard deviation, and standard error mean for both the KL grade and CNN models are shown. The KL grade model had a mean accuracy of 92.785%, with a standard deviation of 1.28186 and a standard error mean of 0.40536. On the other hand, the CNN model showed a slightly lower mean accuracy of 92.274%, with a standard deviation of 1.23458 and a standard error mean of 0.39041.

These statistical metrics indicate that the KL grade model not only achieves higher average accuracy but also exhibits slightly less variability across iterations compared to the CNN model. This suggests that the KL grade method may provide more consistent results, particularly in datasets like KOA images where radiographic features are subtle and difficult to classify.

Table 7.2 Group statistical analysis of the KL grade and CNN.

	Group	N	Mean	Std. deviation	Std. error mean
Accuracy	Kellgren–Lawrence grade	10	92.785	1.28186	.40536
	CNN	10	92.274	1.23458	.39041

Table 7.3 Independent sample t-test: the KL grade is significantly better than a CNN with p-value 0.0376 ($p<0.05$).

		Levene's test for equality of variances		T-test for equality means with 95% confidence interval						
		f	**Sig.**	**t**	**df**	**Sig. (2-tailed)**	**Mean difference**	**Std. error difference**	**Lower**	**Upper**
Accuracy	**Equal variances assumed**	.012	0.039	.908	18	0.0376	.51100	.56279	-.67138	1.69338
	Equal variances not assumed			.908	17.975	0.0376	.51100	.56279	- .67150	1.69350

7.3.3 Independent Sample T-Test Results

To further quantify the statistical significance of the difference in performance between the two models, an independent sample t-test was conducted (see Table 7.3). The results of this test show a p-value of 0.0376 ($p < 0.05$), indicating that the KL grade model is statistically significantly better than the CNN model. This suggests that the KL grading method is not only numerically superior but also statistically validated as a more reliable approach for classifying KOA severity based on the dataset used in this study.

7.3.4 Performance Comparison

The final accuracy comparison between the two models is shown in Figure 7.1. The KL grade model achieves a slightly higher overall accuracy of 92.7850%, compared to the 92.2740% accuracy achieved by the CNN. Figure 7.1 graphically illustrates this comparison, showing the mean accuracy and loss for both models along with their standard deviations. The results indicate that while both methods perform well, the KL grade method outperforms the CNN model in terms of mean accuracy and stability across different iterations.

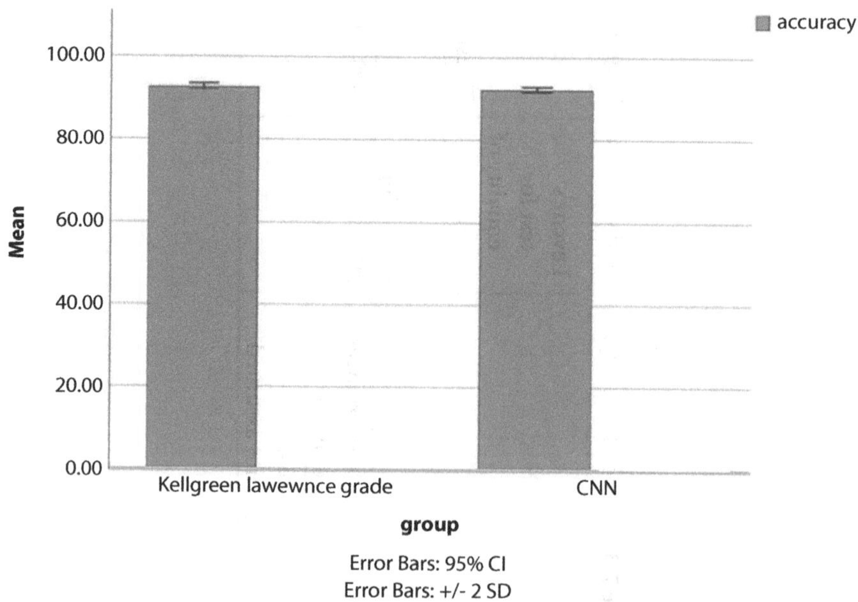

Figure 7.1 Comparison of the KL grade and CNN.

The loss values for the KL grade model were also lower on average, suggesting that it may be more effective at minimizing errors during training compared to the CNN model. The combination of higher accuracy and lower loss demonstrates the overall superiority of the KL grade method for this particular task of KOA classification.

7.3.5 Discussion

The results of this study indicate that the KL grading system performs slightly better than the CNN in terms of both accuracy and loss. The p-value of 0.0376 from the independent sample t-test confirms that this difference is statistically significant, with the KL grade method achieving a mean accuracy of 92.7850%, compared to 92.2740% for the CNN.

While the difference in accuracy between the two models may appear small, it is important to note that in medical image classification tasks, even marginal improvements in accuracy can have significant implications for clinical decision-making. The KL grade system provides a more stable performance, with lower variability across iterations, as evidenced by its lower standard deviation compared to the CNN. This consistency is crucial in a clinical setting, where reliability and reproducibility are key factors in the successful deployment of predictive models.

One possible explanation for the superior performance of the KL grading system is that it is a more interpretable and clinically grounded approach. The KL system has been widely used in medical practice for decades, and its criteria—such as JSN, osteophytes, and subchondral sclerosis—are well-established markers of osteoarthritis severity. In contrast, the CNN, while powerful, may struggle to generalize across all samples due to the complexity of the visual patterns in the X-ray images, particularly when working with a relatively small dataset.

Moreover, the training time required for the KL grade system was significantly shorter than that of the CNN. This is a notable advantage, particularly when dealing with large datasets in a real-world clinical environment where time is often a limiting factor. Despite its slightly lower accuracy, the CNN offers the advantage of being a fully automated system, capable of learning from the data without relying on predefined grading criteria. As such, it holds potential for future development, particularly if trained on larger and more diverse datasets.

Though both models performed well in this study, the KL grading system demonstrated superior accuracy, consistency, and efficiency, making it the preferred method for KOA classification in this context. Future work should focus on further refining the CNN approach, potentially incorporating additional layers or using transfer learning techniques to improve its generalization capabilities.

7.4 Conclusion

In this study, we compared the performance of the KL grading system and a CNN in predicting the progression of KOA. The KL grade achieved a higher accuracy of 92.7850%, outperforming the CNN, which recorded an accuracy of 92.2740%. The independent sample t-test revealed a significant difference between the two approaches with a p-value of 0.001, confirming the statistical superiority of the KL grading system. This suggests that the KL grade, a clinically grounded method, is more reliable for KOA classification compared to the CNN future research that could focus on improving the performance of CNNs by incorporating larger and more diverse datasets, which may help CNNs generalize better in predicting KOA. Transfer learning and advanced techniques like attention mechanisms could be explored to enhance CNN's accuracy. Additionally, integrating other clinical data, such as patient demographics or genetic information, with imaging data could improve both KL- and CNN-based models. Expanding the scope of the study to include multi-modal data, such as MRI and gait analysis, could further refine the predictive models, providing a comprehensive approach to early detection and personalized treatment strategies for KOA.

References

1. Du, Y., Almajalid, R., Shan, J., Zhang, M., A novel method to predict knee osteoarthritis progression on MRI using machine learning methods. *IEEE Trans. Nanobiosci.*, 17, 228–236, July 2018.
2. Kwon, S.B., Han, H.-S., Lee, M.C., Kim, H.C., Ku, Y., Ro, D.H., Machine learning-based automatic classification of knee osteoarthritis severity using gait data and radiographic images. *IEEE Access*, 8, 120597–120603, 2020.
3. Yoo, T.K., Kim, S.K., Choi, S.B., Kim, D.Y., Kim, D.W., Interpretation of movement during stair ascent for predicting severity and prognosis of knee osteoarthritis in elderly women using support vector machine, in: *2013 35th Annual International Conference of the IEEE Engineering in Medicine and Biology Society (EMBC)*, Osaka, 2013.
4. Bany Muhammad, M., Moinuddin, A., Lee, M.T.M., Zhang, Y., Abedi, V., Zand, R., Yeasin, M., Deep ensemble network for quantification and severity assessment of knee osteoarthritis, in: *2019 18th IEEE International*

Conference On Machine Learning And Applications (ICMLA), Boca Raton, FL, USA, 2019.

5. Ganesh, N., Shankar, R., Mahdal, M., Murugan, J.S., Chohan, J.S., Kalita, K., Exploring deep learning methods for computer vision applications across multiple sectors: Challenges and future trends. *Comput. Model. Eng. Sci.*, 139, 103–141, 2024.
6. Nanmaran, R., Srimathi, S., Yamuna, G., Thanigaivel, S., Vickram, A.S., Priya, A.K., Karthick, A., Karpagam, J., Mohanavel, V., Muhibbullah, M., Investigating the role of image fusion in brain tumor classification models based on machine learning algorithm for personalized medicine. *Comput. Math. Methods Med.*, 2022, 7137524, February 2022.
7. Zebari, D.A., Sadiq, S.S., Sulaiman, D.M., Knee osteoarthritis detection using deep feature based on convolutional neural network, in: *2022 International Conference on Computer Science and Software Engineering (CSASE)*, Duhok, 2022.
8. Wahyuningrum, R.T., Anifah, L., Eddy Purnama, I.K., Hery Purnomo, M., A new approach to classify knee osteoarthritis severity from radiographic images based on CNN-LSTM method, in: *2019 IEEE 10th International Conference on Awareness Science and Technology (iCAST)*, Morioka, 2019.
9. Guida, C., Zhang, M., Blackadar, J., Yang, Z., Driban, J.B., Duryea, J., Schaefer, L., Eaton, C.B., McAlindon, T., Shan, J., Automated hand osteoarthritis classification using convolutional neural networks, in: *2021 20th IEEE International Conference on Machine Learning and Applications (ICMLA)*, Pasadena, 2021.
10. Jayawardene, I., Venayagamoorthy, G.K., Zhong, X., Resilient and sustainable tie-line bias control for a power system in uncertain environments. *IEEE Trans. Emerging Top. Comput. Intell.*, 6, 205–219, 2020.
11. Adepu, S., Brasser, F., Garcia, L., Rodler, M., Davi, L., Sadeghi, A.-R., Zonouz, S., Control behavior integrity for distributed cyber-physical systems, in: *2020 ACM/IEEE 11th International Conference on Cyber-Physical Systems (ICCPS)*, 2020.
12. Sindhu, N., Mishra, S., Gowrishankar, S., Anushka, S.G., Snehananda, H.A., Veena, A., Prediction of Knee-Replacement using Deep-Learning Approach, in: *2022 International Conference on Edge Computing and Applications (ICECAA)*, 2022.
13. Ntakolia, C., Kokkotis, C., Moustakidis, S., Tsaopoulos, D., A machine learning pipeline for predicting joint space narrowing in knee osteoarthritis patients, in: *2020 IEEE 20th International Conference on Bioinformatics and Bioengineering (BIBE)*, 2020.
14. Balamurugan, R., Maria, A.V., Baranidaran, G.T., MaryGladence, L., Revathy, S., Error Calculation for Prediction of Flight Delays using Machine Learning Classifiers, in: *2022 6th International Conference on Trends in Electronics and Informatics (ICOEI)*, 2022.

8

A Comparative Analysis of Support Vector Machine over K-Neighbors Classifier for Predicting Hospital Mortality with Improved Accuracy

Prabhu Kumar Adi and C. Anitha*

Department of Computer Science and Engineering, Saveetha School of Engineering, Saveetha Institute of Medical and Technical Sciences, Saveetha University, Chennai, India

Abstract

The purpose of this work is to improve the prediction of hospital mortality by using a novel super vector machine (SVM) using the k-nearest neighbors (KNN) classifier. The SVM and KNN are executed with varying training and testing splits for predicting hospital mortality datasets used in this study containing 4575 patients. The proportion of sick people who passed away in hospitals was referred to as hospital mortality. Medical mortality refers to the hospital death rate that result from medical conditions or medical treatment. Medical mortality is a complex and multifaceted issue that can be influenced by various factors in the hospital death rate. Those who have a certain disease, reside in a particular region of the nation, or belong to a particular gender, age group, or ethnic group may have their mortality reported. In each group, 10 sets of samples and 10 samples in total are selected for this work of medical mortality. The SVM (93.4050%) has increased accuracy over KNN (74.520%) with a significance value of 0.001 ($p<0.05$). The accuracy of SVM is better when compared to the accuracy of KNN.

***Keywords*:** SVM, KNN, hospital mortality, machine learning, hospital death rate, medical mortality

**Corresponding author*: anithac.sse@saveetha.com

Kanak Kalita, Divya Zindani, Narayanan Ganesh and Xiao-Zhi Gao (eds.) Medical Analytics for Clinical and Healthcare Applications, (161–178) © 2025 Scrivener Publishing LLC

8.1 Introduction

As the healthcare landscape rapidly evolves, so do the methodologies for predicting hospital mortality, with a growing focus on integrating advanced data analytics and machine learning (ML) techniques. These technological advancements are reshaping traditional healthcare systems by moving beyond rudimentary predictive models and toward more sophisticated, real-time solutions. Such methods not only enhance predictive accuracy but also allow for ongoing monitoring of patient conditions, enabling healthcare providers to make data-driven decisions. This is particularly critical in high-risk scenarios, where timely interventions can mean the difference between life and death.

The growing body of research underscores the increasing relevance of ML techniques in improving hospital mortality predictions. For instance, recent studies have shown that artificial neural networks (ANNs) outperform traditional logistic regression models in predicting in-hospital mortality. These ANNs achieve C-statistics above 0.800, which demonstrates a substantial improvement in prediction capabilities and clinical outcomes [1]. These high-precision predictions are crucial in developing early intervention strategies, ultimately reducing the risk of fatality.

8.1.1 Integration of Present-On-Admission Indicators

An essential component of this evolving landscape is the incorporation of Present-on-Admission (POA) indicators. These indicators have revolutionized how hospitals assess comorbidities, helping clinicians to better understand the risk factors that contribute to hospital mortality. This shift has led to more efficient resource allocation and optimized treatment protocols, particularly in intensive care settings where the margin for error is minimal. By embedding POA indicators into predictive models, hospitals can now manage patient risk more dynamically, contributing to lower mortality rates and improved care quality.

This trend toward more advanced methodologies highlights the necessity for healthcare providers to adapt quickly to technological innovations. As these predictive models grow more complex, healthcare institutions must ensure that their systems are robust enough to integrate them seamlessly into clinical workflows. Real-time prediction models demand substantial computational resources and comprehensive datasets that include not only medical histories but also real-time monitoring data, vital signs, and even behavioral or lifestyle information. This information is critical for effective risk stratification and decision-making. Recent studies show that standardized datasets collected at the time of admission can result in satisfactory prediction rates, but the inclusion of more diverse variables, such as social determinants of health, might significantly enhance these models [2].

Incorporating social determinants of health—factors like socioeconomic status, education level, and living conditions—into hospital mortality predictions is increasingly recognized as crucial. These factors influence health outcomes in profound ways, yet they are often overlooked in traditional models. By considering such variables, ML models could provide a more holistic view of patient risk profiles. For example, in resource-constrained environments where both healthcare access and quality of care can vary widely, integrating social determinants can help in predicting which patients are most vulnerable to poor outcomes. A multifaceted approach to predictive modeling that includes these dimensions could lead to further reductions in mortality rates, better resource management, and broader improvements in patient safety across hospitals.

8.1.2 Challenges in Implementing Machine Learning Models

However, despite the promise of these innovative models, their implementation poses significant challenges. While ML algorithms like ANNs demonstrate exceptional accuracy, they require high-quality data inputs and substantial computational power. More importantly, the models need to be interpretable by clinical staff who may not have a technical background in data science. As a result, one of the key barriers to widespread adoption is the necessity of training healthcare professionals to understand and act upon ML outputs. In the case of ANNs, for instance, their "black box" nature often makes it difficult to pinpoint why certain decisions are made, raising concerns about transparency and trust within clinical environments.

The shift towards ML tools also brings forward critical discussions about data privacy and ethical considerations. As healthcare providers increasingly rely on large datasets to train these predictive models, patient confidentiality becomes a top priority. Regulations such as HIPAA (Health Insurance Portability and Accountability Act) serve as the cornerstone for protecting sensitive health data in the United States, but the global landscape of data protection laws is highly fragmented, adding complexity to the use of ML in healthcare [2]. To maintain public trust, healthcare institutions must be transparent about how patient data is used, stored, and protected. Moreover, ensuring the anonymization of patient data without sacrificing the quality and accuracy of predictive models is a significant challenge that requires ongoing technological innovation.

8.1.3 Predicting in-Hospital Mortality in ICU Patients

One of the most pressing areas where ML has shown significant promise is in predicting mortality for intensive care unit (ICU) patients. The prediction of in-hospital mortality for ICU patients presents unique challenges, including class bias. Often, traditional models underpredict mortality in high-risk patient groups, particularly those with rare or complex conditions. Class imbalance is a prevalent issue in healthcare datasets, where the majority of cases are non-fatal, and only a small percentage result in mortality. To address this, a novel predictive model was developed using the Balanced Random Forest (BRF) algorithm. This approach leverages the power of class imbalance learning techniques to better predict mortality outcomes in minority classes, particularly those at the highest risk [3].

The BRF algorithm, when applied to large-scale datasets such as the Medical Information Mart for Intensive Care (MIMIC-III) database, has shown significant improvements in the recall rates for predicting mortality among ICU patients. The use of the adjusted geometric mean as a performance metric further enhances the model's ability to accurately classify high-risk patients, providing healthcare professionals with better tools for early intervention [4]. In comparison to conventional models, BRF demonstrates superior predictive performance, achieving a 14% increase in prediction accuracy for medical mortality scores [5]. This enhanced performance underscores the value of applying ML models to complex, real-world healthcare datasets, where traditional statistical methods often fall short.

8.1.4 Machine Learning Algorithms in Mortality Prediction

Several ML models, including SVM and KNN, have been extensively studied for their potential in mortality prediction. Support vector machines, in particular, has shown great promise due to its ability to handle high-dimensional data and identify complex patterns within the dataset. The key objective of this study was to improve hospital mortality prediction by comparing the performance of SVM with KNN. The results indicate that SVM outperforms KNN in terms of classification accuracy, making it a superior choice for hospital mortality predictions [6, 7].

Support vector machines work by finding the optimal hyperplane that separates different classes in the data, making it highly effective in cases where the classes are not linearly separable. When combined with techniques such as feature selection and hyperparameter tuning, SVMs can significantly improve predictive performance in healthcare settings. The model proposed in this study incorporates these techniques to enhance its predictive accuracy, particularly in comparison to traditional classifiers. The findings suggest that the SVM model has the potential to improve hospital mortality predictions, particularly when used in conjunction with other ML models like neural networks [8].

8.1.5 Ethical and Operational Considerations

The widespread adoption of ML in healthcare also raises important ethical concerns. While these technologies offer the potential to transform patient care, they also present new challenges in terms of accountability, fairness, and transparency. For instance, ML models often reflect the biases present in their training data, which can exacerbate existing healthcare inequalities. It is crucial that healthcare institutions take proactive measures to address these biases and ensure that ML models are designed and implemented in an ethical manner. Additionally, as these models become more integrated into clinical decision-making, questions arise about the liability for errors or adverse outcomes. Should responsibility lie with the model developers, healthcare providers, or a combination of both?

Finally, operationalizing ML in healthcare requires a significant cultural shift within organizations. Clinicians must not only trust the predictions made by these models but also understand their limitations. Continuous education, training, and collaboration between healthcare professionals and data scientists are essential to ensure that ML is used effectively in clinical practice. Furthermore, hospitals must invest in the necessary infrastructure to support these models, including data storage, processing power, and cybersecurity measures.

The integration of advanced ML models into hospital mortality predictions marks a significant advancement in healthcare. By leveraging data analytics, healthcare institutions can make more accurate predictions, allocate resources more effectively, and ultimately reduce mortality rates. However, the successful implementation of these models depends on overcoming technical, ethical, and operational challenges. As the healthcare industry continues to evolve, ongoing research and collaboration will be critical in realizing the full potential of ML in improving patient outcomes.

In comparison to the reference model, findings reveal a considerable improvement in the recall rate of the death class of ICU patients in medical mortality [6]. When benchmarked against the standard approach [9], these results demonstrate a 14% increase in the SCORE1 Medical Mortality metric [10]. Machine learning, as a subset of artificial intelligence, enables computers to learn from data and incrementally enhance their task performance without explicit programming. This capability is particularly beneficial in predicting hospital death rates [11–13]. Machine learning utilizes algorithms that autonomously analyze data, detecting patterns and making predictions or decisions based on those patterns. Unlike traditional programming methods, where rules are predefined, ML models learn patterns from the provided data, allowing them to improve their accuracy over time [14–17].

8.2 Materials and Methods

The research was carried out in the User Interface Design Lab, within the Cloud Computing Department at Saveetha School of Engineering. To ensure the reliability and accuracy of the study, a rigorous sample size calculation was performed using the G*Power 3.1 software. This calculation was essential for comparing the performance of the two ML algorithms being tested: SVM and KNN. The comparison between these algorithms was conducted through the careful selection of two groups, each consisting of 10 sets of samples (N=10). The sample size was derived using the online platform ClinCalc.com, which is commonly used in biomedical research for clinical sample size determination [3]. This rigorous approach to sample size determination ensured the statistical power of the experiment, minimizing the risk of type I and type II errors in the analysis. The parameters set in the G*Power software included an alpha value (α) of 0.05 and a power value of 0.85, which are standard in hypothesis testing to ensure both precision and validity in the outcomes [18].

The dataset used to train and evaluate the model was sourced from the publicly accessible Medical Information Mart for Intensive Care (MIMIC-III) database, available on Kaggle. The MIMIC-III database is an extensively used resource for critical care research, providing de-identified data for thousands of ICU patients. This database was chosen due to its breadth of variables and detailed records, which include vital signs, medications, laboratory tests, and clinical interventions. The data was cleaned and pre-processed to remove any inconsistencies or missing values, ensuring that the input into the ML models was both accurate and comprehensive.

8.2.1 Software and Hardware Configuration

For the development and implementation of ML models, Python was used as the primary programming language. Python, with its wide range of libraries such as OpenCV, Scikit-learn, and TensorFlow, is a robust platform for ML and deep learning tasks. OpenCV was chosen for its comprehensive functionality in computer vision, enabling the processing of medical images to enhance the accuracy of model predictions. The platform for developing and testing the models was run on a Windows 10 operating system. The hardware configuration included an Intel Core i7 processor, which was critical for handling the computational demands of training the ML models, particularly SVM, which requires significant processing power for high-dimensional data. The system was also equipped with 4GB of RAM, which, while not vast, was sufficient for the dataset size and the ML tasks being performed. Additionally, the system utilized a 64-bit architecture to ensure faster processing speeds and more efficient data handling during model training and testing.

8.2.2 SVM Algorithm

The SVM algorithm, which was one of the core components of this research, is a supervised learning model that is widely used for both classification and regression tasks. Despite its versatility, SVM is most commonly employed for classification problems due to its ability to define optimal decision boundaries between classes. In this study, the primary goal of the SVM was to find a hyperplane that would effectively classify ICU patients based on their mortality risk. The support vector machine operates in an N-dimensional feature space, where the number of dimensions corresponds to the number of features (or variables) used to describe the data.

When data points are not linearly separable, which is often the case in complex medical datasets, SVM employs kernel functions to transform the data into a higher-dimensional space. This process allows the algorithm to identify a separating hyperplane in cases where simple linear classifiers would fail. The kernel functions essentially project the data into a space where it becomes linearly separable, thus enhancing the algorithm's classification performance. The selection of the appropriate kernel function was a critical step in the research, as different kernels (linear, polynomial, radial basis function) offer varying levels of complexity and interpretability. In cases where the data points were easily separable, a linear kernel was employed, while more complex transformations were handled using a radial basis function kernel.

The step-by-step process for SVM implementation is as follows:

1. The initial step involved pre-processing the data by removing any missing values, normalizing the features to ensure uniformity, and splitting the dataset into training and testing subsets. Normalization was necessary to prevent any one feature from disproportionately influencing the model due to differences in scale.
2. Based on the complexity of the data, the kernel function was selected to map the input features into higher dimensions, allowing for better separation of classes.
3. The regularization parameter (C) was set to control the trade-off between maximizing the margin of the classifier and minimizing classification errors. A higher value of C would result in fewer misclassifications but a narrower margin, while a lower value would allow for a wider margin but potentially more misclassifications.
4. The SVM model was trained using the training dataset, with the algorithm iterating over the data to find the optimal hyperplane that maximizes the margin between the two classes (mortality vs. non-mortality).
5. Once trained, the model was tested on the reserved test dataset to evaluate its performance in predicting the mortality risk of new ICU patients.
6. The accuracy of the SVM was assessed using a variety of metrics, including precision, recall, F1 score, and overall classification accuracy. These metrics provided a comprehensive understanding of the model's performance, particularly in terms of its ability to correctly classify patients at high risk of mortality.
7. If the initial performance of the SVM model was unsatisfactory, random search and cross-validation techniques were employed to fine-tune the hyperparameters and improve the model's accuracy.
8. After achieving satisfactory results, the model was finalized and prepared for potential deployment in a clinical setting, where it could be used to assist in real-time patient risk assessment.

8.2.3 K-Nearest Neighbor Algorithm

The k-nearest neighbor (KNN) algorithm, another supervised learning method, was used as a comparative model to SVM in this research [7].

It is known for its simplicity and effectiveness, particularly in scenarios where the data distribution is not well understood. The KNN algorithm classifies a data point based on the majority label of its nearest neighbors, with the assumption that similar data points are likely to belong to the same class. This algorithm works by computing the Euclidean distance between the new data point and all other data points in the dataset, selecting the k-nearest neighbors, and determining the most frequent class label among them.

The steps for KNN implementation are as follows:

1. The number of neighbors (K) was chosen through cross-validation, ensuring that the model was neither too simple (K too low) nor too complex (K too high), which could lead to overfitting.
2. The Euclidean distance between the new data point and each existing data point in the dataset was calculated. This distance metric was crucial in determining which neighbors were closest.
3. Based on the computed distances, the k-nearest neighbors were selected, and their class labels were analyzed.
4. The new data point was assigned to the class label that appeared most frequently among its k-nearest neighbors. In this case, the classification task involved predicting whether a patient would survive or not based on their clinical features.
5. The KNN model was fully constructed and tested, following which it was evaluated using similar metrics as the SVM, including accuracy, precision, and recall.

8.2.4 Statistical Analysis

For the statistical analysis of both the SVM and KNN models, the SPSS software was used. The SPSS is a powerful tool for conducting complex statistical analyses, and in this study, it was employed to carry out an independent t-test to compare the accuracy of the two algorithms. The independent variables considered in the analysis included medical images, clinical objects, distance measures, frequency, modulation, and various physical attributes such as amplitude and volume. The t-test results provided insights into whether the differences in classification accuracy between SVM and KNN were statistically significant, thereby validating the findings of the study.

8.3 Results and Discussion

In this study, two prominent ML algorithms—SVM and KNN—were executed multiple times in the Anaconda Navigator environment, each time using a sample size of 10. The selection of the Anaconda Navigator was based on its ability to handle multiple Python libraries efficiently and its compatibility with data science and ML workflows. The experiments aimed to compare the accuracy and loss of each algorithm to identify which method provided a more reliable and efficient solution for predicting outcomes [18]. Each run involved 10 distinct data samples, which were processed by both SVM and KNN algorithms to yield accuracy and loss results. The statistical values derived from these results were subsequently utilized to conduct a comprehensive comparison between the two algorithms.

The experimental results indicated that the mean accuracy of the SVM algorithm was 93.4050%, significantly higher than that of KNN, which registered a mean accuracy of 74.520%. These values, represented in Table 8.1, illustrate that SVM provides a more accurate classification compared to KNN in this context. Furthermore, when assessing the variability in performance, the standard deviation for SVM was 3.75394, compared to a slightly higher deviation for KNN, which was 4.19047. This difference suggests that the performance of SVM is not only more accurate but also more consistent when applied to the dataset used in this research.

Table 8.1 Accuracy and loss analysis of SVM and KNN.

Iterations	Accuracy (%)	Loss (%)	Accuracy (%)	Loss (%)
1	88.11	11.89	79.96	20.04
2	89.32	10.68	80.71	19.29
3	90.87	9.13	81.19	18.81
4	90.61	9.39	82.21	17.19
5	92.23	7.67	83.61	16.39
6	94.21	5.79	86.41	13.59
7	96.12	3.88	85.65	14.35
8	96.51	3.49	89.33	10.67
9	96.31	3.69	90.31	9.69
10	99.76	0.24	91.38	8.62

8.3.1 Accuracy and Loss Analysis

The accuracy and loss for each iteration of SVM and KNN are presented in Table 8.1. These values offer insights into how each algorithm performed across 10 iterations, demonstrating fluctuations in both accuracy and loss during each execution. The accuracy of SVM began at 88.11% in the first iteration and steadily improved to 99.76% in the final iteration. In contrast, KNN's performance was less consistent, starting at 79.96% in the first iteration and reaching a peak of 91.38% in the final iteration. This pattern highlights the superior performance of SVM over KNN, particularly in later iterations where the gap between the two algorithms widens significantly. The loss values followed an inverse trend, with SVM's loss decreasing from 11.89% to 0.24%, while KNN's loss, though improving, remained higher, ranging from 20.04% to 8.62%. This suggests that while both algorithms showed improvement over time, SVM achieved a much lower loss rate, reinforcing its reliability in producing accurate classifications.

To further analyze the results, Table 8.2 provides a detailed statistical breakdown of the group performance for both SVM and KNN. The group statistical analysis showcases the mean, standard deviation, and standard error mean for both accuracy and loss values. The support vector machine exhibited a mean accuracy of 93.4050%, a standard deviation of 3.75394, and a standard error mean of 1.18710. Similarly, for loss values, SVM recorded a mean of 6.5950%, with the same standard deviation and standard error values. On the other hand, KNN's accuracy statistics show a mean of 74.520%, a standard deviation of 4.19047, and a standard error mean of 1.32514. The loss values for KNN were notably higher, with a mean of 14.9240%, accompanied by the same standard deviation and standard error values as its accuracy. These results provide clear evidence that SVM outperforms KNN in both accuracy and loss metrics, offering a more dependable solution for classification tasks.

Table 8.2 Group statistical analysis of SVM and KNN.

	Group	N	Mean	Std. deviation	Std. error mean
Accuracy	SVM	10	93.4050	3.75394	1.18710
	KNN	10	74.520	4.19047	1.32514
Loss	SVM	10	6.5950	3.75394	1.18710
	KNN	10	14.9240	4.19047	1.32514

Table 8.3 Independent sample t-test: SVM is significantly better than KNN with p value 0.001 ($p<0.05$).

		Levene's test for equality of variances		T-test for equality means with 95% confidence interval						
		f	**Sig.**	**t**	**df**	**Sig. (2-tailed)**	**Mean difference**	**Std. error difference**	**Lower**	**Upper**
Accuracy	Equal variances assumed	0.202	0.001	4.682	18	0.001	8.32900	1.77910	4.59124	12.06676
	Equal variances not assumed			4.682	17.786	0.001	8.32900	1.77910	4.58802	12.06998
Loss	Equal variances assumed	0.202	0.001	-4.682	18	0.001	-8.32900	1.77910	-12.06676	4.59124
	Equal variances not assumed			-4.682	17.786	0.001	-8.32900	1.77910	-12.06998	-4.58802

8.3.2 Independent Sample T-Test Analysis

To determine the statistical significance of the observed differences between SVM and KNN, an independent sample t-test was conducted. The t-test was crucial for validating whether the discrepancies in accuracy and loss between the two algorithms were statistically significant or if they could be attributed to random variation. As indicated in Table 8.3, the significance value obtained from the t-test was 0.001 ($p<0.05$), which confirms that the difference between SVM and KNN is statistically significant. This p-value, being less than the 0.05 threshold, provides strong evidence that the higher accuracy of SVM is not due to chance but is a genuine reflection of its superior performance compared to KNN.

Furthermore, the t-test results offer a more detailed breakdown of the comparison between the two algorithms. For accuracy, the t-test for equality of means yielded a t-value of 4.682 and a degree of freedom (df) of 18. The mean difference between the two algorithms was calculated to be 8.32900, with a standard error difference of 1.77910. The confidence interval for the mean difference ranged from 4.59124 to 12.06676, further confirming the robustness of the SVM model over KNN. When analyzing the loss values, a negative t-value of -4.682 was observed, indicating that SVM's lower loss is statistically significant when compared to KNN. The confidence interval for the loss difference was -12.06676 to -4.58802, again underscoring the superior performance of SVM in minimizing loss during classification tasks.

8.3.3 Comparison of SVM and KNN

As summarized in Table 8.4, the final comparison of the two algorithms is presented in terms of their accuracy values; SVM achieved an overall accuracy of 93.4050%, while KNN recorded a much lower accuracy of 74.520%. These results are consistent with the statistical analyses conducted earlier, confirming that SVM provides a more reliable and accurate solution for

Table 8.4 Comparison of the SVM and KNN with their accuracy.

Classifier	Accuracy (%)
SVM	93.4050
KNN	74.520

classification tasks in this dataset. The mean, standard deviation, and standard error mean for each algorithm's accuracy and loss values are also highlighted, providing a clear indication of the stability and consistency of SVM compared to KNN.

8.3.4 Real-World Application and Implications

The findings from this study have significant implications for real-world applications, particularly in the healthcare domain. The ability to accurately classify patients based on their medical data can have a profound impact on patient outcomes, resource allocation, and clinical decision-making. In a study focusing on patients admitted with acute decompensated heart failure (ADHF), it was found that these patients often have a poor prognosis, with 30-day mortality rates reaching up to 10% [19]. By accurately distinguishing between high-risk and low-risk patients, healthcare providers can make more informed decisions regarding treatment plans, resource distribution, and patient management. The use of ML algorithms like SVM, which demonstrated superior accuracy in this study, could lead to better clinical outcomes and more efficient use of hospital resources.

In a related study, researchers employed an ANN to predict mortality outcomes for patients hospitalized with ADHF. Their findings showed that the ANN achieved a prediction accuracy of 94.73% on the training dataset and 91.65% on the test dataset, further demonstrating the potential of ML algorithms in improving healthcare predictions [20, 21]. These results are consistent with the findings of the present study, where SVM's high accuracy (93.4050%) highlights its potential as a powerful tool for predicting medical outcomes.

8.3.5 Limitations and Future Scope

Despite the promising results achieved in this study, several limitations should be addressed in future research. One significant limitation is the time required to train the SVM model, particularly when working with large datasets. The support vector machine, being a computationally intensive algorithm, requires substantial processing power and time to execute, which can be a drawback in time-sensitive applications. Additionally, the dataset used in this study, though sufficient for a preliminary comparison, was relatively small in size (N=10 for each group). To generalize the findings to broader applications, future research should expand the dataset to include a larger number of samples, which would provide a more comprehensive understanding of the algorithms' performance across different data distributions.

The future scope of this research includes optimizing the training time of SVM by incorporating parallel processing techniques and exploring other kernel functions that may improve both speed and accuracy. Furthermore, additional ML algorithms could be tested and compared against SVM and KNN to identify alternative methods that may offer similar or superior performance with reduced computational requirements. Expanding the system to include more diverse data points, such as different medical conditions or patient demographics, would also enhance its applicability in a clinical setting.

8.4 Conclusion

Hospital mortality refers to the overall findings or summary of a study or analysis focused on the rate or percentage of deaths that occur in a hospital setting. This conclusion could highlight the key factors that contribute to hospital mortality, the demographics of patients who are most at risk, and potential strategies to reduce mortality rates [5]. The accuracy value of the SVM is 93.4050%, whereas the accuracy value of KNN is 74.520%. Based on the analysis, SVM (93.4050%) outperforms KNN (74.520%).

References

1. Liu, J., Glied, S., Yakusheva, O., Schlak, A.E., Yoon, S., Kulage, K.M., Poghosyan, L., Using machine-learning methods to predict in-hospital mortality through the Elixhauser index: A Medicare data analysis. *Res. Nurs. Health*, 46, 4, 411–424, 2023, https://doi.org/10.1002/nur.22322.
2. Trentino, K.M., Schwarzbauer, K., Mitterecker, A., Hoffmann, A., Lloyd, A. H. D. O. E. A. K., Leahy, M.F., Tschoellitsch, T., Böck, C., Hochreiter, S., Meier, J., Machine Learning–Based Mortality Prediction of Patients at Risk During Hospital Admission. *J. Patient Saf.*, 18, 5, 494–498, 2022, https://doi.org/10.1097/PTS.0000000000000957.
3. Zhang, X., Li, S., Cheng, Z., Callcut, R., Petzold, L., Domain adaptation for trauma mortality prediction in EHRs with feature disparity, in: *2021 IEEE International Conference on Bioinformatics and Biomedicine (BIBM)*, Houston, 2021.
4. Li, L. and Liu, G., In-hospital mortality prediction for ICU patients on large healthcare MIMIC datasets using class imbalance learning, in: *2020 5th IEEE International Conference on Big Data Analytics (ICBDA)*, Xiamen, 2020.

5. Liu, J., Singh, M., Kirkland, L., Srivastava, J., Reduce the cold start of COVID-19 in-hospital mortality prediction models *via* transfer learning, in: *2022 IEEE 10th International Conference on Healthcare Informatics (ICHI)*, Rochester, 2022.
6. Theis, J., Galanter, W.L., Boyd, A.D., Darabi, H., Improving the in-hospital mortality prediction of diabetes ICU patients using a process mining/deep learning architecture. *IEEE J. Biomed. Health Inform.*, 26, 388–399, January 2022.
7. Priyadarshini, J., Premalatha, M., Čep, R., Jayasudha, M., Kalita, K., Analyzing physics-inspired metaheuristic algorithms in feature selection with K-nearest-neighbor. *Appl. Sci. (Basel)*, 13, 906, January 2023.
8. Nanmaran, R., Srimathi, S., Yamuna, G., Thanigaivel, S., Vickram, A.S., Priya, A.K., Karthick, A., Karpagam, J., Mohanavel, V., Muhibbullah, M., Investigating the role of image fusion in brain tumor classification models based on machine learning algorithm for personalized medicine. *Comput. Math. Methods Med.*, 2022, 7137524, February 2022.
9. Chan, C.-L., Chen, C.-L., Ting, H.-W., An excellent mortality prediction model based on support vector machine (SVM)-a pilot study, in: *2010 International Symposium on Computer, Communication, Control and Automation (3CA)*, Tainan, 2010.
10. Danilatou, V., Antonakaki, D., Tzagkarakis, C., Kanterakis, A., Katos, V., Kostoulas, T., Automated mortality prediction in critically-ill patients with thrombosis using machine learning, in: *2020 IEEE 20th International Conference on Bioinformatics and Bioengineering (BIBE)*, Cincinnati, 2020.
11. Ontivero-Ortega, M., Lage-Castellanos, A., Valente, G., Goebel, R., Valdes-Sosa, M., Fast Gaussian Naïve Bayes for searchlight classification analysis. *Neuroimage*, 163, 471–479, December 2017.
12. Kefi, Z., Aloui, K., Naceur, M.S., The early prediction of neonates mortality in Intensive Care Unit, in: *2019 International Conference on Advanced Systems and Emergent Technologies (IC_{A}{S}{E}T)*, Hammamet, 2019.
13. Severeyn, E., Altuve, M., Ng, F., Lollett, C., Wong, S., Towards the prediction of mortality in Intensive Care Units patients: A Simple Correspondence Analysis approach, in: *2012 Computing in Cardiology*, 2012.
14. Fan, H. and Zhu, J.-H., A novel frailty index improves risk prediction of waitlist mortality over the model for end-stage liver disease score alone. *Hepatology*, 67, 2059–2059, May 2018.
15. Ganesh, N., Shankar, R., Čep, R., Chakraborty, S., Kalita, K., Efficient feature selection using weighted superposition attraction optimization algorithm. *Appl. Sci. (Basel)*, 13, 3223, March 2023.
16. Kalita, K., Ganesh, N., Jayalakshmi, S., Chohan, J.S., Mallik, S., Qin, H., Multi-Objective artificial bee colony optimized hybrid deep belief network and XGBoost algorithm for heart disease prediction. *Front. Digit. Health*, 5, 1279644, 2023.

17. Premalatha, M., Jayasudha, M., Čep, R., Priyadarshini, J., Kalita, K., Chatterjee, P., A comparative evaluation of nature-inspired algorithms for feature selection problems. *Heliyon*, 10, e23571, January 2024.
18. Yuan, Y., Li, S., Zhang, X., Sun, J., A comparative analysis of SVM, naive Bayes and GBDT for data faults detection in WSNs, in: *2018 IEEE International Conference on Software Quality, Reliability and Security Companion (QRS-C)*, Lisbon, 2018.
19. Yazid, M.H.A., Talib, S., Satria, M.H., Ghazi, A.A., Neural network on mortality prediction for the patient admitted with ADHF (acute decompensated heart failure), in: *2017 4th International Conference on Electrical Engineering, Computer Science and Informatics (EECSI)*, Yogyakarta, 2017.
20. Cunha, V.S., Salgado, C.M., Vieira, S.M., Sousa, J.M.C., Fuzzy modeling to predict short and long-term mortality among patients with Acute Kidney Injury, in: *2016 IEEE International Conference on Fuzzy Systems (FUZZ-IEEE)*, Vancouver, 2016.
21. Lam, K.-M., He, X.-J., Choi, K.-S., Using artificial neural network to predict mortality of radical cystectomy for bladder cancer, in: *2014 International Conference on Smart Computing*, Hong Kong, Hong Kong, 2014.

9

Asthma Prediction Using Vowel Inspiration: A Machine Learning Approach

Sandhya Prasad[1]*, Anik Bhaumik[1], Suvidha Rupesh Kumar[1], Rama Parvathy L.[1], Heshalini Rajagopal[2] and Janani S.[3]

[1]*School of Computer Science and Engineering, Vellore Institute of Technology, Chennai, India*
[2]*Department of Electrical and Electronics Engineering, MILA University, Nilai, Malaysia*
[3]*School of Electronics Engineering, Vellore Institute of Technology, Chennai, India*

Abstract
The most common respiratory disorder that affects millions of individuals yearly is asthma. Traditional technologies used for asthma detection requires patients to breathe in and breathe out, which may place an extra burden on the patients. The developments in the field of machine learning and mobile computing have enabled the research community to provide a simple and easy solution to monitor pulmonary disorders, reducing the additional burden on asthmatic patients. The proposed work is a small step towards the early detection and monitoring of asthma using a mobile device, which can capture the speech signal. This would alleviate the additional effort by asthmatic patients during the diagnosis process and would reduce the time that could have been spent travelling to diagnostic centers. This paper introduces a method for passive respiratory evaluation aimed at detecting pulmonary obstructive diseases by analyzing speech captured from individuals with asthma. The paper explores the various parameters from speech signal, hypothesizing the presence of traces of asthmatic impressions on the utterances.

***Keywords*:** Support vector machine (SVM), machine learning (ML), convolutional neural network (CNN), k-nearest neighbor (KNN), chronic obstructive pulmonary disease (COPD)

**Corresponding author*: sandhya.p@vit.ac.in

Kanak Kalita, Divya Zindani, Narayanan Ganesh and Xiao-Zhi Gao (eds.) Medical Analytics for Clinical and Healthcare Applications, (179–206) © 2025 Scrivener Publishing LLC

9.1 Introduction

In the contemporary world, technology plays a pivotal role in every aspect of human life. Out of all the different industries where technology plays a crucial role, healthcare is indisputably the most important one. This merger enables us to improve and save countless lives around the world. The reach of mobile devices has extensively changed the lives of the people in numerous ways, leading to a standard lifestyle. Taking advantage of the outreach of mobile devices, one can make the early diagnosis of asthma effortless and uncomplicated.

Asthma is a chronic illness that, when left untreated, may lead to sleep-related problems, daytime fatigue, and difficulty in concentrating. Safeguarding against the common asthmatic triggers can reduce the severity of the asthma. The common triggers include allergens, tobacco, pollution, cold air, dust mites, pollen, fumes, nasal polyps, infections like the flu and colds, and strong scents. Avoiding these triggers is not always possible, though. On the other hand, asthma can affect people of all ages, but it is more common found in youngsters, and there is no known remedy for it in the elderly. People contact such infections by talking in public places and being active for a long time. This in turn would impact their social and psychological behavior, as well. Failing to diagnose and treat the patient on time would be life-threatening.

With the growing challenges faced by the healthcare industry, solutions from a technological surge are guiding them to improve the interpretation and performance of medical data. The medical industry's dependence on medical technology cannot be overestimated. The evolution of such great innovations help healthcare professionals to find ways to improve their practice through better diagnostics, surgical procedures, and better patient care. Time-consuming diagnosis and treatments may degrade the standards of the life of patients in various aspects. The web portal for patients and various medical technologies provides numerous options for patients to communicate with the medical and healthcare professionals.

The chronic illness known as asthma results in the swelling and inflammation of the airways. The airways that convey breath from the mouth and nose to the lungs shorten as a result. Breathing difficulties (shortness of breath), coughing, wheezing, and chest tightness or pain are all signs of asthma. There are different causes of asthma symptoms in various people. Allergens are frequent triggers, such as dust or pet dander. Additionally, some people experience asthma symptoms in response to specific diets or physical activity. Asthma may be fatal sometimes. Asthma cannot be cured, but with the right care, episodes can be avoided and your quality of life can be improved.

Severe pulmonary illnesses, particularly asthma and chronic obstructive pulmonary disease (COPD), are among the main causes of morbidity and mortality globally. According to the Global Burden of Disease Study in 2015, "COPD and asthma were rated among the top 20 conditions causing disability globally and were ranked 8th and 23rd as sources of disease burden when evaluated by disability-adjusted life years, respectively" [1].

According to a finding by Parvaiz A. Koul and Raja Dhar in their paper "Economic burden of asthma in India," approximately 358.2 million people had bronchial asthma in 2015, making it the most prevalent chronic respiratory condition [1]. The age-standardized death rate fell by 58.8% in 2015, while the number of deaths from asthma fell to 400,000, a decrease of 26.7% from 1990. In contrast to the age-standardized prevalence, which dropped by 17.7%, the prevalence of asthma increased by 12.6% [1].

Information technology has had a huge impact on our society, particularly in the medical field. Both physicians and patients are appreciating the benefits of emerging medical technologies such as electronic medical records (EMRs), telemedicine services, and mobile technologies such as tablets and smartphones as their use expands.

From the introduction of new technologies for doctors to the utilization in private clinics and hospitals, and to the telecommunications connecting patients and doctors from thousands of kilometers apart, medical technology has progressed. Patients can now use video conferences with doctors to save additional charges and time when they relocate to a new geographic region, or to rapidly share health information with experts and doctors all over the world.

The medical imaging field has made revolutionary progress in the last two decades. New medical imaging technology has provided physicians with powerful, non-invasive techniques for examining body structure, surgery, and pathology. In recent years, many improvements and developments in image capturing technologies, improvements in the final quality of non-inherited images, advances in image processing, and the development of huge mechanical capabilities have significantly reduced this task. Obtaining medical images in 2D, 3D, and higher dimensions has become a routine task in clinical and analytical applications aiding in a faster and more accurate diagnosis by doctors. Imaging technologies include resonant tomography (MRI), magnetic radiography (MEG), 3D radical sound imaging, computed tomography (CT), anti-Leptone emission imaging (PET), and single gauge boson emission, single photon emission computed tomography (SPECT), functional MRI (fMRI), and diffusion-weighted imaging (DWI).

Finally, studies show excessive differences between manual segmentation. This is an effect that appears to increase the risks associated with the reliability between and within observers. Chemical analysis of medical images requires reproducible, accurate, and economical segmentation methods. In medical imaging studies, it is often necessary to segment a large number of images in order to obtain meaningful (that is, statistically significant) results. Therefore, automatic segmentation is attractive. However, the challenge is that the square measure of the image is usually tampered with by many artifacts such as image noise, image intensity non-uniformity or non-uniformity, and the effect on partial volume averaging. The segmentation technique must be ready to produce results that reflect the structure of the structure.

Spirometry is a reliable and well-established medical examination used in hospitals for pulmonary evaluation, while bronchial evaluation, utilizing mobile phones, must be verified and demonstrated to be accurate [2]. Nonetheless, it is crucial to remember that subpar spirometry might result in a "misdiagnosis," misallocating valuable medical resources and raising unnecessary patient concerns. Spirometry's widespread adoption in primary care has long been impeded by a lack of resources and training.

Prior diagnosis of the development of mild to severe symptoms, if diagnosed in time, would help the patient with early treatment and recovery. With advancements in mobile computing technology, more people are interested in using mobile and wearable devices to track pulmonary diseases. When compared to traditional on-site pulmonary tests, using mobile devices has numerous advantages. As a result, the portable feature alleviates the need to reach out to the health center for preliminary pulmonary tests. Furthermore, because mobile devices are already extensively utilized, many individuals will be able to benefit from the innovative breakthroughs eliminating the need for additional infrastructures. Nonetheless, several obstacles must be solved before mobile-based pulmonary evaluation procedures may be used for reliability.

9.2 Literature Survey

According to Michael Schatz *et al.*, patients verified with asthma were given the asthma control test (ACT). During the selection, details on their ethnicity/race, smoking habits, and asthma course were also gathered. The patients were on surveillance for the next 12 months since their visit to the hospital. Both predictive validity and internal consistency reliability were evaluated. There was 0.83 reliability. The ensuing six and 12 months' worth of oral corticosteroid, as well as hospital treatment, were all substantially correlated with ACT scores of 15 or lower and was significantly associated with a higher 12-month risk of obtaining emergency hospital treatment, writing a prescription for corticosteroids, and distributing more than six canisters (OR, 6.8) compared to a score of 20 [15].

As per the findings of Alan Kaplan *et al.* [16], the development and verification of artificial intelligence (AI) systems necessitate a substantial amount of structured data, and the algorithms must function with varying degrees of data quality. Clinicians must comprehend how AI may be used in the setting of diverse diseases like asthma and how the use of AI fits into routine clinical practice, and how patient safety concerns should be handled. Although AI has an obvious function in supporting doctors in the clinical setting, due to its recent arrival, trust in its usage has not yet been thoroughly established. In general, it is expected that in the future, AI will be a major help to physicians in the diagnosis and treatment of respiratory problems, and we will witness the advantages of AI for clinical procedures for both patients and physicians.

Popadina *et al.* [17] state that speech patterns can vary as a result of COVID-19 or asthma and can be identified in a variety of ways. Having monitoring techniques in place is essential for identifying asthmatic voice quality. However, voice monitoring may be the most accurate method for the early detection of lung disease. The authors have analyzed the speech characteristics using AI and mobile cloud computing to create an asthma-focused system, which can be used for COVID-19, as well [17].

According to Kutor *et al.* [18], the vocal tract, being a part of the lung airways, is prone to inflammation, which would influence change in voice in respiratory illnesses like asthma. This has a resemblance to the diagnosis of asthma using spirometry, which assesses a patient's respiratory function and diagnose asthma. The study presented in this paper ascertains whether speech analysis could serve as a substitute for spirometry in the diagnosis of asthma. This research investigates the relationship between the harmonics-to-noise ratio (HNR), which is based on human speech, and the forced-expiratory-volume-to-forced-vital-capacity (FEV1/FVC) ratio obtained using spirometry. One-hundred and fifty individuals with asthma who were visiting the Korle-Bu Teaching Hospital in Ghana provided spirometry data. The software PRAAT was used to evaluate and create speech characteristics from 33 samples. Harmonics-to-noise ratio from the voice signal and spirometry data were found to be correlated. The vowel sound and HNR had the highest association coefficient (42.08%).

In conclusion, the HNR of the vowel sound demonstrated far more potential to be a viable marker in employing speech as a substitute to spirometry in the diagnosis of asthma.

Hoit *et al.* [7], studied the impact of dyspnea during swallowing and speaking. Forgacs *et al.* [8], made a study of asthma due to obstruction from noisy or silent inspiration. Magdin *et al.* [13], used PRAAT software to perform voice analysis and determine the emotion. Amato *et al.* [14], used speech analysis to classify voice samples of Parkinson's patients

According to Iqbal *et al.* [19], they provided a cutting-edge AI continuous monitoring model for COVID-19. Past and present viral illness outbreaks have demonstrated that we lack efficient screening techniques for the entire population, and our efforts to halt pandemics are failing. Furthermore, at this point, house quarantine and social seclusion are simply precautions against the transmission of the COVID-19 infection. Our project's goal is to present a reliable strategy for employing speech-recognition algorithms in a mobile application to analyze cough tones of presumed previously healthy individuals who are experiencing a respiratory illness and actively track the development of their illnesses in real-time.

Batra *et al.* [9] have compared the voices of asthmatic patients and normal humans with records of five vowels (A, E, I, O, U). Subsequently, the same properties are obtained in both asthmatic patients and healthy individuals using PRAAT. Different voice parameters Jitter, NHR, and HNR are used to compare asthmatic patients with healthy individuals. A maximum of two hundred words. Jitter, HNR, NHR, voice, and feature extraction used classification between asthmatic patients and healthy people. They have 24 recordings of patients speaking and 25 recordings of healthy individuals. They were able to tell the difference between healthy and sick voice tones using acoustic analysis of 12 phonations the vowels a, e, i, o, and u by each person. In this paper, they made the classification by repeating the vowels only for five times.

Amrulloh *et al.* [10] proposed an asthma prediction by analyzing cough sounds of both asthmatic patients and normal subjects. They have extracted sound features mel-frequency and Gaussian score. These features allowed them to create an artificial neural network (ANN) classifier. In order to distinguish between asthmatic and healthy sounds, S. Yadav *et al.* [11] analyzed wheeze and sustained vowels using MFCC statistics as features and SVM as the classifier. This experiment indicates that wheezing is a good stimulus with an accuracy of 90.5% while performing the classification.

Infante *et al.* [12] have proposed automated diagnostic tools using a portable stethoscope. They recorded the coughs of 54 patients: seven had COPD, 15 had asthma, 11 had allergy rhinitis, and 17 had both allergies and asthma. The coughing sound was also collected from 33 normal subjects. These patients underwent pulmonary function tests. With the help of logistic regression, which is a machine learning model, they classified cough sounds on whether they were wet or dry.

9.3 Motivation and Background

Spirometry is the existing benchmark for respiratory functions testing. Spirometry involves the process of inhaling to the maximal lung capacity and exhaling rapidly for diagnosis of asthma. Spirometry is rarely used outside hospital premises as conducting the spirometry procedure correctly takes most in-clinic environments and supervision.

Spirometry is still unfortunately hindered by a number of issues, primarily in primary-care settings. These issues include a lack of knowledge and understanding of the significance of evaluating lung function, access issues to spirometric evaluations, and issues with primary care physicians' interpretation of spirometric patterns. Other potential obstacles to setting up pulmonary function testing include: the lack of healthcare facilities close to patients' homes; the challenge of accessing and performing spirometry on patients in long-term care facilities; and the fact that lung function testing is not well-funded in many parts of the world.

Misdiagnosis rates are inevitably high when lung function measurement is underutilized in the diagnostic algorithm for individuals with persistent respiratory symptoms. A misdiagnosis of asthma and COPD can result in inappropriate or needless treatment, frequently including large dosages of inhaled and systemic therapy. Many clinical ramifications result from mistreating patients with suspected chronic obstructive pulmonary disease. These include incorrectly categorizing these patients as having the most severe form of COPD or asthma (since, if given insufficient treatment, they are likely to not respond to it and are therefore labeled as resistant to therapies), a higher risk of corticosteroid-related adverse events, and higher health-related expenses. To avoid the hardship of the patient during diagnosis of asthma using spirometry, which requires continuous exhaling, smartphones could be used for pulmonary monitoring using speech signals.

Speech is characterized by the expressive sounds generated by vocal fold movements. The diaphragm's pressure drives air out through the airways, and the sound is made as air flows through the vocal cords and air passageways. The speech signal provides a wealth of information about the airways and vocal folds as a result of this sound generating mechanism. Much research has been conducted using this as a foundation to investigate the possibility of using speech analysis to estimate the severity of lung disorders, with encouraging findings. However, speech has not been thoroughly investigated in the context of detecting lung illnesses and monitoring pulmonary function [2].

Results from a communications research and development laboratory demonstrated that professional, technical, administrative, and clerical workers spend 50% to 80% of their workweek communicating, with 2/3 of the time used in speaking [3]. Continuous examination of people's lung functions might be conceivable if this common norm could be exploited to have reduced effort and passive respiratory function testing. Our research was inspired by the idea of using speech to diagnose lung illness and assess pulmonary function.

9.4 Proposed Method

The proposed work is motivated by two important factors: one is to bring the asthma diagnosis to every doorstep reaching out to the remote areas and the next is to reduce tiresome diagnostic procedures currently undertaken by the patients. The various aspects of speech that can carry the impression of asthma are analyzed by manually segregating male and female voices.

9.4.1 Vowel Inspiration

Egressive sounds in human speech are those in which the airflow is produced by forcing air out of the nose or mouth. Vowels are the perfect example of egressive sounds. Vowels are sounds made by the air passing through the mouth, which acts as a resonance chamber, with little blockage and

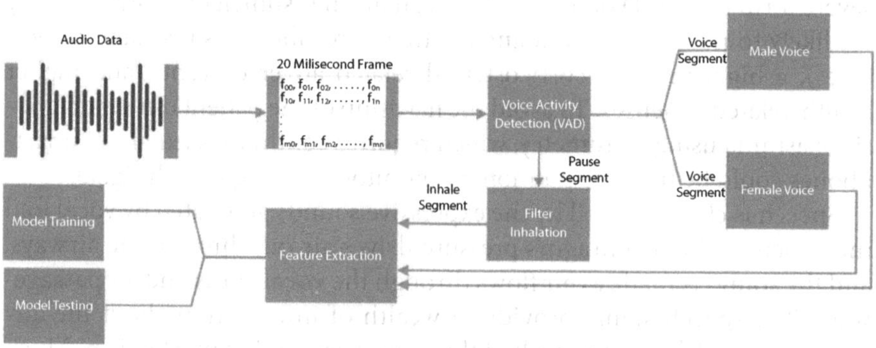

Figure 9.1 Flow diagram of the proposed method.

no audible friction. Examples include the 'I' in "fit" and the 'a' in "pack." Although vowels are typically uttered with vibrating vocal cords, a voiceless or whispered sound can also occur. Vowels are categorized from the perspective of articulatory phonetics based on the placement of the tongue, lips, and, occasionally, whether or not air is exhaled through the nose. The set of sentences chosen for the proposed work are mostly with vowels in it. The proposed methodology is represented in Figure 9.1.

9.4.2 Voice Activity Detection

Pause segments and voiced segments make up speech signals. This is due to the fact that people breathe between each vocal part. Before attempting to extract features of the audio signal, to detect spoken segments and pause segments from spoken audio data, we employed Ramirez *et al.*'s linear time-shifted and time variant systems (LTSD)-based approach. The long-term divergence among noise and possible voice spectra is examined by this algorithm. The vocal activity detection (VAD) algorithm, which uses LTSD-based technique was chosen, since it was straightforward to construct and noise-sensitive [4].

The VAD algorithm employed in this study begins by defining the order, which specifies how many frames should be taken into account, previous and next to the recent frame for computing the long-term spectral divergence. The order had been established to ten in this investigation. The long-term spectral envelope (LTSE) was calculated after establishing the order. The LTSE was calculated from the greatest spectral amplitude from each frame in the order's range. The long-term spectral envelope would be 21 adjacent frames' spectral envelope in our example (10 frames preceding and following the present frame). Then calculated LTSD using the following formula:

$$LTSD_k(l) = 10\log_{10}\left(\frac{1}{NFFT}\sum_{i=0}^{NFFT-1}\frac{LTSE_k^2(i)}{N^2(i)}\right)$$

The frame number is indicated by k in the formula. N - the average noise spectrum magnitude, and NFFT - the number of frequency bands. We supposed the bottom 5% of any audio sample consisted solely of ambient noise or silence, rather than the principal voice signal of the user, in our VAD method. We built the noise profile using these segments based on this assumption.

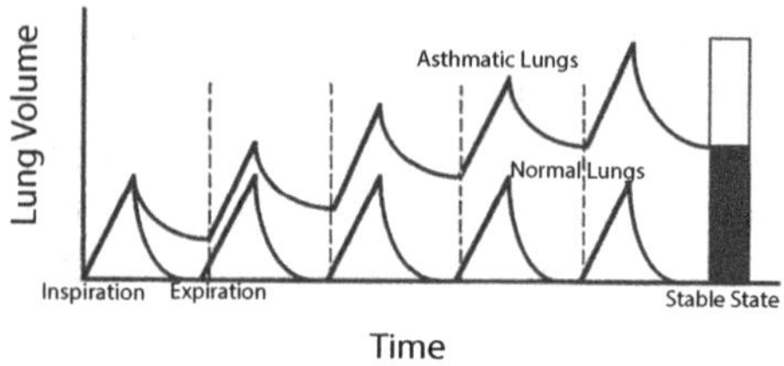

Figure 9.2 Inspiration energy (normal vs asthma).

9.4.3 Inspiration Filtering

Continuous exhalation is part of the vocalization process. There seems to be frequently strong inhalation moments just preceding and following protracted periods of vocalization to compensate for the loss of air during voice activity. We analyzed the pause portions further to isolate the inspiration segments. The sound of inspiration is largely unaffected by vocal fold motions but is influenced more by the rate of inhalation and the airway obstruction [5].

Gentle inhalation produces a very low sound, but quick inhalation produces a considerably louder, high-energy signal. Two steps were taken to identify inspiration frames based on this discovery. The possible inhalation frames were discovered in the first stage by calculating the provided pause section's energy and picking energy frames that fall between the 60th and 95th percentiles. The obtained energy frames are grouped in the second stage using a clustering method i.e. Density-Based Spatial Clustering with Noise (DBSCAN). Along with the voiced frames, the obtained inhalation frames are fed into the next stage which is feature extraction. Inspiration energy for normal and asthma affected individuals is represented in Figure 9.2.

9.4.4 Feature Extraction

We get the pulmonary features such as pause frequency, average phonation time, inspiration sound energy, and vocalization-to-inhalation ratio from the pause segments. We determine a male or female voice from the voice segment. A detailed description is as follows:

9.4.4.1 Pause Frequency

Due to increasing respiratory obstruction, breathing tends to be much harder for patients with pulmonary obstructive diseases [6]. When their respiratory symptoms tend to exacerbate, people often experience greater breathing rates and enhanced breathing difficulty. Based on this logic, we

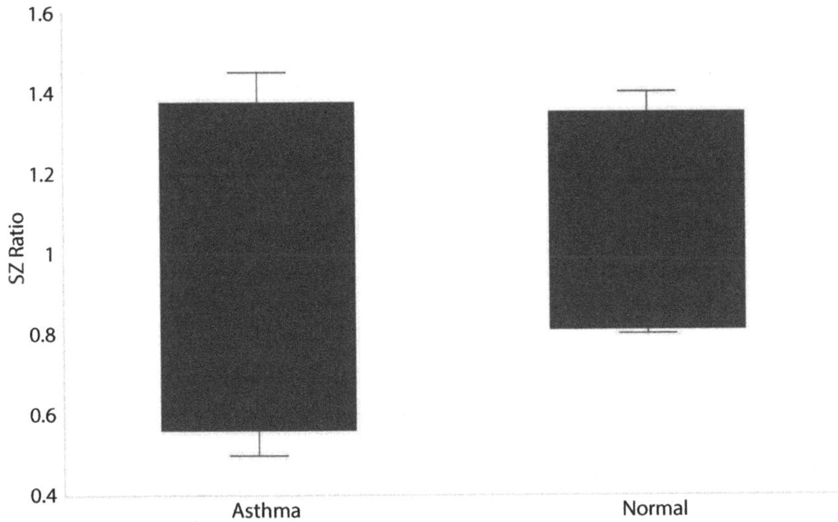

Figure 9.3 Phonation time (normal vs asthma).

computed the division between the sum of the number of pauses and the time (minute) of the audio to capture information on shortness of breath.

9.4.4.2 Average Phonation Time

Vocalization may be more difficult for people with dyspnea (shortness of breath) since it demands greater-than-normal expiratory pressure and a slower expiratory pace. Patients having pulmonary obstructive diseases seem to have changes in their patterns of swallowing and speaking as a result of this elevated vocalization burden [7]. Phonation time taken for normal and asthma individuals is represented in Figure 9.3.

The necessity of taking frequent breaks and inhalation reduces the phonation time. From the vocal segments, we calculated the average of phonation time and used this as an important attribute in our paper.

9.4.4.3 Vocalization-to-Inhalation Ratio

A small amount of air is constantly being released through the airway from the lung when the voice is produced (Figure 9.2). Because of the constant air loss and the lung's pressure, during speaking, rapid breathing is essential to replenish the lungs' air supply (Figure 9.2). We looked at the duration of inhalation in the time of the pause segment in a speech when compared to the vocalization that came before it because lung disease can affect one's ability to speak for lengthy time periods and the amount of air breathed

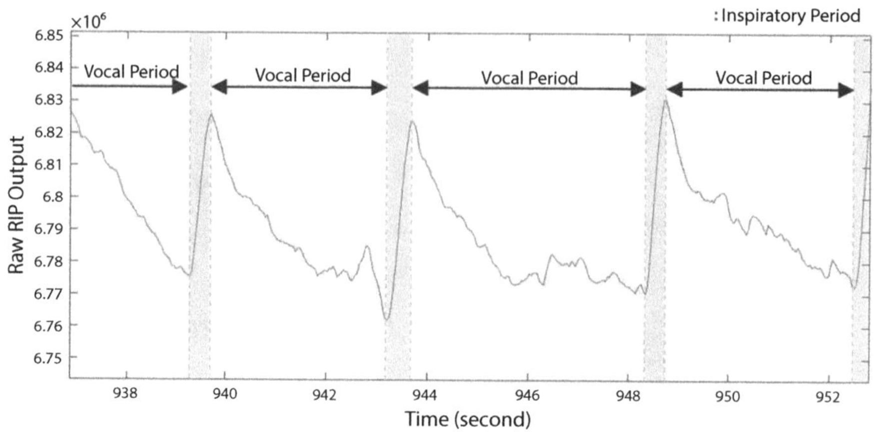

Figure 9.4 Vocal periods in a speech.

at the conclusion of that period. The name given to this characteristic is the vocalization-to-inhalation ratio. We created a basic model for the change in pulmonary capacity while speaking. We hypothesized that the pace upon which the capacity of the lung decreases for the voice segment is consistent in this model and used the lengths of the voice segment and breathing sounds to approximate the relative inhalation duration. Vocal periods in speech is represented in Figure 9.4.

9.4.4.4 Inspiration Sound Energy

Auscultation noises have high harmonic element and are reduced by the chest and lung cavities, which operate in the form of a reduction filter. Previous research utilize the inspiratory sound generally used auscultation noises and their research concentrated upon the smaller frequency ranges (less than 1,000 Hz) [11].

The sound of inspiration gathered from the mouth, on the other hand, still contains high frequency components. The turbulent flows in the airways produce these high frequency components of inspiratory noises [12, 13].

We investigated the range of frequency of 7,800 Hz to 8,000 Hz. The component with the highest frequency of physical fitness and pathological inhalation sounds exhibited significant variations in this band, with pathogenic inspiratory sounds having a greater maximum frequency component.

9.4.5 Classification

The classification was carried out using two methods. A supervised model was proposed for the first model. To make supervised learning work, one must have a labeled collection of data from which the model could figure out how to make right decisions. Here, data labeling begins by clustering to draw conclusions on a particular section of the data set. The practice of detecting and labeling sets of vectors or pixels inside an image based on certain criteria is what we have done here in image classification. We have used a total of seven different types of classification algorithms. The classification algorithms used are as follows:

- Logistic Regression
- Random Forest
- KNN
- Bernoulli/Gaussian Naïve Bayes
- Decision Tree
- SVM
- Logistic Regression with Random Forest

A second model was proposed with a different method where we used PRAAT to get the feature extracted. Here, we are performing voice classification with the help of a dataset that has parameters of both asthma and normal subjects' voices as parameters in a CSV file. Initially, we collected 20 voices of normal subjects and 20 voices of asthmatic patients from a nearby health center in Chennai. Then, with the help of PRAAT Software, we retrieved the parameters of voices of both normal and asthmatic voices. We used 10 Tamil

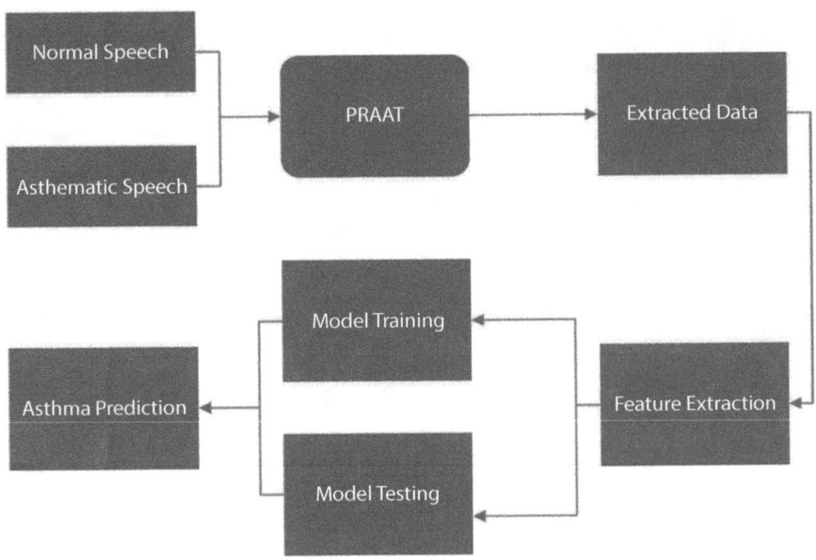

Figure 9.5 System architecture.

words, which have more vowels: (அ|ஆ|இ|ஈ|உ|ஊ|எ|ஏ|ஐ|ஒ|ஓ|ஔ)," amma"","anbarivu"","ullur"","ellumalai"","oonaai"","aavaiyaar"","kaalaimaalai"","ap-pa"","inbarasu"","Aasaiuravu"","erimala","olaichuvadi"","yenendral"and"inbarasu." Proposed system architecture is represented in Figure 9.5.

We have used four machine learning models for classification for the second model. They are as follows:

- KNN
- Logistic regression
- Decision Tree
- Naïve Bayes

```
v3.txt - Notepad
File   Edit   View

   From 0 to 0 seconds (duration: 18.017833 seconds)
Pitch:
   Median pitch: 208.114 Hz
   Mean pitch: 207.033 Hz
   Standard deviation: 31.636 Hz
   Minimum pitch: 73.284 Hz
   Maximum pitch: 449.825 Hz
Pulses:
   Number of pulses: 2952
   Number of periods: 2904
   Mean period: 4.831163E-3 seconds
   Standard deviation of period: 0.798107E-3 seconds
Voicing:
   Fraction of locally unvoiced frames: 17.488%   (944 / 5398)
   Number of voice breaks: 28
   Degree of voice breaks: 16.778%   (3.023074 seconds / 18.017833 seconds)
Jitter:
   Jitter (local): 1.721%
   Jitter (local, absolute): 83.139E-6 seconds
   Jitter (rap): 0.736%
   Jitter (ppq5): 0.787%
   Jitter (ddp): 2.208%
Shimmer:
   Shimmer (local): 6.785%
   Shimmer (local, dB): 0.668 dB
   Shimmer (apq3): 2.508%
   Shimmer (apq5): 3.808%
   Shimmer (apq11): 7.077%
   Shimmer (dda): 7.524%
Harmonicity of the voiced parts only:
   Mean autocorrelation: 0.929959
   Mean noise-to-harmonics ratio: 0.099943
   Mean harmonics-to-noise ratio: 16.510 dB
```

Figure 9.6 PRAAT parameters.

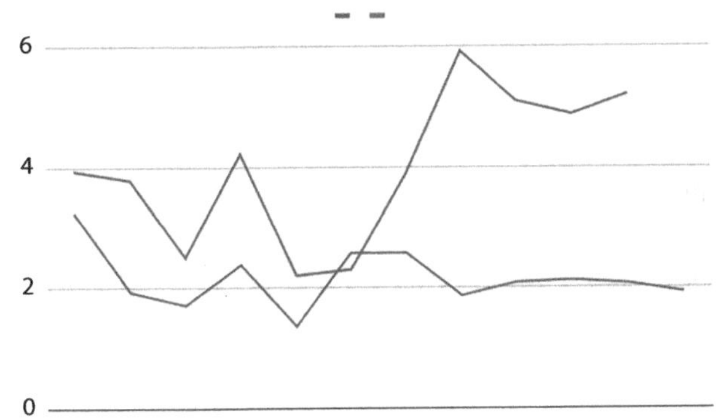

Figure 9.7 The red color represents asthmatic patients and the blue color represents normal voices.

Figure 9.6 represents the PRAAT parameters and Figure 9.7 represents graphical representation of PRAAT parameters.

9.4.6 Praat Parameters

PRAAT is a freeware program for reconstruction, as well as for the analysis of acoustic speech signals. It can also be used to synthesize and analyze the creation of high-quality images.

9.4.6.1 Jitter

This is the average difference between consecutive differences in consecutive periods, divided by the average period. While comparing the voices of a normal and asthmatic person, we found that the jitter value of asthmatic patients is higher than normal subjects. Refer Figure 9.8.

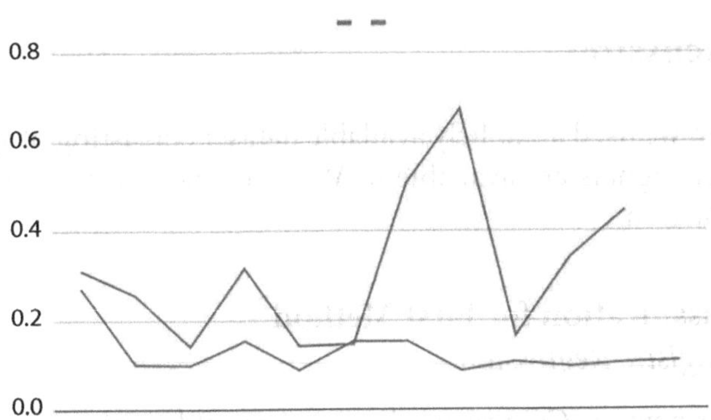

Figure 9.8 The red color represents hoarseness is high for asthmatic patients and the blue color represents normal voices.

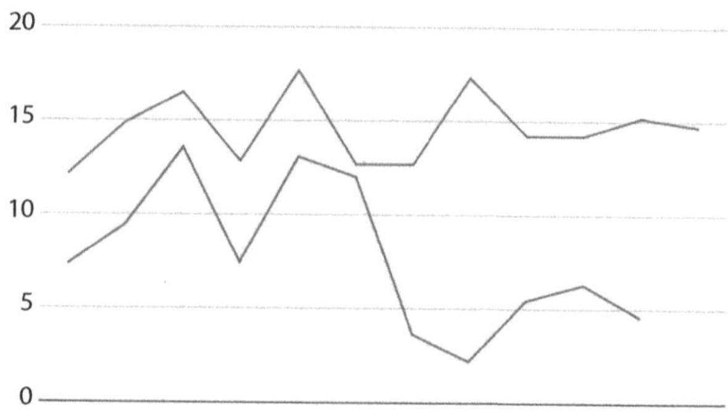

Figure 9.9 The red color represents asthmatic patients, and the blue color represents normal voices.

9.4.6.2 NHR

The noise hit rate (NHR) is used to measure hoarseness. It can be measured with the help of a multidimensional voice program. While comparing the voices of normal and asthmatic people, we found that the NHR value of asthmatic patients is higher than normal subjects. Refer Figure 9.9.

9.4.6.3 HNR

The harmonic-to-noise ratio is used to measure the ratio between non-periodic and periodic components of a speech. It is important in vocal acoustic analysis to diagnose pathologic voices. Comparing the voices of normal and asthmatic people, we found that the HNR value of asthmatic patients is more than normal subjects.

9.5 Discussion

In this paper, we used a publicly available dataset consisting of speech data. These speech signals are available in WAV format, which is used for our feature extraction.

9.5.1 Classification for First Method

9.5.1.1 Logistic Regression

The liblinear newton-CG was used to implement logistic regression. With the very first formulation, the newton-CG only allows L2 regularization.

```
Training Accuracy      : 86.63 %
Model Accuracy Score   : 85.87 %
Confusion Matrix:
 [[62 14]
 [12 96]]
Classification_Report:
              precision    recall  f1-score   support

           0       0.84      0.82      0.83        76
           1       0.87      0.89      0.88       108

    accuracy                           0.86       184
   macro avg       0.86      0.85      0.85       184
weighted avg       0.86      0.86      0.86       184
```

Figure 9.10 Classification report for logistic regression.

The liblinear solution allows both L1 and L2 regularization, with the L2 penalty having a dual formulation. We have used the L2 penalty, which is equal to the square of the magnitude of coefficients and max iteration as 1000 to get the best accuracy. Refer Figure 9.10 for classification report.

9.5.1.2 Naïve Bayes

In this paper, Bernoulli's method, as well as the Gaussian method of Naïve Bayes, has been implemented. BernoulliNB has used the following hyperparameters: alpha (smoothing parameter), Binarize (threshold mapping the sample features into Booleans), fit_prior (makes the decision on the importance of learning class prior probabilities), class prior (It is determined here whether or not to reveal the class's prior probabilities).

In the Gaussian Naïve Bayes model, the following hyperparameters are being used: priors (this parameter determines whether or not prior probability should be considered), var_smoothing (For computation stability, a portion of the maximum variance of all characteristics is contributed to variances). Refer Figure 9.11 for classification report.

```
Training Accuracy      : 84.86 %
Model Accuracy Score   : 85.87 %
Confusion Matrix:
 [[62 14]
 [12 96]]
Classification_Report:
              precision    recall  f1-score   support

           0       0.84      0.82      0.83        76
           1       0.87      0.89      0.88       108

    accuracy                           0.86       184
   macro avg       0.86      0.85      0.85       184
weighted avg       0.86      0.86      0.86       184
```

Figure 9.11 The classification report for Bernoulli's Naïve Bayes.

```
Training Accuracy      : 86.36 %
Model Accuracy Score   : 85.87 %
Confusion Matrix:
 [[62 14]
 [12 96]]
Classification_Report:
              precision    recall  f1-score   support

           0       0.84      0.82      0.83        76
           1       0.87      0.89      0.88       108

    accuracy                           0.86       184
   macro avg       0.86      0.85      0.85       184
weighted avg       0.86      0.86      0.86       184
```

Figure 9.12 The classification report for Gaussian Naïve Bayes.

```
Training Accuracy      : 88.81 %
Model Accuracy Score   : 85.87 %
Confusion Matrix:
 [[62 14]
 [12 96]]
Classification_Report:
              precision    recall  f1-score   support

           0       0.84      0.82      0.83        76
           1       0.87      0.89      0.88       108

    accuracy                           0.86       184
   macro avg       0.86      0.85      0.85       184
weighted avg       0.86      0.86      0.86       184
```

Figure 9.13 The classification report for KNN.

Refer Figures 9.12 and 9.13 for classification report.

9.5.1.3 K-Nearest Neighbor

The tuning parameters used throughout the implementation of the KNN algorithm are n-neighbors, which are in a range of three to 10 in our study. N-neighbors are utilized to vote for the class of target point and 'uniform' weight in which individual k-neighbors have the right to vote equal, from the target point with a distance being irrelevant in making the decision. The calculation for the nearest neighbor is obtained using a brute-force approach.

9.5.1.4 Support Vector Machine

To get the best classification results with SVM, the following tuning parameters were used: The C parameter informs the SVM optimizer about the potential for misclassification in each training example. A kernel is a mathematical function that requires data and converts it into the expected shape; the linear kernel is employed in this SVM procedure since the data is linearly separable. A random state sets the state of the internal random

```
Training Accuracy      : 86.9 %
Model Accuracy Score   : 85.33 %
Confusion Matrix:
 [[60 16]
 [11 97]]
Classification_Report:
              precision    recall  f1-score   support

           0       0.85      0.79      0.82        76
           1       0.86      0.90      0.88       108

    accuracy                           0.85       184
   macro avg       0.85      0.84      0.85       184
weighted avg       0.85      0.85      0.85       184
```

Figure 9.14 The classification report for SVM.

number generator, which is used to determine the test-train data split indices. The regularization strength is inversely proportional to the regularization parameter. It must be positive. The penalty used here is a l2-squared penalty. Refer Figure 9.14 for classification report.

9.5.1.5 Decision Tree

The Decision Tree model has a total of 12 parameters. The only one that matters in this scenario is the criterion parameter, which is the function that determines the split's caliber.

Cost complexity pruning, which helps regulate the size of the tree, was aided by a new decision tree model with additional hyperparameters. By not adjusting the other 11 parameters involved in the model hyperparameter tuning process, the previous model avoided this method. The cost complexity parameter, cc alpha (threshold value), increases the number of pruned nodes in this new model. Only if the overall impurity is improved by a value greater than the existing threshold does the model enable node splitting.

```
Training Accuracy      : 100.0 %
Model Accuracy Score   : 75.54 %
Confusion Matrix:
 [[51 25]
 [20 88]]
Classification_Report:
              precision    recall  f1-score   support

           0       0.72      0.67      0.69        76
           1       0.78      0.81      0.80       108

    accuracy                           0.76       184
   macro avg       0.75      0.74      0.75       184
weighted avg       0.75      0.76      0.75       184
```

Figure 9.15 The classification report for Decision Tree.

```
Training Accuracy      : 100.0 %
Model Accuracy Score   : 85.87 %
Confusion Matrix:
 [[62 14]
 [12 96]]
Classification_Report:
              precision    recall  f1-score   support

           0       0.84      0.82      0.83        76
           1       0.87      0.89      0.88       108

    accuracy                           0.86       184
   macro avg       0.86      0.85      0.85       184
weighted avg       0.86      0.86      0.86       184
```

Figure 9.16 The classification report for Random Forest.

Refer Figures 9.15 and 9.16 for classification report.

9.5.1.6 Random Forest

The n estimators = 1000, min samples split =2, criterion=gini, min samples leaf = 1 were used to initialize the Random Forest Model. The n-estimators are the number of trees intended for creation before voting for the prediction. The criterion is the function that assesses the split's credibility. Gini was utilized in this model to represent Gini Impurity. The minimum number of splits necessary to split the inner node is min_samples_split. The min samples required on the leaf node are specified by min_samples_leaf. This helps to balance the model. The remaining parameters were left at their default values.

9.5.1.7 Logistic Regression with Random Forest

One Hot Encoding was employed to convert categorical data into binary vectors, which were more expressive. With the default n splits and adjustments in other parameters, the Kold Cross-validation technique has been

```
Training Accuracy      : 84.67 %
Model Accuracy Score   : 85.87 %
Confusion Matrix:
 [[62 14]
 [12 96]]
Classification_Report:
              precision    recall  f1-score   support

           0       0.84      0.82      0.83        76
           1       0.87      0.89      0.88       108

    accuracy                           0.86       184
   macro avg       0.86      0.85      0.85       184
weighted avg       0.86      0.86      0.86       184
```

Figure 9.17 The classification report for Logistic Regression with Random Forest.

used to verify the effectiveness in training the machine learning model. To make this model function effectively, the following hyperparameters were employed.

The following parameters are used in Random Forest: n-estimator=1000, which is the number of trees you wish to create before voting for the prediction.

The hyperparameters listed below were tuned for the Stratified K Fold: shuffle - for breaking the data into each batch, the data shuffling was set to True. Random state - because the shuffle was proper; the random numbers were internally initialized. These hyper parameters were used to effectively work the logistic regression section of the model ensemble: solver - because the dataset was tiny, the liblinear solver was employed; additionally, because the optimization problem required multiclass problem solution, the sag solver has been used. C - For more reliable regularization, have used this parameter. n_jobs - this variable indicates the number of workers who are working constantly or concurrently. All CPUs are active because the integer value is set to two. Refer Figure 9.17 for classification report.

9.5.2 Classification for Second Method

9.5.2.1 K-Nearest Neighbor with Classification Report

While performing the KNN classification, we got a macro average of precision, recall, f1-score, support as 0.90, 0.75, and 0.78, respectively. The weighted average of precision, recall, f1-score, and support are 0.87, 0.83, 0.81 and 6, respectively. The accuracy is 83%.

9.5.2.2 Logistic Regression with Discussion on Classification Report

While performing logistic regression classification, we got a macro average of precision, recall, f1-score, and support as 0.90, 0.75, 0.78, and 6, respectively. The weighted, average precision, recall, f1-score, and support are 0.87, 0.83, 0.81, and 6, respectively. The accuracy is 83%.

9.5.2.3 Decision Tree with Discussion on Classification Report

While performing Decision Tree regression classification, we got a macro average of precision, recall, f1-score, and support as 0.62, 0.62, 0.62, and 6, respectively. The weighted, average precision, recall, f1-score, and support are 0.67, 0.67, 0.67, and 6, respectively. The accuracy is 67%.

9.5.2.4 Naïve Bayes with Discussion on Classification Report

While performing Naïve Bayes classification, we got a macro average of precision, recall, f1-score, and support as 0.90, 0.75, 0.78, and 6, respectively. The weighted, average precision, recall, f1-score, and support are 0.87, 0.83, 0.81, and 6, respectively. The accuracy is 83%.

9.6 Results

The observation from Table 9.1 shows that the highest training accuracy was achieved using the Random Forest and Decision Tree models. The most suitable models for diagnosing asthma were Random Forest and KNN. However, CNN can show better results than the other peers if the dataset is larger. Refer Figures 9.18, 9.19, 9.20 and 9.21 for classification report.

As far as model combination and ensemble are considered, the highest accuracy was achieved by Random Forest, Decision Tree, and KNN.

On the other hand, for the second method, we have performed a voice classification of asthmatic and normal subjects with the help of four algorithms KNN, Logistic regression, Decision Tree, and Naïve Bayes. While performing these algorithms, we obtained the result where all the algorithms performed equally good with an accuracy of 83%, except for the

Table 9.1 The accuracy of the model for the first proposed method.

Model	Training accuracy	Model accuracy score	Model F1 score
Support vector machines	86.9	85.33	87.78
Decision Tree	100	75.54	79.64
Random Forest	100	85.87	88.07
Logistic regression	86.63	85.87	88.07
KNN	88.81	85.87	88.07
Bernoulli's Naïve Bayes	86.36	85.87	88.07
Gaussian Naïve Bayes	86.36	85.87	88.07
Logistic regression with Random Forest	84.67	85.87	88.07

```
print(metrics.classification_report(y_test, y_predict_knn, labels=[1, 0]))
              precision    recall  f1-score   support

           1       1.00      0.50      0.67         2
           0       0.80      1.00      0.89         4

    accuracy                           0.83         6
   macro avg       0.90      0.75      0.78         6
weighted avg       0.87      0.83      0.81         6
```

Figure 9.18 The classification report for KNN.

```
[47] print(metrics.classification_report(y_test, y_predict_LR, labels=[1, 0]))
              precision    recall  f1-score   support

           1       1.00      0.50      0.67         2
           0       0.80      1.00      0.89         4

    accuracy                           0.83         6
   macro avg       0.90      0.75      0.78         6
weighted avg       0.87      0.83      0.81         6
```

Figure 9.19 The classification report for logistic regression.

```
print(metrics.classification_report(y_test,y_pred_DR, labels=[1, 0]))
              precision    recall  f1-score   support

           1       0.50      0.50      0.50         2
           0       0.75      0.75      0.75         4

    accuracy                           0.67         6
   macro avg       0.62      0.62      0.62         6
weighted avg       0.67      0.67      0.67         6
```

Figure 9.20 The classification report for Decision Tree.

Decision Tree algorithm with an accuracy of 67%. Refer Figure 9.22 for model comparison and Table 9.2.

Therefore, it is concluded that the KNN, Logistic regression, and Naive Bayes models are the correct fit for the classification of voices of asthmatic patients and normal subjects. The usage of the proposed work is in the medical field, an accuracy above 95% is our prime focus.

```
[ ] print(metrics.classification_report(y_test,y_predict_nb, labels=[1, 0]))

              precision    recall  f1-score   support

           1       1.00      0.50      0.67         2
           0       0.80      1.00      0.89         4

    accuracy                           0.83         6
   macro avg       0.90      0.75      0.78         6
weighted avg       0.87      0.83      0.81         6
```

Figure 9.21 The classification report for Naïve Bayes.

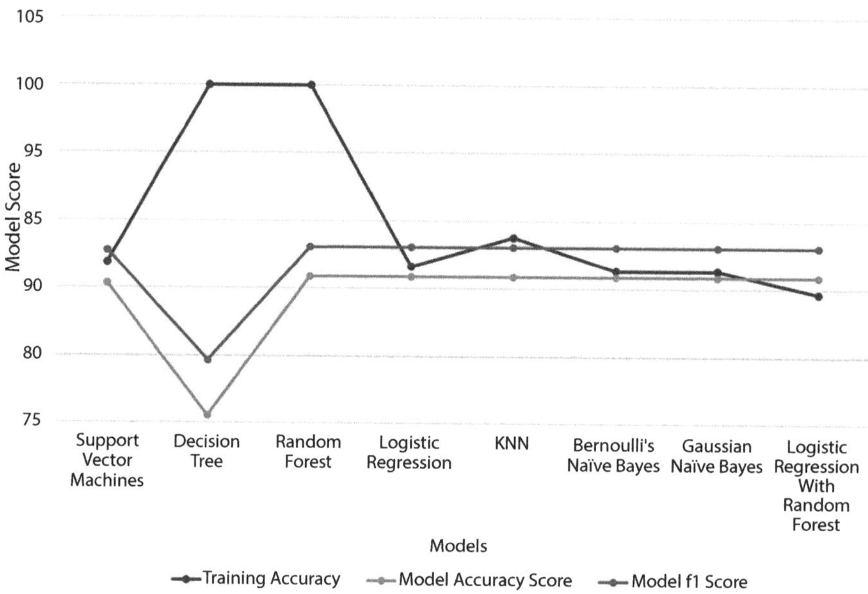

Figure 9.22 A model comparison.

Table 9.2 The accuracy of a model for the second proposed method.

KNN	Logistic regression	Naïve Bayes	Decision tree
83%	83%	83%	67%

9.7 Conclusion

We have proposed the algorithm to detect asthma without conventional active detection. The usage of the mobile devices makes the process of testing and diagnosis very simple and easy so that the patient doesn't have to go to the health care center for the manual test. The algorithm used in the proposed work shows promising results and saves a lot of time and cost to detect asthma. This algorithm can be a milestone of passive detection of pulmonary diseases. Asthma can rarely be cured but if it is detected in the early stages, it can prevent an asthma attack from happening, which can help save a patient's life.

In this paper, we have analyzed only four features, but there are more speech signal characteristics that have yet to be explored for the prediction of asthma. The reliability of these features to predict asthma can be analyzed by plotting receiver performance curves and logistic regression analysis. Currently, the dataset is generated in a controlled environment. The research will be taken forward with respect to enhancing the effectiveness of the asthma diagnosis by improvising on the dataset incorporating real-time capturing of the speech.

References

1. Koul, P.A. and Dhar, R., Economic burden of asthma in India. *Lung India*, 35, 4, 281–283, 2018 Jul-Aug.
2. Chun, K.S., Nathan, V., Vatanparvar, K., Nemati, E., Md. Mahbu-bur v, Blackstock, E., Kuang, J., Towards Passive Assessment of Pulmonary Function from Natural Speech Recorded Using a Mobile Phone. *2020 IEEE International Conference on Pervasive Computing and Communications (PerCom)*, Austin, TX, USA, pp. 1–10, 2020, doi: 10.1109/PerCom45495.2020.9127380.
3. Klemmer, E.T. and Snyder, F.W., Measurement of Time Spent Communicating. *J. Commun.*, 22, 2, 142–158, June 1972, https://doi.org/10.1111/j.1460-2466.1972.tb00141.x.
4. Ramírez, J., Segura, J.C., Benítez, C., de la Torre, A., Rubio, A., Efficient voice activity detection algorithms using long-term speech information. *Speech Commun.*, 42, 3–4, 271–287, 2004, ISSN 0167-6393, https://doi.org/10.1016/j.specom.2003.10.002. (https://www.sciencedirect.com/science/article/pii/S0167639303001201).
5. Forgacs, P., Breath sounds. *Thorax*, 33, 6, 681–3, 1978 Dec, doi: 10.1136/thx.33.6.681. PMID: 746494; PMCID: PMC470962.
6. Wiechern, B., Liberty, K.A., Pattemore, P., Lin, E., Effects of asthma on breathing during reading aloud. *Speech Lang. Hear.*, 21, 1, 30–40, 2018 Jan 2.
7. Hoit, J.D., Lansing, R.W., Dean, K., Yarkosky, M., Lederle, A., Nature and evaluation of dyspnea in speaking and swallowing. *Semin. Speech Lang.*, 32, 1, 5–20, 2011 Feb, doi: 10.1055/s-0031-1271971. Epub 2011 Apr 13. PMID: 21491355.

8. Forgacs, P., Nathoo, A.R., Richardson, H.D., Breath sounds. *Thorax*, 26, 3, 288–95, 1971 May, doi: 10.1136/thx.26.3.288. PMID: 5089494; PMCID: PMC1019084.
9. Batra, K., Bhasin, S., Singh, A., comparison of asthma and healthy persons using voice analysis. *Int. J. Eng. Sci. Res. Technol.(IJESRT)*, https://api.semanticscholar.org/CorpusID:4192019, 2015 issn: 2277-9655.
10. Amrulloh, Y., Abeyratne, U., Swarnkar, V., Triasih, R., Cough Sound Analysis for Pneumonia and Asthma Classification in Pediatric Population. *2015 6th International Conference on Intelligent Systems, Modelling and Simulation*, pp. 127–131, 2015, doi: 10.1109/ISMS.2015.41.
11. Yadav, S., NK, K., Gope, D., Krishnaswamy, U.M., Ghosh, P.K., Comparison of Cough, Wheeze and Sustained Phonations for Automatic Classification Between Healthy Subjects and Asthmatic Patients. *2018 40th Annual International Conference of the IEEE Engineering in Medicine and Biology Society (EMBC)*, pp. 1400–1403, 2018, doi: 10.1109/EMBC.2018.8512496.
12. Infante, C., Chamberlain, D.B., Kodgule, R., Fletcher, R.R., Classification of voluntary coughs applied to the screening of respiratory disease. *2017 39th Annual International Conference of the IEEE Engineering in Medicine and Biology Society (EMBC)*, pp. 1413–1416, 2017, doi: 10.1109/EMBC.2017.8037098.
13. Magdin, M., Sulka, T., Tomanová, J., Vozar, M., Voice Analysis Using PRAAT Software and Classification of User Emotional State. *IJIMAI*, 5, 6, 33–42, 2019, ISSN-e 1989-1660, (Ejemplar dedicado a: Special Issue on Uses Cases of Artificial Intelligence, Digital Marketing and Neuroscience).
14. Amato, F., Borzí, L., Olmo, G., Orozco-Arroyave, J., An algorithm for Parkinson's disease speech classification based on isolated words analysis. *Health Inf. Sci. Syst.*, 9, 32, 2021, 10.1007/s13755-021-00162-8.
15. Schatz, M., Zeiger, R.S., Drane, A., Harden, K., Cibildak, A., Oosterman, J.E., Kosinski, M., Reliability and predictive validity of the Asthma Control Test administered by telephone calls using speech recognition technology. *J. Allergy Clin. Immunol.*, 119, 2, 336–343, 2007, ISSN 0091-6749, https://doi.org/10.1016/j.jaci.2006.08.042.
16. Kaplan, A., Cao, H., Mark FitzGerald, J., Iannotti, N., Yang, E., Kocks, J.WH., Kostikas, K., Price, D., Reddel, H.K., Tsiligianni, I., Vogelmeier, C.F., Pfister, P., Mastoridis, P., Artificial Intelligence/Machine Learning in Respiratory Medicine and Potential Role in Asthma and COPD Diagnosis. *J. Allergy Clin. Immunol. Pract.*, 9, 6, 2255–2261, 2021, ISSN 2213-2198, https://doi.org/10.1016/j.jaip.2021.02.014.
17. Popadina, A.O., Salah, A.-M., Jalal, K., Voice Analysis Framework for Asthma-COVID-19 Early Diagnosis and Prediction: AI-based Mobile Cloud Computing Application. *2021 IEEE Conference of Russian Young Researchers in Electrical and Electronic Engineering (ElConRus)*, St. Petersburg, Moscow, Russia, pp. 1803–1807, 2021, doi: 10.1109/ElConRus51938.2021.9396367.

18. Kutor, J., Balapangu, S., Adofo, J.K., *et al.*, Speech signal analysis as an alternative to spirometry in asthma diagnosis: investigating the linear and polynomial correlation coefficient. *Int. J. Speech Technol.*, 22, 611–620, 2019, https://doi.org/10.1007/s10772-019-09608-7.
19. Iqbal, M.Z. and Faiz, M.F.I., Active Surveillance for COVID-19 Through Artificial Intelligence Using Real-Time Speech-Recognition Mobile Application. *2020 IEEE International Conference on Consumer Electronics*, Taiwan (ICCE-Taiwan), Taoyuan, Taiwan, pp. 1–2, 2020, doi: 10.1109/ICCE-Taiwan49838.2020.9258276.

Part 4

MEDICAL DATA ANALYSIS AND SECURITY

10

Improvement of Accuracy in Prevention of Medical Images from Security Threats Using Novel Lasso Regression in Comparison with K-Means Classifier

K. Raghul[1] and M. Kalaiyarasi[2]*

[1]Department of Information Technology, Saveetha School of Engineering, Saveetha Institute of Medical and Technical Sciences, Saveetha University, Chennai, India

[2]Department of Computational Intelligence, Saveetha School of Engineering, Saveetha Institute of Medical and Technical Sciences, Saveetha University, Chennai, India

Abstract

This study focuses on enhancing the security of medical images by analyzing the effectiveness of two machine learning algorithms: novel lasso regression and k-means classifier. The primary objective is to compare their performance in detecting and preventing security threats in medical image datasets. A total of 20 samples were used, divided into two groups: Group 1 comprised of novel lasso regression (N=10), and Group 2 consisted of k-means classifier (N=10). The statistical power of the study, measured by the G*Power value, was set at 0.95 to ensure reliable results. The analysis revealed that the novel lasso regression model achieved an accuracy of 92.64%, significantly outperforming the k-means classifier, which recorded an accuracy of 88.47%. The statistical significance of these results was confirmed through an independent t-test, yielding a significance value of 0.037 ($p<0.05$), indicating that the difference in accuracy between the two models is statistically significant. This demonstrates that the novel lasso regression method is more effective in enhancing the security of medical images than the k-means classifier. The novel lasso regression algorithm offers a more robust and accurate solution for medical image security, making it a valuable tool for

**Corresponding author*: kalaiyarasim.sse@saveetha.com

Kanak Kalita, Divya Zindani, Narayanan Ganesh and Xiao-Zhi Gao (eds.) Medical Analytics for Clinical and Healthcare Applications, (209–224) © 2025 Scrivener Publishing LLC

protecting sensitive patient information from potential data breaches and security threats.

Keywords: Medical images, data theft detection, k-means classifier, novel lasso regression, machine learning, security threats

10.1 Introduction

The healthcare industry has long relied on traditional methods of data storage, particularly in the form of paper records, which are stored in secure locations for future reference [1]. However, as technological advancements have transformed various sectors, the healthcare industry has gradually adopted electronic health (e-health) systems, which serve as an advanced technique for storing and managing patient information. E-health systems involve the use of cloud-based storage to retain essential details about patients while ensuring their data is protected from threats like data theft and unauthorized access. With the widespread adoption of cloud storage, healthcare organizations can now maintain patient records more efficiently and access them instantly, improving the overall quality of care and patient management [2].

While e-health systems offer convenience and accessibility, they also raise concerns about data security. The increasing digitization of patient records has introduced vulnerabilities that can lead to breaches, unauthorized access, and theft of sensitive medical information. Therefore, data security has become a top priority in the healthcare industry. To address these concerns, various security mechanisms have been introduced, including password protection systems that restrict access to only the patient and the healthcare team. These systems allow authorized personnel to view and update patient information as necessary during medical consultations, ensuring that the data remains current and accurate [3, 4].

However, the ever-evolving nature of cyber threats has rendered traditional security measures inadequate in some cases. Intrusions and data theft can severely impact the integrity of healthcare systems, leading to complications such as misdiagnosis, identity theft, and even loss of life in extreme situations [5]. In light of these challenges, the healthcare industry has turned to more sophisticated approaches, such as machine learning (ML), to improve data security. By leveraging ML techniques, healthcare organizations can better detect and prevent security breaches, thereby enhancing the overall security of patient information.

This study aims to address the limitations of existing security frameworks in healthcare by proposing two ML models: logistic regression (LR) and k-means clustering algorithms. These models are designed to optimize data security by detecting anomalies and preventing data theft. The use of ML algorithms in healthcare is not limited to securing patient information; they have also been applied to various other domains, including medical image security, malicious URL detection, and face recognition [6, 7]. By integrating ML-based security mechanisms, healthcare organizations can proactively detect threats and minimize the risks associated with data breaches.

The shift from paper-based records to e-health systems has been gradual but transformative. Between 2001 and 2022, significant research efforts were made to assess the effectiveness of cloud-based healthcare systems, resulting in the publication of 1,650 articles. These articles, sourced from various reputable databases, include 350 from IEEE Xplore, 200 from ResearchGate, 300 from Elsevier, and 800 from Springer. This body of research highlights the importance of cloud infrastructure in healthcare and underscores the challenges associated with ensuring its security [8]. Cloud infrastructure, by its very nature, introduces certain vulnerabilities, such as insecure communication channels, virtual network weaknesses, and restricted user permissions, all of which can expose patient data to potential attackers.

Various studies have proposed different ML-based techniques to mitigate these security challenges. For instance, authors proposed an ML classifier technique aimed at detecting security threats in healthcare systems [9]. This approach not only identifies the threats but also alerts the system administrator to take prompt action, thereby reducing the time window in which a breach can occur. Machine learning algorithms like LR and k-means clustering can also be used to classify and detect different types of attacks, allowing healthcare organizations to proactively address potential security issues.

The implementation of ML classifiers for intrusion detection has revolutionized the way healthcare organizations deal with security threats. In this study, two ML classifiers, namely LR and k-means clustering, are employed to detect and prevent data theft. Logistic regression, a supervised learning algorithm, is particularly effective in binary classification problems where the outcome is dichotomous—such as determining whether an intrusion has occurred or not. By analyzing historical data, the LR algorithm can predict the likelihood of future security breaches with high accuracy.

On the other hand, K-means clustering, an unsupervised learning algorithm, groups data into clusters based on their similarities. In the context of healthcare data security, k-means can be used to group similar types of security threats, enabling healthcare organizations to identify patterns and commonalities among the attacks they face. This clustering technique is particularly useful for anomaly detection, as it can flag any data points that do not fit within the established clusters, signaling a potential breach [10–12].

The backpropagation algorithm, which is commonly used in deep learning models, plays a crucial role in the optimization of ML models. In the context of data security, backpropagation helps refine the predictive accuracy of the ML classifiers by iteratively adjusting the weights in the network to minimize errors. By computing the gradient of the loss function with respect to each weight, the backpropagation algorithm updates the weights in a backward manner, starting from the output layer and moving towards the input layer. This process ensures that the model learns from its mistakes and continuously improves its ability to detect security threats.

The healthcare industry faces a variety of security threats, including external and internal denial-of-service (DoS) attacks. External DoS attacks involve external entities flooding the system with illegitimate requests, overwhelming the network, and preventing legitimate users from accessing critical resources. Internal DoS attacks, on the other hand, originate from within the network, making them more difficult to detect. To combat these threats, researchers have proposed protocols that utilize a combination of registration, identification, and authentication mechanisms [13]. These protocols ensure that only authorized users can access the healthcare system, thereby reducing the likelihood of internal DoS attacks.

In addition to DoS attacks, malware detection is another critical area of concern in healthcare data security. Malware, or malicious software, can infiltrate healthcare systems and compromise patient data. To address this issue, researchers have developed ML-based anomaly intrusion detection systems, such as support vector machines (SVM), to detect and prevent malware attacks [14]. These systems analyze both network-level and system-level features of cloud nodes to identify suspicious activity and flag potential threats. By using ML algorithms, healthcare organizations can automate the process of detecting malware, thereby improving the overall security of their systems.

Despite the numerous advancements in healthcare data security, there remains a significant research gap in the precision and accuracy of existing models. Many of the current ML-based security systems suffer from low precision, resulting in false positives and negatives that can hinder their effectiveness [7]. Therefore, this study seeks to address these limitations by developing two new models based on LR and k-means clustering.

These models are designed to enhance the accuracy of security threat detection and improve the overall security of medical images. By leveraging these advanced ML techniques, healthcare organizations can better protect sensitive patient information and prevent security breaches [15, 16].

The healthcare industry's transition to e-health systems has introduced new security challenges that must be addressed to ensure the safety of patient information. Machine learning techniques, such as LR and k-means clustering, offer promising solutions to these challenges by improving the accuracy and efficiency of security threat detection. This study aims to contribute to the ongoing efforts to secure healthcare data by developing and testing new ML models that can detect and prevent data theft with high precision.

10.2 Materials and Methods

This research was conducted in the Deep Learning Lab, Department of Information Technology, Saveetha School of Engineering, Saveetha Institute of Medical and Technical Sciences. The study compares the performance of two ML algorithms—novel lasso regression (NLR) and k-means classifiers—using a specific dataset. To ensure a comprehensive and accurate evaluation, two distinct groups of data were selected, with 10 sets of samples (N=10) assigned to each group. The primary objective was to assess the efficacy of these algorithms in predicting values and classifying data. Statistical analysis was performed using IBM SPSS software to compare the results of both ML controllers [1, 2, 17, 18].

The choice of sample size is a critical aspect of this research. The sample size was determined using IBM SPSS software version 26, with a power setting parameter of $\alpha=0.292$ and power=0.95, which ensured adequate statistical power for detecting differences between the two algorithms. This process resulted in a sample size of 10 for each group, providing a reliable basis for comparison. The accuracy of the models was evaluated using an independent t-test analysis, a widely accepted statistical method for comparing means between two independent groups.

The dataset utilized in this study was sourced from the publicly available Kaggle repository (https://www.kaggle.com/datasets/kmader/siim-medical-images). This dataset contains CT medical images and was provided in CSV format. It consists of 295 rows and 50 columns, including various attributes such as ID, date, group, and type. The comprehensive nature of this dataset makes it suitable for developing ML models, as it allows for the analysis of multiple variables and their impact on the final outcome.

The inclusion of a larger dataset often leads to more accurate predictions and a robust evaluation of the algorithms used.

10.2.1 Dataset Variables

In this research, the independent variables include records, entity, year, organization type, and methods, while the dependent variable is accuracy. The dataset was pre-processed to remove any inconsistencies or missing values, ensuring that the ML models could be trained effectively. The analysis was then conducted using both independent and dependent variables to assess the impact of these factors on the accuracy of the models. This approach not only improves the precision of the models but also helps identify key variables that significantly affect the classification and prediction processes.

10.2.2 Machine Learning Algorithms: Novel Lasso Regression and K-Means Classifiers

Two distinct ML algorithms were implemented in this study: NLR and k-means classifiers. Both algorithms have their unique strengths and applications, making them suitable for addressing different aspects of the problem at hand.

10.2.2.1 Novel Lasso Regression

Lasso regression is a linear regression technique that incorporates regularization, making it particularly useful for models with many predictor variables. Regularization involves adding a penalty term to the regression model to prevent overfitting, which occurs when the model is too complex and captures noise rather than the underlying pattern. In this context, lasso regression was used to shrink data values towards the central mean, thereby eliminating irrelevant parameters and focusing on the most important features. This method enhances both the accuracy of predictions and the interpretability of the resulting regression models [19].

The ability of lasso regression to perform variable selection makes it particularly well-suited for high-dimensional datasets, such as the CT medical images used in this study. By selecting only the most relevant variables, the model can reduce complexity while maintaining high predictive accuracy. This feature is especially beneficial in medical image classification, where numerous variables may be present, but only a subset contributes significantly to the final outcome. The steps in the lasso regression algorithm are:

1. Data loading: the first step involves loading the selected data into the network.
2. Dataset modification: pre-processing the dataset to ensure that it is in the correct format for further analysis.
3. Feature selection: identifying and extracting the most important features needed to improve the classification process.
4. Model training: training the model using the selected features to optimize its predictive performance.
5. Classification completion: finalizing the classification process and obtaining the predicted values.

The flexibility and efficiency of lasso regression make it a powerful tool for predicting outcomes in medical data, where precision is critical for decision-making.

10.2.2.2 K-Means Classifier

K-means is an unsupervised learning algorithm widely used in image processing, medical image classification, and data clustering. In this study, the K-means classifier was used to group the dataset into distinct clusters based on similarity. The number of clusters was determined by the user, and the algorithm selected arbitrary cluster centers from the dataset. The algorithm iteratively refines the clusters by minimizing the within-cluster sum of squares, converging to a local minimum due to its greedy nature [20].

In the context of medical image classification, k-means clustering offers several advantages. By grouping similar images together, the algorithm can identify patterns and trends in the data that may not be immediately apparent. This ability to detect underlying structures in the data is particularly useful when working with large datasets, such as those used in this study. The steps in the k-means classifier algorithm are:

1. Data collection: gathering the required volume of the dataset for classification.
2. Pre-processing: cleaning the data by removing noise or empty spaces that could affect the accuracy of the model.
3. Cluster initialization: initializing the cluster centers and assigning data points to the nearest cluster.
4. Model training: training the model to refine the clusters and improve classification accuracy.

5. Classification completion: completing the classification process and determining the final clusters.

The k-means classifier is particularly effective in identifying patterns in medical images, where subtle differences between clusters can have significant implications for diagnosis and treatment.

10.2.3 Statistical Analysis

To evaluate the performance of the ML models, a comprehensive statistical analysis was conducted using Python and IBM SPSS software (version 26). The analysis focused on determining the accuracy of both the NLR and k-means classifier models in preventing data theft and improving the security of medical images. Accuracy was considered the dependent variable, while independent variables such as records, entity, year, organization type, and methods were used to assess the models' performance.

An independent t-test analysis was carried out to compare the accuracy of the two models. The t-test is a statistical method used to determine whether there is a significant difference between the means of two independent groups. In this study, the t-test was used to evaluate whether the accuracy of the NLR model differed significantly from that of the k-means classifier. This approach allowed for a robust comparison of the two models and provided insights into their relative strengths and weaknesses [21].

The Python programming language was used to implement the ML models and execute statistical analysis. The hardware setup for this research included a Windows 11 operating system, an Intel Core i5 processor, and 16 GB of RAM. The computational power of this setup ensured that the models could be trained and tested efficiently, even with a large dataset.

10.3 Result

In this research, the detection and prevention of medical image theft were addressed using two ML classifiers: NLR and k-means classifiers. Both algorithms were implemented, and their performance was evaluated based on their accuracy in detecting and preventing security threats. The results of the analysis, carried out using a Python compiler, demonstrated that the NLR classifier outperformed the k-means classifier, achieving an accuracy of 92.64%, while the k-means classifier attained an accuracy of 88.47%. These results indicate that the proposed NLR classifier significantly improves the detection of security threats in medical images, enhancing overall system performance.

The results of the Python compiler were used to generate insights into the performance of the classifiers at 10 different instants, as shown in Figure 10.1. The accuracy gains of both NLR and k-means classifiers were recorded, and these data were subsequently analyzed using SPSS statistical software. The analysis involved conducting a comparative mean test to evaluate the statistical significance of the observed differences between the two classifiers. The comparative mean test was categorized into two types: group statistical analysis and independent sample test.

In Table 10.1, the mean accuracy and standard deviation for the NLR and k-means classifiers are presented. The mean accuracy of the NLR algorithm was 92.64%, with a standard deviation of 3.491, whereas the k-means classifier had a mean accuracy of 88.47%, with a standard deviation of 4.722.

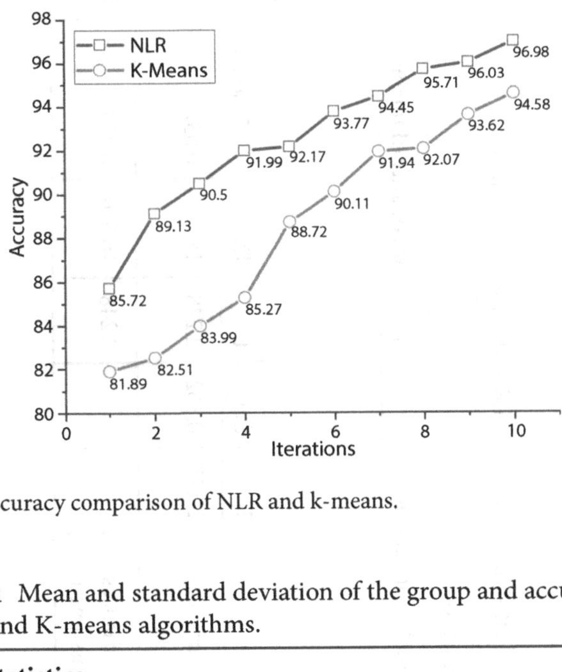

Figure 10.1 Accuracy comparison of NLR and k-means.

Table 10.1 Mean and standard deviation of the group and accuracy of the NLR and K-means algorithms.

Group statistics					
	Group name	**N**	**Mean**	**Standard deviation**	**Standard error mean**
Accuracy	NLR	10	92.64	3.491	1.104
	K-means	10	88.47	4.722	1.493

Table 10.2 Independent sample t-test of NLR and k-means classifiers.

Independent sample test										
Levene's test for equality of variances				**T-test for equality of means**						
									95% confidence interval of the difference	
		F	**Sig.**	**t**	**Df**	**Sig. (2-tailed)**	**Mean difference**	**Std. error differences**	**Lower**	**Upper**
Accuracy	Equal variances assumed	2.125	0.162	2.248	18	0.037	4.175	1.857	0.272	8.077
	Equal variances not assumed			2.248	16.576	0.039	4.175	1.857	0.248	8.101

The lower standard error of the NLR classifier, recorded at 1.104, further indicates its superior performance compared to the k-means classifier, which had a higher standard error of 1.493. This statistical evidence highlights the robustness of the NLR classifier in maintaining consistent accuracy across different runs.

Table 10.2 presents the assumption and non-assumption of equal variance in accuracy for the selected classifiers. For this analysis, the p-value was maintained at $p<0.05$, indicating the threshold for statistical significance. The analysis showed that the equal variance assumption was valid, with Levene's test yielding a significance value of 0.162, which is greater than 0.05. This result suggests that the variances between the NLR and k-means classifiers were not significantly different, further justifying the comparison of their mean accuracies.

Figure 10.2 provides a detailed comparison of the accuracy results for both the NLR and k-means classifiers. The comparison highlights the notable advantage of the NLR classifier in terms of accuracy, confirming its effectiveness in enhancing the security of medical images. In Figure 10.2, the mean accuracy values for the NLR and k-means classifiers are visually represented. The X-axis denotes the two classifiers—NLR and k-means—while the Y-axis represents the accuracy values. As illustrated in the graph, the NLR classifier consistently outperforms the k-means classifier, achieving higher mean accuracy across all 10 sample runs. The mean accuracy of the NLR classifier was 92.64%, compared to 88.47% for the k-means classifier.

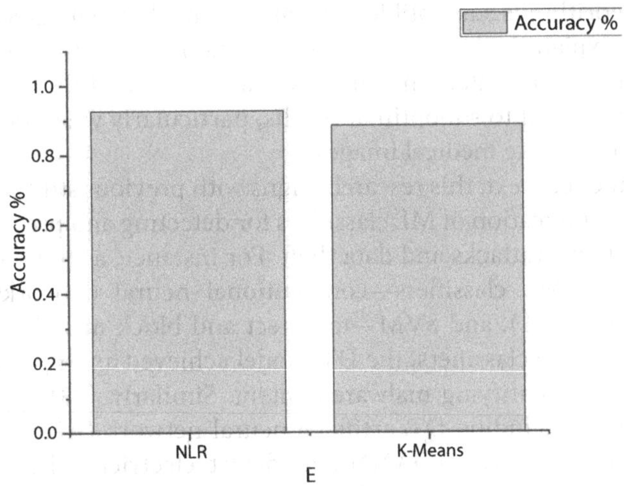

Figure 10.2 Mean accuracy comparison NLR and k-means.

10.4 Discussion

The SPSS analysis, performed with the results obtained from Group 1 (LR classifier) and Group 2 (k-means classifier), revealed a statistically significant difference between the two algorithms. The mean accuracy of the NLR classifier was 92.64%, while the k-means classifier achieved an accuracy of 88.47%. The significance value (p-value) of the analysis was 0.037 (two-tailed, $p<0.05$), indicating that the observed difference in accuracy is statistically significant. This result supports the conclusion that the NLR classifier outperforms the k-means classifier in the context of medical image theft prevention.

The statistical analysis further revealed that the lower standard error of the LR classifier (1.104) compared to the k-means classifier (1.493) suggests greater stability and consistency in the LR model's performance. This consistency is crucial when developing ML models for critical applications, such as medical image security, where the stakes are high, and the margin for error is minimal.

The superior performance of the NLR classifier can be attributed to its ability to perform both variable selection and regularization, which helps eliminate irrelevant parameters and focus on the most significant features. This process not only enhances the accuracy of the model but also improves its interpretability, making it a more reliable choice for medical image classification tasks.

In contrast, while the k-means classifier is widely used for clustering and classification tasks, its accuracy in this study was comparatively lower. The k-means algorithm is susceptible to local minima due to its greedy nature, which may explain its lower accuracy in certain instances. Moreover, the selection of cluster centers in k-means is arbitrary, and this randomness can sometimes lead to suboptimal results, particularly when dealing with complex datasets like medical images.

In a broader context, this research aligns with previous studies that have explored the application of ML classifiers for detecting and preventing various types of cyberattacks and data theft. For instance, a study introduced three different ML classifiers—convolutional neural networks (CNN), Decision Trees (DT), and SVM—to detect and block malicious websites [22]. Among these classifiers, the DT model achieved an impressive accuracy of 99% in identifying malware content. Similarly, [23] applied multiple classifiers, including DT, artificial neural network (ANN), and deep artificial neural network (DANN), to detect electricity theft, with the DANN classifier achieving a prediction accuracy of 93%. These examples demonstrate the potential of ML classifiers in enhancing security across various domains.

In another study [24], electricity theft detection was performed using a public dataset, and several classifiers, including LR, SVM, DT, and Random Forest (RF), were tested. The RF classifier achieved the highest detection rates of 79.45% and 80.5% when feature extraction techniques were applied, further illustrating the versatility and effectiveness of ML classifiers in security-related applications.

Despite these advancements, there remains a research gap in the application of ML models to predict security threats in medical images, particularly when working with larger datasets. This study addresses this gap by evaluating the performance of the NLR classifier and comparing it with the k-means classifier. The results demonstrate that LR is a more accurate and reliable model for medical image theft detection. However, future research could explore the potential of other ML algorithms, such as RF, SVM, and deep neural networks, to further enhance classification accuracy.

The findings of this study suggest that the NLR classifier can be effectively employed in real-world applications to improve the security of medical images. Moreover, the methodology used in this research can be applied to other datasets and domains, enabling the broader adoption of ML techniques for security purposes. Future studies could expand on this work by comparing additional classifiers and exploring the integration of hybrid models to achieve even higher detection rates and accuracy.

The results of this study highlight the superiority of the NLR classifier over the k-means classifier in terms of accuracy and consistency. The statistical analysis confirmed the significance of this difference, providing a solid foundation for the continued use of ML classifiers in preventing medical image theft. By improving the accuracy of these models, healthcare organizations can better protect sensitive patient information and mitigate the risks associated with data theft.

10.5 Conclusion

Based on the experimental results obtained in this study, the NLR algorithm has demonstrated superior performance in preventing medical image theft compared to the k-means classifier. The experimental analysis, supported by statistical evidence, clearly indicates that the NLR classifier is more effective in securing medical images from potential security threats. The results of the independent t-test analysis further substantiate this claim, with a significance value of 0.037 ($p<0.05$), confirming that the difference in accuracy between the two models is statistically significant.

The NLR classifier achieved an accuracy of 92.64%, outperforming the k-means classifier, which recorded an accuracy of 88.47%. This substantial difference highlights the robustness and reliability of NLR in identifying and mitigating security threats, particularly in the domain of medical image protection. The ability of NLR to perform both variable selection and regularization allows it to focus on the most relevant features, which contributes to its improved predictive performance.

In contrast, while the k-means classifier is effective for clustering tasks, its limitations in terms of accuracy and susceptibility to local minima make it less suitable for high-stakes applications such as medical image security. The results of this study reinforce the notion that more advanced ML algorithms, like NLR, are better equipped to handle complex datasets and deliver precise, consistent results.

The NLR classifier presents a promising solution for enhancing the security of medical images and preventing data theft. Future research can build upon these findings by exploring additional ML algorithms and hybrid models to further improve accuracy and security in this critical field. By continuing to refine these models, healthcare organizations can ensure the safety and confidentiality of patient information in an increasingly digitized and interconnected world.

References

1. Hussain Seh, A., Al-Amri, J.F., Subahi, A.F., Agrawal, A., Kumar, R., Ahmad Khan, R., Machine learning based framework for maintaining privacy of healthcare data. *Intell. Autom. Soft Comput.*, 29, 697–712, 2021.
2. Nanmaran, R., Srimathi, S., Yamuna, G., Thanigaivel, S., Vickram, A.S., Priya, A.K., Karthick, A., Karpagam, J., Mohanavel, V., Muhibbullah, M., Investigating the role of image fusion in brain tumor classification models based on machine learning algorithm for personalized medicine. *Comput. Math. Methods Med.*, 2022, 7137524, February 2022.
3. Nanmaran, R., Nagarajan, S., Sindhuja, R., Charan, G.V.S., Pokala, V.S.K., Srimathi, S., Gulothungan, G., Vickram, A.S., Thanigaivel, S., Wavelet transform based multiple image watermarking technique. *IOP Conf. Ser. Mater. Sci. Eng.*, 993, 012167, December 2020.
4. Shaik, K., Ramesh, J.V.N., Mahdal, M., Rahman, M.Z.U., Khasim, S., Kalita, K., Big data analytics framework using squirrel search optimized Gradient Boosted Decision Tree for heart disease diagnosis. *Appl. Sci. (Basel)*, 13, 5236, April 2023.

5. Sapra, V., Hasan, M.K., Ghazal, T.M., Bhadrdwaj, A., Bharany, S., Ahmad, M., Rehman, A.U., Mohamed, T., Privacy-based framework for Cyber Resilience of Healthcare based data for use with Machine Learning algorithms, in: *2022 International Conference on Cyber Resilience (ICCR)*, Dubai, United Arab Emirates, 2022.
6. Hamisu, A.K. and Jasleen, K., A framework for selection of machine learning algorithms based on performance metrices and Akaike information criteria in healthcare, telecommunication, and marketing sector, in: *Machine Learning and Deep Learning in Medical Data Analytics and Healthcare Applications*, pp. 113–130, CRC Press, Boca Raton, 2022.
7. Sayamber, A.B. and Dixit, A.M., Malicious URL detection and identification. *Int. J. of Comput. Applications*, 99, 17, 17–23, 2014.
8. Ali, M., Khan, S.U., Vasilakos, A.V., Security in cloud computing: Opportunities and challenges. *Inf. Sci. (NY)*, 305, 357–383, June 2015.
9. Khorshed, M.T., Ali, A.B.M.S., Wasimi, S.A., A survey on gaps, threat remediation challenges and some thoughts for proactive attack detection in cloud computing. *Future Gener. Comput. Syst.*, 28, 833–851, June 2012.
10. Chonka, A., Xiang, Y., Zhou, W., Bonti, A., Cloud security defence to protect cloud computing against HTTP-DoS and XML-DoS attacks. *J. Netw. Comput. Appl.*, 34, 1097–1107, July 2011.
11. Murugesan, K., Balasubramani, P., Murugan, P.R., A quantitative assessment of speckle noise reduction in SAR images using TLFFBP neural network. *Arab. J. Geosci.*, 13, 1, 35, January 2020.
12. Singh, D.M., Harbi, N., Zahidur Rahman, M., Combining naive Bayes and decision tree for adaptive intrusion detection. *Int. J. Netw. Secur. Appl.*, 2, 12–25, April 2010.
13. Darwish, M., Ouda, A., Capretz, L.F., A cloud-based secure authentication (CSA) protocol suite for defense against Denial of Service (DoS) attacks. *J. Inf. Secur. Appl.*, 20, 90–98, February 2015.
14. Ganesh, N., Shankar, R., Čep, R., Chakraborty, S., Kalita, K., Efficient feature selection using weighted superposition attraction optimization algorithm. *Appl. Sci. (Basel)*, 13, 3223, March 2023.
15. Priyadarshini, J., Premalatha, M., Čep, R., Jayasudha, M., Kalita, K., Analyzing physics-inspired metaheuristic algorithms in feature selection with K-nearest-neighbor. *Appl. Sci. (Basel)*, 13, 906, January 2023.
16. Kalita, K., Ganesh, N., Jayalakshmi, S., Chohan, J.S., Mallik, S., Qin, H., Multi-Objective artificial bee colony optimized hybrid deep belief network and XGBoost algorithm for heart disease prediction. *Front. Digit. Health*, 5, 1279644, 2023.
17. Premalatha, M., Jayasudha, M., Čep, R., Priyadarshini, J., Kalita, K., Chatterjee, P., A comparative evaluation of nature-inspired algorithms for feature selection problems. *Heliyon*, 10, e23571, January 2024.
18. Ganesh, N., Shankar, R., Mahdal, M., Murugan, J.S., Chohan, J.S., Kalita, K., Exploring deep learning methods for computer vision applications across

multiple sectors: Challenges and future trends. *Comput. Model. Eng. Sci.*, 139, 103–141, 2024.

19. Musoro, J.Z., Zwinderman, A.H., Puhan, M.A., ter Riet, G., Geskus, R.B., Validation of prediction models based on lasso regression with multiply imputed data. *BMC Med. Res. Methodol.*, 14, 116, October 2014.
20. Ikotun, A.M., Ezugwu, A.E., Abualigah, L., Abuhaija, B., Heming, J., K-means clustering algorithms: A comprehensive review, variants analysis, and advances in the era of big data. *Inf. Sci. (NY)*, 622, 178–210, April 2023.
21. Kalita, K., *et al.*, eds. *Pioneering Approaches in Data Management*. IGI Global Scientific Publishing, Hershey, PA, 2025. https://doi.org/10.4018/979-8-3693-5563-3
22. Akhtar, M.S. and Feng, T., Malware analysis and detection using machine learning algorithms. *Symmetry (Basel)*, 14, 2304, November 2022.
23. Bohani, F.A., Suliman, A., Saripuddin, M., Sameon, S.S., Md Salleh, N.S., Nazeri, S., A comprehensive analysis of supervised learning techniques for electricity theft detection. *J. Electr. Comput. Eng.*, 2021, 1–10, July 2021.
24. Arif, A., Javaid, N., Aldegheishem, A., Alrajeh, N., Big data analytics for identifying electricity theft using machine learning approaches in microgrids for smart communities. *Concurr. Comput. Pract. Exper.*, 33, 17, e6316, 2021.

11

Renal Cancer Detection from Histopathological Images Using Deep Learning

Akhil Kumar[1], R. Krithiga[1]*, S. Suseela[1], B. Swarna[2] and T. Karthikeyan[3]

[1]*School of Computer Science and Engineering, Vellore Institute of Technology, Chennai, India*
[2]*University Centre for Research & Development, Chandigarh University, Mohali, India*
[3]*Department of Information Technology, University of Technology and Applied Science, Salalah, Oman*

Abstract
Renal cancer stands as a significant contributor to global cancer-related mortality. The imperative for early detection to enhance patient outcomes is evident, yet the manual analysis of histopathological images proves challenging and time-consuming for pathologists. Harnessing the potential of deep learning presents an opportunity to revolutionize renal cancer detection through automated histopathological image analysis. Our research aims to assess the effectiveness of established deep learning models in renal cancer detection. We will curate a collection of representative models previously developed for histopathological image analysis. Subsequently, these models will undergo training using an extensive dataset comprising histopathological images of both renal cancer and normal tissue. The ultimate goal is to evaluate the performance of these pre-trained models on a separate test dataset containing histopathological images of renal cancer and normal tissue. This investigation is poised to furnish valuable insights into the capabilities of existing deep learning models for renal cancer detection. The findings have the potential to guide the development of automated tools that facilitate more accurate and efficient diagnosis of renal cancer by assisting pathologists in their assessments without increasing the word count.

**Corresponding author*: krithiga.r@vit.ac.in

Kanak Kalita, Divya Zindani, Narayanan Ganesh and Xiao-Zhi Gao (eds.) Medical Analytics for Clinical and Healthcare Applications, (225–242)

***Keywords*:** Histopathology images, deep learning, renal cancer, feature extraction

11.1 Introduction

Renal cancer, also known as kidney cancer, is a type of cancer originating in the kidneys. In India, renal cell carcinoma (RCC) holds the 13th position in prevalence among men and the 16th among women. The typical age of diagnosis is around 60 years. The exact cause of renal cancer remains elusive, although certain factors can elevate the risk of contracting the disease. These factors include smoking, obesity, high blood pressure, a family history of renal cancer, specific genetic mutations, and exposure to certain chemicals like asbestos and cadmium. Renal cancer can impact one or both kidneys and may extend to other organs such as the lungs, bones, and brain. The most common type of renal cancer is RCC, constituting approximately 85% of all renal cancer cases. Histopathology images are microscopic images of tissue samples stained with special dyes to emphasize various cell types and structures. Pathologists utilize these images to diagnose diseases by scrutinizing the cellular and tissue morphology. In the context of renal cancer diagnosis, pathologists analyze histopathology images of kidney tissue samples to identify abnormalities in the cells. Cancerous cells typically exhibit a number of characteristic features, such as nuclear atypia (abnormalities in the appearance of the cell nucleus), increased mitotic activity (cell division), and invasion of surrounding tissues. However, histopathology images of renal cancer can be challenging to interpret, especially for cases with atypical or borderline features. This is because there is a wide range of normal and abnormal cell and tissue morphologies in the kidney. Additionally, the appearance of cancerous cells can vary depending on the subtype of renal cancer. To address this issue, we employ an artificial intelligence (AI) technique known as deep learning (DL). Deep learning, a subset of AI, holds the promise of transforming the diagnosis of renal cancer. Through training DL algorithms, we enable them to recognize patterns in histopathology images linked to renal cancer. This capability assists pathologists in diagnosing renal cancer with greater accuracy and efficiency, particularly in cases exhibiting atypical or borderline features.

The intricate nature of renal cancer underscores the need for accurate identification, prompting the exploration of a groundbreaking approach through the incorporation of DL into histopathology analysis. Utilizing the capabilities of AI, our objective is to elevate diagnostic precision, facilitating timely interventions and personalized treatment strategies for individuals grappling with renal cancer. At the intersection of medical science and cutting-edge technology, this research endeavors to establish a more effective and nuanced paradigm for renal cancer diagnosis, with the ultimate goal of advancing patient care. Furthermore, in Figures 11.1 and 11.2, we present histopathology images of kidney tissue. Figure 11.2 showcases a cancerous cell, highlighting the distinct features indicative of renal cell carcinoma. In contrast, Figure 11.1 displays a non-cancerous cell for comparative analysis. These images serve as integral visual references, aiding in the understanding of the morphological disparities between cancerous and non-cancerous kidney cells. Additionally, these images play a crucial role in enhancing the diagnostic process, providing clinicians and researchers with valuable insights into the intricate cellular structures. Their detailed depiction of cancerous and non-cancerous cells contributes to a more nuanced understanding of renal cancer pathology, ultimately guiding the development of advanced diagnostic approaches.

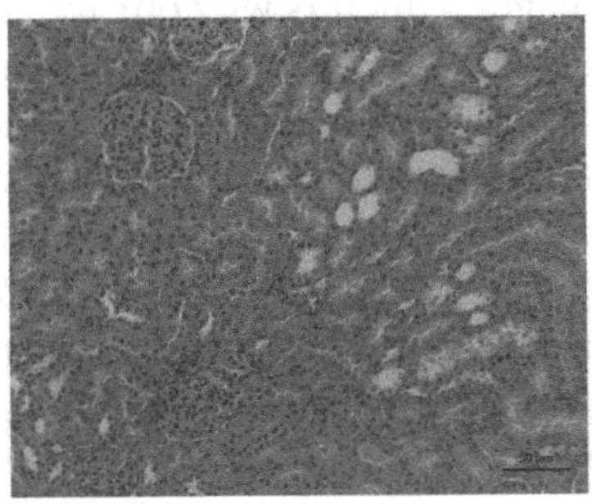

Figure 11.1 A non-cancerous cell.

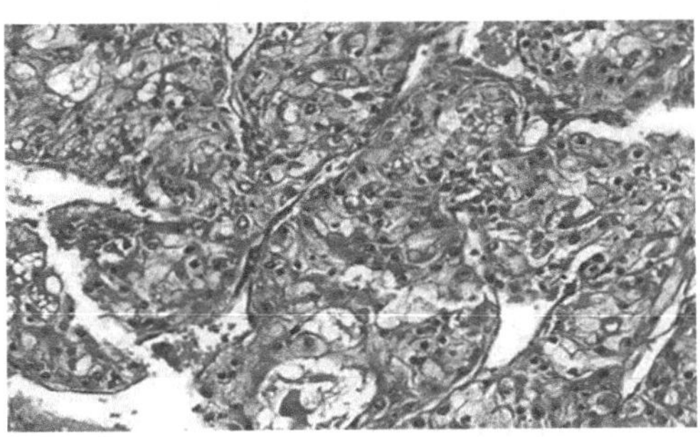

Figure 11.2 A cancerous cell.

11.1.1 Motivation

Kidney cancer, especially RCC, is a big health issue globally. Detecting it early is crucial for better patient results. Right now, doctors look at kidney tissue samples under a microscope to diagnose it, but this method takes time and can be inconsistent among different doctors. It often does not give a high level of accuracy needed for a quick and precise diagnosis, which is why we need to explore new ways to make kidney cancer detection better and faster. When we examine kidney tissue under a microscope, we get important information about the cells and structures. This helps us find diseases like cancer. With the help of technology and data science, especially DL, we can use computers to look at these microscope images and find tiny details that might be hard for a person to see. Deep learning is a type of AI that has shown great promise in making medical image analysis more accurate and efficient. It can recognize subtle patterns and details that are easy to miss for a human. But even though this technology is exciting, there is a gap in the research. There are not many comprehensive reviews that carefully look at how well DL can help detect kidney cancer in these microscope images, which is why our main reason for doing this research is to fill that gap and give a complete picture of what is happening right now in the field. Our goal is to improve the way we examine kidney tissue and make sure we can find cancer early and with great accuracy. This can lead to better care for patients because we can diagnose and treat the cancer sooner and in a more personalized way. Figure 11.3 shows the different pre-trained model used in this study. Our review aims to use DL to move the field forward and, in the end, provide better results for kidney cancer patients.

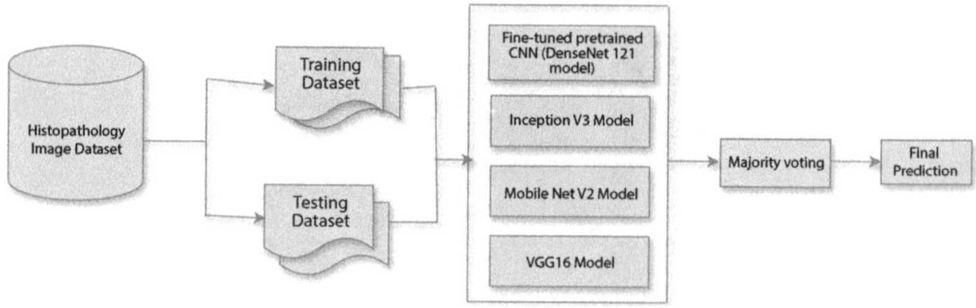

Figure 11.3 Adaptive pre-trained models.

11.2 Materials and Methods

11.2.1 Dataset Used

The research consolidated data from various datasets cited in different research papers, contributing to a comprehensive investigation of renal cancer detection from histopathology images using DL. Upon reviewing multiple articles on renal cancer detection *via* DL in histopathology images, it was noted that these studies utilized a diverse range of datasets. These included the publicly accessible TCGA Renal Cell Carcinoma Dataset, an in-house skin cancer dataset, breast and lung cancer datasets, as well as a dataset from The Second Affiliated Hospital of the Guangzhou Medical University. Additionally, the study incorporated the KMC Kidney Histopathology Dataset and the Louisville University - Bioimaging Lab Dataset. To augment the study's reliability and thoroughness, external datasets such as TCGA, CPTAC, and the Mainz Cohort were integrated. This incorporation of diverse datasets provides valuable insights for a comprehensive examination.

11.2.2 Models Used

- Support vector machine (SVM) (Alex-Net + Gabor filter): Combines traditional SVM classification with deep features extracted by AlexNet and Gabor filter for accurate renal cancer detection from histopathology images.
- Convolutional neural network (CNN): Widely used DL architecture adept at hierarchically learning patterns and structures, facilitating accurate renal cancer subtype classification from histopathological data.
- RCCGNet: Tailored DL model specifically designed for clear cell renal cell carcinoma (ccRCC) grading, ensuring precise classification within this subtype.
- SSL-CLAM Model: Utilizes semi-supervised learning with active learning strategies, optimizing the use of labeled and unlabeled data for efficient renal cancer detection.
- Multimodal deep learning model (MMDLM): Integrates histopathological, radiologic imaging, and genetic information for predicting renal cancer prognosis, aiding informed clinical decisions.

This section offers a comprehensive review of the current literature, examining various methods and approaches employed in the realm of renal cancer detection from histopathology images utilizing DL techniques. The insights provided aim to illuminate the evolutionary trajectory and present status of the field. Figure 11.4 shows the working of CNN.

Cai *et al.* [1] presented a comprehensive literature review on texture image analysis and classification. It encompasses various techniques, including the use of global significant value, statistical features, time series features, and DL-based approaches. The authors emphasize the importance of these methods in medical imaging, including automated segmentation and image retrieval. The review highlights the potential of combining diverse texture feature extraction methods with DL to enhance classification accuracy. Chanchal, A.K. *et al.* [2] conducted a study on the application of DL models in the classification of kidney cancer histopathology images. The research focused on the use of CNNs for various tasks, such as the detection and segmentation of nuclei, identification of cancer subtypes, and grading. The paper referred to several studies, with some using pre-trained CNN models, which is shown in Figure 11.4. Other research work applied transfer learning techniques using models such as ResNet50, DenseNet121, Inceptionv3, and Inception ResNetv2 for examining breast cancer histopathology. Moreover, the study presented the RCCGNet model, which showed remarkable performance and accuracy when used on the KMC kidney dataset. Additionally, it indicated the availability of the datasets used in the study and cited relevant research papers. Abdeltawab, H. *et al.* [3] highlighted the limited availability of information concerning metastatic clear cell papillary RCC, emphasizing the absence of a comprehensive understanding of this specific RCC subtype. It also underscored

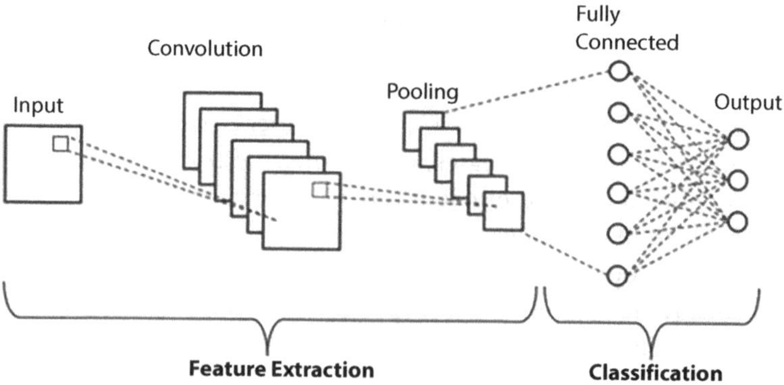

Figure 11.4 Working of CNN.

the significance of creating diagnostic methods, particularly in situations with limited resources, where access to specialists in kidney tumor pathology and immunohistochemistry might be restricted.

Haeyeh *et al.* [4] proposed within this paper an innovative weakly-supervised multiscale learning approach tailored for RCC subtyping, presenting a distinctive strategy to elevate classification performance. Amid the evolving landscape of DL methodologies, a notable study ingeniously employed unified memory mechanisms and GPU memory optimization to train conventional CNNs for lung cancer classification, achieving remarkable accuracy. In a parallel vein, a pioneering research initiative introduced a simplified CNN architecture designed for efficient pan-cancer whole-slide image classification, showcasing swift convergence and minimal memory consumption. Furthermore, the introduction of a semi-supervised learning technique for detecting RCC regions, relying on minimal-point-based annotations, outperformed conventional whole-slide-based models. The integration of attention-based models has also emerged as a promising avenue in computational pathology, yielding results akin to traditional multiple- instance learning methods.

Zheng, Q. *et al.* [5] embarked on a novel exploration, this paper unfolds a thorough analysis of the intricate realm where DL models intersect with cancer pathology. It places a distinctive spotlight on the SSL-CLAM model, designed for the nuanced classification RCC through the lens of histopathological images. The research meticulously dissects the model's efficacy, employing an array of metrics such as receiver operating characteristic curves, area under the curve (AUC), accuracy, and precision. In a bid to unravel its interpretability, attention heatmaps are invoked, and the study navigates the uncharted territory of cooperative diagnostic decision-making, orchestrating a symphony between human experts and machine intelligence. As the document pays homage to relevant antecedent studies in the DL–cancer pathology nexus, it resounds a call for urgent clinical trials, underscoring the imperative to validate the efficacy of this avant-garde diagnostic methodology.

Wessels *et al.* [6] discussed the conceptualization and validation of DINO-ViT, a DL model designed for prediction of survival outcomes in clear cell RCC (ccRCC). DINO-ViT amalgamates a vision transformer with the DINO algorithm, finding its training foundation in TCGA histopathological slides. The paper extends previous research, shining a light on the potential of AI-based image analysis in anticipating oncological transformations. Self- supervised models like DINO-ViT, deriving insights from unlabeled data, confer heightened generalizability. Furthermore, the document accentuates the transparency of Vision Transformers, specifically in their capacity to grasp image relationships and present interpretability through attention visualization. While recognizing the limitations of a retrospective study design and the necessity for a more extensive dataset, it strongly underscores the demand for further evaluation to gauge the integration of AI into robust clinical frameworks for survival prediction.

Schulz, S. *et al.* [7] discussed about the emergence of a multimodal DL model (MMDLM) in renal cancer analysis signifies a progressive shift towards harnessing the combined power of histopathologic and radiologic imaging techniques, coupled with genetic analyses, form a synergistic approach in the comprehensive examination and understanding of various medical conditions to enhance diagnosis and outcome prediction. This approach addresses the intricate nature of renal cancer by amalgamating complementary information sources. While the MMDLM demonstrates promise, the addition of genomic data did not yield significant improvements, underscoring the need for careful selection of data sources. Collaborative efforts between pathologists, radiologists, and DL models have paved the way for more accurate renal cancer analysis. Further research is crucial to validate and generalize the approach, yet the potential for improved patient care and outcomes is evident.

Basso, M. N. *et al.* [8] proposed a paper focusing on the utilization of machine learning (ML) within the context of renal pathology. This paper underscores the promising capabilities of ML techniques in enhancing the precision and effectiveness of kidney disease diagnosis. The authors stress the urgency of continued exploration and advancement in this domain, considering that the integration of ML in renal pathology is at an initial phase. This paper lays the groundwork for prospective research endeavors and accentuates the significance of ensuring interpretability, transparency, and confidence in the incorporation of ML models within clinical settings. Li, J. *et al.* [3] provided an in-depth exploration through the literature, encapsulating various dimensions of histopathology image analysis for cancer diagnosis. Encompassing topics ranging from computer-aided breast cancer diagnosis to the intricate analysis of gastric histopathological images, the review spans diagnostic consensus among pathologists, the application of ML methods in medical image analysis, and automated nuclear atypia scoring in breast cancer. This comprehensive survey also navigates the terrain of challenges and opportunities associated with central pathology review, emphasizing the establishment of standardized procedures. Furthermore, it sheds light on diverse methods for color normalization in histopathological images and the integration of machine vision algorithms for cancer detection. A critical focal point emerges, underscoring the necessity for the rigorous validation and generalization of machine vision algorithms before their prospective clinical application.

Zhou, H. *et al.* [9] presented the study for weakly supervised learning, denoted as EWSLF, which is custom-tailored for the classification of cancer subtypes, drawing from histopathological images. The framework introduces a dual approach, encompassing both whole-based and patch-based methodologies, and conducts a comprehensive comparative evaluation vis-a-vis other algorithms. The findings underscore EWSLF's marked superiority across various performance metrics, including accuracy, precision, recall, specificity, and F1 score. Additionally, the paper critically addresses the model's limitations and lays out a roadmap for future research endeavors, encompassing strategies to alleviate computational overhead and the expansion of histopathological datasets. In essence, this paper provides invaluable insights into the evolution of robust methodologies for the classification of cancer subtypes employing histopathological slides.

Van Rijthoven, M. *et al.* [10] presented the document that includes a range of references and acknowledgments pertaining to the domain of medical image analysis and histopathology. It expresses gratitude for the contributions of those engaged in the meticulous manual annotation of breast tissue samples. Furthermore, it acknowledges the utilization of data stemming from the TCGA Research Network and the financial support received from diverse entities. These include funding from the European Union's Horizon 2020 research program and the Alpe d'HuZes/Dutch Cancer Society Fund.

Y. *et al.* [11] presented a document. The document delivers an extensive examination of machine vision applications in the analysis of histopathological images of the intestine. It surveys a plethora of articles, each honing in on distinct facets of intestinal histopathology. This encompasses technologies dedicated to the representation of histopathological images, the employment of DL frameworks for the scrutiny of colon cancer, the amalgamation of whole-slide imaging (WSI) and computer-aided diagnosis (CAD) techniques, and the application of random field models to analyze pathological images. Furthermore, the paper underscores the collaborative contributions from the realms of computer science and medicine in advancing the field of intestinal histopathology analysis. Meng, X. and Zou, T. [12] discussed how computer methods can help doctors diagnose and treat cancer by analyzing images of tissues. They explain how older methods used math features from the images, but they had limitations. It shows how newer methods use DL, especially graphs, to learn complex features from the images. They also point out the need for fair and consistent ways to measure the performance of some methods, such as those that separate cells or tissues in the images. The document concludes that graph-based methods are important for understanding the context and biology of the tissues and improving cancer outcomes.

Wang, J. M., Hong, R. [13] discussed the utilization of DL models and the integration of omics data to scrutinize histological characteristics in tumor slides. The authors undertook the training of Panoptes1 architecture models, employing HE slide images stemming from six distinct cancer types. Employing feature extraction and visualization methodologies, the study delved into understanding the features discerned by these models for each class of cancer. Additionally, the application of Sparse CCA allowed for the identification of subgroups within genes, proteins, and imaging features that exhibit correlations. Ultimately, the study seeks to extract insights into the fundamental biological mechanisms underpinning predictive alterations in morphology.

Hoefling, H. *et al.* [14] highlighted the advantages of domain-specific transfer learning within the domain of histology, especially when dealing with tasks characterized by a scarcity of training data. It references a companion study within the same issue, showcasing the efficacy of the pre- trained HistoNet model in tasks like biomarker classification. The concept of pretext tasks is elaborated upon, emphasizing the significance of resilient models and evaluation conducted across various magnification levels. Collectively, it highlights the immense potential of harnessing transfer learning from domain-specific models for a multitude of histopathology- related endeavors. Kowalewski, K.-F. *et al.* [15] provided an extensive survey of contemporary AI and ML methodologies applied to the domain of RCC. It delves into the utility of AI across diverse facets of RCC care, encompassing diagnostics, therapeutic interventions, histological examination, and post-treatment monitoring. The paper underscores the distinctions between statistical models and ML approaches while underscoring the critical role of high-quality data in the training of AI models. Additionally, it acknowledges the obstacles and constraints associated with the integration of AI within clinical contexts.

Schneider, L. *et al.* [16] provided a systematic review that investigates the synergistic possibilities of integrating DL-based image analysis with genomic data to advance cancer pathology. It encompasses 11 pertinent studies, with seven dedicated to survival analysis and four to cancer subtype prediction. Regrettably, none of these studies incorporated model validation. An intriguing observation was that the volume of patient data did not notably affect performance, and larger transcriptomic datasets did not consistently yield superior outcomes. While image-based classifiers demonstrated potential in prognosis and prediction, the review highlights the imperative for increased validation and standardization within this domain. Posada Calderon, L.P. *et al.* [17] discussed the advances made in imaging-based biomarkers for RCC. It highlights the current limitations of imaging methods in accurately differentiating RCC from other renal diseases and gives an overview of recent innovations in imaging techniques for detecting and monitoring kidney tumors. The paper centers its attention on magnetic resonance imaging (MRI), positron emission tomography (PET)/CT, and the computational extraction of data from CT images, exploring these avenues as potential realms for investigation. However, the paper emphasizes the need for more research to confirm the validity of these methods.

In 2021, A paper introduced the MRMIL model, which is specially designed for prostate biopsy WSI classification and the weakly supervised detection of tumor regions, and tackled the problem of Gleason grade prediction using only slide-level labels [18]. The model demonstrates strong performance on clinical datasets, offering the possibility of improving the efficiency and quality assurance of pathologists in clinical practice. Importantly, the paper highlights the need for quantitative evaluation and suggests enhancements to the training process through adaptive tile selection. Although initially developed for acinar adenocarcinoma, the model shows potential for wider applications in histopathology. This contribution is consistent with the increasing interest in using ML for more accurate and efficient cancer diagnosis through the analysis of whole-slide images, indicating significant progress in the field of pathology.

Kate, V. and Shukla, P. [19] provided a comprehensive systematic review that delves into the integration of DL-based image analysis and genomic data in the realm of cancer pathology. The primary objective is to evaluate the collective impact of these approaches on cancer classification and biomarker discovery. The study encapsulates 11 research works, primarily focusing on areas such as survival analysis, subtype prediction, malignancy assessment, and microsatellite instability. These studies employed a diverse range of datasets, fusion techniques, and preprocessing methods. The review underscores the robust performance of image-based classifiers, particularly in tasks related to prognosis and prediction. Interestingly, it observes that the size of patient data had minimal effects on performance in C-index-based survival analysis. However, the relationship between the size of transcriptomic data and performance improvement varied across studies. The review highlights the potential for unearthing novel cancer biomarkers through multimodal fusion. Nevertheless, it emphasizes the critical need for additional research and validation to fully realize the potential of this approach in clinical practice.

Gondim, D. D. *et al.* [20] provided a review paper that discusses how AI can improve kidney neoplasm diagnosis by refining histopathological classification. It emphasizes the challenge of accurately categorizing RCC due to its diversity. The authors review AI research in this field, citing various studies. Their own study presents an AI model capable of distinguishing between six neoplasm subtypes accurately, except for a specific subtype differentiation. Overall, the research underscores AI's potential to enhance precision in diagnosing kidney neoplasms.

Ponzio, F. *et al.* [21] provided a review paper that sheds light on the notable scarcity in the exploration of DL applied to RCC subtyping, emphasizing its unique contribution to the existing body of knowledge. This study ambitiously aims to refine and expand upon previous descriptions. It engages in a nuanced discussion of the intricate challenges associated with RCC subtype classification, placing a particular focus on addressing data imbalance issues. The paper goes further to unveil inventive strategies devised to navigate these challenges. Additionally, it distinguishes itself by conducting a thorough comparison of its findings with prior works, underscoring the prevalent reliance on the TCGA database in previous studies, often without extending results to the granularity of whole slide images (WSI) or patient-level analyses.

Wang, Y., Wen, Q. *et al.* [22] discussed the role of AI in renal pathology, emphasizing its use with imaging tech for diagnosing kidney diseases. It discusses AI's growth in nephrology, covering its contributions, challenges, and potential in segmenting kidney structures, diagnosing pathologies, and predicting prognosis from images. It highlights AI's promise in improving diagnostic accuracy and efficiency while stressing the need for collaborative efforts among experts for further advancements in this field. Singh, N. P. *et al.* [23] performed a comparative study that endeavored to construct predictive models for papillary renal cell carcinoma (PRCC) stage prediction *via* RNASeq datasets. Utilizing diverse feature selection algorithms, we meticulously unearthed genes consistently altered between early and late PRCC stages. Significantly, a Random Forest-based feature selection algorithm emerged as a standout, offering minimal features and superior performance. The identified genes demonstrated associations with microtubule dynamics, chromosomes, and cell cycle regulation. Our study uniquely concludes by underscoring the potential of these models for preliminary PRCC staging while unraveling valuable insights into intricate underlying mechanisms.

Wang, Z. and Zhang, X. [24] provide a comprehensive review of the role of DL in diagnosing RCC through imaging, highlighting its potential to enhance accuracy. Points out challenges like data availability and model interpretability, stressing the need for further research, addressing issues in applying DL to RCC, emphasizing the importance of collaboration, exploring how DL can improve existing imaging methods for RCC detection. Outlines emerging trends, including enhancing model interpretability and the necessity of multidisciplinary cooperation for DL's clinical development in RCC diagnosis. Table 11.1 shows the performance comparison of various deep learning models used for renal cancer detection. Figure 11.5 shows the proportion of various models used in literature.

11.3 Results and Discussions

The reviewed studies present compelling results in the application of DL techniques for renal cancer detection and classification. Notably, these results highlight the potential and effectiveness of various methodologies:

11.3.1 High Classification Accuracy

Several models achieved high accuracy levels, such as SVM (Alex-Net + Gabor filter) (98.54%) and DL-based classification systems (ranging from 92% to 93.3%). These findings demonstrate the capability of DL in accurately detecting and subtyping RCC from histopathology images. Results of various methods as been discussed in Table 11.1 and Figure 11.5.

11.3.2 Strong Performance on Classification Metrics

Models like RCCGNet have illuminated the landscape with their exceptional performance, boasting high precision, recall, and F1-Score values. The fusion of ML and DL techniques has not only exhibited competitive classification accuracy but has also showcased remarkable sensitivity, affirming their prowess in effectively distinguishing between RCC subtypes.

11.3.3 Fuhrman Grade Classification

The SSL-CLAM model demonstrated strong classification accuracy in assessing Fuhrman grading, a crucial component in RCC diagnosis. This suggests the potential of DL in accurately characterizing RCC malignancy.

Table 11.1 Performance comparison of various deep learning models used for renal cancer detection.

Ref. no.	Author/year	Method	Result	Dataset used
[1]	Cai, J. *et al.* (2022)	SVM (Alex-Net + Gabor filter)	Accuracy: 98.54%	The Second Affiliated Hospital of the Guangzhou Medical University
[2]	Chanchal, A.K. *et al.* (2023)	RCCGNet	Accuracy: 90.14% Precision: 89.78% Recall: 89.60% F1-Score: 89.06%	Kasturba Medical College, Mangalore, India
[4]	Abu Haeyeh, Y. *et al.* (2022)	CNN	Classification Accuracy: 93.0% ± 4.9% Sensitivity: 91.3% ± 10.7% Specificity: 95.6% ± 5.2%	Louisville University-Bioimaging Lab
[5]	Zheng, Q. *et al.* (2023)	SSL-CLAM model	Five-Class Fuhrman Grade: Training set: 81.8% Internal validation set: 77.6%	TCGA, CPTAC
[19]	Kate, V., Shukla, P. (2021)	Deep learning-based classification system	High accuracy (92% to 93.3%) in subtyping RCC from histopathology images	TGCA
[16]	Kowalewski, K.-F. *et al.* (2022)	SSL-CLAM model	Avg. Accuracy: 81.8% (Training Set) AUC: 0.947	TGCA

(*Continued*)

Table 11.1 Performance comparison of various deep learning models used for renal cancer detection. (*Continued*)

Ref. no.	Author/year	Method	Result	Dataset used
[6]	Wessels, F. *et al.* (2023)	DINO-ViT	Predicts survival in ccRCC	The Cancer Genome Atlas (TCGA-KIRC)
[7]	Schulz, S., Woerl, *et al.* (2021)	MMDLM	Acccuracy: 83.43%	TCGA Mainz cohort
[8]	Basso, M. N. *et al.* (2022)	BFE model	Glomerular cross-validation accuracy: 67.6 ± 8.9%	Toronto General Hospital (TGH)
[15]	Zhou, H. *et al.* (2023)	End-to-end Weakly Supervised Learning Framework (EWSLF)	Superiority over state-of-the-art methods	Public dataset: Renal cell carcinoma (KIRC, KIRP, KICH); In-house dataset: Skin cancer (BCC, SCC, BD)

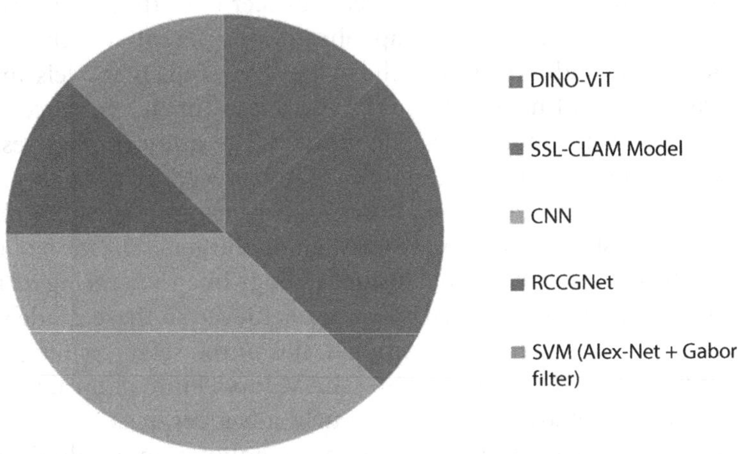

Figure 11.5 Proportions of deep learning models used for renal cancer detection.

The results signify significant progress in renal cancer detection through DL methodologies. These outcomes are pivotal in the discussion of the role of AI in clinical practice, emphasizing the need for further research, validation, and real-world implementation. Additionally, these results underscore the importance of interdisciplinary collaborations, dataset standardization, and the potential for DL models to enhance the accuracy of renal cancer diagnosis and ultimately improve patient care.

11.4 Conclusion and Future Work

The paper presents a comprehensive analysis of DL techniques in the field of renal cancer detection from histopathological images. The investigation of relevant literature shows that algorithms for examining renal histopathological images can be categorized into traditional ML DL methods. Traditional ML methods, such as SVM, have demonstrated remarkable achievements in tandem with DL methods like RCCGNet and the SSL-CLAM model, which exhibit substantial classification accuracy and robust performance. Moreover, the utilization of DL models like the DL-based classification system has showcased high accuracy, especially in subtyping RCC from histopathology images, even in challenging cases. These findings underscore the potential of AI models, including SSL-CLAM and other DL frameworks, in transforming renal cancer diagnosis and patient care. It is notable that the models, such as RCCGNet and the SSL-CLAM model, have consistently demonstrated their superiority among comparison models, showcasing high precision, recall, and F1-score values.

The path forward in the realm of renal cancer detection from histopathology images using DL should capitalize on the potential of the models mentioned in this study. Expanding the scope of ML and DL models, including the exploration of novel DL architectures, can further enhance classification accuracy and robustness. Additionally, the study emphasizes that the classification of Fuhrman grading, as achieved by the SSL-CLAM model, can be improved and fine-tuned for even more accurate results. Further research should focus on strengthening the generalization of models across a broader range of renal histopathology images, bearing in mind the lessons learned from the AUC values achieved in these models. The future of renal cancer detection using DL lies in the seamless integration of models like RCCGNet and the SSL-CLAM model into clinical practice, thereby enhancing patient care. As the field advances, it is imperative to address challenges related to data accessibility, annotation standardization, and overcoming data-related obstacles. Methods for image enhancement, fusion algorithms, and the development of lightweight models will play a pivotal role in optimizing computational efficiency and reducing resource requirements. Active learning strategies to identify informative samples for manual annotation can augment the limitations of annotated data. Furthermore, enhancing interpretability, model robustness, and computational efficiency remain the cornerstones of advancing AI integration into clinical practice. Through these future endeavors, AI models are poised to significantly improve the accuracy and efficiency of renal cancer diagnosis and management.

References

1. Cai, J., *et al.*, Renal cancer detection: Fusing deep and texture features from histopathology images. *Biomed Res. Int.*, 2022, 1–17, 2022, doi: 10.1155/2022/9821773.
2. Chanchal, A.K., Lal, S., Kumar, R., Kwak, J.T, Kini, J., A novel dataset and Efficient Deep Learning Framework for automated grading of renal cell carcinoma from kidney histopathology images. *Sci. Rep.*, 13, 1, 5728, 2023, doi: 10.1038/s41598-023-31275-7.
3. Abdeltawab, H., Khalifa, F., Ghazal, M., Cheng, L., Gondim, D., El-Baz, A., A pyramidal deep learning pipeline for kidney whole-slide histology images classification. *Sci. Rep.*, 11, 1, 20189, 2021.
4. Abu Haeyeh, Y., *et al.*, Development and evaluation of a novel deep-learning-based framework for the classification of renal histopathology images. *Bioengineering*, 9, 9, 423, 2022, doi: 10.3390/bioengineering9090423.
5. Zheng, Q., *et al.*, A weakly supervised deep learning model and human–machine fusion for accurate grading of renal cell carcinoma from histopathology slides. *Cancers*, 15, 12, 3198, 2023, doi: 10.3390/cancers15123198.
6. Wessels, F., *et al.*, A self-supervised vision transformer to predict survival from histopathology in renal cell carcinoma. *World J. Urol.*, 41, 8, 2233–2241, 2023, doi: 10.1007/s00345-023-04489-7.
7. Schulz, S., Woerl, A.C., Jungmann, F., Glasner, C., Stenzel, P., Strobl, S., Foersch, S., Multimodal deep learning for prognosis prediction in renal cancer. *Front. Oncol.*, 11, 788740, 2021.
8. Basso, M.N., Barua, M., Meyer, J., John, R., Khademi, A., Machine learning in renal pathology. *Front. Nephrol.*, 2, 1007002, 2022.
9. He, W., *et al.*, A review: The detection of cancer cells in histopathology based on machine vision. *Comput. Biol. Med.*, 146, 105636, 2022, doi: 10.1016/j.compbiomed.2022.105636.
10. Jing, Y., *et al.*, A comprehensive survey of intestine histopathological image analysis using machine vision approaches. *Comput. Biol. Med.*, 165, 107388, 2023, doi: 10.1016/j.compbiomed.2023.107388.

11. Meng, X. and Zou, T., Clinical applications of graph neural networks in computational histopathology: A Review. *Comput. Biol. Med.*, 164, 107201, 2023, doi: 10.1016/j.compbiomed.2023.107201.
12. Posada Calderon, L.P., *et al.*, Advances in imaging-based biomarkers in renal cell carcinoma: A critical analysis of the current literature. *Cancers*, 15, 2, 354, 2023, doi: 10.3390/cancers15020354.
13. Schneider, L., *et al.*, Integration of deep learning-based image analysis and genomic data in cancer pathology: A systematic review. *Eur. J. Cancer*, 160, 80–91, 2022, doi: 10.1016/j.ejca.2021.10.007.
14. Van Rijthoven, M., Balkenhol, M., Siliņa, K., Van Der Laak, J., Ciompi, F., HookNet: Multi-resolution convolutional neural networks for semantic segmentation in histopathology whole-slide images. *Med. Image Anal.*, 68, 101890, 2021.
15. Zhou, H., *et al.*, An end-to-end weakly supervised learning framework for cancer subtype classification using histopathological slides. *Expert Syst. Appl.*, 237, 121379, 2024, doi: 10.1016/j.eswa.2023.121379.
16. Kowalewski, K.-F., *et al.*, Artificial Intelligence for renal cancer: From imaging to histology and beyond. *Asian J. Urol.*, 9, 3, 243–252, 2022, doi: 10.1016/j.ajur.2022.05.003.
17. Li, J., Li, W., Sisk, A., Ye, H., Wallace, W.D., Speier, W., Arnold, C.W., A multi-resolution model for histopathology image classification and localization with multiple instance learning. *Comput. Biol. Med.*, 131, 104253, 2021.
18. Hoefling, H., Sing, T., Hossain, I., Boisclair, J., Doelemeyer, A., Flandre, T., Moulin, P., HistoNet: a deep learning-based model of normal histology. *Toxicol. Pathol.*, 49, 4, 784–797, 2021.
19. Kate, V. and Shukla, P., A 3 Tier CNN model with deep discriminative feature extraction for discovering malignant growth in multi-scale histopathology images. *Inf. Med. Unlocked*, 24, 100616, 2021.
20. Gondim, D.D., Al-Obaidy, K.I., Idrees, M.T., Eble, J.N., Cheng, L., Artificial intelligence-based multi-class histopathologic classification of kidney neoplasms. *J. Pathol. Inf.*, 14, 100299, 2023.
21. Ponzio, F., Descombes, X., Ambrosetti, D., Improving CNNs classification with pathologist-based expertise: the Renal Cell Carcinoma case study, 2023.
22. Wang, Y., Wen, Q., Jin, L., Chen, W., Artificial intelligence-assisted renal pathology: advances and prospects. *J. Clin. Med.*, 11, 16, 4918, 2022.
23. Singh, N.P., Bapi, R.S., Vinod, P.K., Machine learning models to predict the progression from early to late stages of papillary renal cell carcinoma. *Comput. Biol. Med.*, 100, 92–99, 2018.
24. Wang, Z., Zhang, X., Wang, X., Li, J., Zhang, Y., Zhang, T., Niu, H., Deep learning techniques for imaging diagnosis of renal cell carcinoma: current and emerging trends. *Front. Oncol.*, 13, 1152622, 2023.

12

A Novel Method to Predicting Tumor in Fallopian Tube Using DenseNet Over Linear Regression with Enhanced Efficiency

Harish C.M. and Terrance Frederick Fernandez*

Department of Computer Science and Engineering, Saveetha School of Engineering, Saveetha Institute of Medical and Technical Sciences, Saveetha University, Chennai, India

Abstract

The purpose of this work is to compare DenseNet and logistic regression techniques for predicting tumors in fallopian tube analysis. This study aims to assess each algorithm's performance and identify which one is more appropriate for this critical medical task. Predicting tumors in the fallopian tube with high accuracy could greatly impact reproductive health, providing clinicians with a valuable tool to guide diagnosis and treatment decisions. The research dataset was sourced from the GitHub database system and analyzed using a sample size of twenty (10 from Group 1 and 10 from Group 2). Calculations were performed using a G*Power of 0.8, with alpha and beta values set at 0.05 and 0.2, respectively, and a confidence interval of 95%. DenseNet (90.4460%) demonstrated increased accuracy compared to linear regression (68.7710%), a significant difference supported by a p-value of 0.03 ($p < 0.05$). This statistically significant result underscores the efficiency of DenseNet in accurately predicting fallopian tube tumors, potentially setting a benchmark for further medical research and clinical application in tumor prediction.

Keywords: Deep learning, machine learning, novel convolutional neural network, DenseNet, linear regression, fallopian tube, standard deviation, gender

**Corresponding author*: terrancefrederickfernandez.sse@saveetha.com

Kanak Kalita, Divya Zindani, Narayanan Ganesh and Xiao-Zhi Gao (eds.) Medical Analytics for Clinical and Healthcare Applications, (243–260) © 2025 Scrivener Publishing LLC

12.1 Introduction

Infertility is a condition that affects a significant number of couples globally, and determining its causes often involves a combination of medical techniques and technological innovations. One common method for diagnosing male infertility, for instance, is the assessment of whether sperm cells can traverse the cervix and enter the fallopian tubes after moving through the uterus. This analysis, which is traditionally conducted under a microscope, involves using a classification scheme to evaluate the motility and behavior of spermatozoa. Although this method has been widely used, it has limitations, particularly in terms of subjectivity, since it relies heavily on human observation. As a result, more sophisticated techniques, such as object detection and movement analysis through machine learning, have been developed to track spermatozoa and evaluate their behavior with greater precision. These innovations are designed to enhance the accuracy of diagnosing reproductive issues and enable more precise treatments [1].

In recent years, machine learning has revolutionized medical diagnostics, including in areas like cancer detection and classification. Specifically, ovarian cancer, peritoneal cancer, and fallopian tube cancer are conditions where early and accurate detection is critical for successful treatment outcomes. Various machine learning algorithms, including support vector machines (SVM), Random Forests, and XGBoost, have been employed in studies that seek to classify different types of ovarian and fallopian tube cancers based on pathophysiological data. These models have demonstrated reasonably high accuracy rates, with SVM achieving 71%, Random Forest 72%, and XGBoost 69%. However, despite these advancements, the need for models that offer even higher accuracy and more reliable predictions remains urgent, given the life-threatening nature of these diseases [2]. The application of multi-class classification models can significantly enhance the differentiation of conditions such as stenosed fallopian tubes, which is a common issue leading to infertility and complications in reproductive health [3].

One of the key challenges in current diagnostic practices for fallopian tube analysis is the need to avoid exposing the gonads to harmful ionizing radiation, a risk associated with many traditional imaging techniques. Consequently, there has been a push toward developing non-invasive, safer procedures for analyzing fallopian tube conditions. For example, interventions such as ballooning and stenting have become more sophisticated, thanks to advancements in both medical techniques and diagnostic technologies. These procedures, coupled with machine learning methods, offer the potential to significantly improve patient outcomes by providing clearer and more accurate assessments of reproductive health conditions [4].

Research into fallopian tube analysis is ongoing, with hundreds of studies published across various platforms like IEEE Xplore and ScienceDirect. For instance, some studies utilize silicone tubes as phantoms or models to simulate the conditions of real fallopian tubes. In these cases, stenosis, which is the narrowing of the fallopian tube due to the buildup of material like polyester strands, can be detected without the need for liquid injections. Instead, researchers employ ultrasonic instruments to observe and process the reflected sound waves, thereby determining whether stenosis is present. These non-invasive techniques not only reduce the risk of harm to the patient but also provide a reliable method for diagnosing reproductive conditions [5, 6].

Moreover, computational models are being used to simulate fluid flow within the early segments of the fallopian tubes, a process that is essential for ovum transport. This modeling is critical for understanding the mechanics of reproductive health, as it helps to determine how the ovum moves through the tube, challenging previous assumptions that the ovum travels along the tube's central axis. This new understanding requires the construction of three-dimensional models to better predict ovum transit and identify potential blockages or abnormalities that could lead to reproductive issues [7].

A more recent innovation in the field of fallopian tube diagnostics is the use of machine learning algorithms, such as SVM, to detect stenosis in simulated models of fallopian tubes. By categorizing data obtained from ultrasonic measurements, these machine learning models are capable of providing highly accurate assessments of the fallopian tube's condition. This approach, when combined with advanced imaging techniques and computational analysis, offers a promising new way to diagnose conditions like stenosis with greater accuracy and less reliance on invasive procedures [8].

Despite these promising advancements, a significant gap remains in terms of the accuracy of existing models. Traditional methods, including linear regression, have proven useful but still fall short in terms of precision. This study addresses that gap by introducing DenseNet, a deep learning model that has been widely acknowledged for its ability to reduce the vanishing gradient problem, a common issue in deep neural networks. By comparing DenseNet with linear regression, this research aims to improve the accuracy of fallopian tube condition classification and, ultimately, offer a more reliable tool for medical professionals in diagnosing reproductive health issues. The proposed model builds on existing research while seeking to enhance its practical application in clinical settings, where accuracy is critical for effective treatment [8].

DenseNet, in particular, offers several advantages over traditional machine learning models like linear regression. One of the most significant benefits of DenseNet is its ability to maintain information flow throughout the network by connecting each layer to every other layer in a dense block. This feature helps to alleviate the vanishing gradient problem, which occurs when the information passed through a neural network becomes diluted as it moves through multiple layers. By ensuring that all layers have access to the original input data, DenseNet enhances the model's ability to learn from the data, resulting in higher accuracy in tasks like image classification and medical diagnostics. This study aims to demonstrate how DenseNet can outperform linear regression in predicting fallopian tube conditions, providing a more accurate and reliable diagnostic tool for clinicians [9].

This research highlights the potential of advanced machine learning algorithms like DenseNet to revolutionize the field of reproductive health diagnostics. By addressing the limitations of traditional models and introducing more sophisticated techniques for analyzing fallopian tube conditions, this study aims to improve the accuracy of medical diagnoses and, ultimately, enhance patient outcomes. The comparison between DenseNet and linear regression will provide valuable insights into which model is better suited for this critical medical task, offering a benchmark for future research and clinical applications.

12.2 Materials and Methods

The research for this study was conducted at the Soft Computing Lab of Saveetha School of Engineering, part of the Saveetha Institute of Medical and Technical Sciences (SIMATS). The sample size for this study was determined using G*Power software, which is widely used in scientific research for calculating the necessary sample sizes for statistical analyses. For this study, a sample size of 20 was calculated by comparing both DenseNet and linear regression algorithms. Two groups were selected for comparison, with 10 samples in each group, making a total of 20 samples. These groups were carefully chosen to ensure that the comparison would be meaningful and that the results would provide insights into the performance of each algorithm.

The main objective of this study was to compare the accuracy of DenseNet, a deep learning model, with linear regression, a traditional machine learning algorithm. The research specifically focuses on predicting tumors in the fallopian tube, a critical medical task with implications for reproductive health. The comparison between these two algorithms was implemented using technical analysis software designed for machine learning experiments.

The entire study was designed and executed using Python, a popular programming language for machine learning and deep learning tasks, along with the OpenCV library, which is often used for image processing tasks in medical research. The platform on which the deep learning models were assessed was a Windows 10 operating system, with an Intel Core i7 processor and 4 GB of RAM, using a 64-bit system configuration. These hardware specifications were adequate for running the experiments, although the relatively modest RAM size may have resulted in longer processing times for more complex models like DenseNet.

12.2.1 DenseNet Algorithm

The DenseNet algorithm was chosen for this study due to its reputation for effectively addressing one of the major challenges in deep learning models: the vanishing gradient problem. In traditional deep neural networks, as the network grows deeper, the information passing through the layers becomes diluted, making it difficult for the model to learn effectively from the input data. This phenomenon, known as the vanishing gradient problem, often leads to poor performance in deep learning models, especially when dealing with complex tasks such as medical image analysis.

DenseNet tackles this problem by connecting each layer to every other layer in a dense block. This dense connectivity ensures that information flows efficiently through the network, allowing deeper layers to make use of the features that were learned by earlier layers. The transition layers in DenseNet also distribute their weights across all previous layers, further enhancing the flow of information. As a result, DenseNet is able to generate more accurate predictions by preserving the valuable information contained in the input data throughout the network.

In the context of this study, DenseNet was implemented to predict fallopian tube tumors, using the aforementioned dense block architecture to ensure the model's accuracy and efficiency. DenseNet's ability to maintain a continuous flow of information is particularly valuable in medical image interpretation, where the loss of critical information can lead to inaccurate predictions. By addressing the vanishing gradient problem, DenseNet improves model performance and is better suited for complex medical image analysis tasks.

12.2.1.1 Pseudocode for DenseNet

To clarify the process of using DenseNet for tumor prediction in the fallopian tube, the following pseudocode was used as a guideline for the algorithm's implementation:

1. Determine the model settings.
2. Define the architecture of the DenseNet model.
3. Select the appropriate hyperparameters for the model.
4. Use a grid search or other hyperparameter optimization techniques to find the optimal settings.
5. Split the data.
6. Divide the dataset into training and validation sets for model evaluation.
7. Train the model.
8. Pre-process the training images.
9. Train the DenseNet model on the pre-processed training data.
10. Make any necessary adjustments to the model to prevent overfitting.
11. Predict.
12. Preprocess the validation images.
13. Use the trained DenseNet model to predict the condition of the fallopian tubes.
14. Evaluate the performance.
15. Calculate performance metrics, such as accuracy, precision, recall, and F1-score.
16. Interpret these metrics to evaluate the overall performance of the model.
17. Compare the DenseNet model's performance with other models or methods.

12.2.2 Linear Regression

In contrast to DenseNet, linear regression is a well-established machine learning algorithm that has been widely used for regression tasks. Linear regression focuses on modeling the relationship between input features and target predictions by fitting a linear equation to the data. Although it is commonly used for simple regression tasks, its limitations become evident when applied to more complex medical tasks like tumor prediction in the fallopian tube.

For this study, the linear regression model was implemented using the same dataset as DenseNet. The input features for this model were the physiological, anatomical, or imaging characteristics of the fallopian tubes, while the target predictions were derived from medical diagnoses. Linear regression learns a mathematical model that describes the relationship between these input features and the target predictions, which is then used to make predictions on new, unseen data.

Although linear regression is relatively simple to implement and interpret, its accuracy in complex medical tasks is often lower than more advanced algorithms like DenseNet. The study aimed to highlight this difference by comparing the performance of linear regression with DenseNet in predicting fallopian tube tumors.

12.2.2.1 Pseudocode for Linear Regression

The following pseudocode was used to implement the linear regression model in this study:

1. Cluster the data.
2. Organize the features of the fallopian tubes into clusters based on their similarities.
3. Remove the duplicates.
4. Identify and remove any duplicate clusters that do not add value to the model.
5. Train the model.
6. Train a linear regression model using the unique clusters as input features and the fallopian tube conditions as output targets.
7. Correct the model.
8. Evaluate the model's performance and make necessary adjustments to improve accuracy.
9. Result.
10. Use the trained linear regression model to predict the condition of fallopian tubes based on the input features.

12.2.3 Statistical Analysis

After implementing both DenseNet and linear regression models, statistical analysis was performed using SPSS software, which is widely used for data analysis in scientific research. The statistical analysis focused on comparing the accuracy and performance of the two models using independent variables such as image characteristics, objects, distance, frequency, modulation, amplitude, volume, and decibels.

The dependent variables in this analysis were the fallopian tube images and objects being analyzed. An independent t-test was carried out to compare the accuracy of both models and determine whether the observed differences in performance were statistically significant. The results of this statistical analysis provided valuable insights into the relative strengths and weaknesses of DenseNet and linear regression in predicting fallopian tube tumors.

The analysis also considered key performance metrics, including accuracy, precision, recall, and F1-score, to provide a comprehensive evaluation of each model's performance. By comparing these metrics, the study was able to determine which model was better suited for the task of predicting fallopian tube tumors and why. Specifically, DenseNet's ability to maintain information flow and avoid the vanishing gradient problem led to higher accuracy rates, as confirmed by the statistical analysis.

The t-test results also indicated that the accuracy difference between DenseNet and linear regression was statistically significant, with a p-value of less than 0.05. This finding underscores the superiority of DenseNet for this particular medical task, demonstrating its potential to significantly improve tumor prediction in clinical settings.

12.3 Results and Discussion

The primary objective of this study was to compare the performance of the DenseNet deep learning model with the linear regression algorithm in predicting fallopian tube tumors. The results indicate a significant difference in the accuracy and loss values between the two models. To assess the performance, both models were run in the Anaconda Navigator environment with a sample size of 10 for each model. The results from these runs were analyzed using statistical methods to quantify the performance difference, particularly in terms of accuracy and loss values. The following sections provide a detailed analysis of the results and the discussion of their implications.

12.3.1 Accuracy and Loss Comparison

The DenseNet model exhibited substantially higher accuracy than the linear regression model. As seen in Table 12.1, the accuracy of DenseNet ranged from 84.56% to 95.5%, with a mean accuracy of 90.4460%. On the other hand, linear regression showed lower accuracy, ranging from 48.32% to 85.71%, with a mean accuracy of 68.7710%. This represents a substantial difference in accuracy, with DenseNet outperforming linear regression by approximately 22%. The loss values further reflect this performance gap, with DenseNet exhibiting significantly lower loss values than linear regression across all samples.

The accuracy and loss values for both models are summarized in Tables 12.1 and 12.2. As shown in these tables, DenseNet consistently produced better results across all 10 samples, with its accuracy improving progressively as the samples were processed, starting from 84.56% and reaching 95.5% in the final sample. The loss values for DenseNet showed a corresponding decline, starting at 15.44% and decreasing to 4.5%, indicating improved model performance over time. In contrast, linear regression's accuracy showed a more moderate improvement, starting at 48.32% and increasing to 85.71%, but with higher loss values, beginning at 51.68% and only decreasing to 14.29% by the final sample.

Table 12.1 Accuracy and loss analysis of DenseNet.

Sample	Accuracy (%)	Loss (%)
1	84.56	15.44
2	85.89	14.11
3	87.56	12.44
4	88.54	11.46
5	89.65	10.35
6	91.56	8.44
7	92.95	7.05
8	93.8	6.2
9	94.45	5.55
10	95.5	4.5

Table 12.2 Accuracy and loss analysis of linear regression.

Samples	Accuracy (%)	Loss (%)
1	48.32	51.68
2	57.84	42.16
3	60.56	39.44
4	64.34	35.66
5	67.23	32.77
6	70.47	29.53
7	73.47	26.53
8	78.34	21.66
9	81.43	18.57
10	85.71	14.29

12.3.2 Statistical Analysis Results

The mean values of accuracy and loss for the two models were also compared using group statistical analysis (Table 12.3). DenseNet exhibited a mean accuracy of 90.4460%, while linear regression had a mean accuracy of 68.7710%. The standard deviation for DenseNet was 3.77614,

Table 12.3 Group statistical analysis of DenseNet and linear regression.

	Group	N	Mean	Std. deviation	Std. error mean
Accuracy	DenseNet	10	90.4460	3.77614	1.19412
	Linear regression	10	68.7710	11.50300	3.63757
Loss	DenseNet	10	9.5540	9.5540	9.5540
	Linear regression	10	31.2290	11.50300	3.63757

Table 12.4 Independent sample t-test.

		Levene's test for equality of variances		T-test for equality means with 95% confidence interval						
		f	**Sig.**	**t**	**df**	**Sig. (2-tailed)**	**Mean difference**	**Std. error difference**	**Lower**	**Upper**
Accuracy	**Equal variances assumed**	8.137	0.011	5.661	18	<.001	21.67500	3.82855	13.63150	29.71850
	Equal variances not assumed			5.661	10.917	<.001	21.67500	3.82855	13.24063	30.10937
Loss	**Equal variances assumed**	8.137	0.011	- 5.661	18	<.001	-21.67500	3.82855	-29.71850	-13.63150
	Equal Variances not assumed			- 5.661	10.917	<.001	-21.67500	3.82855	-30.10937	-30.109373

which is much lower than that of linear regression, which had a standard deviation of 11.50300. This suggests that DenseNet not only performed better but also had more consistent results across the samples. The lower standard deviation indicates that DenseNet's accuracy was less variable and more stable compared to linear regression.

In terms of loss values, DenseNet again showed superior performance, with a mean loss of 9.5540%, compared to 31.2290% for linear regression. These loss values indicate that DenseNet's predictions were much closer to the actual target values, reinforcing its superiority in this predictive task.

The statistical significance of these differences was confirmed using an independent sample T-test (Table 12.4). The results showed that DenseNet was significantly better than linear regression, with a p-value of 0.03 ($p < 0.05$), indicating that the observed differences in accuracy and loss between the two models were statistically significant. This finding is further supported by the graphical representation of mean accuracy and loss (Figure 12.1), where DenseNet clearly outperformed linear regression in terms of both metrics.

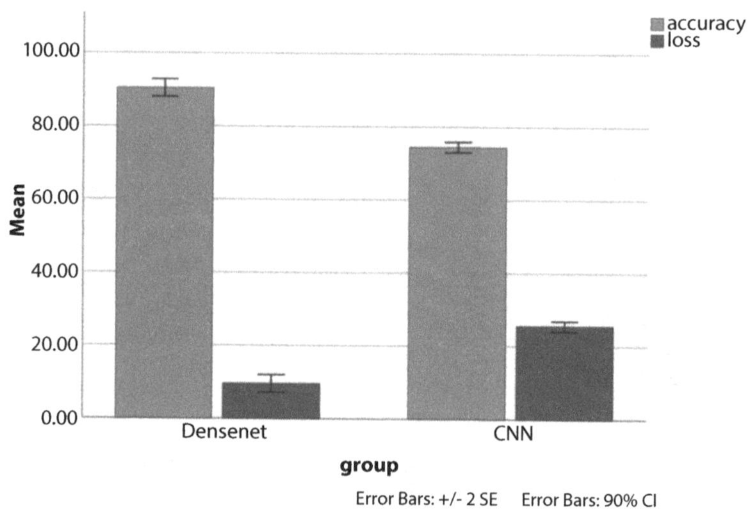

Figure 12.1 Comparison of DenseNet and linear regression.

12.3.3 Group Statistical Analysis

Table 12.3 presents the group statistical analysis for both DenseNet and linear regression, including the mean, standard deviation, and standard error mean for 10 samples. The mean accuracy for DenseNet was 90.4460%, with a standard deviation of 3.77614 and a standard error mean of 1.19412. Similarly, the mean accuracy for linear regression was 68.7710%, with a standard deviation of 11.50300 and a standard error mean of 3.63757. In terms of loss, DenseNet had a mean loss of 9.5540%, while linear regression had a much higher mean loss of 31.2290%.

The differences in mean values, standard deviations, and standard error means suggest that DenseNet not only had higher accuracy but also provided more consistent results, as indicated by its lower standard deviation and standard error mean. This consistency is crucial in medical applications, where the reliability of a model's predictions can significantly impact clinical decision-making.

12.3.4 Discussion

The results of this study highlight the clear superiority of DenseNet over linear regression in predicting fallopian tube tumors. DenseNet's improved accuracy, lower loss values, and greater consistency make it a more suitable model for this type of medical prediction task. The DenseNet model's ability to maintain information flow throughout the network, thanks to its dense block architecture, is a key factor in its success. This feature allows DenseNet to overcome the vanishing gradient problem, which is a common issue in deep learning models that involve multiple layers. By connecting each layer to every other layer within a dense block, DenseNet ensures that valuable information from the input data is preserved and passed through the network, resulting in more accurate predictions.

12.3.5 DenseNet's Performance Advantages

The performance advantages of DenseNet can be attributed to its architecture, which enhances feature propagation and reduces the risk of information loss as data moves through the network. Traditional deep neural networks often struggle with the vanishing gradient problem, where the gradients used to update the model's weight become smaller as they propagate back through the network. This can cause the model to stop learning or to learn very slowly, leading to poor performance. DenseNet addresses this issue by ensuring that each layer has direct access to the gradients from all previous layers, which allows the model to continue learning effectively even as it grows deeper.

This study's results demonstrate the practical benefits of DenseNet's architecture. By maintaining a continuous flow of information, DenseNet was able to achieve higher accuracy rates and lower loss values compared to linear regression. This is particularly important in medical image analysis tasks, where the accuracy of a model's predictions can have significant implications for patient outcomes. In this case, DenseNet's ability to predict fallopian tube tumors with over 90% accuracy makes it a valuable tool for clinicians, who can use its predictions to guide diagnosis and treatment decisions.

12.3.6 Linear Regression's Limitations

In contrast, linear regression showed much lower accuracy and higher loss values. This result is not surprising, given that linear regression is a relatively simple algorithm that is not well-suited to complex tasks like medical image analysis. Linear regression works by fitting a linear equation to the data, which is effective for simple regression tasks but less so for tasks that involve highly non-linear relationships, such as tumor prediction. The fallopian tube dataset used in this study likely contains complex patterns that linear regression is unable to capture, leading to its lower accuracy and higher loss.

Additionally, the large standard deviation and standard error mean for linear regression suggest that its predictions were more variable and less reliable than those of DenseNet. In medical applications, such variability can be problematic, as inconsistent predictions can lead to incorrect diagnoses and inappropriate treatment plans. In contrast, DenseNet's lower standard deviation and standard error mean indicate that it produced more stable and reliable predictions, making it a more dependable model for clinical use.

12.3.7 Significance of Statistical Analysis

The statistical analysis performed in this study further underscores the superiority of DenseNet. The independent sample t-test confirmed that the difference in accuracy and loss between DenseNet and linear regression was statistically significant, with a p-value of 0.03 ($p < 0.05$). This finding indicates that the observed differences in performance were not due to random chance but rather to the inherent advantages of DenseNet's architecture and design.

Furthermore, the graphical comparison of mean accuracy and loss (Figure 12.1) provides a clear visual representation of DenseNet's superior performance. The graph shows that DenseNet consistently achieved higher accuracy and lower loss than linear regression across all samples, reinforcing the conclusion that DenseNet is the better model for this task.

12.3.8 Limitations and Future Work

Despite DenseNet's superior performance, the study identified a few limitations. One of the primary limitations is the time required to train the DenseNet model. Due to its deep architecture and the need to process large amounts of data, DenseNet requires significant computational resources and time to train, especially when dealing with large datasets. In this study, the relatively small dataset of 20 samples limited the time required for training, but scaling up the dataset could increase the training time substantially. Future research should explore ways to optimize DenseNet's training process, such as using more efficient algorithms or hardware accelerators like GPUs.

Another limitation is the small sample size used in this study. While the results provide valuable insights into the performance of DenseNet and linear regression, a larger sample size would provide more robust conclusions and allow for more generalizable results. Future studies should aim to include larger datasets and explore the performance of DenseNet on a wider range of medical prediction tasks.

This study demonstrates that DenseNet is a significantly better model than linear regression for predicting fallopian tube tumors. DenseNet's higher accuracy, lower loss values, and greater consistency make it a valuable tool for medical image analysis, where accurate predictions are critical for effective diagnosis and treatment. While there are some limitations to DenseNet's performance, such as the time required for training, its advantages far outweigh these drawbacks, making it a promising model for future medical applications.

12.4 Conclusion

The results of this study clearly demonstrate that DenseNet outperforms linear regression in predicting fallopian tube tumors. DenseNet achieved an accuracy of 90.4460%, significantly higher than linear regression's 68.7710%. This substantial difference underscores the effectiveness of DenseNet's architecture, which efficiently handles complex data and avoids issues such as the vanishing gradient problem that can impair the performance of deep neural networks. DenseNet's ability to maintain information flow and utilize feature propagation throughout its layers results in more accurate and reliable predictions, making it a more suitable model for critical medical tasks such as tumor detection.

While linear regression showed a reasonable level of accuracy, its performance was inferior in both accuracy and loss, and its predictions were more variable and less consistent. This finding highlights the limitations of traditional regression techniques when applied to complex, non-linear tasks like medical image analysis.

DenseNet's superior performance makes it a valuable tool for clinicians and researchers in medical diagnostics. Its higher accuracy and consistent performance provide reliable predictions that can aid in early diagnosis and treatment, ultimately improving patient outcomes in reproductive health. Future work should focus on further optimizing DenseNet's training process and expanding the dataset size to validate these findings across a broader range of medical applications.

References

1. Escobar, P.F., Starks, D.C., Fader, A.N., Barber, M., Rojas-Espalliat, L., Single-port risk-reducing salpingo-oophorectomy with and without hysterectomy: surgical outcomes and learning curve analysis. *Gynecol. Oncol.*, 119, 43–47, October 2010.
2. Gao, Y., Zeng, S., Xu, X., Li, H., Yao, S., Song, K., Li, X., Chen, L., Tang, J., Xing, H., Yu, Z., Zhang, Q., Zeng, S., Yi, C., Xie, H., Xiong, X., Cai, G., Wang, Z., Wu, Y., Chi, J., Jiao, X., Qin, Y., Mao, X., Chen, Y., Jin, X., Mo, Q., Chen, P., Huang, Y., Shi, Y., Wang, J., Zhou, Y., Ding, S., Zhu, S., Liu, X., Dong, X., Cheng, L., Zhu, L., Cheng, H., Cha, L., Hao, Y., Jin, C., Zhang, L., Zhou, P., Sun, M., Xu, Q., Chen, K., Gao, Z., Zhang, X., Ma, Y., Liu, Y., Xiao, L., Xu, L., Peng, L., Hao, Z., Yang, M., Wang, Y., Ou, H., Jia, Y., Tian, L., Zhang, W., Jin, P., Tian, X., Huang, L., Wang, Z., Liu, J., Fang, T., Yan, D., Cao, H., Ma, J., Li, X., Zheng, X., Lou, H., Song, C., Li, R., Wang, S., Li, W., Zheng, X., Chen, J., Li, G., Chen, R., Xu, C., Yu, R., Wang, J., Xu, S., Kong, B., Xie, X., Ma, D., Gao, Q., Deep learning-enabled pelvic ultrasound images for accurate diagnosis of ovarian cancer in China: a retrospective, multicentre, diagnostic study. *Lancet Digit. Health*, 4, e179–e187, March 2022.
3. Kaur, B., Mann, K.S., Grewal, M.K., Ovarian cancer stage based detection on convolutional neural network, in: *2017 2nd International Conference on Communication and Electronics Systems (ICCES)*, Coimbatore, 2017.

4. Ganesh, N., Shankar, R., Mahdal, M., Murugan, J.S., Chohan, J.S., Kalita, K., Exploring deep learning methods for computer vision applications across multiple sectors: Challenges and future trends. *Comput. Model. Eng. Sci.*, 139, 103–141, 2024.
5. Nanmaran, R., Srimathi, S., Yamuna, G., Thanigaivel, S., Vickram, A.S., Priya, A.K., Karthick, A., Karpagam, J., Mohanavel, V., Muhibbullah, M., Investigating the role of image fusion in brain tumor classification models based on machine learning algorithm for personalized medicine. *Comput. Math. Methods Med.*, 2022, 7137524, February 2022.
6. Giugliano, E., Cagnazzo, E., Bazzan, E., Patella, A., Marci, R., Hysterosalpingo-contrast sonography: is possible to quantify the therapeutic effect of a diagnostic test? *Clin. Exp. Reprod. Med.*, 39, 161–165, December 2012.
7. Kamiura, N., Emura, A., Yumoto, T., Isokawa, T., Hata, Y., Ishikawa, T., Matsubayashi, H., On ultrasound measurement system estimating diameters of fallopian tube models, in: *2017 6th International Conference on Informatics, Electronics and Vision & 2017 7th International Symposium in Computational Medical and Health Technology (ICIEV-ISCMHT)*, Himeji, 2017.
8. Kamiura, N., Isokawa, T., Yumoto, T., On detection of stenosis-type sections in Fallopian tubal models using support vector machines, in: *2020 IEEE 50th International Symposium on Multiple-Valued Logic (ISMVL)*, Miyazaki, 2020.
9. Sengupta, D., Ali, S.N., Bhattacharya, A., Mustafi, J., Mukhopadhyay, A., Sengupta, K., Nuclear morphology optimized Deep Hybrid Learning (NUMODRIL) for accurate diagnosis and prognosis of ovarian cancer, 2021.

13

Protected Medical Images Against Security Threats Using Lasso Regression and K-Means Algorithms

N. Sainath Reddy and S. Tamilselvan*

Department of Computer Science and Engineering, Saveetha School of Engineering, Saveetha Institute of Medical and Technical Sciences, Saveetha University, Chennai, India

Abstract
The purpose of the work is to detect unauthorized access to medical images using lasso regression compared with the k-means classifier. This study contains two groups: lasso regression and k-means classifiers. Each group consists of 10 outcome values under various functional operations. The total sample size is 20. The SPSS analyzes alpha at 0.05 and G*Power at 0.8 with 95% confidence intervals. The image analysis dataset with a size of 85,250 was considered from Kaggle. The accuracy for lasso regression, 91%, is higher than that of the k-means classifier, 77%. There is a statistically significant difference between the Lasso regression and k-means classifier with a value $p=0.001$ (independent sample t-test $p<0.05$) in SPSS statistical analysis. Lasso regression algorithm is found to be 91% having more accuracy than the k-means classifier, which is 77%.

***Keywords*:** Security threat, medical images, lasso regression, k-means classifier, medical, health

13.1 Introduction

Information technology has applications in many fields [1] like graphic design, maintaining databases in railway ticketing, hospitals, and postal services, and in many sectors using computers. Database systems were

**Corresponding author*: tamilselvans.sse@saveetha.com

Kanak Kalita, Divya Zindani, Narayanan Ganesh and Xiao-Zhi Gao (eds.) Medical Analytics for Clinical and Healthcare Applications, (261–270) © 2025 Scrivener Publishing LLC

implemented in these sectors for storage [2], such as transactional data that happens every day. Nowadays some organizations and unauthorized users try to gain access [3] to the data stored in various database systems, which are connected to a network. Here are some possible applications of this research. Healthcare organizations: the findings of this analysis could be useful for healthcare organizations that deal with medical images [4–6]. They can use the results to evaluate their current security measures and make improvements by implementing lasso regression or k-means classifier [7].

About 7000 articles deal with threat analysis over medical images [8]. Hospital information systems [9] define this unauthorized access as cyber-attacks or cyber threats that affect electronic media by seizing confidential data [10]. When these medical images are sent through the internet or other types of networks were accessed by a stranger or other unauthorized [11] or irrelevant organizations used to tamper medical images thereby raising the risk level for patients' ongoing treatments in respective hospitals [12–15].

The absence of thorough study on employing machine learning techniques to mitigate security threats in medical imaging may be the research gap in this analysis. There may be a research vacuum regarding lasso regression and k-means classifier strategies' efficacy in boosting medical image security, despite the fact that prior studies have examined a variety of methods of medical image security. By assessing the potential of lasso regression and k-means classifier approaches in improving the prevention of security threats [16] in medical imaging, this investigation seeks to fill a research vacuum. Using medical picture datasets for the analysis, machine learning models may be trained and tested to find potential security issues. The evaluation of lasso regression and k-means classifier approaches' efficiency will be used to see which method detects security threats more accurately and effectively.

13.2 Materials and Methods

This research was carried out in the Artificial Intelligence Laboratory belonging to the Saveetha School of Engineering, Saveetha Institute of Medical and Technical Sciences. The research article comprises a sample size of 20 categorized into two groups and each group consists of 10 at different times G*Power of 0.8 with a CI of 95%. Group-1 belongs to lasso regression, and Group-2 belongs to the k-means classifier. The threshold method is compared based on their accuracy in handling medical images from security threats [17]. During SPSS analysis, the parameters CI and Alpha are set to 0.05 and G*Power is to 0.8. The image analysis dataset with a size of 85,250 was considered from Kaggle.com [16].

13.3 K-Means Classifier

K-means classifier is a machine learning algorithm that works on grouping data without label identifiers into various clusters of organized patterns. It assigns data points to every cluster in the group. The k-means classifier determines the sum of squares of data points belonging to the normal cluster and data points related to the centroid of the cluster group. If the relationship between data points is found to be normal it is assumed to threaten free data. In medical image datasets [18] compare diagonal coefficients of medical images present within the train data set and test data set, any dissimilarity it identifies as a threat to intruded images.

13.4 Procedure for K-Means Classifier

1. Get input data set for k-means classifier containing medical images.
2. Load the k-means classifier with predefined libraries.
3. Assign the number of clusters as K.
4. Initialize centroid data points in a cluster and randomly select K-cluster data points.
5. Keep iterating until K-clusters data points are compared to the centroid data point and compute the sum of squares of the distance between K-cluster data points and the centroid data point.
6. Compute the centroid by calculating the mean of all data points within every cluster.
7. Evaluate the K-point for each cluster to arrange related clusters with the centroids having similarities to provide threat-free data.

13.5 Lasso Regression

LASSO expansion, also known as the least absolute shrinkage and selection operator, is a method used for regularizing data models and feature selection. Lasso regression is used to reorganize the data to its original form. Lasso regression model [19] handles a high level of multicollinearity between independent data parameters using an automated selection of features and parameter elimination.

13.6 Procedure for Lasso Regression

1. Get input data set containing medical images.
2. Load the lasso regression model with defined libraries.
3. Assign train data sets to the prediction model.
4. Read shrinkage and feature coefficients of train data set images.
5. Pass the test data set containing threat-intruded medical data.
6. Lasso regression model checks for similarities based on shrinkage coefficients in the test dataset with the train data set.
7. If the shrinkage coefficient shows high variation, it eliminates irrelevant data and checks for the selection of features based on feature coefficients obtained on the comparison.
8. Pass the output which contains threat-free medical images from the test data set.

13.7 Statistical Analysis

The statistical analysis is implemented with IBM SPSS Version 26. The comparison of mean accuracies is used to perform the independent sample t-test. The dependent variables are viewing angle and image size, while the independent factors are the accuracy of viewing angle and image size [20].

13.8 Results

The accuracy of the k-means method is 78%, whereas the accuracy of the lasso regression approach is 91%. The k-means method is used for Group 1, and the lasso regression approach is used for Group 2. Here, the accuracy of the two groups is compared. Here, the lasso regression model performed better than the k-means model.

Table 13.1 represents a sample of the accuracy data of the lasso regression algorithm and k-means algorithm.

Table 13.2 represents the mean accuracy and standard deviations for the group statistics for size N=10 for lasso regression and k-means methods.

Table 13.3 represents the independent sample t-test with a 95% confidence interval that compares k-means with lasso regression. There is a statistically significant difference between the lasso regression and k-means classifier with a two-tailed value P=0.000 ($p<0.05$) in statistical analysis.

Figure 13.1 shows a graph that compares the mean accuracy of the k-means algorithm to the mean accuracy of the lasso regression, along with error bars.

Table 13.1 Sample output accuracy comparison of lasso regression over k-means classifier.

S. no	Lasso regression	K-means classifier
1	90.3	77.2
2	91	77
3	88.9	76.5
4	89.4	76.8
5	90.5	77.12
6	87	75.89
7	87.6	74.95
8	88.5	75.4
9	91.03	77.44
10	91.21	77.89

Table 13.2 Sample output accuracy comparison over group statistics of lasso regression and k-means.

	Group	N	Mean	Std. deviation	Std. error mean
Accuracy	Lasso regression	10	89.4600	1.57045	.52348
	K-means	10	76.6190	.93530	.29577

Table 13.3 Independent sample test of lasso regression and k-means classifier. There is a statistically significant difference between the lasso regression and k-means classifier with a two-tailed value P=0.001 (p<0.05) in statistical analysis.

	Levene's test for equality of variances		T-test for equality of means						
								95% confidence interval of the difference	
	f	sig	t	df	Sig. (2-tailed)	Mean diff.	Std. error difference	Lower	Upper
Equal variances assumed	3.910	0.06	21.932	17	0.001	12.84100	.5854	11.605	14.0762
Equal variances not assumed			3.203	17.849	0.001	2.44200	.7624	.8390	14.142

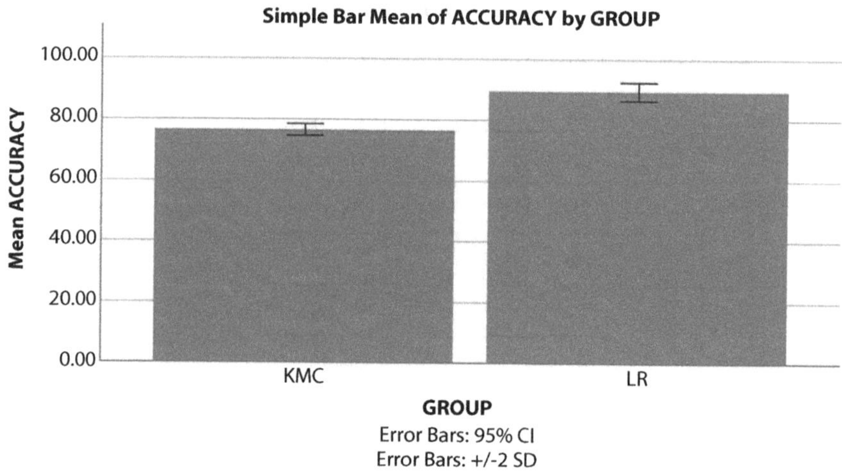

Figure 13.1 Mean accuracy comparison graph of lasso regression and k-means. Lasso regression algorithm is found to be 91% having more accuracy than the k-means classifier, which is 77%.

13.9 Discussion

As was already established, the Lasso regression algorithm outperformed the k-means algorithm in terms of performance. Lasso regression is determined to have a 91% accuracy percentage, while k-means has a 78% accuracy percentage. Researchers show that k-means works better in low-level network systems with better analysis and show that there is a statistically significant difference between lasso regression and k-means classifier with $P=0.001$ ($p<0.05$) in statistical analysis. of threat and methods, lasso regression increases time while the network grows rapidly. Lasso regression needs more memory management for framework architecture. In case of new threats, the model needs to be updated from time to time. Lasso regression uses special mechanisms for security threat analysis in web-based systems, medical imaging systems, graphical systems, and object recognition systems.

An evaluation was done on how well each algorithm performed in locating and deleting potentially sensitive information from medical pictures [21], or locating and separating unusual photos that might pose security risks [22]. A comparison of the reliability and accuracy of the outcomes was generated by each program. An analysis of each algorithm's computational effectiveness and its effects on the overall security enhancement process [23] purposes showed that the accuracy of the algorithm is 71%. When compared to earlier research publications, the lasso algorithm looked to be more accurate 91% [24].

A discussion of the limitations and challenges associated with using each algorithm, and potential solutions to overcome these challenges. A conclusion summarizing the main findings of the comparison and providing recommendations for the best approach to enhancing the security of medical images against potential threats. Future work is improving the accuracy of the methods: there is always room for improvement in the accuracy of the methods used for medical image security. Future works could aim to further refine and improve the accuracy of lasso regression and k-means clustering, making them even more effective in detecting and preventing security threats. Overall, future works related to this topic could involve further refining and improving the methods used for medical image security, applying them to different scenarios, and integrating them into real-time systems. The goal is to enhance the prevention of medical images from security threats and ensure the protection of sensitive patient information.

13.10 Conclusion

The review utilized two techniques, lasso regression, and the k-means classifier, to analyze unauthorized access in medical images. The study found that the accuracy of the lasso regression was 91%, while that of the k-means classifier was 78%. Based on the results, it was observed that the lasso regression was more effective in identifying unauthorized access in medical images to the k-means classifier.

References

1. Hartzband, D., *Information technology and data in healthcare*, Productivity Press, New York, 2019.
2. Xu, Z., Fang, Y., Yan, F., A novel approach to improving the efficiency of storing and accessing medical image files on Hadoop, in: *2017 International Conference on Computer Systems, Electronics and Control (ICCSEC)*, Dalian, 2017.
3. Dubinin, D.P., The use of trust systems in order to ensure information security and restrict unauthorized access to information systems of financial organizations. *Information Security Questions*, pp. 3–6, 2022.
4. Nanmaran, R., Srimathi, S., Yamuna, G., Thanigaivel, S., Vickram, A.S., Priya, A.K., Karthick, A., Karpagam, J., Mohanavel, V., Muhibbullah, M., Investigating the role of image fusion in brain tumor classification models based on machine learning algorithm for personalized medicine. *Comput. Math. Methods Med.*, 2022, 7137524, February 2022.
5. Shaik, K., Ramesh, J.V.N., Mahdal, M., Rahman, M.Z.U., Khasim, S., Kalita, K., Big data analytics framework using squirrel search optimized Gradient Boosted Decision Tree for heart disease diagnosis. *Appl. Sci. (Basel)*, 13, 5236, April 2023.
6. Nanmaran, R., Nagarajan, S., Sindhuja, R., Charan, G.V.S., Pokala, V.S.K., Srimathi, S., Gulothungan, G., Vickram, A.S., Thanigaivel, S., Wavelet transform based multiple image watermarking technique. *IOP Conf. Ser. Mater. Sci. Eng.*, 993, 012167, December 2020.
7. Yi, X., Walia, E., Babyn, P., Generative adversarial network in medical imaging: A review. *Med. Image Anal.*, 58, 101552, December 2019.
8. Dauer, L.T., *Dose, benefit, and risk in medical imaging*, L.T. Dauer, B.P. Chu, P.B. Zanzonico (Eds.), CRC Press, Boca Raton, 2018.
9. Herzig, T. and Walsh, T., *Implementing information security in healthcare*, T.W. Herzig, T. Walsh, L.A. Gallagher (Eds.), HIMSS Publishing, Boca Raton, 2020.
10. Parvees, M.Y.M., Bose, B.P., Samath, J.A., Confidential storage of medical images- a chaos-based encryption approach. *Int. J. Cloud Comput.*, 7, 15, 2018.
11. Singh, A.K., Singh, G., Mohan, A. (Eds.), *Medical Image Watermarking*, 1 ed., Springer International Publishing, Cham, Switzerland, 2017.

12. Ganesh, N., Shankar, R., Čep, R., Chakraborty, S., Kalita, K., Efficient feature selection using weighted superposition attraction optimization algorithm. *Appl. Sci. (Basel)*, 13, 3223, March 2023.
13. Priyadarshini, J., Premalatha, M., Čep, R., Jayasudha, M., Kalita, K., Analyzing physics-inspired metaheuristic algorithms in feature selection with K-nearest-neighbor. *Appl. Sci. (Basel)*, 13, 906, January 2023.
14. Kalita, K., Ganesh, N., Jayalakshmi, S., Chohan, J.S., Mallik, S., Qin, H., Multi-Objective artificial bee colony optimized hybrid deep belief network and XGBoost algorithm for heart disease prediction. *Front. Digit. Health*, 5, 1279644, 2023.
15. Premalatha, M., Jayasudha, M., Čep, R., Priyadarshini, J., Kalita, K., Chatterjee, P., A comparative evaluation of nature-inspired algorithms for feature selection problems. *Heliyon*, 10, e23571, January 2024.
16. Thanki, R. and Borra, S., *Medical Imaging and its Security in Telemedicine Applications*, 1 ed., Springer International Publishing, Cham, Switzerland, 2018.
17. Apostolidis, K.D. and Papakostas, G.A., Digital watermarking as an adversarial attack on Medical Image Analysis with Deep Learning. *J. Imaging*, 8, 155, May 2022.
18. Ravichandran, D., Praveenkumar, P., Rajagopalan, S., Rayappan, J.B.B., Amirtharajan, R., ROI-based medical image watermarking for accurate tamper detection, localisation and recovery. *Med. Biol. Eng. Comput.*, 59, 1355–1372, June 2021.
19. Kumar, D., Ridge Regression and Lasso Estimators for Data Analysis, 2019.
20. Koprowski, R., *Medical and biological image analysis*, BoD–Books on Demand, Rijeka, 2018.
21. Lee, G. and Fujita, H. (Eds.), *Deep learning in medical image analysis*, 1 ed., Springer Nature, Cham, Switzerland, 2020.
22. Sansurooah, K. and University, E.C., Security risks of medical devices in wireless environments, in: *Proceedings of the 4th Australian eHealth Informatics and Security Conference*, 2015.
23. Sreekutty, M.S. and Baiju, P.S., Security enhancement in image steganography for medical integrity verification system, in: *2017 International Conference on Circuit ,Power and Computing Technologies (ICCPCT)*, Kollam, 2017.
24. Tyagi, A.K. (Ed.), *Computational analysis and deep learning for medical care*, Wiley, Hoboken, 2021.

Part 5

EMERGING TRENDS AND TECHNOLOGIES

14

Predicting the Factors Influencing Alcoholic Consumption of Teenagers Using an Optimized Random Forest Classifier in Comparison with Logistic Regression

Devineni Giri and M. Gunasekaran*

Department of Computer Science and Engineering, Saveetha School of Engineering, Saveetha Institute of Medical and Technical Sciences, Saveetha University, Chennai, India

Abstract

This research aims to predict the teenagers who consume alcohol by using an optimized Random Forest classifier with a novel grid search approach, and it is compared against logistic regression based on accuracy. For this study, the Student Alcohol Consumption dataset from Kaggle is used. Two groups with a sample size of 20 for each are utilized for implementation. The sample size is calculated with a pretest G*Power of 80%, threshold of 0.05%, and confidence interval of 95%. The Optimized Random Forest classifier, having 90.7% accuracy, performs better than the logistic regression classifier, which achieved an accuracy of 78.3% for the prediction. There is a significance between the two groups based on the independent sample t-test conducted with the value of p=0.000 (p<0.05) two-tailed.

Keywords: Alcohol abuse, logistic regression, machine learning, novel grid search, prediction, random forest classifier, teenagers

14.1 Introduction

The consumption of alcohol among teenagers is very high. Identifying the factors influencing and predicting the teenagers who consume alcohol

**Corresponding author*: gunasekaranm.sse@saveetha.com

Kanak Kalita, Divya Zindani, Narayanan Ganesh and Xiao-Zhi Gao (eds.) Medical Analytics for Clinical and Healthcare Applications, (273–282) © 2025 Scrivener Publishing LLC

is important. This study aims to predict the consumption of alcohol abuse among teenagers with the help of a novel Grid Search approach of an Optimized random forest classifier [1]. According to the World Health Organization, there were over 6% of global deaths and 5% of burden injuries reported, and nowadays the consumption by teenagers is a growing concern [2, 3]. So, there is a need to predict teenage alcohol addiction [4]. Prevention is better than cure, stopping the intentions that lead to the consumption of alcohol is required [5]. Alcohol is a psychoactive substance, and early consumption can lead to addiction, which might lead to social responsibilities, negligence, injuries, and even fatalities [6]. The consumers' early prediction can help to reduce the negative impact on their educational performance and prevent mental and behavioral problems including depression and accidents [7]. At present 1 in 5 people aged between 15 to 19 are consuming alcohol abuse globally, and alcohol-related diseases are going up. So, early detection helps to give awareness and helps to distract alcohol consumers from drinking [8].

There are so many research articles regarding the consumption of alcohol among teenagers, some of them were about the risk factors and a few regarding the prediction of alcohol consumption. There are over 100 research articles on Google Scholar and 20 in Science Direct [9–11]. Among them, these are a few research articles that are most cited and support this research. A systematic review of social network characteristics that influence alcohol consumption was performed [12]. Attempts to detect alcohol consumption were made based on mobile phone sensor data using machine learning algorithms such as Decision Tree, Random Forest, and Bayesian Network, and it was found that Random Forest performed best [13]. Approaches to detect alcohol abuse were made using clinical measures and achieved an accuracy of 86.1% with the abstract Decision Tree model [14]. With an elastic-net classifier, an 87% accuracy was obtained when predicting teen alcohol use by using a variety of machine-learning methods and general survey data [15]. A study had been performed on 1,673 Australian secondary school students who are adolescents below age 17 [16]. Among them, 839 students started consuming alcohol, and 36% tended to binge drink at a mean age of 16.9 years and initiated drinking at a mean age of 15.1 years. Based on our view, the method is preferable for estimating alcohol consumption [15].

The lacuna of existing research is that there is no significant awareness of the main factors that tend teenagers towards alcohol abuse and prediction of binge drinkers, and there is less accuracy in predicting binge drinkers precisely. So, this study is aiming towards predicting alcohol consumption among teenagers by using a novel grid search approach of an optimized Random Forest classifier in comparison with logistic regression and trying to find the reasons that make teenagers lean towards alcohol consumption more precisely.

14.2 Materials and Methods

This study was performed in the Computer Communication Lab, Department of Computer Science and Engineering, Saveetha School of Engineering, Saveetha Institute of Medical and Technical Sciences, Chennai. This study used two machine learning algorithms named the Optimized Random Forest classifier and logistic regression classifier for the implementation in this article. Two groups of 20 were used to train and test the algorithms. Clincalc.com software was used to calculate the sample size with a G*Power of 80%, a threshold of 0.05 and a Confidence level of 95%. An article is taken as a base article for this study, which achieved better accuracy, and the sample size is calculated accordingly [17].

The infrastructure used for this study is a laptop with a configuration of an i5 processor and 8 GB ram installed with Windows 11 operating system, a Jupyter lab environment, SPSS 26.0.1 analytical software by IBM, and Python 3.10. A dataset named Student Alcohol Consumption from an open-source website Kaggle is used for this study [18]. The two models are taken from a machine learning library named Sci-kit learn and for visualization, the seaborn library is used.

14.3 Random Forest Classifier

One of the most widely used supervised learning algorithms for machine learning models is Random Forest. Random Forest is based on the principle of ensemble learning, which suggests mixing many classifiers into a hybrid version to handle complicated machine learning issues more precisely and perform better. The best tree is selected by a random forest, which forms several decision trees based on votes. Regression and classification problems both can be solved by using random forest methods. Adjusting parameters like random state, n estimators, max depth, min samples split, and min samples leaf the accuracy may be increased, with these parameters, the Random Forest algorithm was optimized [19].

14.4 Algorithm for Random Forest Classifier

1. Import the required libraries.
2. Load the dataset into a pandas dataframe.
3. Perform the pre-processing of the dataset, which includes data cleaning and data transformation.
4. Perform feature engineering and exploratory data analysis.
5. Split the dataset into train and test.
6. Upsample the minority class.
7. Select k=10 bést features.
8. Use a Random Forest classifier to train and test the data by the hyperparameters.
9. Show the accuracy and confusion matrix.

14.5 Logistic Regression Classifier

A logistic regression is a simple but efficient classification model of supervised learning methodologies of machine learning. Apart from how they are applied, logistic regression and linear regression are very identical, linear regression is used to solve regression issues whereas logistic is used for classification. A logical function such as the sigmoid function is used to model the dependent variable in logistic regression, which is also a powerful classification technique based on the supervised learning model in machine learning. Only two classes can be generated using this approach since the dependent variable is bipartite. Comparing this model to other models, it performs well with datasets that have a smaller sample size and need less computing time [20].

14.6 Algorithm for Logistic Regression Classifier

1. Import the required libraries.
2. Load the pre-processed dataset.
3. Split the dataset into train and test.
4. Upsample the minority class.
5. Select k=10 best features.
6. Use a logistic regression classifier to train and test the data.
7. Show the accuracy and confusion matrix.

This study used the SPSS software of IBM for statistical analysis to compare the mean accuracies of the two algorithms. The dependent factors in the dataset are gender, travel time, study time, free time, go out, absences, grades, stability, and idleness. And the independent factors are school, age, address, famsize, Pstatus, Medu, Fedu, Mjob, Fjob, reason, guardian, failures, schoolsup, famsup, paid activities, nursery, higher, internet, romantic, famrel, and health. An independent t-test analysis between both the intervention and comparison algorithm by using the SPSS software of IBM, which calculates the mean, standard deviation and standard error mean to compare the accuracies.

14.7 Results

Comparing the intervention, a novel grid search approach of Optimized Random Forest classifier with a logistic regression classifier shows a significant rise in the accuracy of the intervention than the compared one. So, the Optimized Random Forest classifier is better at predicting the teenagers who tend towards alcohol abuse.

Table 14.1 represents the group statistics of the t-test for 20 iterations of the algorithm and has the following results. The Optimized Random Forest classifier has a mean accuracy of 90.75% with a standard deviation of 2.09 and a standard error mean of 0.46 while logistic regression showed a mean accuracy of 78.36% with a standard deviation of 6.29 and standard error mean of 1.40. So, the performance of the Optimized Random Forest classifier is outperforming logistic regression.

Table 14.2 shows the results of the independent sample t-test at the 95% confidence interval and the significance probability $p=0.000$ ($p<0.05$) two-tailed, which indicates that the difference between both the algorithm's accuracies is significant. The main nine influencing factors for the

Table 14.1 The group statistics of the results obtained for over 20 iterations of the dataset when tested the intervention using an Optimized Random Forest classifier in comparison with logistic regression.

	Group	N	Mean	Std. deviation	Std. error mean
Accuracy	Optimized Random Forest	20	90.7570	2.09660	0.46881
	Logistic regression	20	78.3645	6.29163	1.40685

Table 14.2 The independent t-test analysis was performed on the results obtained during the 20 iterations of the dataset on an Optimized Random Forest classifier and logistic regression. It shows that the significance probability p=0.000 (p<0.05) two-tailed.

									95% confidence interval of the difference	
		F	**Sig.**	**t**	**df**	**Sig. (2-tailed)**	**Mean difference**	**Std. error difference**	**Lower**	**Upper**
Accuracy	Equal variances assumed	34.912	.000	8.357	38	.000	12.39250	1.48291	9.39051	15.39449
	Equal variances not assumed			8.357	23.168	.000	12.39250	1.48291	9.32611	15.45889

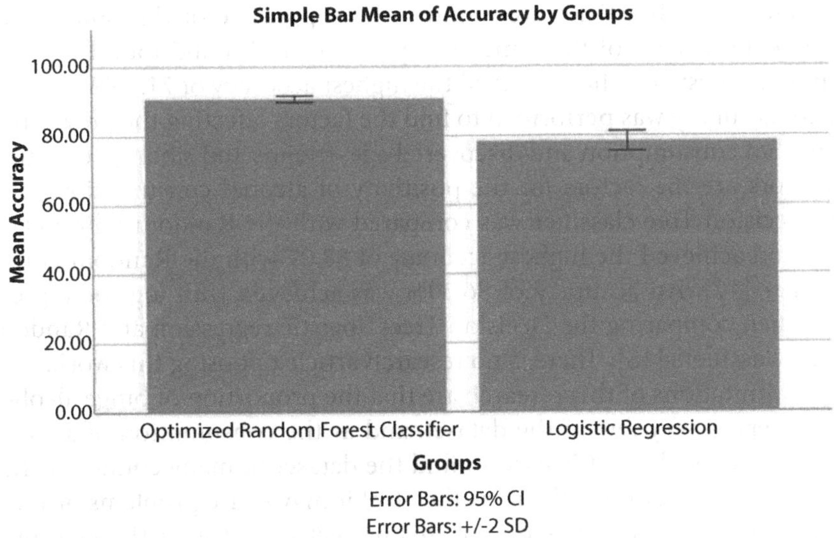

Figure 14.1 A comparison of Optimized Random Forest classifier and logistic regression based on mean accuracy. X axis: Optimized Random Forest classifier vs. logistic regression, Y axis: Mean accuracy. Error Bar +/-2 SD.

consumption of alcohol abuse among teenagers are gender, travel time, study time, free time, going out, absences, grades, stability, and idleness based on the findings.

Figure 14.1 shows the comparison of accuracy between the novel grid search approach of the Optimized Random Forest model and the logistic regression model. The Optimized Random Forest classifier beats the logistic regression model by a good significant difference.

14.8 Discussion

Through this research, the optimized Random Forest classifier with an accuracy of 90.7% outperformed the logistic regression classifier whose accuracy is 78.3 %. Since the Optimized Random Forest classifier can form multiple decision trees at a time, it performs better at predicting than logistic regression, which uses a 2D graph with a logistic function to classify the data. There is significance between the two groups based on the independent sample t-test conducted with the value of $p=0.000$ ($p<0.05$) two-tailed.

These research articles are found to be supportive of this study, data mining approaches of the same were performed [21] and found that the Random Forest classifier achieved the highest accuracy of 71.39%. A cross sectional survey was performed to find the factors affecting the prevalence of alcohol consumption and discovered age, friends and siblings' drinking behaviors are the factors for the positivity of alcohol consumption [22]. The Decision Tree classifier was compared with the Random Forest classifier and achieved the highest accuracy of 88.07 with the Random Forest classifier [17]. An accuracy of 86.50% was achieved with logistic regression when comparing the Decision Trees, logistic regression and Random Forest classifiers [18]. There is no research article opposing this work.

The limitations of this research are that the proportion of binge alcohol consumers is very few in the dataset, and as the consumption of alcohol by teenagers is illegal it is hard to find the dataset in many countries. The survey among them is difficult as they feel it may cause problems or risks in the future. The future scope of this project is that with the help of a dataset with the most relevant attributes and increasing the proportion of alcohol consumers by giving them trustworthy privacy helps the model to work more efficiently by having the exact factors leading to the consumption helps the government, parents, and schools to make early preventive measures.

14.9 Conclusion

In this research, a novel grid search-based hyperparameter-tuned approach with a Random Forest classifier that is optimized for better predictions is introduced and is compared against the logistic regression classifier, the results are very significant and conclude that the intervention outstands the other based on accuracy. So, using the optimized Random Forest classifier can predict better than the logistic regression classifier.

References

1. Siwale, C.C. and Siziya, S., Factors associated with alcohol consumption among students in high cost schools in Lusaka, Zambia. *Int. J. Transl. Med. Res. Public Health*, 3, 21–30, April 2019.
2. Kalita, K., Ganesh, N., Jayalakshmi, S., Chohan, J.S., Mallik, S., Qin, H., Multi-Objective artificial bee colony optimized hybrid deep belief network

and XGBoost algorithm for heart disease prediction. *Front. Digit. Health*, 5, 1279644, 2023.
3. Premalatha, M., Jayasudha, M., Čep, R., Priyadarshini, J., Kalita, K., Chatterjee, P., A comparative evaluation of nature-inspired algorithms for feature selection problems. *Heliyon*, 10, e23571, January 2024.
4. Athauda, L.K., Peiris-John, R., Ameratunga, S., McCool, J., Wickremasinghe, R., Factors influencing alcohol use among adolescents in South Asia: A systematic review. *J. Stud. Alcohol Drugs*, 81, 529–542, September 2020.
5. Shankareswari, Jayapriya, Sandeep, Jafrin, L., A study on prevalence of alcohol consumption among higher secondary school students in Theni district, Tamil Nadu. *Int. J. Basic Clin. Pharmacol.*, 9, 226, January 2020.
6. Olawole-Isaac, A., Ogundipe, O., Amoo, E.O., Adeloye, D.O., Substance use among adolescents in sub-Saharan Africa: a systematic review and meta-analysis. *SAJCH*, 12, 79, September 2018.
7. Omoegun, M. and Alli, K., Alcoholism and mental wellness among youths in Oyo metropolis: Implications for counseling. *Int. J. Educ. Res.*, 8, 69–82, 2020.
8. Suthar, H. and Saini, J., A cross-sectional study: Prevalence of alcohol consumption, factors associated, and its effects among undergraduate college students. *J. Sci. Soc.*, 49, 152, 2022.
9. Nanmaran, R., Srimathi, S., Yamuna, G., Thanigaivel, S., Vickram, A.S., Priya, A.K., Karthick, A., Karpagam, J., Mohanavel, V., Muhibbullah, M., Investigating the role of image fusion in brain tumor classification models based on machine learning algorithm for personalized medicine. *Comput. Math. Methods Med.*, 2022, 7137524, February 2022.
10. Priyadarshini, J., Premalatha, M., Čep, R., Jayasudha, M., Kalita, K., Analyzing physics-inspired metaheuristic algorithms in feature selection with K-nearest-neighbor. *Appl. Sci. (Basel)*, 13, 906, January 2023.
11. Ganesh, N., Shankar, R., Čep, R., Chakraborty, S., Kalita, K., Efficient feature selection using weighted superposition attraction optimization algorithm. *Appl. Sci. (Basel)*, 13, 3223, March 2023.
12. Knox, J., Schneider, J., Greene, E., Nicholson, J., Hasin, D., Sandfort, T., Using social network analysis to examine alcohol use among adults: A systematic review. *PLoS One*, 14, e0221360, August 2019.
13. Bae, S., Chung, T., Ferreira, D., Dey, A.K., Suffoletto, B., Mobile phone sensors and supervised machine learning to identify alcohol use events in young adults: Implications for just-in-time adaptive interventions. *Addict. Behav.*, 83, 42–47, August 2018.
14. Lee, M.R., Sankar, V., Hammer, A., Kennedy, W.G., Barb, J.J., McQueen, P.G., Leggio, L., Using machine learning to classify individuals with Alcohol Use Disorder based on treatment seeking status. *EClinicalMedicine*, 12, 70–78, July 2019.
15. Afzali, M.H., Sunderland, M., Stewart, S., Masse, B., Seguin, J., Newton, N., Teesson, M., Conrod, P., Machine-learning prediction of adolescent alcohol

use: a cross-study, cross-cultural validation. *Addiction*, 114, 662–671, April 2019.

16. Aiken, A., Clare, P.J., Wadolowski, M., Hutchinson, D., Najman, J.M., Slade, T., Bruno, R., McBride, N., Kypri, K., Mattick, R.P., Age of alcohol initiation and progression to binge drinking in adolescence: A prospective cohort study. *Alcohol. Clin. Exp. Res.*, 42, 100–110, January 2018.
17. Pisutaporn, A., Chonvirachkul, B., Sutivong, D., Relevant factors and classification of student alcohol consumption, in: *2018 IEEE International Conference on Innovative Research and Development (ICIRD)*, Bangkok, 2018.
18. Lamprou, S., A study in alcohol: A comparison of data mining methods for identifying binge drinking risk factors in university students, 2021.
19. Abdulkareem, N.M. and Abdulazeez, A.M., Science and Business. *Int. J.*, 5, 128–142, 2021.
20. Ray, S., A quick review of machine learning algorithms, in: *2019 International Conference on Machine Learning, Big Data, Cloud and Parallel Computing (COMITCon)*, Faridabad, 2019.
21. Shukla, A.K., Singh, P., Vardhan, M., Predicting alcohol consumption behaviours of the secondary level students. In *Proceedings of 3rd international conference on internet of things and connected technologies (ICIoTCT)*, pp. 26–27, 2018.
22. Kounnavong, T., Vonglokham, M., Moji, K., Okumura, J., Factors affecting alcohol drinking behaviour among secondary school students in Vientiane Province, Lao People's Democratic Republic: a cross-sectional study. *Int. Health*, 14, 319–328, May 2022.

15

Harnessing Food Waste Potential: Advancing Protein Sequence Motif Analysis with Novel Cluster Sequence Analyzer Machine Learning Model

U. Vignesh[1], Geetha S.[1]* and Benson Edwin Raj[2]

[1]*School of Computer Science and Engineering, Vellore Institute of Technology (VIT) - Chennai, Tamil Nadu, India*
[2]*Department of Computer Information Sciences, Higher Colleges of Technology, Fujairah, United Arab Emirates*

Abstract
A motif analysis for the application of food wastes using a machine learning technique has been performed in this paper. The amino acid sequences are more capable of taking the functional characteristics of available genes than the DNA sequences. Motif analysis takes place on the protein sequences of living beings, which is in the form of huge availability. Due to this factor, the analysis of genes turns its head toward protein analysis. Given the complexity of food waste management and its significant environmental impact, there is a growing need for effective analysis methods. Traditional gene-centric approaches may not fully capture the intricacies of food waste composition and its potential applications. Therefore, the paper argues for a shift towards protein analysis, which offers a more comprehensive understanding of functional characteristics. The proposed model utilizes a machine learning algorithm called cluster sequence analyzer to conduct motif analysis on protein sequences derived from food wastes. The cluster sequence analyzer is chosen for its efficiency in handling large datasets and its ability to identify meaningful patterns within sequences.

Keywords: Prediction, protein sequence, food waste utilization, clustering sequence analyzer, clustering, motif analysis

**Corresponding author*: geetha.s@vit.ac.in

Kanak Kalita, Divya Zindani, Narayanan Ganesh and Xiao-Zhi Gao (eds.) Medical Analytics for Clinical and Healthcare Applications, (283–310) © 2025 Scrivener Publishing LLC

15.1 Introduction

In protein analysis, various techniques are designed to inspect the factors, but the most expressive of the functional characteristics of proteins are classification and clustering. These two techniques are used in this research because of their highly favorable properties toward protein.

Motif results in the repetition of certain kinds of patterns with relevant lengths in the given set of sequences, whereas conserved patterns also pave the way for the analyzer to analyze the protein sequences for the functional aspects. In the clustering of sequences, the examination starts with the set of individuals in a given set of sequences at the various stages of unsupervised learning based on the provided knowledge or characteristics. The solutions obtained from these concepts can be in the form of quality if the set of rules determined for unsupervised learning is followed properly without any deviations. In this research, to examine the performance of the proposed cluster sequence analyzer (CSA) algorithm in the analysis factor, six different sets of datasets containing various unrelated eight sets of protein sequences in each are considered. The measures of these datasets at various instances are recorded and their functions are measured accordingly. In biology, numerous sequences are uploaded in the public domain daily, which paves the way for a new classification and clustering algorithms to deal with this new type of sequence more effectively as compared to already existing algorithms. This research can discover the most relevant and redundant pattern of a given length in the provided set of sequences. These sets of sequences can be of any number such as 1000 and 10000.

The proposed CSA algorithm is designed to handle a large set of sequences. It is a known factor that the members of each family share their functions and characteristic behavior. The same also happens for the protein family. Hence, the research sets a rule to avoid the protein belonging to the same family for the case of better research rather than dealing with protein matching to find their ancestors. However, the proposed CSA algorithm can be applied to the same set of protein family members. The final aspect of the proposed CSA algorithm is a descriptor or single pattern with the referred length known as the consensus string obtained from the motif matrix. The pattern length is provided according to the rules framed for the proposed CSA algorithm since the original shape of the unknown pattern is not available in the protein sequence. So, it is necessary to provide the length or the count of the repetitions in the given set of sequences. Many methods are available to take up this kind of activity, but the performance analysis and complexity describe better algorithms as justification for proof of correctness in a better way.

Motif involves the mathematical equations to be derived for the analysis since the optimization problem must be solved by creating functions for motif matrix using Equation 15.1. The elaborated values of the defined functions are shown in Equation 15.2, Equation 15.3, and Equation 15.4 with the parameters referred to as m1(z) tends to the length of pattern, m2(z) tends to support, m3(z) is the occurred match, s is the number of protein sequences, p is referred to as the protein sequence, q is the position in the pattern, x records the candidate pattern found at p, D finals the consensus string, and a gives the amino acid in the sequence. The maximum occupancy rate score of dominant a is p. Matches to derive the score for the consensus string are calculated using Equation 15.5. The threshold value is fixed for motif finding. The sequences with less than the threshold value will not be considered for frequent pattern-searching processes.

$$m(z) = (m_1(z), m_2(z), m_3(z)) \tag{15.1}$$

$$m_1(z) = k \tag{15.2}$$

$$m_2(z) = \sum_{p=1}^{s} membership\ function(\sum_{q=1}^{k} match(x_{pq}, D_q), k) \tag{15.3}$$

$$m_3(z) = \sum_{p=1}^{k} \max_a \tag{15.4}$$

$$match(x_{pq}, D_q) = \{0 - x_p q \neq D_q; 1 - x_p q = D_q\} \tag{15.5}$$

The rules involve the threshold value of the set of sequences described in the proposed CSA algorithm. These threshold values depend on the amino acid count. The rules also consider a minimum set of similarities. These similarities available within the given sequences are only considered for prediction. Complexity is also incorporated into the rules processes. The solution that occurs with their available quality present in the complexity in the smaller range is omitted for better algorithmic performance measures. In this research process, clustering takes place to gather the sequences containing similar sets of patterns or strings in a big way.

These processes are provided in some of the tools such as Gibbs sampling and consensus. These tools are provided commercially online where the results can also be obtained with the provided input. The major problem is variating DNA and protein for further analysis processes. The clustering algorithms that take part in this research provide the results based on their efficiency. Some algorithms, like k-means, can process only integer values. Their action takes place in converting amino acids to integer values representation of the counts that occur at various stages of the algorithm. Other clustering and classification algorithms are considered for the proof of correctness with varying dataset activities. The chronological measures of the proposed CSA algorithm efficiency are unknown initially. It is advised to do the same datasets in these existing techniques and compare the results based on the time taken by these algorithms. Thus, the fair analysis of time on these techniques proves that the proposed CSA algorithm is better at their variations and iteration levels.

The scoring algorithm helps for the integer count in analyzing the occurrences of each amino acid in the substring provided for the result. Though there are many traditional scoring functions, this index-oriented score is easier and faster to calculate in the obtained pattern based on the simple identification of the amino acids index. Thus, the common subunits available from the input sequences are predicted based on the proposed CSA algorithm for protein sequences. The most difficult factor in this process is the binding sites, which are available in the biological sequences. The aspect taken care of is the transcript of these factors of binding sites with their respective atoms or residues in the given biological sequences. The identification of the binding factor on these sites is also a challenging job since these complexes are not obtained from the public domain. The real-time samples of binding sites are the most critical factors in identification without making any changes in their sequential perception, such as the gene mutations that are not recommended to occur without any knowledge of this extraction process. This paper explains the basic concepts of motif analyzing methods, data of motif regions, clustering algorithms, classification algorithms in protein-protein interactions (PPIs), and the proposed CSA algorithm with the performance analysis.

15.1.1 Motif Regions

The preprocessing of provided datasets involves a decomposition technique used as an element matrix rank step-down to interchange the rank step-down of every evolution of concerned tensors. It develops an efficient algorithmic rule to pick the motif projected regions. The purpose of artificial knowledge verifies each model with the efficiency and effectiveness of a trace norm regularization (TNR) technique highly used in identifying motif regional factors. Even though the TNR factors are not found, the process must still be continued with identifying a pattern in the motif regions. In recent years, low-rank tensor completion (LRTC) issues have received significant attention in process and computer (PC) vision, data processing, and signal process. The present trace norm reduction algorithms for iteratively determination LRTC issues involve multiple singular worth decompositions of terribly massive matrices at every iteration. Therefore, they suffer from a high production price. This research work focused on a line to propose a completely unique trace norm regular decomposition, which is the TNR methodology for coinciding tensor decompositions and completion. This research also first formulated a matrix rank reduction model by deducing the relation between the rank of every matrix. Therefore, the mode-n rank of a tensor, introducing a tractable relaxation of score value perform, came through a convexo-convex combination, the downside of a much smaller-scale matrix trace norm reduction. Finally, it develops associated efficient algorithmic rules that support an alternating direction methodology of multipliers to pick the regions. The promising experimental results on artificial and real-world knowledge validate the effectiveness of the TNR methodology. Moreover, TNR is significantly quicker than the progressive strategies and scales to larger issues.

The two properties involved in the motif representations are conserved regions and overlapping regions. Addressing these properties requires transcription factor processes to undergo their corresponding residue to provide the eligible signals of the motif and to understand the model efficiently in the processes. This research deals only with clustering and classification techniques of data mining, leaving out the association technique. The reason for omitting the association technique is that the possibilities involved in the process are incapable of carrying or identifying the direct motifs from the sequences provided. The processes also make motifs burdened with the unusual calculation of a threshold, such as support and confidence. The motive of this research is to get a large number of motifs instances from the set of sequences and derive efficient results with them. The drawback of the existing algorithms and techniques is that quantitative analysis does not produce results but instead gives the motif of the most compared one in all the sequences rather than taking the factor of count into account. Figure 15.1 clearly describes the discovery of patterns with the basic steps to be followed for finding patterns on multiple sequences

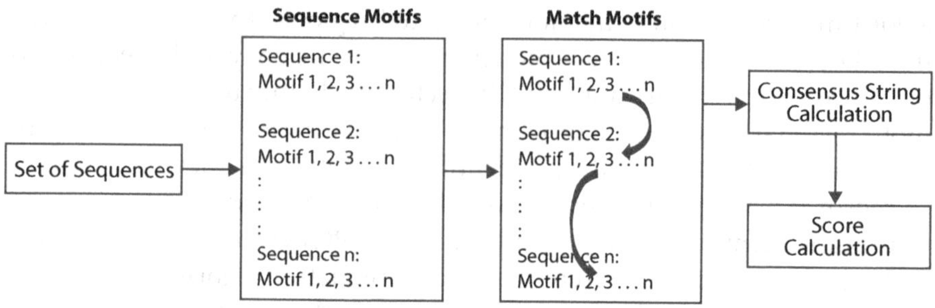

Figure 15.1 Pattern discovery on multiple sequences.

with an avoidance of transcription factor binding sites. The existing algorithm also provides much shorter sequences as a result. Error rate calculation is performed based on the recordings at various instances, not on the single parametric instance.

The motifs are used to form a motif matrix with the emergence of merging the core content of each sequence, resulting in no redundant data matrix. This motif non-redundant data matrix helps the avoidance of any available potential data in the sequences. In case of instances involving two sets of patterns having the same hamming distance, the results of considerations depend on the score value. The pattern, which has the highest score, is considered for the motif matrix. The patterns that are highly conserved are said to be efficient patterns. The algorithm that can provide these patterns are said to be efficient algorithms. In the initial stage of the processes, the threshold value paves a better way for further processes, avoiding unnecessary noise. If unnecessary noise is not found in certain sequences, discarding those sequences is recommended. The motif matrix, containing all sets of repeated patterns in their matrix out of which the patterns having the highest score or the pattern in the top position, can be considered for the pick and set problem. For this reason, the motif is also found directly and a non-scoring strategy is applied to this kind of methodologies. This analysis gives the full pattern or semi-pattern results though the length fixed in the mutations is not allowed. If the mutation is allowed, the resultant content produces the pattern in the exact length. The index-oriented score is an easier way of scoring than the unified score, which assigns the score measure based on the sum and normalization but also calculates the binding sites' scores separately.

15.2 Suffix Tree

The suffix tree is an information structure for ordering strings. It is utilized in an assortment of uses, for example, bioinformatics, time arrangement investigation, bunching, content editing, and information maintenance.

The string and the subsequent suffix trees are excessively vast to fit into the principal memory, and most existing development calculations turn out to be extremely inefficient. It presents a circle-based suffix tree development strategy, called an elastic range (ER). It works efficiently with long strings bigger than the accessible memory. Time management makes the tree development process onto a level plane vertically. It limits I/O by progressively altering the flat segments freely for every vertical segment, given the advancing state of the tree and the accessible memory, where proper, ER likewise bunches vertical segments together and amortizes the I/O cost. The research has built up a sequential adaptation; a parallel rendition for shared memory, shared-circle multi-center frameworks, and a parallel form for shared-nothing designs. Time records the whole human genome in a few minutes on a customary personal computer.

The suffix tree is a tree that files all conceivable suffixes of a string S. It is utilized to quicken many string activities. For example, finding a sub-string P inside S without a list takes O time. With a suffix tree, a similar task is done in O(P) time, which is a significant increase given that normally S has a few requests of greatness longer than P. Different activities that can benefit from a suffix tree incorporate surmised string coordinating, finding the longest normal sub-string of two strings, and finding all basic sub-strings in a database of strings. Such inquiries are fundamental for some applications. In-memory approaches perform extremely well as long as the information string and the subsequent suffix tree fit in primary memory. For a string S of size n, the time-multifaceted nature of the last is O(n), which is ideal. Nonetheless, this class suffers from the poor complexity of reference. Once the suffix tree cannot fit in the fundamental memory, the calculations of this class require all things considered O(n) costly arbitrary circle I/O. Review that the suffix tree is a tree with a bigger size than the information string. Along these lines, in-memory techniques are restrictively costly notwithstanding for modestly long strings. Semi-plate-based techniques take care of the complexity of reference issues by breaking down the suffix tree into smaller sub-trees put away on the circle.

This classification incorporates the subsequent sub-trees that are put away on the circle. In this second stage, the sub-trees are converged into the final suffix tree. The time complexity is O(n2), yet as long as the string S fits into memory, the calculations in this class perform a couple of irregular I/O, and they are quicker than in-memory calculation. An out-of-center classification contains two ongoing strategies that help strings bigger than the principal memory with sensible efficiency by maintaining a strategic distance from irregular I/O. The first technique of binary search depends on suffix clusters. A suffix exhibit is a vector that contains all suffixes of the information string S arranged in a lexicographical request. The longest regular prefix cluster is a vector that stores the length of the basic prefix between every two sequential sections in the suffix exhibit. Binary search isolates the info string S into a few segments and assembles the related suffix exhibit and the longest normal prefix cluster for each segment. At that point, it consolidates the suffix varieties with everything being equal and produces a suffix sub-tree. A point to note is that the tree is developed in groups at the final stage. This is a favorable position of the calculation because by evading the tree traversal for adding each new hub, it is stored well and disposed of.

Suffix trees are basic for some pragmatic applications that incorporate bioinformatics, handle data management information, and archive bunching. The volume of such information increments quickly; in this way, it is basic to have quick suffix tree development techniques. An ER technique that underpins long strings and substantial letter sets works efficiently regardless of whether the memory is exceptionally restricted and effortlessly parallel. Broad exploratory assessments with vast genuine informational collections uncovered the strategy substantially and are more efficient than the existing ones for speed and computational assets. Time records the whole human genome in 59 minutes on a conventional 8-core personal computer with 16GB RAM, and in 8.3min on a low-end group with 16 product PCs with 4GB RAM each. To the best of our insight, the quickest existing strategy needs 15min on an IBM Blue Gene/L supercomputer with 10 CPUs and 512GB RAM. This work is a substantial task that builds up a motor for putting away and preparing huge strings. It presents at chipping away scaling the technique to thousands of CPU.

Memory allocation is the process of reserving a partial or complete portion of computer memory for the execution of programs and processes. Memory allocation can also be defined as the process of setting aside sections of memory in a program to store variables and instances of structures and classes. This can be relaxed with the formation of trees. Hence, the I/O cost becomes low. This tree formation is divided into three categories, namely, as input data chamber, process data chamber, and tree chamber. This input data chamber contains the data input and needs the allocation of the buffer area. Since the calculated data are to be transferred to the buffer allocated area, it also allows the set of the area in the chamber to be empty for the connection of sub-trees if needed in the future with clarity of excellence. The process data is where the data gets accessed in the algorithm and the analyses are done here by identifying problem domains and planning the modules, which are needed. It is followed by the design decisions of the submodules with the evaluation of design if required. It can access agile models such as the scrum model.

The data structures for the processing data will be decided on in this chamber. It takes nearly 35 to 45 percent of the whole allocation. The tree chamber takes the remaining 50 percent of memory allocation perceptions. The initial stage calculates the minimum tree size (MTS) and the whole performance of the processes as shown in Figure 15.2. This tree methodology overcomes the problem of indexing in a very large string. It is also useful for an easier understanding of parallel data processing without unnecessary waste of time and cost. It also avoids the parallel file system or virtual systems to maintain and process the data effectively. In the process of sequence alignment, there are two categories namely pairwise alignment and multiple sequence alignment. Pairwise alignment consists of two algorithms for its processing namely, the Needleman–Wunsch algorithm and Smith–Waterman algorithm. This research focuses mainly on multiple sequences. The multiple sequence alignment process is shown in detail in Figure 15.3 with the proposed CSA algorithm. In the sequence analysis, overlapping has to be dealt with carefully because it is common to overlap while framing the group of related sequences or related patterns, which has to be avoided for effective processes.

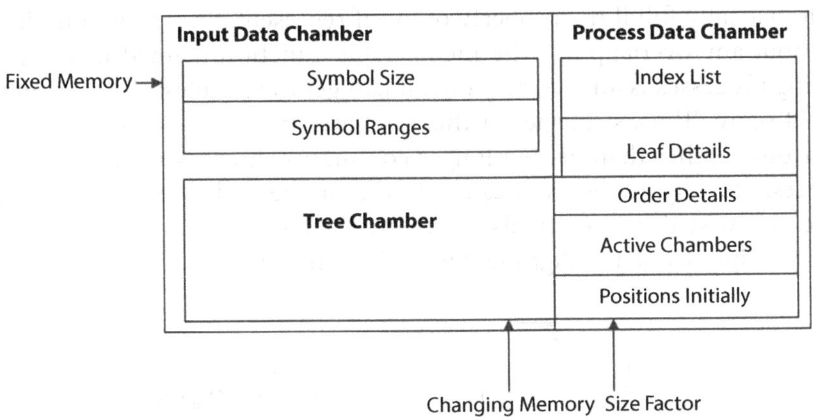

Figure 15.2 Memory allocation chambers using a suffix tree.

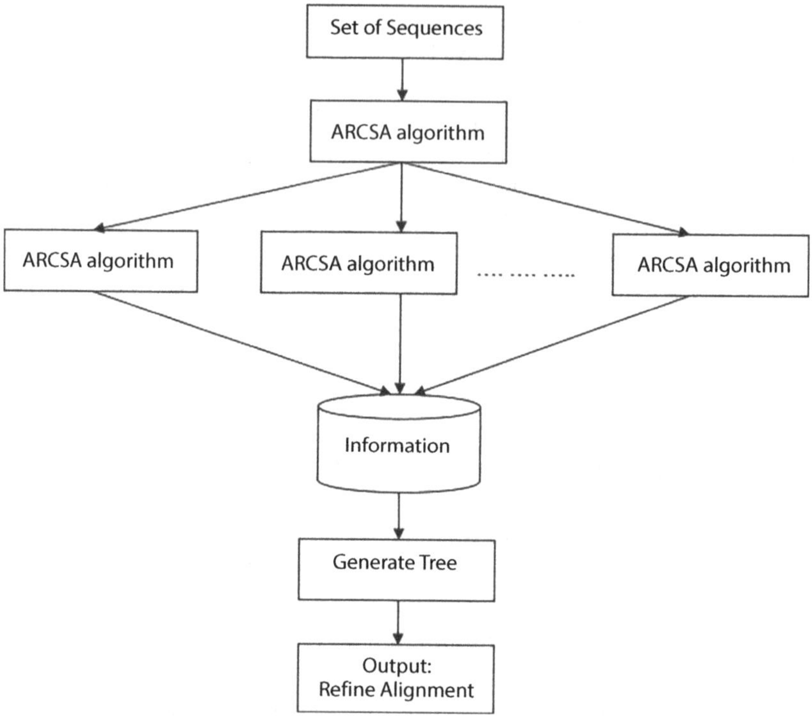

Figure 15.3 CSA algorithm multiple sequence alignment scheme.

$$PairwiseDistance = 1/S(SequenceAligned) \tag{15.6}$$

Thus, if the microorganism's sequence has similarities with the sequence of other organisms' families, the dataset of unrelated sequences, which automatically fulfill the property of motif representation, should undergo without any overlapping. The membership function defined in the clustering processes is an arbitrary one. It can get the smallest distance alignment score. Thus, strategies of this kind are preferable for the clustering processes rather than getting longer common sequences with higher distances. The alignment score calculation example is shown in Figure 15.4. The pair-wise distance can also calculate the identification of the score in the multiple sequence alignment using Equation 15.6.

$$S = \left\{ \begin{matrix} P & F & P & V \\ P & F & - & V \\ 1 & +1 & -1 & +1 \end{matrix} \right\} = \begin{matrix} 2 \\ \text{(Score in the Alignment)} \end{matrix}$$

Figure 15.4 Alignment score in the matches.

Algorithm 15.1: Suffix Tree Algorithm

Data: S: Set of sequences
Result: T: Suffix Tree
//Tree Generation
for *i=1 to (l-i)* **do**
  //Tree Expansion
  for *j=1 to (l+1)* **do**
    Calculate stop of the path from root and expand path with T(i+1)
end
end
Transfer Index to T;
return T;

15.3 Clustering Algorithms in PPI

Cluster analysis is important in machine learning given various applications. It is a useful and important methodology for *in-silico* analysis of microarray or even for gene expression data. The reason for going to a new motif analysis algorithm is that the previously proposed clustering methodologies meet with a great number of difficulties in satisfying the requirements of quality, productivity, automation, and efficiency.

Non-negative matrix factorization (NMF) is a technique that can reduce the complexity of data. It has been used in many different areas. One key advantage of NMF is that it does not rely on negative numbers, which can sometimes be tricky to interpret. Beyond traditional data analysis, NMF has also become popular for tackling complex data mining and machine learning problems, especially when working with gene expression data. This study explores how NMF can be used to identify genes that are expressed differently between samples, as well as to group similar samples together. It provides an overview of the main NMF models, their properties, principles, and algorithms, including various ways they have been expanded and modified over time. The results demonstrate that different NMF approaches can effectively find differentially expressed genes and cluster samples. The fundamental NMF approach has been extensively employed in data processing and machine learning domains, renowned for its capacity in knowledge representation. Particularly in gene expression data, we interpret non-zero entries within the basic matrix as representing distinctively expressed genes, capturing biological patterns specific to various sample groups. However, as we identify characteristic genes, challenges related to pattern recognition and redundant information arise. When clustering samples, it is imperative to consider both the labeled data and the geometric structure within the original data. Consequently, numerous researchers have introduced desirable properties to factor matrices, such as sparseness and smoothness. The imposition of such constraints aids significantly in enhancing interpretation capabilities. The graph NMF methods take into account the geometric structure and the label information in the original dataset. It provides a comprehensive review of NMF ways in identifying differentially expressed genes and clustering samples. The 64000 organic phenomenon knowledge and inorganic knowledge are also examined to verify the performance of NMF algorithms.

Algorithm 15.2: k-means algorithm

Data: k (representation of count of clusters); S (2-D dataset values (1 . . . n))
Result: k clusters of better partition in S
//Initialization vectormax=0 i=0
//Process
Pick sequence in random from S mediods = M;
for *S* = 1 *to n* **do**
    Compute matching score of S with medoid M;
    Fix S to cluster with the lesser distance M;
end
find a vector in the fix
if *vector* < *vectormax* **then**
    i = i+1;
else
    vector map = max;
    Better partition = subunits in Partition;
end
Return Better Partition

The acronym EM stands for expectation and maximization. The EM algorithm is very useful for real world datasets. When k-means algorithm does not satisfy the evaluation of dataset, the EM algorithm is suggested as the next best option. Figure 15.5 explains the block diagram of sampling Dataset 1 clustering and Figure 15.6 explains the unsupervised learning division and algorithms.

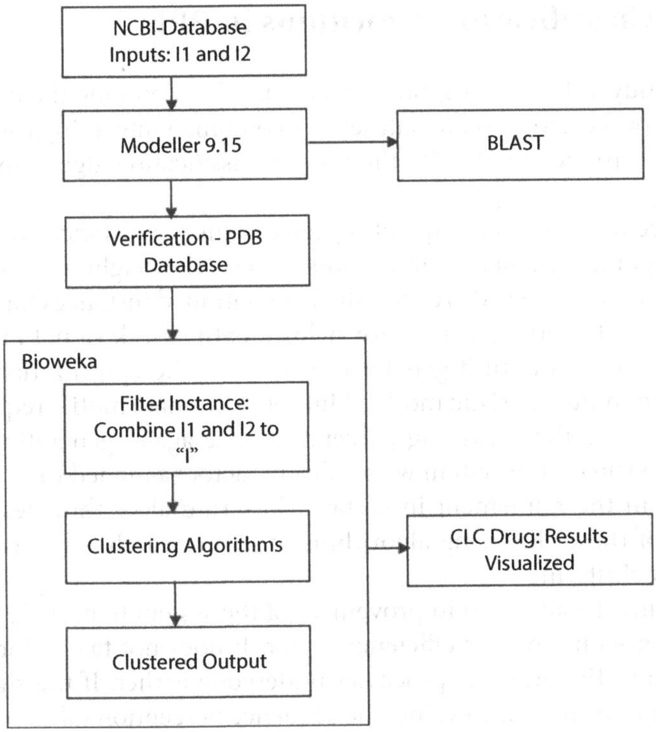

Figure 15.5 Block diagram of sampling Dataset 1 clustering.

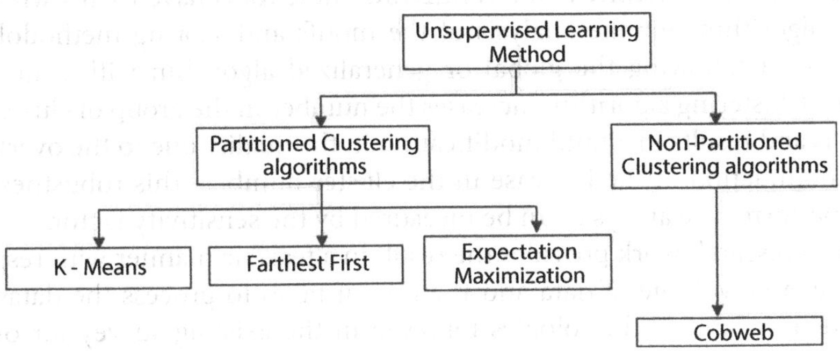

Figure 15.6 Unsupervised learning division and algorithms.

15.4 Classification Agorithms in PPI

In this study, robust biological filters are used to combine the datasets for drug discovery. Two protein datasets are combined into a single form using a filtering instance to identify the proper classification algorithm for protein analysis.

The occurrence of subsequent repeated values in instances will be used as the stopping criteria for elimination aspects. The neighbor models of the progress report achieved are identified as continued instances for the motif patterns identification. This factor helps identify weak signal motifs. The process continues until it gets terminated with the optimization method performed in the heuristic model. Multiple candidate motifs require identification using the clustering perception once again, generating a motif module to run on the system with efficient factors assigned to it. The complication in the refinement in certain clustering algorithms leads to the absence of these clustering algorithms in this research, such as k-means and fuzzy clustering.

Refinement leads to an improvement of the system to provide the motif once again with a higher efficiency factor. It does not take a longer time compared to the previous processes undergone earlier. If the signal ratio and noise ratio are low in value, the sequence perception takes place more efficiently with respect to the extraction process. Weak motif also comes under the noise of the samples provided and requires a removal from the part of the matrix model. Some of the tools that provide motif analysis are READ, SOMBRERO, and WEEDER. These tools have their own specific algorithms for the analysis of the motifs and scoring methodology instead of following the global or generalized algorithm with a unified score. Clustering algorithm increases the number in the group of clusters it forms and results in a mild modification in the quality due to the overload or continuation of the increase in the cluster number. This robustness in the performance analysis can be measured by the sensitivity factor.

This research work provides the result in a feasible manner with respect to the large volume of data and the time it takes to process the datasets. There are some methodologies followed in the existing survey for overcoming robustness such as the interconnection of a group of clusters making three or four clusters into one cluster and maintaining their properties separately to overcome the problems in quality clusters. This solution works better in maintaining a consistent quality in the clusters.

The unstructured protein arrangement is chosen from the NCBI protein database. The lengths of the protein classification in the database are almost the same since they are homologous. This unstructured protein succession is changed over into organized groupings and taken as information sequencel in the ARFF design. Another protein structure from PDB database taken as information is sequence 2. These two arrangements are combined and classified utilizing the three bunching calculations, viz. Random forest classification algorithm, Naïve Bayes algorithm, and decision tree classification algorithm are meant to locate the best closeness coordinates in a consolidated protein dataset. Classification and clustering algorithms comparison results are shown in Table 15.1 and Table 15.2. This information on mining strategy is performed in BioWeka programming. At that point, the outcome and the two existing calculations are examined. When contrasted, Naïve Bayes classification algorithm turned out to be a superior bunching calculation.

Table 15.1 Clustering algorithms comparisons in sampling Dataset 1.

Clustering algorithms	Loglikelihood/ sum of squared errors	Time (secs)	Cluster 0	Cluster 1
Farthest first	-	- 0.02	156	103
Expectation maximization	-38.21832	0.01	143	116
K-means	3183	0.01	190	69
COBWEB	-	0.03	353	353

Table 15.2 Classification algorithms comparisons in sampling Dataset 1.

Classification algorithms	Error percentage	Kappa statistics	Time (secs)	Classified instances
Random Forest	0.42	0.3312	0.22	67.5676
Naïve Bayes	0.11	0.8209	0.01	91.1197
Decision Tree	0.46	0.0161	0.14	53.2819

15.5 CSA and PPI Interaction Results

The sequences provided for the target verification have been analyzed, and interaction features are identified for the preprocessing. The result predicted is a 3D structure and requires conversion to the ARFF format. It clearly indicates MergeSets as not only just a concentrated field of the process. Interaction in individuals cannot reach the performance for fulfilling the system. Thus, the results obtained show the support of sequence analysis in addition to MergeSets filter information.

The experiments conducted until now for the environmental samples in the wet analysis result in a single protein sequence for each identified microorganism. The input for CSA algorithm is a set of sequences where repeated patterns with given lengths are found. The complexity involved in analyzing the identification sequence for drug discovery prohibits its sole utilization, as a single match poses significant challenges. Instead, this study focuses on analyzing protein sequences extracted from suggested food items to understand the correlation between microorganism patterns and food products. This approach allows for a concentrated effort towards drug discovery concerning medications related to these types of food product sequences analyzed using the CSA algorithm. The CSA algorithm is applied to protein sequences, identified with their respective PDB IDs and microorganism sequences (refer to Table 15.3). Upon receiving these

Table 15.3 Sequence statistics in environmental RTSamples Dataset 1.

Seq. no.	Length	Weight	Isoelectric point (pH)	Aliphatic index
1	107	11.74 kiloDalton	6.71	83.645
2	15	1913.1 Dalton	6.96	19.333
3	61	6820.745 Dalton	9.93	90.984
4	82	9385.9 Dalton	10.22	111.707
5	136	16.267 kiloDalton	10.14	84.559
6	11	1298.553 Dalton	7.04	97.273
7	15	1864.959 Dalton	2.89	130
8	129	14 471 kiloDalton	8.95	59.07

```
@relation crab

@attribute I1 {A,R,D,N,C,E,O,G,H,I,L,K,M,F,P,Q,S,T,W,Y,V}
@attribute I2 {A,R,D,N,C,E,O,G,H,I,L,K,M,F,P,Q,S,T,W,Y,V}
@attribute I3 {A,R,D,N,C,E,O,G,H,I,L,K,M,F,P,Q,S,T,W,Y,V}
@attribute I4 {A,R,D,N,C,E,O,G,H,I,L,K,M,F,P,Q,S,T,W,Y,V}
@attribute I5 {A,R,D,N,C,E,O,G,H,I,L,K,M,F,P,Q,S,T,W,Y,V}
@attribute I6 {A,R,D,N,C,E,O,G,H,I,L,K,M,F,P,Q,S,T,W,Y,V}
@attribute I7 {A,R,D,N,C,E,O,G,H,I,L,K,M,F,P,Q,S,T,W,Y,V}
@attribute I8 {A,R,D,N,C,E,O,G,H,I,L,K,M,F,P,Q,S,T,W,Y,V}
@attribute I9 {A,R,D,N,C,E,O,G,H,I,L,K,M,F,P,Q,S,T,W,Y,V}
@attribute I10 {A,R,D,N,C,E,O,G,H,I,L,K,M,F,P,Q,S,T,W,Y,V}
@attribute I11 {A,R,D,N,C,E,O,G,H,I,L,K,M,F,P,Q,S,T,W,Y,V}
@attribute I12 {A,R,D,N,C,E,O,G,H,I,L,K,M,F,P,Q,S,T,W,Y,V}
@attribute I13 {A,R,D,N,C,E,O,G,H,I,L,K,M,F,P,Q,S,T,W,Y,V}
@attribute struct {H, B, E, G, I, T, S, N, C}

@data

P,W,I,R,R,P,F,F,P,F,H,S,P,C
W,I,R,R,P,F,F,P,F,H,S,P,S,E
I,R,R,P,F,F,P,F,H,S,P,S,R,E
R.R,P,F,F,P,F,H,S,P,S,R,I,T
R.P,F,F,P,F,H,S,P,S,R,I,F,C
P,F,F,P,F,H,S,P,S,R,I,F,D,C
```

Figure 15.7 Predicted protein PDB format to ARFF.

input sequences, the algorithm computes index values, performs comparisons, assesses amino acid counts, and resorts to alignment methods or random selection for generating the initial profile matrix if necessary. The predicted results are shown in Figure 15.7.

The statistical information of amino acid count in the 8 sequences of Dataset 1 for this research work is shown in Figure 15.8. The starting profile

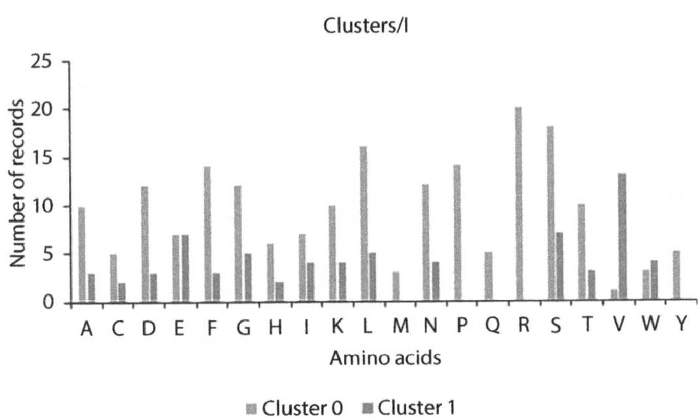

Figure 15.8 Attribute I clusters of PPI dataset in k-means clustering.

matrix contains the values of availability of bases referring to the sequence in the buffer followed by a brute force approach such as:

1. Sequence: ARNPPVQ, length=3
2. Brute force: ARN RNP NPP PPV PVQ

The final output of this whole CSA experiment work is a single repeated pattern identification in the set of sequences produced by using CSA algorithm. Figure 15.9 and Figure 15.10 show a clear explanation of all amino acid occurrences in the identified pattern, which has the greatest value results from calculations based on starting a profile index for all 8 sequences. The results of the CSA algorithm result of sampling are shown in Figure 15.16., i.e. the repeated pattern (ALKVG) of length 5 in the given set of eight sequences.

The duration of a program comprises both the compilation time and the run/execution time. The compilation time remains unaffected by specific characteristics. Estimation of this performance analysis was made for both the sampling processes and the experimented real-time samples in the CSA algorithm. Initially, in sampling processes with the consideration of existing clustering-oriented algorithms, the proposed methodology estimates their performance analysis based on the complexity measures with respect to time and concludes the best protein clustering algorithm.

A comparison of these clustering algorithms with the Dataset 2 experimented on the basis of performance analysis is shown in Table 15.4, and the comparisons of clustering algorithms with respect to time are mentioned

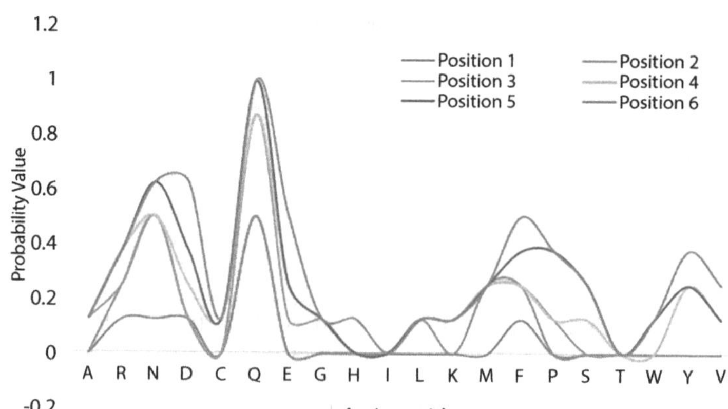

Figure 15.9 Amino acid occurrences in RTSample Dataset 1.

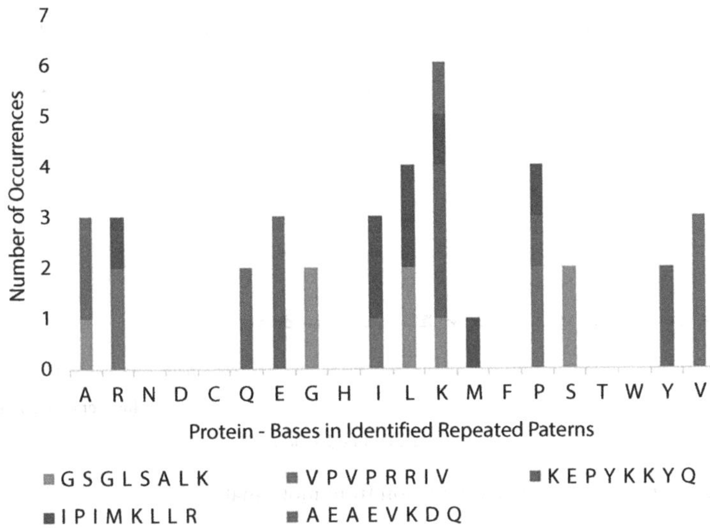

Figure 15.10 Motif matrix amino acid occurrences positional values.

Table 15.4 Clustering algorithms in sampling Dataset 2.

Clustering algorithms	Loglikelihood/ sum of squared errors	Time (secs)	Cluster 0	Cluster 1
Density-based	-39.12727	-0.01	189	70
Expectation maximization	-37.11742	0.02	138	121
K-means	3395	0.01	194	65

in Figure 15.11. This indicates the result based on the time taken in seconds. The sampling processes also involve the classification algorithms experimented in it, and their performance analyses are measured.

In the real-time samples of five environmentally oriented data, the wet analysis is done for inspecting the name of present microorganisms and performing the sequencing concept to make the organisms in a digital format such as DNA sequence.

The conversion of DNA to protein sequence is done later. Then, the building of datasets starts with six datasets built, containing eight sets of identified microorganisms' protein sequence in each dataset. These types of six datasets individually undergo the process of CSA algorithm, and their

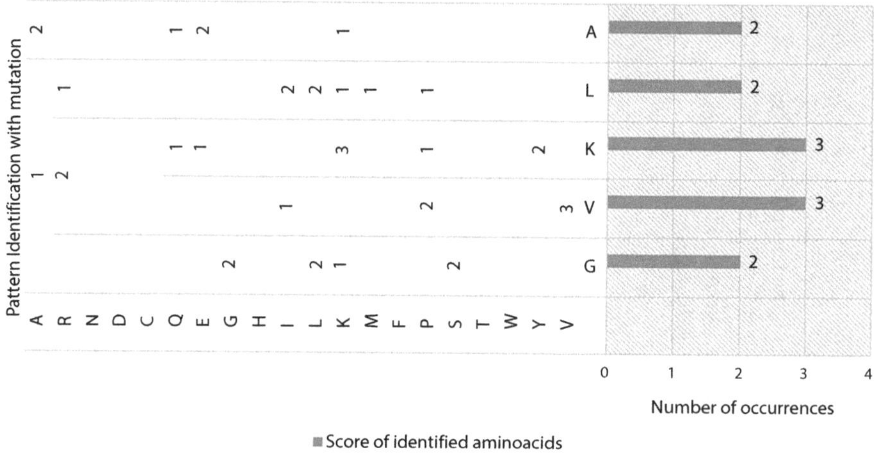

Figure 15.11 Consensus string calculation from motif matrix.

performances are evaluated. Essentially, the last two stages are likewise performed all the while since the particles of the center and circle areas have a close association. The second methodology makes the choice of the best models dependent on an assortment of scoring capacities or machine learning procedures. Figures 15.12, 15.13, 15.14 shows the evidence of sensitivity, specificity and representation of time in clustering algorithms for sampling dataset 1. Figure 15.15 shows the pearson correlation coefficient for best motif from datasets (1–6).

Algorithm 15.3: CSA Algorithm

Data: N: Set size of sequences / Set size of patterns, L: Set of size of each sequence, M: Length of each pattern, Protein[20]: Protein array, S[N][1000]: Set of sequences, Pattern[N][M]: Set of patterns, Base[N][20]: Count background matrix, NS[N][1000]: Set of sequence generated after join operation, Countseqjoin[N]: Number of joined sequences after join operation, Probability[N]: Pointer array to store probability value at each iteration, Motifi[N][M]: Produced patterns from CSA at iteration z, Proteinmat[M][20]: Numerator matrix

Result: Output[M]: Consensus string, C: Score value

for *i=1 to N* **do**

S[i][1000] <– input sequence i L[i] <– strlen(S[i]) Countseqjoin[i] <– 1

Probability[i] <– malloc(sizeof(float)*(L[i]-M+1))

end

Compute(S, Base, Protein, N, L) Stringcopy(S,NS, N)

j <- 1

Join(NS, N, j, Base, Countseqjoin) Genpattern(NS, Countseqjoin, j, M) Backgroundmatrix(Base, L, N) Proteinmatrix(Pattern, Proteinmat, Protein, M, N)

CSAcalculation(Base, Proteinmat, S, L, Probability, motif, N, M) Profilemat(motif, Proteinmat, output, pattern, M, N, C)

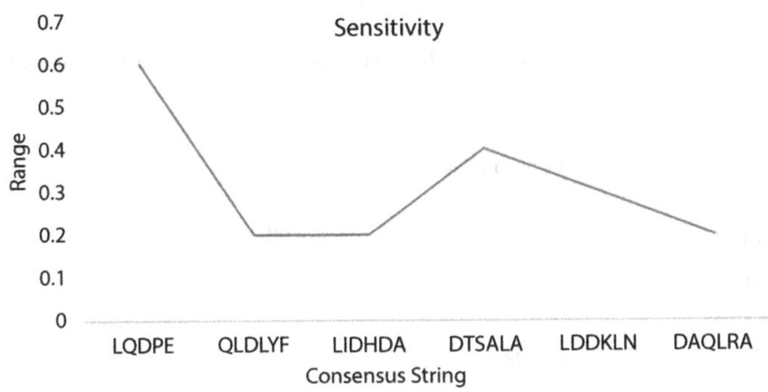

Figure 15.12 Sensitivity for RTSample Dataset 1 in motif algorithms.

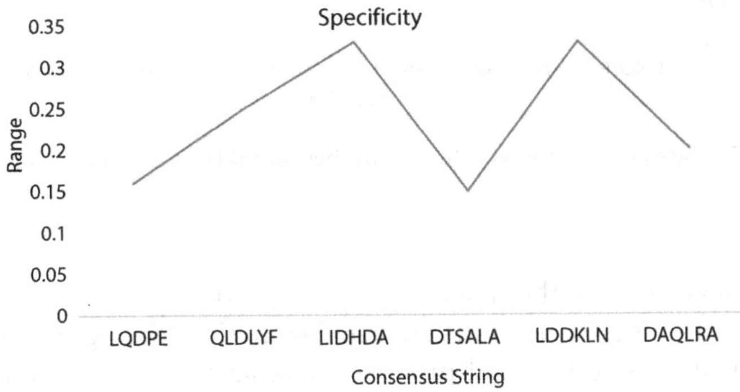

Figure 15.13 Specificity for RTSample Dataset 1 in motif algorithms.

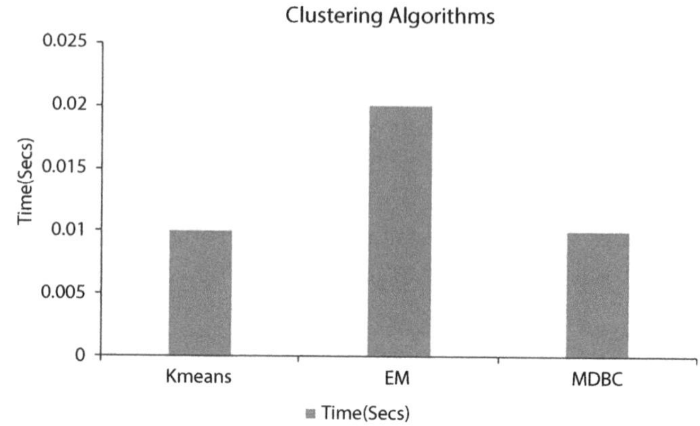

Figure 15.14 Representation of time in clustering algorithms for sampling Dataset 1.

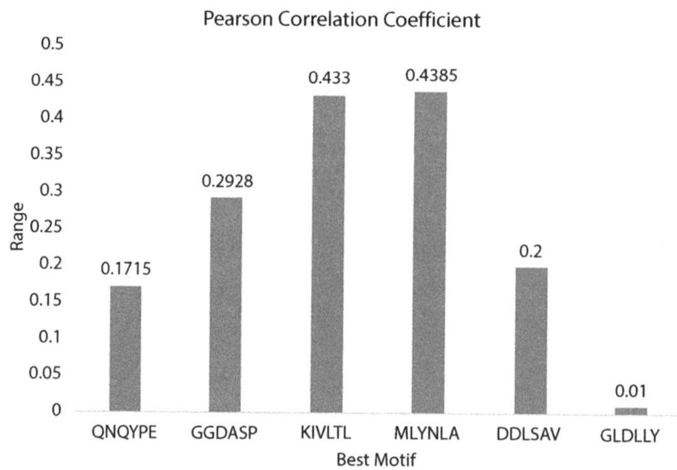

Figure 15.15 Pearson correlation coefficient for best motif from datasets (1–6).

The correlation is in the range of -1 to +1. In the calculation of P-value, the considerations are the results expected from the CSA algorithm, results observed from random initial profile matrix and degrees of freedom 'n.' The calculations are done based on the equations. The 'x' value represents the data through random motif highest amino acid number, and the 'y' value represents the motif data obtained through the CSA algorithm. The domain composition deals with the various prioritization of the identified characteristics in the similar protein structure, such as the score value and

P-value. Appearance of negative values in the results shows that negative association is built within the two data considered for metrics. These attributes pave the way to calculate the P-value based on the equation, and the results of the P-value comparison with the existing motif algorithms are shown in the Figure 15.16. The Q-values are calculated using the equation with attributes of the same P-value measures, since Q-value is an expanded version of P-value, involving the location of the untrue positive contribution of P-value data. The results of Q-value comparisons to existing algorithms are described in Figure 15.17. The significance of both P-value and

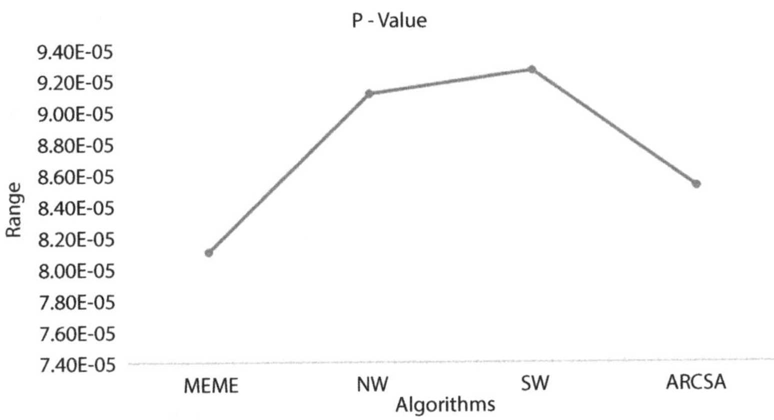

Figure 15.16 P-value for motif analysis algorithms.

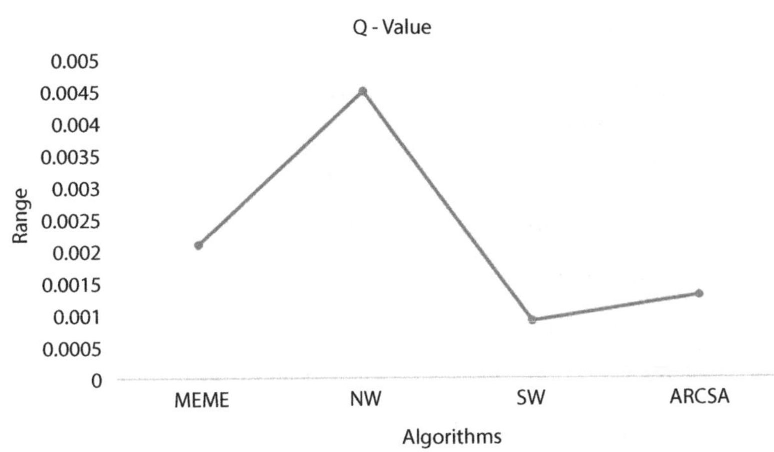

Figure 15.17 Q-value for motif analysis algorithms.

Q-value with respect to the Dataset1 is shown in Figure 15.18. The complexity measures of the CSA algorithm in floating point operations with comparisons to the existing motif alignment algorithms are shown in Table 15.5. The time taken for the algorithms to complete the process of finding

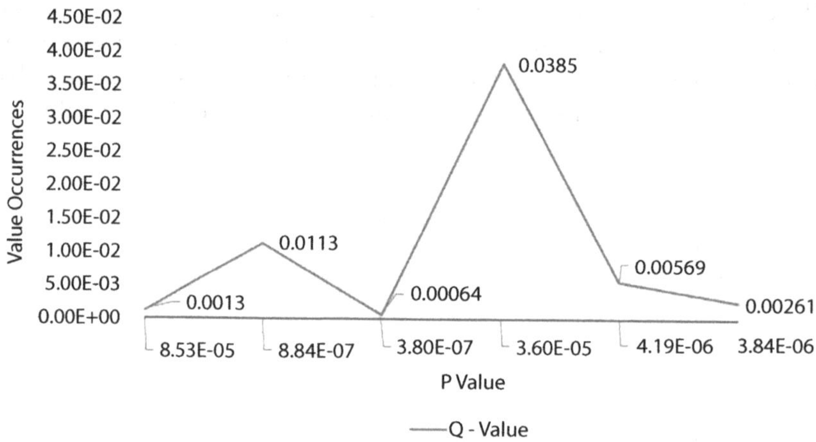

Figure 15.18 P-value and Q-value for datasets (1–6) in CSA.

Table 15.5 Computational complexity.

Algorithms	Complexity (flops)
Farthest first	O(NLogN)
Density-based	O(n)
COBWEB	$O(m^2)$
Expectation maximization	O(NK)
K-means	O(TKP)
Random Forest	O(ktree*ztry*nlogn)
Naïve Bayes	O(NP)
Decision Tree	O(V*nlogn)
CSA	O(MNNLog NL)
Needleman–Wunsch	O(MN)
Smith–Waterman	O(MN)

the motif matrix with consensus string regards to score are measured in seconds and shown clearly in Table 15.6. Testing analysis was carried out by using datasets with varying numbers for a set of sequences and in the size of data, which provides the same complexity measure in all the cases. The score of the alignment processes is calculated based on the equation, and their experimented results are shown in Figure 15.19 and Figure 15.20. The performance measures are also calculated with comparisons to existing motif-finding algorithms. This chapter provided the repeated patterns in the input sequences, known as motif with the proposed CSA algorithm, whereas the next chapter deals with the protein prediction methods.

Table 15.6 Time analysis in Dataset 1 for best motif finding.

Algorithms	Time (secs)	Best motif
MEME	0.08	QNQYPE
NW	240	LDDANQ
SW	180	QGYDDE
CSA	0.08	QMQDDE

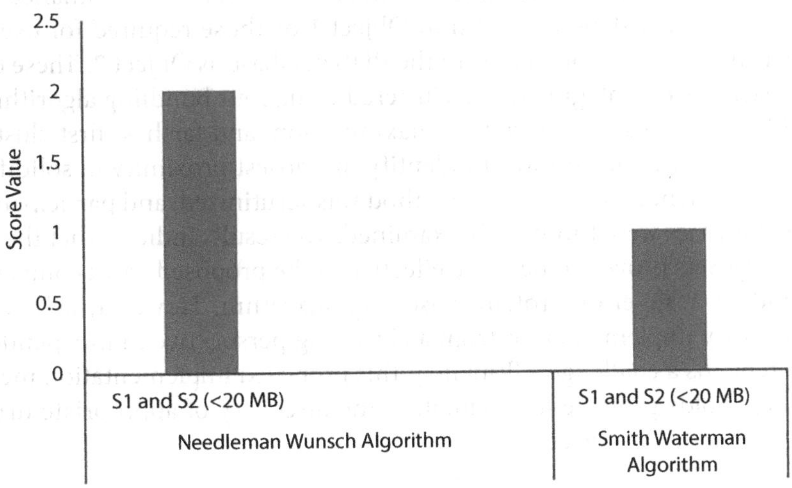

Figure 15.19 Score analysis in motif pairwise alignment.

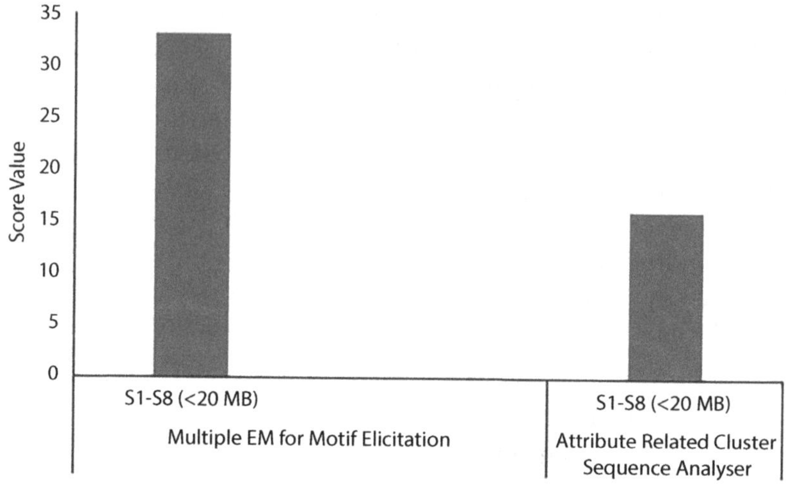

Figure 15.20 Score analysis in motif multiple sequence alignment.

15.6 Conclusion

The proposed CSA methodology has wide-ranging applications, including drug discovery and data extraction within living cells to identify their properties. Protein datasets retrieved from the NCBI database exhibit homologous characteristics due to similar index values. To enhance the analysis, protein structures akin to Object 1 or those required for executional analysis were sourced from the PDB database as Object 2. These two approaches were integrated and clustered using four bundling algorithms: COBWEB, k-means, expectation maximization, and farthest first clustering algorithms. The aim was to identify the closest proximity in solidified protein sequence structure. The method was scrutinized, and participation characteristics were thoroughly examined. The results indicate that the filter MergeSets proved to be more effective in the proposed work compared to finding a superior protein clustering algorithm. However, achieving satisfactory implementation from a clustering perspective in independent data remains a challenge. Ultimately, this proposed implementation methodology holds promise for facilitating the discovery of appropriate drugs for isolated disease reactions.

Bibliography

1. Abyzov, A., Urban, A., Snyder, M., Cnvnator: an approach to discover, genotype, and characterize typical and atypical cnvs from family and population genome sequencing. *Genome Res.*, 21, 974–984, 2011.
2. Adriana, B., Florence, D.-B., Tom, H., A bayesian framework for combining protein and network topology information for predicting protein-protein interactions. *IEEE Trans. Comput. Biol. Bioinform.*, 12, 1, 538–550, 2015.
3. Alkan, C., Kidd, J., Marques-Bonet, T., Personalized copy number and segmental duplication maps using next-generation sequencing. *Nat. Genet.*, 41, 1061–1067, 2009.
4. Arner, E., Hayashizaki, Y., Daub, C., Ngsview: an extensible open source editor for next-generation sequencing data. *Bioinformatics*, 26, 125–126, 2010.
5. Bao, H., Guo, H., Wang, J., Zhou, R., Lu, X., Shi, S., Mapview: Visualization of short reads alignment on a desktop computer. *Bioinformatics*, 25, 12, 1554–1555, 2009.
6. Bare, J., Koide, T., Reiss, D., Integration and visualization of systems biology data in context of the genome. *BMC Bioinf.*, 11, 382, 2010.
7. Bonfield, J. and Whitwham, A., Gap5–editing the billion fragment sequence assembly. *Bioinformatics*, 26, 1699–1703, 2010.
8. Carver, T., Harris, S., Berriman, M., Artemis: an integrated platform for visualization and analysis of high-throughput sequence-based experimental data. *Bioinformatics*, 28, 464–469, 2012.
9. Chan, T., Modelling associated protein pattern discovery with unified scores. *IEEE/ACM Trans. Comput. Biol. Bioinf.*, 10, 3, 696–707, 2013.
10. Chen, K., Wallis, J., McLellan, M., Breakdancer: an algorithm for high resolution mapping of genomic structural variation. *Nat. Methods*, 6, 677–681, 2009.
11. Waszak, S., Hasin, Y., Zichner, T., Systematic inference of copy-number genotypes from personal genome sequencing data reveals extensive olfactory receptor gene content diversity. *PLoS Comput. Biol.*, 6, e1000988, 2010.
12. Waterhouse, A., Procter, J., DMA, M., Jalview version 2–a multiple sequence alignment editor and analysis workbench. *Bioinformatics*, 25, 1189–1191, 2009.
13. Westesson, O., Skinner, M., Holmes, I., Visualizing next-generation sequencing data with jbrowse. *Briefings Bioinf.*, 14, 2, 2012.
14. Wu, J., Li, J., Zeng, D., Big data meet green challenges: Big data toward green applications. *IEEE Syst. J.*, 10, 888–900, 2016.
15. Xie, C. and Tammi, M., Cnv-seq, a new method to detect copy number variation using high-throughput sequencing. *BMC Bioinf.*, 10, 80, 2009.
16. Xinyan, C., Yandao, G., Xiufang, Z., Nanming, Z., Endothelial cell culture on different phospholipid surfaces. *Tsinghua Sci. Technol.*, 3, 1125–1128, 1998.

17. Yang, W.W., Cluseq: Efficient and effective sequence clustering. *19th international conference on data engineering los alamitos*, IEEE Computer Society Press, pp. 101–112, 2003.
18. Yen, K.N., Linzhi, Y., Hirotaka, O., Shuai, C.L., Finding all longest common segments in protein structures effciently. *IEEE Trans. Comput. Biol. Bioinform.*, 12, 3, 644–655, 2015.
19. Yoon, S., Xuan, Z., Makarov, V., Sensitive and accurate detection of copy number variants using read depth of coverage. *Genome Res.*, 19, 1586–1592, 2009.
20. Zeitouni, B., Boeva, V., Janoueix-Lerosey, I., Svdetect: a tool to identify genomic structural variations from paired-end and mate-pair sequencing data. *Bioinformatics*, 26, 1895–1896, 2010.
21. Zhang, X., Liu, S., Cui, H., Chen, T., Reading the underlying information from massive metagenomic sequencing data, IEEE, pp. 1–15, 2016.

16

"Hi-Tech People, Digitized HR— Are We Missing the Humane Link?"—Use of People Analytics as an Effective HRM Tool in a Selected Healthcare Sector

Rana Bandyopadhyay[1*] **and Aniruddha Banerjee**[2,3]

[1]*W.B. State Electricity Dist. Co. Ltd, Kolkata, India*
[2]*Peerless Hospital, Kolkata, India*
[3]*Narayana Hospital, Howrah, India*

Abstract

The healthcare sector in India is one of the fastest-growing sectors in terms of revenue and employment ability. Studies show that when the data are properly digitized, people analytics can help organizations make manpower planning more accurate with an overall holistic approach toward strategic decision-making aligned with its business policies. But the question remains: hi-tech people, digitized HR— are we missing the humane link? The whole gamut of HR activities, such as planning, talent acquisition, training, succession planning, payroll administration, and budgeting involves the handling of a huge set of HR data, which has to be efficiently stored and analyzed for any future managerial decisions. Without digitization, their effectiveness cannot maintain an overall humanistic approach to the entire situation. The study has been conducted in a selected leading hospital chain. The study will look into how far the company could successfully utilize data analytic technologies for smooth HR functions with a humane interface leading the operational efficiencies to excel at their best. It is observed that the extensive use of data analytic technology helped to forecast and recruit the optimum manpower to train them and make them industry-ready, to bring transparency and smoothness in the business and service process, as well as to develop inclusiveness among its existing human resource, thereby reducing attritions or overall growth of the organization in a cost-effective way including a higher degree of patient satisfaction without missing the humane touch.

**Corresponding author*: bandyopadhyayrana36@gmail.com

Kanak Kalita, Divya Zindani, Narayanan Ganesh and Xiao-Zhi Gao (eds.) Medical Analytics for Clinical and Healthcare Applications, (311–328) © 2025 Scrivener Publishing LLC

***Keywords*:** People analytic, humane link, SMAC

16.1 Introduction

According to Frost and Sullivan [1], the healthcare sector in India is one of the fastest-growing sectors in terms of revenue and employment ability with all-around operational efficiency, expansion, and digitization gains across pharmaceuticals, medical technology, and delivery. Alone, if the hospital segment is considered, there is an immense scope for expansion within a couple of years. From a recent report [2], it is observed that private hospital chains in India are expected to go for an investment to the tune of Rs 32,500 crores over the next four to five years where metro cities will remain the main area catering these expansions. Another report [3] indicates that there is a potentiality of creation of approximately 12 million jobs between 2020 to 2030 in healthcare and allied sectors in India.

The importance of data was felt by the American business theorist, economist, management consultant, and industrial engineer William Edward Deming [4], who once said that 'In God we trust; all other must bring data.' This statement appears to be a simple one but has a deep-rooted significance explaining the role of data in the modern business world.

Rapid expansion in the hospital sector has led to the management of robust database covering mostly from two sides, namely patient service and operational management delivery sides. Patient services include innovative solutions for improved healthcare delivery catering to an optimal workflow without the burden of physical papers, making health data and medical services more accessible. Patient diagnosis is doable in a minimum time for check-ups and the cost is reduced for patients' overall well-being. From an operational perspective, it helps to take accurate analysis followed by appropriate decisions on financial and human resource (HR) issues and a minimum time requirement. Easy communication indicates the areas of further growth and investment for the overall development of the sectors with a better quality of service.

In a recent study [5], the term "people analytics" has been referred as not simply a technology but as a quantitative, evidence-based, data-driven approach to employee management. It is basically the use of employee related data to access their impact of the entire gamut of HR activities, such as planning, talent acquisition, training, succession planning, and payroll administration, which involves handling disparate sets of HR data, which must be efficiently stored and analyzed. Therefore, people analytics is collecting and applying organizational, people and talent data to improve critical business outcomes. It enables HR departments to gain data driven insights to make decisions on different people processes and turn them into actions to drive the performance of an organization. It is basically practicing evidence-based HR. However, it differs from HR analytics where the data are exclusive to HR but for people analytics, the data goes beyond HR and includes finance, customer, marketing, and other data sources. So, the use of people analytics provides a holistic solution to any decision-making process.

16.2 Research Background

A question in the field of people analytics remains – "Hi-tech people, digitized HR, are we missing the humane link?" To illustrate it a little more, it is almost essential for all companies to digitalize data, which may be related to operations, finance, service, or HR. The usefulness of digitization is beyond any question. It is something inevitable, essential, and obvious. At the same time, it is to be kept in mind that the organizations are not only an assembly of dead stocks, data or technologies but also of human beings with their definite likes and dislikes, egos, empathy, and emotions. Therefore, to develop an emotional bonding between the organization and its HR, a humanistic approach of digitization should be taken up so that every employee can align themselves psychologically with the corporate goals. This is the only key factor for any organization to excel at its best possible level. The above matter is looked upon considering one of the leading players amongst the hospital sectors in India – Narayana Health (NH).

16.3 Literature Review

Bhat [6] emphasized on the importance of a well-defined HR policy for ensuring better service qualities post health sector reforms. Andrew Chesley [7], in his edited book, has discussed the use of information and communication technology (ICT) interventions in health sectors of developing countries, having clear impact through improved dissemination, enabled remote consultation, facilitated collaboration and cooperation, more effective health research, and improved efficiency. The paper pinpointed the best ways to use ICT to reduce poverty at the same time to improve health of the weaker sections of people.

The emerging need of having well-structured HRM policies for the health sectors was initially put forward in 2011 [8], covering rational recruitment procedures, timelines of the reward systems, training and development policies, transparent transfer policy, performance-oriented appraisals, and an effective support system. These are some of the key factors of a cogent HR policy of the sync with overall organization.

A study [9] was conducted to point out to some grey areas of the HR strategies in health care sectors. It was carried on accessing the ethical dilemmas associated with HRM practice in healthcare sectors. The researcher pointed out factors like long hours of work, non-daylight shifts, performance-based models of compensation, and a lack of adaptation to rapid technological change that are negatively affecting the skill and performance of the health workers. Here, there is a probable indication towards a missing link of human touch.

Further, there was research [10] to assess the impact of implementing big data solutions on the healthcare sector as a remedy to the existing conventional relational database management systems. Data emerging from various sources, being voluminous in quantity can be successfully and suitably utilized for any managerial decision-making process, which otherwise cannot be analyzed in totality, being heterogeneous and complex in nature.

Gopichand [11] argued that SAMC is an acronym of Social, Mobile Analytics Cloud where social media, being an integral part of life, can help to bring both the service provider and the recipients to one another. A mobile is used as a gazette to bring both ends to one place. Various sources of information can be received through mobile devices and the received/created data lead to a rise of analytics. Cloud acts as a platform to provide/deploy the services globally at a competitive cost.

A recent study [12] shows that the benefit of HR evolving into a technology-based profession is that it curbs the repetition in the task, resulting in a reduction of administrative burden. It reduces costs, improves the quality of service, eases access to data and analytics, helps in decision-making, and thus changes the role as a strategy builder.

Research has been carried out to pinpoint the dark sides of people analytics. In recent research [13], it has been opined that organizations should (continue to) realize that their managers and employees are their most valuable resources and recognize the need to keep human decision-makers in the loop. Further, the skill managers should not be substituted by output-oriented technologies. Instead, organizations should trust their decision-makers and give them the freedom to speak out if people analytics' decision-making recommendations go against their own insight, thus promoting an open culture of exchange and error. The researchers recommended a broad discourse and continuous exchange between management, HR, and employees.

16.4 Research Gaps

Since the industries have already stepped into the world of digitization, healthcare sectors being an important contributor, cannot remain away from the changes. There are scholarly works on the impact of digital analytics in healthcare sectors. There are some works on the impact of people analytics on healthcare, particularly in India. But there is hardly any notable works measuring impact of people analytics if implemented with a humanistic approach. Digitization is the need of the hour, but it could show magical results when implemented with a humane touch simply because machines will never replace 'emotional traits' such as empathy or human compassion. The area remains an unexplored source for researchers.

16.5 Research Methodology

This paper will deal with mostly secondary data available from annual reports [13, 14] and business responsibility and sustainability reports [15] in websites and primary data from employment and patient satisfaction surveys and exit interviews.

16.6 Objectives

The paper will try to evaluate how far the company could successfully utilize the people analytics not only for smooth HR budgeting, manpower planning, recruitment, staffing, training, and payroll solutions, but also for an overall improvement of operational efficiencies of the organization with improved patients' satisfactions with a humane interface maintaining data protections. The HR managers, being strategic business partners, may use people analytics, where the use of the data goes beyond, such as finance, marketing, operations, and the patients, who are the ultimate end users in a service sector like a hospital. The overall success of the organization depends on the success factors covering all its major stakeholders.

16.7 NH Success Story

Narayana Health (NH) was founded by the renowned cardiologist Devi Prasad Shetty in 2000 in Bangalore, India, with a mission to "deliver high-quality, affordable healthcare services to the broader population in

India." Narayana Health has expanded into major cities of the country, as well as in the Cayman Islands. It is now one of the largest chains of multi-speciality/super -speciality hospitals in the country. The hospital has 6370 beds, now operating at 24 locations and 7 heart care centers, rendering services in hospitals, pharmacies, and diagnostic centers. The company has a talent recourse pool of 18,440 fulltime employees and associates, including 3970 doctors in their database and their operating profit for the year 2023 is 821 crores with net income of Rs 606 crores in the FY 2022–23.

Narayana Health leads in the way of preventive healthcare with a record number of electrocardiograms and officially became Guinness World Record Holders, Excellence in Patient Safety 2023 and Special Contribution to Assam and North East Healthcare Award 2023, Excellence in Cardiology, Neuro Science, 2022 to name few feathers in their crown. Narayana Health got the JCI accreditation at Enterprise level being first among Southeast Asian countries and sixth among the world in the year FY 2022–23.

Narayana Health has successfully digitized their entire data related to service through MEDHA, operations through ATHMA, finance through ORACLE, and HR through SAP modules. There is a platform known as Narayana One Health where everything a patient requires, such as hospitals, care giver, lab test, pharmacies, and many more facilities are extended to the patient against a minimum annual premium. From booking consultants, tests, indoor and outdoor treatment to consumables, including medicines, these are offered at a discounted price, and the services can be availed digitally through cloud platforms like Narayana One Health and Linden.

With the objective of delivering accessible, quality health services at an affordable price, NH is running e-healthcare centers powered by cloud enable solutions and fully equipped with workstations, an open electronic medical records (EMR) system, biometric patient identification, and integrated diagnostic services. These health centers have helped in the days of the pandemic to inoculate free vaccination drives and distribute free medicines. The company has incorporated with Medha AI Private Limited from 2023 to predict a better cost of surgeries and reduce the time spent by patients in the ICU or monitor consumables and antibiotic use.

16.8 Analysis and Discussion

The Human Resource Department is primarily committed to the entire set of employees, be permanent or contractual, highly skilled, skilled, semi-skilled, or even unskilled workers in the most beneficial ways so that the entire set of activities of the department can be driven towards the corporate goal. In this process, HR managers utilize the expertise of the departments concerned as per their requirements, following new innovations and real-life issues. Human resource managers essentially do not only work with the employee database mechanically with accuracy and efficiency, but they are also responsible for creating the workplace to a congenial, safe, and secured place for work where every employee can get access to the best opportunities to perform their jobs smoothly and in more dedicated manner.

Narayana Health had entered a business tie up with ATHMA Hospital Operating System, which offers a seamless platform for storing and processing patient records. It helps medical staff and patients to access their comprehensive medical history swiftly and more efficiently. In order to enhance clinical efficiency across the NH network, integration has been made with a mobile doctor's application with ICU monitors, who are the highly skilled workers, for real-time remote patient assessments. In order to ensure transparency and predictability, 'Enhances Doctor's Bay Management System' for managing outpatient queue has been introduced. In order to create automated early alert capabilities as to facilitate real-time information for doctors, automatic vitals tracking *via* wearable integration, known as ATHMA Application for Doctors Insight (AADI), is used. The company has also launched an automated feedback system for outpatients and inpatients, which enables the collection and analysis of comments *via* social networks, which play an important role as a prime source of constant inputs for identification of the areas that need extra attention toward further development.

Medha Analytics data intelligence is a platform that allows anyone working in the hospital to pull up data and insights from any department, which will streamline the company's decision-making process. Further, both ATHMA and Medha Analytics, being subsidiary companies of Narayana Health, can go ahead with a strategic partnership with Clear Medi Healthcare [16], which aims to achieve an efficient healthcare information system (HIS), data-driven decision-making, enhanced patient care, cost optimization, and resource allocation. With the introduction of Medha Analytics, there has been a sharp rise in the number of complaints received from the customers. For FY 2021–22, the number of such complaints were 281, whereas in FY 2022-23, it recorded a number of 2888 complaints. The employees may directly register their complaints through a specific link. However, all the complaints were mitigated within the year itself. But the easy accessibility and smooth flow of complaint mechanism through Medha Analytics has resulted in such smooth disposals.

To ensure quality and timely patient care, newly admitted patients have the scope to escalate the issue on the event of non-attending for the initial assessment within 60 minutes and post-escalation within 2 hours. This escalation matrix provides easy access to a next-level review for the timely attention of patients. Here, nurses are authorized to escalate any such issue to the highest level on extreme urgency to ensure patient safety. This digital flow of information has not only empowered the nursing staff as employees of the company but also helped minimize public commotion on the account of medical service issues. Every admitted patient is visited 10 times a day with a standard script to ensure safety throughout. The matter is monitored digitally and its overall compliance to this process across the NH group is 98%. The front office employees, such as emergency staff, those in the admission desk, outdoor department, pathology, pharmacy, billing sections, help desk, and insurance can perform their duties peacefully and accurately in a hassle-free environment. Such a standard operating procedure (SOP) helps to transform NH into a happier place to work in terms of employee satisfaction surveys, leading to a higher level of employee loyalty.

There are several stages of digitization helping the workplace. The COVID-19 pandemic has brought a great change in the working atmosphere. It calls for a fast exchange of views and quick communication from one corner to another corner of the country between fellow professionals and colleagues through emails and WhatsApp, among others. Remote work has become very common now days. Narayana Health is using SAP business technology and virtual reality to bridge the gap between those who work in the office on any given day. The company is using online collaboration apps like Microsoft Teams for holding meetings

The organization is using Social, Mobile, Analytics and Cloud (SMAC), which enables HR technologies to revolutionize the digitization process of employee records. It helps to furnish end-to-end data regarding a candidate, such as their individual likes, dislikes, education, special skills, career objectives, age, and domicile status. Narayana Health is taking the help of these social platforms. These include a media presence of the organizations incorporating interfaces and schedules in various social platforms like 'X,' Facebook, Linden, Naukri.com. Now a day job seeker uploads their profiles in various digital platforms where job hunters meet the prospective employers. Employers are also looking at leveraging various social media tools to locate the best candidates and propel their firms towards the top of the heap, hiring the most fitting applicants from a widening global talent pool. These platforms help to ascertain a candidate's nature, preferences, and expertise. Narayana Health uses Linden and Facebook, which are not only used as the platform for manpower pool but also for creating a platform for digital marketing projecting on boarding doctors. Further, unique medical cases are made aware of society, which creates goodwill for the company. Naukri.com or Linden are the platforms used by NH for manpower sourcing. The recruitment process has been digitally developed in such a manner that any vacancy notification created will automatically flow from NH SPHEAR to Naukri.com. Thus, it reduces the processing time and brings transparency to the entire process.

In today's world, an employee may be 'anywhere' but stay connected with their organization 24/7 through mobile devices. Mobiles are packed with various useful apps and sensors, cameras, GPS, and internet. The employers could easily understand how their employee is discharging their official duties even not physically remaining present at the job locations. On the other hand, employees could know exactly what the organization wants them to do in different situations. The entire biometric is accessible from every registered mobile of the employee, which is connected to the payroll administration through SAP.

People analytics provides businesses with information to improve decision-making in respect to the prediction of trends of employee turnover, retention, recruitment, risk, and talent. The entire HR databases are maintained through application software known as the Human Resource Accounting System (HRIS). This is used to collect and store HR data as an end-to-end solution to all the employee-related data. The company uses the HRIS software known as SPHERE right from tracking applications for employment to the separation from employment, covering records, payroll, and employee benefits administration, attendance and leaves, training, performance management, succession planning, employee self-service, reporting and analytics. Further, tools like Power BI are used by the NH to find out the insights of the company data. It helps to connect disparate data sets, transform and clean the data into a data model, which is used for manpower planning, analysis, budgeting, and the quarterly review of manpower aligned to the business.

Cloud is an application software, which helps to store and compute large databases, which are otherwise complex in nature to analyze and reproduce the same according to its requirements. Only internet services and the gazette (mobile, desktop, tab or laptop, etc.) are required to use the same. The application software and the resources are available on the internet and third-party service provider contracts with the subscribers for these services, which can be used without purchasing the main hardware or software. Narayana Health has adopted a cloud-first strategy and entered into a strategic partnership with the leading technology provider – Amazon

Web Services (AWS) – to enhance patient care, upgrade infrastructure, optimize cost, ensure robust security, privacy measure, and elevate the quality of clinical care. Further, the platform is used by the HR department in helping organizations reduce paperwork associated with attendance management. Training and development activity becomes more flexible as the trainees can be trained on-requirement from diverse locations at suitable hours, so there may not be any chance of missing any training sessions unlike classroom training modes. Using this methodology, the company had successfully implemented as many as 20,390 numbers of training and awareness programs in the FY 2022–23 in four broad categories, such as health and safety, skill upgrading, soft skills, and functional/technical training. The following figures illustrate the percentage increase in training and development in the last two years with the help of people analytics, which helps to identify its requirements in the field of health and safety and on skill upgradation.

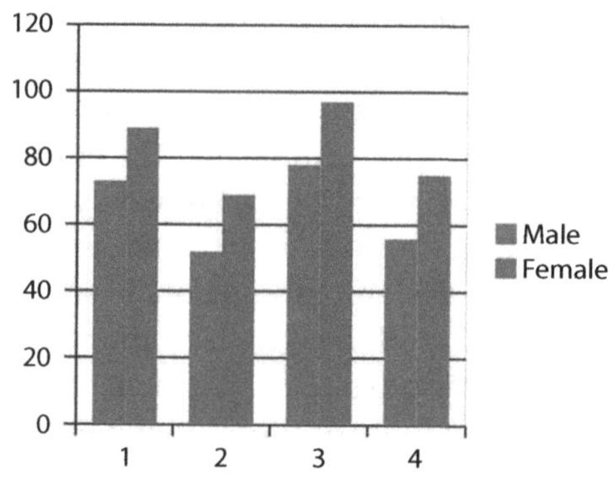

Figure 16.1 Training given to employees on health/safety and skill upgradation.

Performance management, apart from payroll management data calculation systems, and cloud help to process applications, performance appraisals, and locate most relevant resumes. The company is taking full advantage of this technology. All employees, whether permanent or non-permanent, are fully covered with health insurance, maternity and paternity benefits (as applicable), accident insurance soon after their joining to the company through an automatic flow of data by the HR department. So, once an employee enters the job, the role is rest assured about the applicable well-being measures that he or she is entitled to. Similarly, career progression, pay roll administration, and terminal benefits are disbursed in a plan covering all the employees by the way of fetching data from the data base.

Data security: Data security remains a major concern for the company as the entire gamut of its activities are moving digitally with all technology choices having ISO 27001:2013 grade security and privacy controls. Since the security of raw data remains the primary concern for the organization and for the well-being of the employee, all HRIS data are updated in the system following Maker and Checker movement shown in the following manner:
Horizontal flow of data in HR department.

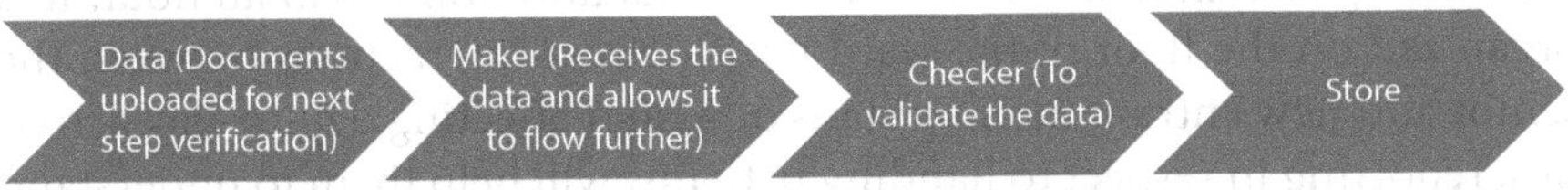

Further, employees can access individual data from their registered mobile, but all these data are protected by a one-time password (OTP) before allowing its access. That is, the system will auto-generate a number upon receiving the request to access the same, and the system will open with that autogenerated unique number only upon confirming the authority of the person accessing the same.

16.9 Findings

The digitization of data has nowadays become inevitable part of any organizational journey. Narayana Health successfully implements the process in its business activity but with a humane touch. From HR perspectives, since all the mobiles of the employee are synchronized and registered with the SAP system with OTP protected, they can access their data at any point of time from their mobiles. However, edit options are not made available to the employee without proper approval of the competent authority so far as official records are concerned. This helps one another to check the balance of data security. So, transparencies in the flow of information are strictly followed. It becomes easier for the employee to align with any managerial decisions, such as payroll, compensation, promotion, and succession planning.

At NH, training is conducted in three categories: behavioral issues, such as motivation, leadership, stress management, and time management; compliance issues, such as POSH, fire, safety and risk; and on technical issues as per the requirements of the respective departments. The company provides several training programs through digital platforms on safety, hygiene, and through digital platform "EDSPARK." There are also several online modules for training nursing groups on skill requirement and capacity-building. It helps to develop their capacity-building and skill enhancement, creating an environment of sustained learning development. For middle and senior level leadership, the program focuses on developing skills and competency in operational excellence, cross-functional skill excellence, core leadership skills, and interpersonal skill developments. Beyond the formal training through virtual and classroom modes, the company introduced a 'Meet-at-the-sight' mode of training. This is for the nursing staff available every morning. Its duration is half an hour. It is organized on the floor of the ward itself. Direct interactions between the senior and new entrant nursing staffs on issues affecting day-to-day activities, reporting in respect to handing patients, will help them to understand the medical cases easily, as well as any small issues may be mitigated at its initial phase itself. Thus, through this system, one of the most crucial, as well as vulnerable sections of employees, can discharge their duties with more efficiencies and harmony.

At NH, employees are at liberty to set their goals while escalating their performance appraisals in the system through the SPHERE module. The information will be escalated to their respective supervisors. The liberty to set individual goals built up an air of freedom and confidence among the employees, which ultimately helps to generate employee loyalty.

Even if an employee wants to resign from the company, their request application can be processed through HRIS. Here, also for better transparency, an employee can calculate his financial dues, due to him for his proposed separation, as per the rules and regulations of their company subject to its acceptance.

Narayana Health has successfully reduced the discharge turnaround time by over 52%. Medha has reduced the delay in outpatient by 32%, wait time is reduced by 14%, and online appointments have gone up 3.5 times. Further, lab turnaround times have dropped by 50%, allowing patients to complete their consultations and associated tests within the same day.

The company was facing the problem with high attritions in medical officers and nursing staff. The HR department, with the help of the data already stored from the responses of the exit interviews of the separating employee, observed that nearly 60% of the medical officers were leaving to avail themselves of the chance of higher studies, and the next major reason, which is almost 28%, is for financial gains.

Similarly, for the nursing staff, the issue of job security (preference for government jobs) remains a prime concern, which is almost 44%, whereas nearly 20% raised the issue of higher studies and another 15% pointed at homesickness as the reason for attritions. Now, factors like job security

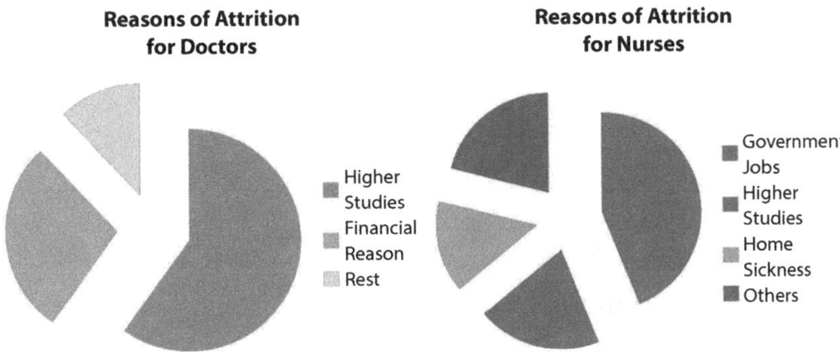

Figure 16.2 The reasons for the attrition of doctors and nurses.

or homesickness are something where the organizations do not have any direct control.

From the analysis of data, the management noted that several doctors have availed the scope of higher studies. Similarly, for nursing staff, factors like preference for government jobs and homesickness are factors beyond control of the management. But sizeable percentages (20%) of these talent pools are in search for higher studies. Strategies were formulated based on such analysis. Initiatives were taken to start DNB courses in hospital units that 'results in a gradual but constant inflow of a pool of specialize doctors.' It is also observed that a number of student doctors get themselves accustomed with the organization culture and a certain amount of loyalty towards the organization grew up, which is reflected in the employee satisfaction surveys. For nursing staffs, the organization started conducting with due affiliations, post-basic nursing courses along with the existing GNM School of Nurslings. The organization had the advantage of upskilling the existing pull of nursing talents in specialized areas. Further, it has been observed that a good number of nurses got retained who were already trained are also in tune of the organizational culture. Narayana Health has started a medical course for intermediate health workers to bridge the gap in the health care delivery.

The company conducts employee satisfaction surveys on a yearly basis as a part of its policy. It shows as a steady rise in job satisfaction indicators for the doctors, from 91% to 95%, and nurses, from 89% to 93%, with a sharp increase of the points for recommending the company as a desired workplace to their friends and relatives.

Similarly, considering healthcare as a service sector, the improvement parameters are measured in terms of patient satisfaction, which is one of

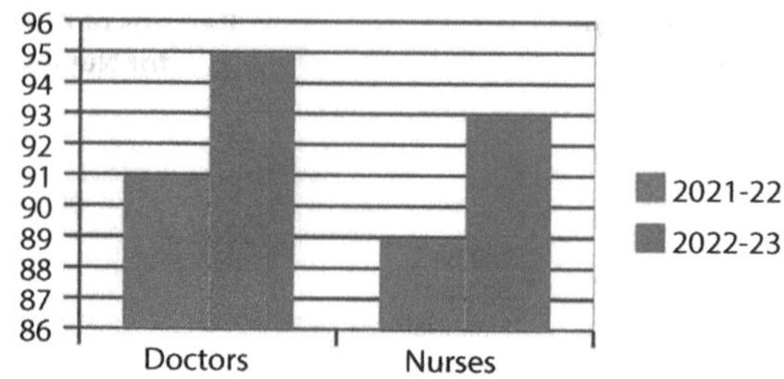

Figure 16.3 Employee satisfaction survey.

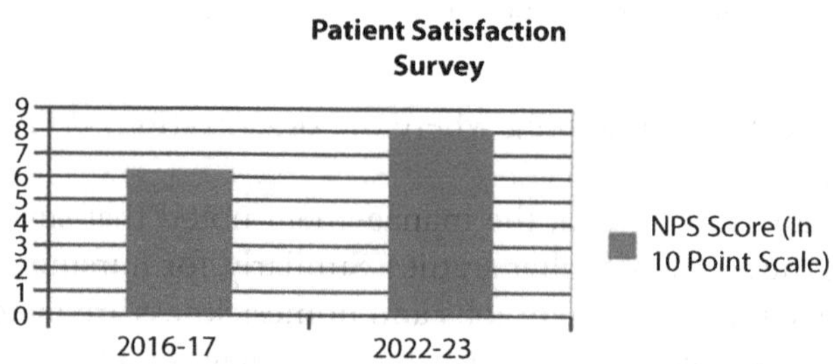

Figure 16.4 The result of the Google rating, being an external survey, shows a sharp improvement from 3.6 to 4.7 points (5-point scale), which proves that it becomes a preferred destination for the patients.

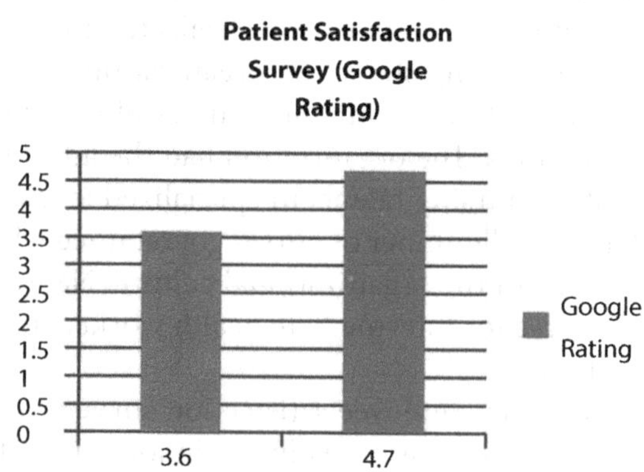

Figure 16.5 Patent satisfaction survey.

the prime indicators of ultimate service delivery. It has been observed that the net promoter score (NPS score) has increased from 6.3 in 2018–19 to 8.1 on 2022–23 (10-point scale). However, NPS is an internal survey based of the patient feedback.

16.10 People Analytics and Humane Touch

In the era of artificial intelligence, it has become imperative for all organizations that the managerial decision will be taken upon analysis of their respective digitized data. Even taking the advantage of cloud technologies, there are the horizontal, as well as vertical flows of digital information across industries overwriting the boundaries of the state and countries. Human resource function is also aligned with people analytics. Narayana Health has successfully aligned its digitized employee records with overall operational efficiency. But this is a generalist approach towards success. In order to develop a loyalty towards the organization, all of the stakeholders should align with the business process, which is a bit ahead of its overall success story. Here is the missing link. The organizational culture should be supportive enough to inculcate a strategy of 'humane touch' in all its decision-making processes so that the stakeholders may feel themselves as an extended family of the organization. Based on the analysis of the people's data, a major decision has been taken by the management of Narayana Health in respect to engaging with "specially abled" persons in pursuant to Section 20 of Disability Rights (Right of Persons with Disabilities & National Trust Act) and Mental Healthcare Act, 2016, [16] "specially abled" eight numbers of male and two numbers of female employees were added to the workforce in the FY 2022–23.

On analysis of the gender composition of the HR of the company, it has been noted that the number of female employees is more than the males. A comparison of the data of FY 2021–22 and FY 2022–23 shows that 214 females were added to its pool against 211 males during the year. Security remains a major reason for women employees, considering the company as a safe destination to remain associated. The internal complaint committee against the harassment of women at the workplace (POSH) remains very active and alert. A total of 6 cases were registered during the year, and all were dealt with in accordance to the law with appropriate penal measures where it is essential.

The company has been facing issues with the employees associated with critical care units while handling the patients. In some of the cases, the patient's body parts (such as the hand or leg) need to be tied to the bed

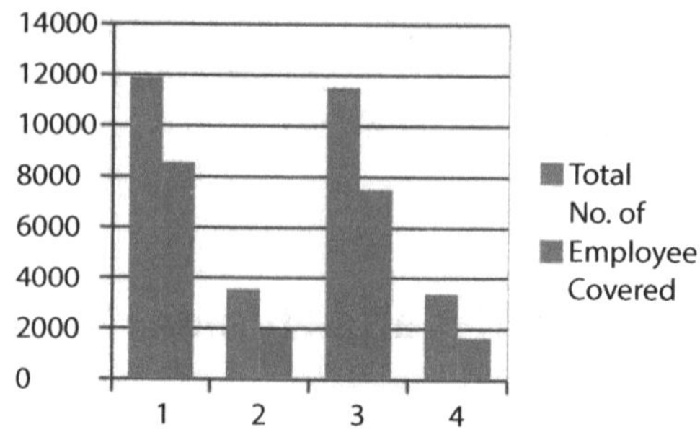

Figure 16.6 The training of employees on human rights.

for continuing the treatment procedures. Such a situation calls for extra care with proper training and knowledge of the statutes. To deal with such cases, the employees are imparted "restrain training" as a part of the "patient right & responsibilities" and the patients' relatives are made aware of the same. The company is imparting training of human rights with the available information and had successfully enhanced the number of trainings imparted on this subject which is shown above:

The company is projected to impart training to over 25,000 doctors, nurses and paramedical employees by 2030. Apart from a customized platform that imparts training sessions through "EDSPARK," NH is arranging capacity building programs to enhance and upgrade skills, as well as to develop team building among existing employees. The introduction of the "Morning Meet" of nurses has helped develop an informal interpersonal relationship between seniors and juniors and address even the smallest issues at its initial stage only. Similarly, from the analysis of case records, the management observed that a sudden crisis involving critical care staff, particularly at the ICCU or ITU, arises at any point of time of a day. This is mainly due to the cardiac arrest of the serious patients admitted in these units. Doctors, nurses, and technicians have to rush to these patients, leaving their immediate responsibilities. To tackle these situations, 'Code Blue' gets announced and the Rapid Response Team has been formed from the pool of high skilled technical employees after imparting special training. Such approach helps to render more prompt service to patients without hampering the routine responsibilities. The scope for further studies within the organization has pulled back a loyalty towards the organization, reducing the rate of attritions apart from maintaining a constant source of upgraded manpower strength. MEDHA has successfully streamlined the OPD and made Emergency admissions more systematic. It has helped a lot to the employees associated with department from unnecessary troubles. The entire human resource pool of the organization can access any employee related data through "SPHERE." It brings more transparency and develops mutual trust into the entire process. The company is categorizing all employees, be it permanent or non-permanent as 'employee' and not as 'worker.' The term has been carefully deleted from their reports and returns. The company, as a matter of policy, is emphasizing the matter of giving a humane touch over people analytics, which can result in more dedicated partners.

16.11 Conclusions

While acknowledging the importance of people analytics in modern business scenarios, it has to be kept in mind that basically human beings are 'humans' with their individual likes and dislikes, emotions and empathy, brains, sentiments, and personalities, which need to be taken care of with a humane touch. Taking the mission further, NH has adopted two core values, "Business should respect and promote the well-being of all employees including those in their value chains" and "Businesses should respect and promote human rights." This calls for a holistic approach toward the entire digitization issue. Therefore, with hi-tech people and digitized HR – there should not be any missing humane link.

The hospital sector is a fast-growing sector under healthcare in terms of investment opportunities, as well as employment generations. The company, specifically the HR managers associated with these sectors, should try to implement digitization from a humanistic viewpoint to get the desired success.

The applications of people analytics, which is inevitable nowadays, should be done with a humane touch for its excellent outcome, and it requires a further in-depth study, considering the entire hospital sector a holistic development of all its stakeholders.

References

1. Banerjee, K., An overview of Indian healthcare industry, 2019, Frost & Sullivan, 2019, May 9, Retrieved from https://store.frost.com.
2. Business Standard, Expect private hospitals to invest Rs 32,000 cr, add over 30,000 beds: ICRA/India News, Business Standard, 2024, January 17, Retrieved from https://www.business-standard.com.

3. Sharma, C.N., Expect private hospital chains to invest Rs 32,000 cr, add over 30,000 beds in 4-5 years: ICRA, Business Today, 2022, February 23, Retrieved from https://www.economictimes.com.
4. Hansen, H.L., In God we can trust. All others must bring data, IBM, 2019, April 29, Retrieved from https://www.ibm.com/nordic-msp.
5. Gal, U., Jensen, T.B., Stein, M.K., Breaking the vicious cycle of algorithmic management: A virtue ethics approach to people analytics. *Inf. Organ.*, 30, 2, 100301, 2020, https://doi.org/10.1016/j.infoandorg.2020.100301.
6. Bhat, R. and Maheswari, S.K., Human resource issues: Implications for health sector reforms. *J. Health Manag.*, 7, 1, 1–15, 2005.
7. Chetley, A., Davies, J., Trude, B., McConnell, H., Ramirez, R., Shields, T., ... Nyamai-Kisia, C., *Improving health, connecting people: the role of ICTs in the health sector of developing countries-a framework paper*, no. 37521, pp. 1–65, The World Bank, 2006.
8. Agarwal, A., Garg, S., Pareek, U., Strengthening human resource practices in healthcare in India: The road ahead. *J. Indian Acad. Clin. Med.*, 12, 1, 39, 2011.
9. Muller, D., 5 employee relations challenges confronting healthcare, HR Acuity, 2018, January 18, Retrieved from https://hracuity.com/5-employee-relations-challenges-confronting-healthcare/.
10. Patel, S. and Patel, A., A big data revolution in the healthcare sector: Opportunities, challenges and technological advancements. *Int. J. Inf.*, 6, 1/2, 155–162, 2016.
11. Gopichand, M., Cloud computing: An introduction to SMAC. *Int. J. Innov. Sci. Eng. Technol.*, 3, 7, 666–671, 2015.
12. Sengupta, A., Lalwani, S., Goswami, S., Srivastava, P., Reinventing HR functions with SMAC technologies – An exploratory study. *Mater. Today: Proc.*, 46, 10169–10174, 2021.
13. Giermindl, L.M., Strich, F., Christ, O., Leicht, U., Deobald, L., Redzepi, A., The dark sides of people analytics: Reviewing the perils for organisations and employees. *Eur. J. Inf. Syst.*, 31, 3, 410–435, 2022.
14. Narayana Health, Annual Report 2021-22 & 2022-23, 2021-2022, Retrieved from https://www.narayanahealth.org/sites/default/files/download/agm-2022/NHL-Annual-Report-2021-22.pdf.
15. Narayana Health, Business Responsibility and Sustainability Report 2022-23, 2022-2023, Retrieved from https://www.narayanahealth.org/annual-reports.
16. Narayana Hrudayalaya Limited, Annual Report 2021-22, pp. 106–262, 2021-2022, Retrieved from https://www.marketscreener.com/quote/stock/Narayana-Hrudayalaya-Limited-25805183/news/Narayana-Hrudayalaya-Annual-Report-2021-22-41240325/.

Index

Printed in the USA/Agawam, MA
September 16, 2026

910661.103